PRAISE FOR *CRIMES THAT CHANGED OUR WORLD*

"Paul H. Robinson and Sarah M. Robinson relate captivating tales about how outrageous and highly publicized crimes produced legal reform and social change, usually for the better. Both specialists and novices will be fascinated by the role crime has played in improving our world." —**Douglas N. Husak**, distinguished professor of philosophy and law, Rutgers University; author, *The Philosophy of Criminal Law*

"By tracing the connections between so many significant legal reforms and the outrage over the crimes that provoked them, Paul and Sarah Robinson offer many important insights for those pursuing law reform at every level." —**Gerald F. Uelmen**, professor of law and dean emeritus, Santa Clara University School of Law; board of directors, Catholic Mobilizing Network

"What do the Triangle Factory Fire, Lindbergh kidnapping, Watts riots, attempted assassination of Ronald Reagan, and the Enron scandal all have in common? The answer, according to this fascinating book, is that the public outrage provoked in each case (as well as fifteen other cases discussed) led to a radical, and often sudden, legal reform—including, respectively, the promulgation of building safety codes, federalization of criminal law enforcement, militarization of the police, changes in the insanity defense, and tougher enforcement of financial crime laws. In twenty absorbing chapters, the authors offer a broad sweep of history, legal and social analysis, and human drama." —**Stuart Green**, distinguished professor of law, Rutgers University

"A fascinating analysis of a remarkable range of criminal cases that, for better or worse, triggered significant changes in American law and policy—ranging from building safety regulations to the 'war on terror,' from drunk-driving laws to financial crimes. The cases are described in vivid, often moving, detail, and their social and political significance through the public outrage that they provoked is illuminatingly explained." —**Antony Duff**, professor emeritus, University of Stirling

"Immensely readable and informative, *Crimes That Changed Our World* provides readers with an in-depth look at some of the most fascinating, tragic, and ultimately consequential crimes in the history of modern American criminal justice. From their effects on everything from building safety codes to the insanity defense to our modern system of 911, the authors show how a handful of salient and terrible crimes helped to transform the landscape of American criminal law in profound ways that are still felt—and often hotly debated—today." —**Richard A. Bierschbach**, dean and professor of law, Wayne State University Law School

"Thomas Carlyle famously argued that human history boiled down to a chronicle of the achievements of outstanding individuals. In this fascinating and accessible book the Robinsons show that notorious crimes and disasters caused by stupid people or stupid laws have the potential to mobilize public demands for reform that lead to legal and social change. Sometimes the changes are for the better (like building codes), sometimes for the worse ('three strikes' sentencing laws), sometimes a mix of good and bad (enhanced drunk-driving laws) and sometimes, as with airport security efforts, one just can't tell. This book will be a valuable resource to those interested in law and social reform, and deserves a wider readership among all who want to understand the drivers of social change." —**Daniel D. Polsby**, professor of law, Antonin Scalia Law School, George Mason University

"*Crimes That Changed Our World* vividly recounts twenty infamous crimes that reshaped the law—from the triangle shirtwaist factory fire and the Lindbergh kidnapping to the Reagan assassination attempt and 9/11. The Robinsons combine careful research with fast-paced storytelling to reconstruct the impact each crime had on an indignant public. They also bring to life the reformers who skillfully channeled popular outrage into support for legal reforms with far-reaching consequences, most for good, and some for ill. A compelling read, this book is also an indispensable primer for aspiring reformers, showing how policy ideas can shape public perceptions of events to catalyze change." —**Guyora Binder**, distinguished professor, Law School, University at Buffalo

Crimes That Changed Our World

Crimes That Changed Our World

Tragedy, Outrage, and Reform

Paul H. Robinson and Sarah M. Robinson

ROWMAN & LITTLEFIELD
Lanham • Boulder • New York • London

Published by Rowman & Littlefield
A wholly owned subsidary of The Rowman & Littlefield Publishing Group, Inc.
4501 Forbes Boulevard, Suite 200, Lanham, Maryland 20706
www.rowman.com

Unit A, Whitacre Mews, 26-34 Stannary Street, London SE11 4AB

British Library Cataloguing in Publication Information Available

Library of Congress Cataloging-in-Publication Data

Names: Robinson, Paul H., 1948– author. | Robinson, Sarah M., author.
Title: Crimes that changed our world : tragedy, outrage, and reform / Paul H.
   Robinson and Sarah M. Robinson.
Description: Lanham, Maryland : Rowman & Littlefield, [2018] | Includes
   bibliographical references and index.
Identifiers: LCCN 2017048534 (print) | LCCN 2017048633 (ebook) | ISBN
   9781538102022 (Electronic) | ISBN 9781538102015 (cloth : alk. paper)
Subjects: LCSH: Criminal law—History. | Criminal justice, Administration
   Of—History. | Crime—History.
Classification: LCC K5032 (ebook) | LCC K5032 .R63 2018 (print) | DDC
   364.10973—dc23
LC record available at https://lccn.loc.gov/2017048534

∞™ The paper used in this publication meets the minimum requirements of
American National Standard for Information Sciences—Permanence of Paper
for Printed Library Materials, ANSI/NISO Z39.48-1992.

Printed in the United States of America

Dedicated to
Ronald Gainer, a man of principle,
—PHR
and
Juleann Miller, a force for good.
—SMR

Contents

Acknowledgments

We are very much indebted to many people for their help with this book, especially Mitchell Heyland, Daniel Atlas, Morgan Schusterman, and Melanie Young of the University of Pennsylvania Law School. Many very capable University of Pennsylvania undergraduate research assistants have also provided an enormous amount of help, especially Taryn MacKinney, Todd Costa, Jack Hostager, Pei Hsuan Sherry Tseng, Aaron Wolff, and Iman Charania.

We must acknowledge Silvana Burgese, Kelly Farraday, and Nesha Patel of Penn Law's Faculty Support Services for their endless help in the preparation of the manuscript; Edwin Greenlee, Merle J. Slyhoff, and Joseph Parsio of the Penn Law Library for their monumental efforts to find us all manner of materials, old and new, common and rare; and Penn Law deans Michael Fitts, Wendell Pritchett, and Ted Ruger for their unstinting support for this work. We are indebted to them all.

In the effort to make these issues accessible to the general reader, we asked some friends to read and comment on early drafts. We thank them all, especially George Sevier, Catherine McAlpine, Larry Cusack, Atticus Robinson, and Nancy Bray. We also had the good fortune to be found by Mary Whisner who volunteered to be our proofreader. John Alcorn, of Trinity College, in Hartford, provided a useful opportunity to explore these issues with an audience by making the book the subject for the 2017 Wassong Lecture.

Preface

As we go through our daily routines, all but the Pollyannas among us see flaws in our existing world. We may try to avoid dwelling on them, but they are there, and they bother us, sometimes a lot. What is easy to miss, without the perspective of even recent history, is that the flaws are generally minor, even trivial, compared to the often appalling state of affairs that existed in the same space just decades ago.

Within the memory of living persons, our world was one with no system of food or drug safety, essentially no building or fire codes, woefully ineffective criminal law enforcement, no protection of the environment, the appalling treatment of some people based on race or other group characteristic, rampant drunk driving, rampant domestic violence, rampant sexual assault, and a host of other conditions that we would now find intolerable.

What can seem almost bizarre to us is that people of not that long ago accepted this state of affairs as perhaps regrettable but tolerable. When we examine that not-too-distant past, we frequently end up scratching our heads wondering, "What were they thinking?"

Of course, this has always been the way of progress. You can be sure that in our not-too-distant future, people will be scratching their heads wondering about us, "What were they thinking?" We may each have our pet theory on what their source of wonderment will be, but more likely than not, if history is any judge, most of us will guess wrong. Our successors will find appalling and intolerable things that we as a society are presently quite willing to tolerate.

This process of the continuous march of progress—of increasing and shifting expectations and ever-rising baselines—is an interesting story in itself. One might think it is the natural result of hundreds or thousands of small steps of gradual improvement over time. And in some cases it is. But it turns out that the march of progress also has some sharp turns in it. The path of the march may be a long series of course corrections, but sometimes it is a quick turn or an unexpected lurch. Sometimes our present circumstances seem entirely acceptable—until they aren't. Then, in a flash, we suddenly feel differently about things, and often just as suddenly do something about it.

This book is about that fiery dynamic—changes that come quickly, sometimes suddenly, sometimes unpredictably, and sometimes inexplicably. Our focus will be on a particular group of triggers of change that we think are the most interesting, the most powerful, and sometimes the most unexpected: *crimes*.

In the cases we explore, the general dynamic is the same: a terrible crime provokes public outrage that in turn produces important reforms. But there are many differences in how the dynamic works and what drives it. Why do some crimes trigger a turn from the current path while similar crimes only a year or two before did not? Or, why didn't the turn wait until a similar crime several years or decades down the path? Or why a turn at all, rather than many gradual course corrections?

The exact nature of the crime-outrage-reform dynamic can take many forms, and we will explore those differences as we work through some of the most important cases of the past century. Each case is in some ways unique, but there are repeating patterns that can offer important insights about how change comes, and how in the future we might best manage it.

But what these extraordinary cases have in common is that all of them deal with crimes that changed our world.

Chapter One

1911
Triangle Factory Fire

Building Safety Codes

It is a pleasant early spring afternoon, and you are standing on the side-walk at 27 Washington Place in New York City. The building in front of you is a beautiful neo-Renaissance specimen ten stories tall. Situated on the corner of Green Street and Washington Place, on the New York University campus, hundreds of people use it every day in comfort and safety.

If you were standing at that same spot on the early spring afternoon of March 25, 1911, at 4:45 p.m., you would be dodging an onslaught of burning, screaming bodies, mostly of young women. The crowd in the street around is also screaming, but some of this is drowned out by the roar of the fire on the top three floors of the Triangle Shirtwaist Factory. Young women are hanging out of the windows and standing on ledges trying to escape the flames. In many cases their dresses are already on fire.

Like watching a suicide jumper but times a hundred, you are help-less to do anything. The flaming bundles are now falling in doubles and triples, all hitting the pavement with a sickening thud. When the rain of horror is over, 146 people are dead. Perhaps most striking about the hor-rific event is that there is nothing terribly unusual about the factory on the upper floors. It is like hundreds of other factories in the city.

The building's façade looks the same today as it did one hundred years ago, but it is very different on the inside. Its safety and comfort is as typi-cal of today's buildings as the danger of the Triangle Shirtwaist Factory was common in the factories of its day.

How did we get from there to here? In large measure, it was due to the horror of those falling flaming bodies.

THE TRAGEDY

On the afternoon of March 25, 1911, as the sun sinks toward the west over the New York City skyline, a fire breaks out in the ten-story Asch Building. The top three floors of the building are occupied by six hundred employees, mostly young women, of the Triangle Shirtwaist Company. True to its name, the company manufactures shirtwaists, a type of women's blouse or dress with details similar to those in men's shirts. It is about fifteen minutes before the five o'clock closing time. Someone drops a still-burning cigarette into a wood box under one of the cutting tables on the eighth floor. The box is filled with cloth cuttings that ignite. Workers at the cutting tables run to get buckets of water to extinguish the fire. The company has some twenty-seven buckets of water distributed throughout the thirty thousand square feet of its three floors. Before they can extinguish the flames, the fabrics hanging on a wire above the cutting tables catch fire.[1]

The factory is perfectly designed to fuel a massive fire. The floors, tables, and chairs are all made of wood. Cotton cloth in bolts, half-finished garments, and piles of scraps are everywhere. The sewing machines drip oil that coagulates on the factory floor; flammable fabrics and templates are everywhere. The factory is practically built to burn, and it does. The fire is quickly out of control, far beyond the reach of a few buckets of water.

In theory, there are several routes of escape: two staircases, a fire escape, and two elevators. But the reality is different. One of the stairwells is locked. Management locks the door to prevent employees from taking breaks without permission or stealing company property. The other stairway is unlocked but narrow. At less than three feet wide, there is only enough room for a single-file procession. The fire escape is even narrower. It descends to the second floor above a small courtyard that serves primarily as an air and light shaft. The two service elevators carry only ten people each.

A bookkeeper on the eighth floor calls the tenth floor and tells them about the fire. The tenth floor is occupied by the company's management and owners. There are only sixty employees on the tenth floor, and they are able to evacuate onto the roof where a New York University professor and some students from the next building help them get away from the burning Asch building. The same bookkeeper tries to call the ninth floor but no one answers. Workers on that floor don't realize there is a fire until they see smoke billowing up past their windows.

Rebecca Feibish, a seventeen-year-old émigré from Romania three years before, is at work on the ninth floor. She is the third of seven children, and her annual salary of $300 is the highest in the family. When she realizes the danger, she grabs her friend, Sylvia Riegler, and the two try to find a way out. Sylvia is not able to master her terror, but Rebecca pulls her forward, pleading with her to make the effort.

There are some 275 people on the eighth floor and another 300 on the ninth. Those on the eighth floor have already jammed the escape routes before those on the ninth even know of the danger. A hundred or so people escape via the unlocked staircase but the well-fueled fire fills the stairwell with smoke. Some workers descend the narrow fire escape, but a large metal shutter blocks their way at the eighth floor landing. The desperate employees try to climb around the shutter, but the going is slow, and soon a crowd jams the stairs behind it. The fire escape sags under the weight, then falls away from the buildings, sending bodies, some aflame, tumbling into the courtyard below.

The elevator operators are trying to do their best to ferry as many people as possible out of the building but they can only do so much. Soon the elevators fail. Gaspar Mortillalo, one of the operators, can't force his elevator past the seventh floor to reach the fire because heat has warped the elevator tracks. As the elevator descends, Mortillalo hears the thud of bodies landing on its roof. As fire continues to consume the building and the heat becomes unbearable, agonized workers slide down the elevator cables. Some jump down the elevator shafts. Joseph Zito, the other elevator operator, can no longer get his elevator to ascend due to the accumulated weight of bodies on top of it.

The factory becomes a veritable furnace. The heat hits one thousand degrees as the fire reaches out with its tentacles, enveloping the building and grabbing at the clothes and hair of the hapless factory workers. People are forced out the windows by the flames. They fall or jump, many with clothes afire, down to the street below. Rebecca jumps. The teenager survives the fall but the doctors are unable to save her, and she dies at the hospital. Sylvia, too fearful of heights to stand in the window, heads back into the burning factory.

James P. Meehan of Traffic Division B is riding his horse through Washington Square Park that afternoon. He gets into a conversation with his superior, Lieutenant William Egan. A boy runs up to the pair gesturing wildly in the direction of the Asch building. Meehan rides toward the building, halting his horse in front of 23 Washington Place. Smoke is issuing thickly from the eighth floor. A bystander tells the policeman that he saw something looking "like a bale of dark dress goods" fall out of the window. "Someone's in there all right. He's trying to save the best cloth,"[2] the man says.

Another cloth bundle falls from an open window. A gust of wind catches the bundle and it bursts open. It is not a bundle of cloth at all, but

the falling body of a girl whose dress is on fire. More people come running, summoned by the screaming onlookers. One man, John H. Mooney,
runs to Fire Box 289 at the corner of Greene Street and raises the first
alarm at 4:45 p.m.

Patrolman Meehan runs into the building and bounds up the stairs two
at a time. He meets a mass of scared girls coming down, and he squeezes
himself against the wall so they can pass. Moving further up, he trips on
an unconscious girl between the seventh and eighth floors. He revives her
and sends her down the stairs. By the time he gets to the eighth floor, he
sees that the fire is only a few feet away from the door to the stairwell.
He directs several more girls down the stairs with the help of a machinist
named Louis Brown. Brown has worked his way to the front of a pack of
girls and is able to force a door open. Sylvia had found her way to that
area and is right behind Brown as it opens. Brown, Meehan, Sylvia, and
the girls rushing out behind them are able to make it down the stairs.[3]

As they descend, Meehan hears banging coming from the other side of
the sixth floor door. Giving it everything he has, he shoulders the door
and it springs open. The floor is filled with terrified women. The employees who took the fire escape down from above discover that it is not a
path to safety. They reenter the building at the sixth floor and eventually
fight their way down to the street. By this time, fire engines and police
vehicles are arriving. One witness, a coroner named Dr. D. C. Winterbot-
tom runs to a store and grabs a telephone. He freezes for a moment before
he can collect himself enough to scream at the operator: "For God's sake,
send ambulances."[4]

As medical personnel arrive on the scene, they stare in horror at the
ghastly scene. Dozens of women are hanging from ledges. Some, their
dresses ablaze, jump out of windows. The sounds of fire whistles and
bells resound through the streets. Men on the streets yell up to the women
not to jump. Wildly waving their arms, they yell "Here they come!" referring to the emergency personnel. Some men bring over blankets to catch
the falling women. The bodies land on the blankets with such force that
they rip the cloth out of the hands of the would-be saviors. They fall with
tremendous force, crashing onto the sidewalk with sickening momentum.
Where there are iron grates in the sidewalk, the bodies hit with such force
that they smash through the grates. People are jumping in ones, twos, and
threes, falling, and then crashing with the bone-crushing thumps.

Bodies begin to pile up on the sidewalk. Some are on fire, and firefighters douse them with their hoses. The water runs red with the blood. The
bodies soon bury the fire hoses, forcing the firefighters to clear the bodies
out of the way before they can continue to fight the fire.

Firefighter Captain Howard Ruch tells his men to open up life nets to
catch the people who keep jumping as the fire pushes more and more

Figure 1.1.   Bodies of victims collect on the sidewalk, 1911. *Kheel Center, Cornell University, photo by: Brown Brothers*

workers out of the windows and off the ledges. The men unfurl the nets and loop their arms in. The first net is ready just in time to catch three falling bodies. The bodies hit with eleven thousand pounds of force, and the firemen are knocked off their feet, and some tumble into the net. The nets rip and some start burning. People are now jumping in threes and fours. The nets are useless. Even the smallest bodies go right through. One woman survives the jump and Chief Edward J. Worth sends her across the street. She walks ten feet before collapsing, dead. The firemen try to raise ladders, but the ladders don't reach past the sixth floor. One worker tries to grab at a ladder as she falls past it, but she misses and plummets downward, her clothes ablaze.

A girl walks out on a ledge, moving away from the window. She takes off her wide-brimmed hat and throws it out, away from the building. She then takes some coins and bills from her handbag and casts them out over the street. The coins bounce on the cobblestones, and she plunges after them. A young man on the ninth floor holds a girl out of the window away from the heat and drops her. He takes another girl in his arms and drops her, too. Then he takes a third, as if, to quote reporter William

Shepherd, he was helping her "into a street car instead of into eternity."
The man sees "that a terrible death awaited them in the flames and his
was only a terrible chivalry."[5] The man takes one more girl in his arms
and she puts her arms around him and they kiss. The man drops his lover
and then casts himself out over the piles of the dead below.

On the Washington Place side, people are jumping feet first from
the open windows. On the Greene Street side, people are stuck inside,
crushed up against closed windows. The windows finally break, and
from the empty frames, a torrent of fiery bodies pours out in a stream
plummeting to the street.

At 4:57, no more than twenty minutes after the fire started, the last
body, a young girl wreathed in burning clothes, jumps from a ledge on
the ninth floor. She catches on an iron hook sticking out at the sixth floor
and hangs there, burning, before something gives, and she falls to the
sidewalk.

The number of dead is 146, mostly women, many of them very young.

THE OUTRAGE

Why is the Triangle Waistcoat Factory in a condition that allows this
monstrous disaster? Owned by Joseph J. Asch, the structure was built in
1901 at the cost of $400,000. The building is 135 feet tall. Were it fifteen
feet taller, the law would require metal trim around the door and window
frames as well as stone or concrete floors, all of which would provide
greater structural support in a fire, but at 135 feet, its entirely wood construction is legal. The building has ten thousand square feet on each floor,
which, according to the law, requires three stairwells for exit. But the law
seems to be applied in this instance according to personal interpretation.
The architect successfully argued that "the staircases are remote from
each other and, as there is a fire escape in the court[yard], it practically
makes three staircases, which in my opinion is sufficient."[6]

The Asch building's "third staircase," the fire escape, runs from the
top floor and stops at the second story, leaving a one-story gap, but as
Manhattan borough president George McAneny puts it, the law "leaves
enormous discretionary power with the Building Department." An expert
in fire insurance and prevention, Arthur E. McFarlane, points out during
the investigation that a lot of builders "decided to build their loft buildings without any fire escapes at all. Others put them in the air shaft which,
in case of fire, becomes its natural flue. Others bolted on all-but-vertical
18-inch ladder escapes such as could not legally have been placed upon
even a three-story tenement house." (The law for commercial buildings
like Asch is different from the law for residential buildings.)

State law dictates that doors in factories "shall be so constructed as to open outwardly, where practicable, and shall not be locked, bolted or fastened during working hours." In the Asch building, the stair landings are too narrow to allow the doors to open outward. Thus, outward-opening doors are judged not "practicable." The dangers of inward-opening doors have been established by earlier fires where people pushing to exit from a fire make it impossible for the doors to open inward. Panic bars, developed in response to the problem, were commercially available in 1911, but not legally required.

In 1911, New York City doesn't have laws mandating fire sprinklers in factories. It is not that the value of such systems is doubted. Fire Chief Edward F. Crocker notes that there has never been a death in a building with a sprinkler system. It is simply that it is up to the person who must pay for the devices to decide to install them. Additionally, fire equipment of the day can't combat fires higher than eighty-five feet up. That means that the top three floors of the Asch building, the entirety of the Triangle Factory, is out of reach of the fire hoses.

Chief Crocker has previously testified before the New York State Assembly to these building safety failings: "I think if you want to go into the so-called workshops . . . twelve, fourteen or fifteen story buildings they call workshops, you will find it very interesting to see the number of people in one of these buildings with absolutely not one fire protection, without any means of escape in case of fire."[7]

Even cheap fixes, such as fire drills, are not mandated. P. J. McKeon, a fire prevention expert who lectures at Columbia University, inspects the Triangle Shirtwaist Factory in 1909. The factory owners are trying to increase their insurance coverage. McKeon is worried about the crowded top three floors of the building. Upon learning that the building has never had a fire drill so workers will know how to respond to a fire, McKeon recommends such a drill, but no drill is organized.

On October 15, 1910, just months before the deadly fire, fireman Edward F. O'Connor inspects the Asch building. Based on the then-current building codes, he reports that the fire escape and stairways are "good." Further, the building, a veritable matchbox, is legally considered "fireproof." So, after the tragedy, Joseph Asch is able to accurately tell reporters "I have obeyed the law to the letter. There was not one detail of the construction of my building that was not submitted to the Building and Fire Departments. Every detail was approved and the Fire Marshall congratulated me." After the fire, Albert G. Ludwig, the chief inspector and deputy superintendent of the Building Department says that the Asch building "could be worse and [still] come within the requirements of the law."[8]

The rain of burning women is not quickly forgotten. The Collegiate Equal Suffrage League holds a rally at Cooper Union on the Friday after the fire.[9] A banner across the speakers' platform reads, "Votes for women. Locked doors, over-crowding, inadequate fire escapes. The women could not, the voters did not alter these conditions. We demand for all women the right to protect themselves."[10] The event's program includes a speech from Dr. Anna Shaw, a well-known suffragist.

"As I read the terrible story of the fire," Dr. Shaw says to the emotionally raw crowd, "I asked, 'am I my sister's keeper?' For the Lord said to me, 'where is thy sister?' And I bowed my head and said, 'I am responsible.' Yes, every man and woman in this city is responsible. Don't try and lay it on someone else. . . . You men—forget not that you are responsible! As voters it was your business and you should have made it your business." (Women did not get the vote until nine years later, in 1920.)

Dr. Shaw faults the law: "Something's got to be done to the law," she argues to applause. "And if it's not constitutional to protect the lives of workers then we've got to smash the constitution! It's our 'instrument,' and if it doesn't work, we've got to get a new one!"[11] The crowd learns that over fifty thousand workers die every year in work accidents, around a thousand a week. As for the owners of the Triangle Shirtwaist Factory, "Mr. Harris and Mr. Blanck were there at the time the fire broke out. They escaped. We congratulate them. My friends, what a tremendous difference between the captains of ships and the captains of industry!"[12]

Chief Crocker, the perpetual critic of weak fire safety codes, sends a note that is read to the assembly. Crocker wants the crowd to understand that choices are being made. These deaths are not the wrath of God or an accident: "It comes down to dollars and cents against human lives no matter how you look at it."[13]

The National Women's Trade Union League holds a similar rally in the Metropolitan Opera House on April 2, 1911. They attempt to channel the outrage into creating safer conditions for factory workers. The International Ladies' Garment Workers' Union (ILGWU) organizes a funeral procession to mourn the women who died in the fire.[14]

A commemorative funeral march of over one hundred twenty thousand people is held on April 5, a Wednesday. It is a frigid, rainy morning eleven days after the fire. The city essentially shuts down for the event. Three hundred thousand people line the route, paying tribute as empty coffins roll by. The funeral parade takes four hours to pass by. With the dead duly honored, the raw emotion of the public becomes focused on the perceived negligence of the owners, Max Blanck and Isaac Harris.

Two weeks after the fire, the owners are charged with first and second degree manslaughter for locking the doors that prevented the workers from escaping. They are indicted and brought to trial. The prosecutors must prove that Harris and Blanck either locked the doors or ordered them to be locked. Their defense is easy, simply noting that they took no such action and had no knowledge of it being done. On December 27, they are judged not guilty. Angry crowds yell "Murderers!" as they leave the courthouse.[15]

Several survivors and dozens of family members of those who died bring civil cases against Harris and Blanck. Most families cannot afford the legal fees required to bring a civil suit. There is no such thing as Workers' Compensation in 1911, but the owners eventually settle, agreeing to give the twenty-three litigants seventy-five dollars per victim or the equivalent of five weeks' wages.

Under existing law, the owners have not done anything so bad or so different from what others do to be singled out for criminal punishment. Nor are any officials found to have done wrong. The law's expectations for building safety are low. Chief Crocker seethes. He testifies: "The fault in New York City is that there is nobody responsible for anything. The Fire Department is not responsible; the Building Department is not responsible; the Police Department is not responsible; the Health Department is not responsible. If anything happens they are all stepping from under."[16]

THE REFORM

On the day of the fire, Frances Perkins is having tea with friends just down the street from the Asch Building. The group hears the fire engines and goes into the street to investigate. Perkins, a Mount Holyoke graduate, watches, helpless to prevent the deaths.

Perkins is the executive secretary of the New York Consumers League. Her work in economics and social work combines with her deep personal convictions to make her an effective lobbyist. She has long had a vision of doing "something about unnecessary hazards to life."[17] Summoning her considerable talents, Perkins quickly starts the process for reform.

She taps into the public outrage of the moment and calls on politicians generally and Governor John Dix in particular to act. Recounting her eyewitness memories of the fire, she reminds everyone, "I can't begin to tell you how disturbed the people were everywhere. It was as though we had all done something wrong. It shouldn't have been. We were sorry. Mea culpa! Mea culpa! We didn't want it that way. We hadn't intended to have 147 girls and boys killed in a factory. It was a terrible thing for the people of the City of New York and the State of New York to face."[18]

Governor Dix, who understands the real source of power in New York, suggests that Perkins consult Tammany Hall—the Democratic machine that controls New York City at the time—and its powerful bosses, Assemblyman Alfred Smith and Senate Majority Leader Robert F. Wagner. The powers of Tammany Hall decide that, given the continuing unrest, they will support legislation that promotes worker safety. On June 30, 1911, an appropriation is made to establish the Factory Investigating Commission (FIC), and the first state-sponsored investigation into worker safety is underway. Perkins is appointed executive secretary to lead the commission's work.

Perkins uses the momentum of growing public discontent to obtain funding to study more than just the safety of garment shops in Manhattan. The FIC examines firsthand the working conditions and safety of 1,836 factories across the state, interviewing hundreds of civic and union leaders, factory workers, and public officials over four years.

The commission does not lose sight of the headline event, the source of the outrage that created it, and its primary focus remains fire hazards. Ex-Chief Crooker, the longtime critic of existing regulations, testifies alongside many other experts regarding the inadequate codes and the impossibly confusing overlapping mandates across different city departments and agencies. Armed with these frontline reports, the FIC is able to get fifteen separate reforms enacted at the state level.

The New York City Board of Aldermen also uses the FIC report to justify creation of the Bureau of Fire Prevention. The city enacts the Sullivan-Hoey Fire Prevention law, which clarifies the responsibilities of the different city agencies with respect to code promulgation, inspections, and enforcement. The city's Municipal Building Code becomes more safety oriented: sprinkler systems must now be installed in all factories, as well as lighted exit signs, exit doors that open outward, and onsite firefighting equipment. Systemic issues are also addressed, including the problems of evacuating large groups from high-rises and the storage of flammable materials in public buildings.

New York State follows New York City's lead. Over several rounds of legislation, laws are put into place that reorganize the New York State Department of Labor and assign broad powers to the department. A new industrial board is empowered to promulgate an industrial code that will carry the force of law.

In turn, New York's unprecedented response to the Triangle Shirtwaist Factory fire prompts many states to enact similar reforms.

On paper, the situation in New York City improves greatly. The Tammany bosses Wagner and Smith (the latter will soon become governor) work with Perkins in part because they want to change the image of their political machine and are seeking a broader political base. However, they still need the support of business owners. The cost of implementing the reforms would fall on owners, and sprinkler systems, fire extinguishers, and redesigned egress do not come cheap. The ultimate solution to their dilemma: strong laws but weak enforcement.

Violations of the new codes frequently are not taken seriously. In 1913, Blanck and Harris, the owners of the Triangle Shirtwaist Factory, are running a new factory where the doors are again being chained, trapping 150 women inside without means of escape in case of fire. The result: Blanck is fined twenty-five dollars. He understands the game. Later that same year, on December 23, Blanck is again found to be violating the law and is issued a warning. On this occasion he is not fined.

Nationally the movement brings real change to fire prevention and public safety. New York is the nation's leader in passing fire-safety legislation. Even though its own enforcement is weak, its legislative action sets an example to inspire others, whose enforcement is not so weak.

Tammany boss Wagner continues with his worker-safety reform movement when he becomes a U.S. senator. Frances Perkins also becomes a national power, as secretary of labor under President Franklin Roosevelt, and adds an informed voice to the federal efforts toward fire safety. As the state and federal reforms take shape, Perkins reflects on the efforts, noting that they are "based really upon the experience that we had in New York State and upon the sacrifice of those who, we faithfully remember with affection and respect, died in that terrible fire on March 25, 1911."[19]

BEYOND REFORM

While the Triangle fire is effective in starting the reform movement for building safety and spreading it beyond New York, the movement remains primarily reactive.[20] Each forward step requires a new tragedy. There is still no proactive search for codes that will avoid tragedies *before* they happen.

In March of 1937, a natural gas explosion at the New London School kills 298 people in Texas. Most of the victims are children. Natural gas is not commonly used as a commercial heating fuel at the time, but waste gas from a nearby oil field is piped into the school building to heat it at essentially no cost. Natural gas is colorless and odorless, so when a leak occurs in the school's system, no one notices. A shop teacher turns on an electric sander, providing the spark, and sets off the explosion. The building seems to lift into the air, then smashes to the ground, its walls collapsing. Its roof falls in, burying its victims under brick, steel, and concrete. A two-ton concrete slab flies two hundred feet from the building before landing on and crushing a 1936 Chevrolet. The explosion is heard four miles away.[21] Once the cause of the fire is understood, Texas passes legislation requiring that odorous mercaptans be added to natural gas. By giving natural gas a distinct odor, similar to garlic or rotten eggs, dangerous leaks become easier to detect. The reform quickly spreads.[22]

In 1942, a fire at the Cocoanut Grove nightclub kills 492 people. The firefighters have difficulty getting into the building because the doors, which open inward, are blocked by stacks of bodies. Further, the exits are too narrow to manage the volume of fleeing patrons, and decorative draperies cover the exit signs. The club also has highly flammable finishes.[23] Within a few years, commercially viable flame retardants for fabrics are developed. Interior finishes of buildings become regulated.

The flammability of fabrics in other contexts is not immediately considered, however. Yet, all over the country children are regularly injured by seemingly benign sources. Items such as costume cowboy chaps quickly melt and burn the child if exposed to even moderate heat, yet are legally sold. After many children are injured, the federal government enacts the Flammable Fabrics Act of 1953, forbidding the use of dangerously flammable textiles in making clothes. Consumer Product Safety Commission tests impose flammability standards for all clothing.[24] The Children's Sleepwear Standard of 1972 goes on to subject children's sleepwear to special regulation.[25]

On December 7, 1946, a fire breaks out in the Winecoff Hotel in Atlanta, Georgia, killing 119 people. It remains the worst hotel fire in United States history. After the deaths, changes are made to building codes for hotels. The changes apply the same rules already mandated in many other types of buildings, such as requiring fire-retardant finishes, multiple exit stairways, and fire doors to seal off stairwells.

In 1958, ninety-two school children and three nuns die when their school, Our Lady of Angels, burns. The building was not built to be a school and thus not legally bound to meet school building codes. While the school is clean and well run, a pile of cardboard somehow ignites and goes unnoticed. The school has a fire-safe brick exterior but the interior is made almost entirely of combustible wooden materials—stairs, walls, floors, doors, roof, and cellulose fiber ceiling tiles. Moreover, the floors have been repeatedly coated with flammable varnish and petroleum-based waxes. There are only two (unmarked) fire alarms in the school. The four fire extinguishers are mounted seven feet in the air and thus unreachable to many. The only fire escape is beyond reach because the well-fueled fire quickly fills the hallway with suffocating smoke and superheated gases.

Sweeping changes in school fire-safety regulations are thereafter enacted, including fire-safety doors at stairwells to slow the spread of a fire. Some 16,500 older school buildings in the United States are brought up to meet the new codes within one year after the disaster. The head of the National Fire Protection Agency gives voice to the larger issue: "There are no new lessons to be learned from this fire; only old lessons that tragically went unheeded."

As awareness of fire danger grows, new problems are exposed. In the 1970s, a new gadget makes its way into most American kitchens, drip coffeemakers. They are wonders of convenience; set it up and coffee is made and kept warm all day. By the mid-1980s, tracking the causes of fires becomes common, and the numbers reveal a grim story: hundreds of fires are being caused by the innocent-looking coffee devices. In 1996 alone, five hundred residential fires are started by the machines.[26] An inexpensive thermo-coupler, which is known to fail with regularity, is found to be the problem. Mr. Coffee, pitched by baseball hero Joe DiMaggio, is the most famous brand of drip coffeemakers and has many recalls of its machines. But in fact, almost all brands are fire hazards.

Regulating consumer goods to prevent fire hazards soon becomes common. Appliances are now tested and must meet safety standards before reaching retail shelves. The cost is passed on to the consumer, often at pennies per item.

Building safety, on the other hand, remains a maze of problems with no easy fix. Throughout the United States, model building codes are developed by a wide range of organizations, including local government officials, insurance underwriters, private groups, union organizations, and the federal government, without much thought to uniformity or guiding principles. The United States has no national building code. Rather, state, tribal, or local governments are left to decide for themselves what to do or not to do.[27]

To make it easier for governments to formulate reasonable practices, in 1994, the overarching International Code Council (ICC) is formed to coordinate comprehensive codes for building construction safety and fire prevention. The ICC is an umbrella organization comprising a family of international codes including the International Residential Code (IRC), the International Building Code (IBC), and the International Existing Building Code (IEBC). In the United States, each state and many municipalities still decide for themselves which specific codes they will adopt, but the model codes provide at least a nudge toward greater uniformity. The "Eurocode," in contrast, is now in force in the entire EU, superseding all national codes. The model codes are constantly being improved. Today, all fifty states, the District of Columbia, and every United States territory have adopted some ICC codes.

The fire-safety reforms sparked by the Triangle Factory fire have indeed changed our world. At the time of the 1911 fire, workers died at a rate of about 1,000 per week in the United States, while the nation's population stood at 94 million. One hundred years later, the U.S. population is 322 million, yet the weekly on-the-job death toll is down to 90, less than a tenth of what it was, even though the population is now more than three times larger.[28] The numbers are compelling: the odds of dying on the job in 1911 were 1 in 1,800; the odds that a given worker will be killed this year are 1 in 69,000. As a point of comparison, it is more likely that today's worker will be killed crossing the street, a chance of 1 in 54,538.[29]

A LARGER PERSPECTIVE

What does the Triangle fire and its aftermath tell us about the tragedy-outrage-reform dynamic? Why did the Triangle fire have the effect that it did? Why was *it* the trigger for reform rather than one of the many other earlier fires, some of which were even larger disasters?

The 1903 Iroquois Theater fire killed more people, 602. And it was equally horrendous. Families were at the theater for a holiday show. The stage curtains caught fire, which spread instantly to the ceiling and quickly engulfed the entire building. With the flames racing through the building, people panicked. Women and children screamed as the living tried to climb over those trampled to death at the exits. The piles of corpses reached seven feet high and became walls that penned in the living. By the time firefighters arrived, no one remained alive.

One might speculate that, while the theater fire was horrific, the horror was private. We could only imagine after the fact the terrible sufferings but only after officials later reconstructed the events that must have occurred. The Triangle Factory fire, in contrast, was public. Nothing can match the riveting effect of raining flaming bodies, where it is the bystanders on the sidewalk who are doing the screaming.

But this is a cheap answer, we think. More likely, it was the social and political environment that changed between the 1903 theater fire and the 1911 factory fire. The real cause for the change lay with Theodore Roosevelt, an aggravated Tammany Hall, and a presidential assassin.

The political bosses of New York found the energetic, young Governor Roosevelt a troublesome man. His commitment to ridding the state of corruption and his desire to improve the lives of average citizens interfered with the Tammany Hall way of doing business. To get rid of Roosevelt, they promoted him to obscurity—he became vice president under William McKinley. But the plan went awry when McKinley was assassinated and Roosevelt, at forty-two, became the youngest president this country has ever had.

With him, Roosevelt brought to power the Progressives, who had previously been a more intellectual movement than political one. His "Square Deal" promised the average citizen a government of fairness, which would break the trusts, regulate the railroads, and provide pure food and drugs. The goal of building safety fell squarely within the nature of the Progressive agenda.

On the other hand, while the rise of the Progressives created kindling, it is doubtful that the dramatic string of building safety reforms would have happened without the spark of the Triangle fire. The Progressives had an endless list of ways in which average citizens' lives could be improved. But this is where raining flaming bodies trumped the others on the list.

The striking horror of that Saturday afternoon occurred in a sea of raised expectations. The outrage was strong and sustained because the average citizen was now less likely to accept such horrible disasters as simply a terrible accident, as just one more bad thing in a tough, unforgiving world of many inevitable bad things. A tragedy of this nature and dimension touched people's hearts in a way that could not be ignored because it so vividly conflicted with their new feelings of hope and expectation.

The "progressive" agenda may have now run its course. Dramatically increasing the minimum wage hardly has the moral force of preventing falling flaming bodies, and may not even be good for the people it is trying to help. (Does it cost jobs? Does it increase the cost of living for low-income people?) But no matter what one may think of progressivism today, the original movement did play an important role in converting the public outrage over the Triangle Factory into practical reforms that have improved all of our lives.

As we shall see in other chapters, every "trigger case" has its own unique story, partly a product of human nature generally and partly a product of the social and political context of the moment.

Chapter Two

1915
Chloroform Killer
Medical Examiners

THE TRAGEDY

In 1914, Carl Menarik leaves his name and his home in Vienna.[1] As Fred-erick Mors, the young man settles in Yonkers, New York City. He works as a porter in Unionport at the German Odd Fellows Home, a facility that is part orphanage and part old-folks home. The facility is used for hous-ing some two hundred and fifty waifs and a hundred pensioners. Here Mors makes a meager salary of eighteen dollars per month, plus room and board—about $425 in today's currency. Nonetheless, Mors enjoys the work because it allows him to cultivate his interest in medicine. He feels good about all the responsibility he is given, and is "made practically a nurse because the men over me realized that I knew something about nursing and was better educated than most orderlies."[2] The busy city takes little notice of Mors, and history certainly would have forgotten him had he not stopped by a police station in January of 1915.

A slight man, Mors fights the unusual cold of this New York winter—which has frozen the trolleys in their tracks and put fifteen thousand men to work as "snow fighters" clearing the streets—to arrive at the police sta-tion. He now paces in front of investigator Louis Gray, who immediately notices the man is not an ordinary New Yorker. Mors is dressed in an old-school European hunting costume, complete with a heavy corduroy jacket, knee breeches, knee-length stockings, and a fine feathered hat.[3] Mors is blue eyed, bearded, and smokes Egyptian cigarettes. Clouded by his cigarette smoke, Mors has a story to tell and seems frustrated, "Oh, I wish I spoke English better," he mutters in a thick accent.[4] But his English is clear enough for Mors to confess to murder.

Mors explains to investigators that he has killed eight residents of the Odd Fellows Home. The victims are, in his words, "superannuated octogenarians."[5] Mors conveys to the authorities that he sees that medical care offers them no hope. "They were all in great pain that could not be relieved. There was no chance for them. Also they were not pleasant physically or mentally to themselves or anyone else."[6] After his confession, he is jailed.

Once in custody, Mors's story evolves. Now he claims that he undertook the killings at the behest of his boss Adam Banger, the superintendent of the home. Banger recently fired Mors, and Mors has come to the police because he fears that the superintendent plans to put the blame on him. He says Banger affirmatively tasked him with the "removal"[7] of the elderly residents who were in the worst health. Those patients were a drain on resources. Though the command feels daunting, Mors understands that "it was really a kind-hearted thing to do."[8] The police arrest the superintendent and three other employees of the home and launch an investigation into Mors's account. They discover little physical evidence that corroborates his story, but there are circumstantial hints. For example, in his home, there is a German-language poison handbook.

There is no shortage of witnesses who come forward to speak about Mors's suspicious behavior. The embalmer believes Mors to be "indifferent to the suffering and deaths of those in the home." Several of the older residents state that they are afraid of Mors, especially those individuals who require more care. "If you don't stop making so much trouble," he'd been heard saying to one ninety-one-year-old man, "I'll send you to where there is more heat than you want."[9] The boy who watches the dispensary tells the police that Mors has described elderly residents as useless. The boy says that Mors has told him that disposing of them "would be a good thing." Now several people state that they have long known Mors to be a murderer. One woman rang her bell too frequently, and Mors is reported to have told her she'd be sorry if she did it again. The next day, she was dead.

The embalmer also claims that Mors had been sloppy in at least one of the killings. Mors applied too much chloroform to the cloth he used to kill a man, which inflamed the sensitive skin around the man's mouth. The embalmer is suspicious enough to confront Mors about the markings. Mors shrugs it off, attributing the markings to a rag used around the man's mouth postmortem to keep it shut. The embalmer is unconvinced. In his view, the marks are chloroform scars, just like the ones he found on people who'd died during surgery from chloroform inhalation.

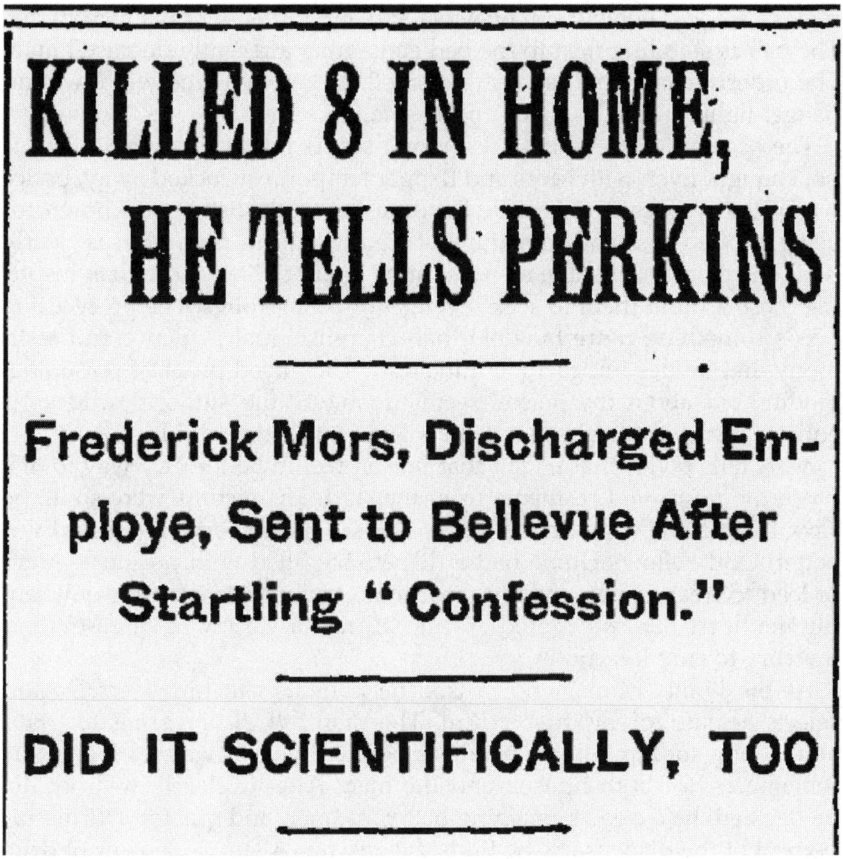

KILLED 8 IN HOME, HE TELLS PERKINS

Frederick Mors, Discharged Employe, Sent to Bellevue After Startling " Confession."

DID IT SCIENTIFICALLY, TOO

Figure 2.1. Frederick Mors came to the police, 1915. *New York Times*

One of the orderlies—an attendant at the hospital—reports to police that he noticed Mors putting Vaseline around a man's mouth. The orderly asked Mors about this and Mors explained that the Vaseline would make it easier to shave the dead man's face. The orderly is startled—the man in front of him is alive. Then sure enough, death arrives within a few hours.

Mors does not deny the interaction with the orderly. In fact, after the conversation with the orderly, Mors tells the police, he learned his lesson. He begins using a more subtle method: he stuffs chloroform-drenched cotton balls in his victims' ears and nose. The police find cotton balls and tweezers in his coat.

At least one orderly believes the story that Mors has been following orders. This orderly relates an incident to police. Having been instructed to remove a body, he walks in on Mors and superintendent Banger talking. The pair is standing next to the bed containing a recently deceased man. The orderly comments on a sweet smell, Mors opens the window, and Banger lights a cigar to cover up the smell.

The accumulating witness testimony seems pretty damning, but it is not enough. Even with Mors and Banger temporarily locked away, police worry that witnesses might be bending the truth. Banger is known for being a rotten boss and something of a bully. For his part, Mors is clearly odd. The pair of unlikable men might be guilty of little more than inspiring those around them to seek revenge for past wrongs. The prosecution needs something more tangible than circumstantial evidence and testimony that invites impeachment in court. They need proof of poisoning. Finding out about the poison seems doable to the authorities: Mors is entirely forthcoming about who he killed and how he did it.

Mors tells police that he felt that poison would be the best way to dispatch the unwanted residents from the start. His victims were so ill, he says, that no one would be terribly surprised if they suddenly died. Even better, Odd Fellows Home had a dispensary filled with poisons—sugar of lead to treat rashes, codeine, morphine, opium, atropine for quickening the heart rate, powdered arsenic to treat a variety of diseases, and mercury to cure infections.

At the home, Mors, who insists the patients call him Herr Doctor, selects arsenic for his first victim. The man fell ill, lingering for days and slowly succumbing to paralysis before dying. It was terrible, Mors remembers, for both himself and the man. Arsenic clearly will not do, he decided; he'd need something better, cleaner, and quieter. During his perusal of the dispensary, he finds the answer. A simple, powerful drug called chloroform. "When you give an old person chloroform," he tells the police, "it's like putting a child to sleep."[10]

Chloroform—an effective sedative with a distinctively sweet smell—has been around since 1847, discovered by Scottish doctor James Young Simpson as an alternative to ether. Though chloroform had been the drug of choice for physicians for over fifty years, it is dangerous. Even in small doses, chloroform kills one in three thousand people, and its effects are unpredictable. People put under chloroform for surgery are known to die on the operating table before a surgeon has time to make the first incision. By the early 1900s, the British Medical Association labeled chloroform the "riskiest anesthetic"; the American Medical Association advised hospitals to stop using it. While hospitals found alternatives, it continued to appear in pharmacies across the nation—and in places such as the Odd Fellows Home.

Detectives must prove that Mors has actually done what he claims and is not simply a nutcase. They decide to dig up Mors's first victim. According to Mors, this patient was killed with arsenic, and it is well understood how to find arsenic in a body after death. Unfortunately, the authorities learn that the Odd Fellows Home uses arsenic tonic on patients regularly. If everyone has been given doses of arsenic, finding arsenic in the corpse will prove nothing, so the plan is scrapped.

Now the detectives wonder about the possibility of detecting chloroform in the other victims. They turn to the New York City coroner, Patrick Riordan, who informs the police that there is no way to detect a chloroform killing. Chloroform, he maintains, leaves no telltale markers on a corpse, so digging up the buried bodies for analysis is pointless. "We might do this in some cases, but Mors has said that he chloroformed the persons he killed in Westchester, and the fact that a person has been chloroformed cannot be proven by an autopsy," Riordan unhesitatingly explains. "Therefore we can establish nothing by exhuming the bodies. Mors may have given each of his victims a quart of chloroform but we couldn't prove it by an autopsy."[11] Riordan also adds doubt to Mors's claims. Contrary to Mors's accounts that his victims died within minutes, Riordan informs the police that death by chloroform poisoning takes at least ten minutes. The case against Mors seems to be slipping away.

Police come to expect little from Patrick Riordan. He is an irritable man with a taste for liquor, and the Mors case arrives at a bad time for him. It's mid-January, and he is very busy fending off accusations that he'd been drunk on the job. Less than a month earlier, Riordan had been on call during a terrible train crash in the city. Two passenger trains collided, and the station platform—seventy-five feet above the ground—burst into flames. Screaming passengers clambered down the stairs to the street below, and dozens of wounded passengers were rushed to hospitals.

Two men, Joseph Collins and Gottlieb Minnick, both train workers, were killed in the crash. Their bodies were taken to the police station to await the coroner, but Riordan was nowhere to be found. Hours passed. Finally around two in the morning—some eight hours after the crash— Riordan stumbled into the station, so drunk he could hardly walk. When someone read the names of the victims, Riordan grumbled, "It's a shame that two such names should pull us out on a night like this."[12]

Journalists seize the opportunity to mock one more city official who owes his job not to skill but only to patronage. The next day, Riordan's drunkenness lands him in the newspaper, and the city reacts explosively at his disrespect for the victims. By January, Riordan is struggling to talk himself out of formal charges. He really does not need the Mors case to add to his woes.

Drunkenness is not Riordan's only pitfall: the coroner simply does not have the medical knowledge to be effective in his current position. Unbeknownst to the inept Riordan, chloroform poisoning *can* be detected in a corpse. Chloroform poisoning is actually relatively easy to detect in dead bodies. "Chloroform," reads one toxicology book of the time "not only withstands but also impedes putrefaction."[13] Animals killed with chloroform could have the poison in their tissues for weeks afterward, and their brains could have it for months. A buried corpse would be even more likely to retain the poison, as the compound couldn't evaporate easily. The drug leaves internal tissue red and inflamed, causes blood to darken and clot, and swells vessels in the brain, lungs, kidney, and liver.

Beyond observational markers, there are also chemical tests to identify the toxin. In one such test, tissue is ground up, purified with steam, and boiled with lye and benzene. If the "syrup"[14] contains chloroform, it turns yellowish-red and glows yellowish-green under ultraviolet light. In a different process, the tissue can be heated and mixed with hydrochloric acid to break up the chloroform into its disparate elements. Riordan is also wrong to tell the police that chloroform is not a quick killer: published scientific studies show that chloroform can kill in less than a minute.

But what do the police know? They are untrained in medicine and oblivious to Riordan's error. They have been told that they can't prove that Mors is the killer. Seeing no way forward the district attorney is unwilling to move against Mors or his boss. But given the veracity of his confession, the police are not comfortable setting Mors free. If they can demonstrate that Mors is insane, they can lock him away without a criminal conviction. The district attorney sends Mors to Bellevue Hospital.

Though now famous for its respectable psychopathic unit, the hospital has a dark place in the city's mythology. "It gathers the dead and dying from river and streets," a *New York Times* reporter once writes, "and is kept busy night and day with the misery of the living."[15] The psychiatric ward is especially feared, despite the best efforts of the ward's head, Dr. Menas Gregory.

When Mors arrives at the hospital, Gregory studies him closely. After ten days, Gregory acknowledges that while Mors is "not well mentally,"[16] he's not crazy, and he certainly may have had the capacity to commit murder. At a minimum, according to the doctor, these killings are not hallucinations.

For the investigators, the input from Gregory seems to remove all doubt as to Mors's guilt; even the prosecutor admits that Mors likely killed the eight people he claimed to have killed—and perhaps more, as the police find evidence of nine more suspicious deaths.

It is not enough. As the Bronx district attorney says, "Mors' fellow employees and others have given circumstantial evidence, they have told of deaths under suspicious circumstances, they have even told of smelling the odor of chloroform about Mors' person, but nothing they have said would be accepted by a judge or jury as proof of the fact that a crime had been committed in the manner described by Mors."[17] There are plenty of people saying he did it, but why did none of them come forward if they all knew it was occurring? It seems like a barrier that is too formidable to navigate around. The disheartened prosecutor decides not to press charges.

Officials still believe Mors to be dangerous, so they decide to move him to Hudson River Valley Hospital for the Insane in Poughkeepsie. In May of 1915, Mors strolls out of the asylum. He is never seen again.[18]

THE OUTRAGE

In January of 1915, the New York City Commissioner of Accounts, Leonard Wallstein, publishes a scathing report on the city coroner system, which he calls "a joke, a travesty, a disgrace, a public scandal, and a sheer waste of taxpayers' money."[19] Wallstein's prominent case study is Patrick Riordan, the incorrigible drunk who sips from a flask during criminal trials and failed in the Frederic Mors case. Death reports from his office are comically ambiguous: "could be suicide or murder," "either assault or diabetes," "diabetes, tuberculosis or nervous indigestion," and an "act of God." Sometimes the cause of death is left blank. In about half of the eight hundred cases that Wallstein, the city's accounts man, examines, "there is a complete lack of evidence to justify the certified cause of death."

Incredibly, Riordan's incompetence isn't unusual. Riordan is a symptom of a much larger problem—a problem rooted in politics. Coroners are elected, but elections are rigged, with winners determined by New York City's political bosses. Coroners work on salary and receive a commission, earning extra money per body. Corruption is rampant; one assistant coroner repeatedly dumps the same drowned man into the Hudson River to rack up extra money. Among other moneymaking schemes, some coroners will only return bodies to their families after extracting a promise from them to use certain funeral homes, which in turn give a kickback to the coroner. Some coroners even issue fake death certificates to those willing to pay, meaning citizens with resources are able to hide suicides, murders, spouse abuse, and abortions.

Coroners also have access to some financial resources and therefore have some power to give out favors. In some states, the coroner empanels the jury. Whereas the average laborer earns two dollars per day, those appointed by a coroner as a juror earn five dollars per trial. Some men become professional jurors serving on hundreds of panels. The coroner's jury was created to increase the public's confidence in the coroner's determination, but it is the coroner who appoints the jury. Being caught in the act with a corpse in the morgue did not prevent one necrophiliac juror from being called for future hearings.[20]

Even coroners who are not trying to game the system are likely to be unsuited for the job due to ignorance. Coroners aren't required to have medical knowledge, and indeed, most of the New York City coroners aren't doctors: between 1898 and 1915, the position of coroner is filled by two saloon keepers, two plumbers, a milkman, a lawyer, and a host of men from other nonmedical occupations. Doctors who do become coroners usually do so because they have no better option, for example, after losing their license due to malpractice.

The National Research Council describes the average American coroner as an "untrained and unskilled individual, popularly elected to an obscure office for a short term, with a staff of mediocre ability and inadequate equipment."[21] The council suggests eliminating the coroner position, calling it "an anachronistic institution which has conclusively demonstrated its incapacity to perform the functions customarily required of it."[22] The system is expensive, too: according to Wallstein's report, the city squanders $172,000 annually on "unqualified coroners, their mediocre physicians and their personal clerks, who spend most of their time on private affairs."[23]

THE REFORM

Frederic Mors's disappearance is the final straw, and city officials demand change. To Commissioner Wallstein, the logical first step is to simply abolish the coroner system.[24] The governor forces Riordan to resign as New York City coroner in 1915; in the same year, New York passes a law eliminating the coroner system. The city assembles a new system and with it, a new position: the medical examiner. Unlike the coroner, the medical examiner is required to have a medical degree and some background in diseases. And the position is not elected. An applicant for the new position of medical examiner must prove his or her expertise through a series of examinations.

The changes are strong, but the new system will not be implemented for three years. Those opposing the bill hope that, by January of 1918, the public's angry demand for change will fade. There is also the hope that the current wave of reform-minded politicians will give way to the former machine politics that put Riordan in office.

Unfortunately, their hopes turn out to be true. In 1917, reform-minded mayor John Mitchel, who is credited with cracking down on the city's corruption and improving institutions like the fire department, is running for reelection. Mitchel's opponent is Judge John Hylan, a friend of the New

York political machine. Hylan's campaign is remarkably successful, and he beats reformer Mitchel by an overwhelming majority.[25] On one of his first days in office, Hylan announces, "We have had all the reform that we want in this city for some time to come."[26] For Hylan, the reform stipulated by the 1915 law is hardly more than background noise, a dispensable change. In January of 1918, when the change officially becomes law, Hylan appoints Riordan, the former coroner, as the medical examiner of New York City.

Commissioner Wallstein is appalled.[27] Riordan is the poster child for the necessity of a medical examiner, a terrifying example of the dangers posed by putting someone with no medical knowledge in a medical official's job. Worse, Riordan's appointment is a blatant violation of the new law, as he lacks medical experience and skipped the required examinations. Hylan does not foresee the strength of the reaction.

Almost immediately, Wallstein threatens a lawsuit against Hylan. The *New York Times* enters the fight when it publishes an article attacking Riordan's drinking habits and poor record as coroner. The article details the multiple misconduct hearings in which "witness after witness testified that Riordan was incompetent and was repeatedly intoxicated while on duty." As the article becomes widely circulated, public outrage is on the rise again.[28] Civic groups take turns reminding Hyland and the public that Riordan lacked even the most basic qualifications for the job. To make matters worse, it comes to light that the list of potential candidates includes Dr. Otto Schultz, a professor of medical jurisprudence, Dr. Douglas Summers, a professor of pathology, and Dr. Charles Norris, the chief of laboratories at Bellevue and Allied hospitals. All three had sought the position of chief medical examiner,[29] all three passed the exams that Riordan had avoided, and all three had backgrounds in pathology. Under the new law, all three doctors should have been given priority. Instead, the only man who had been fired from the job for his incompetence is given the position.

To get out of the jam, Mayor Hylan appoints a civil service commission to prove the other doctors' ineligibility.[30] The commission declares that it is illegal for the doctors to perform the autopsies required by the exam. Therefore, anyone who actually took the exam is a criminal and unfit to serve. Mayor Hylan claims he appointed the only man who wanted the job who was not also a criminal.

The public outcry grows; even politicians like Governor Whitman call Hylan's actions embarrassing, illegal, and insincere.[31] Hylan sees no way to hold onto Riordan and his own credibility. On January 31, 1918, Mayor Hylan sacks Riordan and appoints Dr. Charles Norris to be the chief medical examiner.[32]

Dr. Norris is immediately popular with the public, and for good reason: his dedication is unrivaled, and his improvements to the system are marked. He's a passionate advocate for improving health in New York City, and his financial generosity is unparalleled, even spending his own money on the job, and he hires medically and scientifically trained staff to boost the department's success. Most importantly, he becomes an irreplaceable asset in criminal investigations. Norris's dramatically improved system ushers in a new era of death investigation.[33]

Within a few short years, Dr. Norris's standard of excellence spreads across the nation. In 1928, a national report dubbed "The Coroner and the Medical Examiner" recommends dramatic nationwide changes.[34] The coroner system, it declares, should be abolished throughout the country, replaced by scientifically trained medical examiners with expertise in pathology. The report recommends good salaries to attract scientists, as well as a staff with knowledge of toxicology, bacteriology, and the like. The committee also recommends that medical examiners develop relationships with hospitals and universities.

In 1956, the National Conference of Commissioners on Uniform State Law drafts and releases the Model Post-Mortem Examination Act. The act recommends that states adopt the medical examiner system to "provide a means whereby greater competence can be assured in determining causes of death where criminal liability may be involved."[35]

The act's guidelines are extensive, ranging from staff qualifications to laboratory maintenance. The chief medical examiner, it provides, should be a licensed physician with at least two years of postgraduate training. The coroner office should be abolished, and coroners that remain should work under the authority of the medical examiner's office.[36] The act also outlines the deaths that require examination, including violent, sudden, or suspicious deaths; deaths related to employment; and deaths that might impact public health. If an autopsy does indeed impact the public, then the examiner should work alongside legal officials.

THE LIMITS OF REFORM

The act's recommendations are well researched, and it is commonly anticipated that states will jump on board. But change is slow: after thirteen years, only twelve states have adopted the medical examiner system. The sluggish state response surprises many. In 1968, the National Research Council Committee on Forensic Pathology releases a report that explores potential reasons behind states' lack of action, citing budget shortages and variable levels of training.[37] In 1985, the National Association of Counties publicizes the benefits of medical examiners; in 2003 and 2009, the Medicine Workshop and National Research Council do the same.

And yet only three more states adopt the reforms by 2000, and by 2015, only sixteen states and the District of Columbia have a centralized medical examiner system.[38] The barriers to adoption are simply too steep. To make the change requires building a working system that often takes power away from politicians, who give up a source of patronage and influence. Even when the political obstacles can be overcome, few eligible doctors elect to become medical examiners. Death investigations are notoriously difficult, dirty, and gruesome. The position of medical examiner lacks prestige, and the standard working conditions reflect this: offices are usually understaffed, the cases are time-consuming, and medical examiners are often on call 24/7. Furthermore, despite the difficult work, time in court, and pricey education, medical examiners are paid far less than other doctors. A medical examiner averages about $100,000 annually, while the salaries of hospital pathologists can exceed $300,000. Other doctors shy away from the profession because of its connection to politics that can create conflicts with medicine. In some states, medical examiners are elected just as corners were elected.

Nonetheless, the trend toward professionally trained medical examiners has dramatically improved the system of death investigation in the United States. Though statistics vary by jurisdiction, about 92.5 percent of deaths are due to natural causes; the remaining are accidents, suicide, and homicide.[39] Impressively, less than one percent of investigated deaths remain undetermined—a bold contrast to the bumbling guesses of coroners in 1915.

With the right conditions and the right skill set, the vast majority of deaths can be ascribed to a designated cause. But this is not always a good thing. The technological and professional advances in death investigation, especially after being touted and exaggerated on the popular television series "CSI" (*Crime Scene Investigation*), have created expectations in juries that are often unrealistic. The "CSI effect," as it is called, leads to wrongful acquittals even in the presence of good evidence that in the past would have persuaded a jury beyond a reasonable doubt. But when juries expect the kind of technical razzle-dazzle that they see on television, even the advanced technology of the real world may pale in comparison. As one forensic science official from Massachusetts, John Grossman, put it, "I think it makes it much harder for the experts. Juries now expect high-level science to be done on lots of cases where again we don't have the resources to do them and in many cases, the science doesn't exist to do them."[40]

Despite such complications, professional death investigation has clearly improved our current situation, and the days of drunken coroners are long gone. Today's professionals conduct autopsies, determine cause of death, issue death certificates, and often play crucial roles in trials. Medical examiners also help to identify bodies, using information derived from the autopsy and the ever-growing databases of missing persons. Additionally, insight gleaned from autopsies has gradually made the world a safer place. For example, several medical examiners noticed that people were dying from ethylene glycol (commonly known as "antifreeze") poisoning. The coroners demonstrated that the sweet taste of the substance made it an easy way to poison an unsuspecting victim and recommended that the taste be changed. Starting in 2013, the bitter compound known as "denatonium benzoate" must be added to all products containing ethylglycol.

Statistically, 2.4 million Americans will die this year. Of those deaths, approximately 450,000 will be investigated and certified by professionals.[41] Reforms have drastically reshaped the nature of death investigations since 1915, with better training, less corruption, and clearer professional expectations. The questions that stymied the Mors investigation would be easily resolved today.

Chapter Three

1932
Lindbergh Kidnapping and Dillinger Robberies

Federalization of Criminal Law Enforcement

THE TRAGEDY—LINDBERGH KIDNAPPING

Late in the morning of March 1, 1932, a nurse named Bessie Gow heads to her employer's home in Hopewell, New Jersey.[1] A devoted nanny, she's been called to watch the couple's twenty-month-old son, a curly-haired boy named Charles Jr. At quarter to six that evening, she takes the infant upstairs to his nursery. The boy is suffering from a cold, so Gow gives him some medicine and prepares a warm supper before dressing him for bed. Sensing that the baby still isn't comfortable, Gow brings out some cloth and sews up a warm flannel nightshirt for the lad. At around half past seven, the boy is tucked into his crib. Gow, with the help of the baby's mother Anne, closes the window shutters in his room. The thick wooden shutters on the southeast window—apparently warped—will not close properly. The women pull them closed as best they can before leaving at eight o'clock.

Just before ten, Gow heads upstairs to check on her charge. She cracks the door enough to allow a sliver of light from the hall to enter the room, enters, turns on the heater, and heads to the baby's bed. Knowing that the cold has been troubling the child, she pauses over the crib to listen to his breathing. Is the medicine she gave him helping? She listens for any strain in his breathing. Instead, she hears silence. Her heart drops. She reaches for the baby but only finds sheets. The baby is gone.

Nanny Gow hurries from the room to find Anne. Does she have the baby? No—Anne is alone. Perhaps Charles Sr. has taken him downstairs.

29

Anne directs Gow to the library, where Charles Sr.—a handsome, stern-faced man—is reading at his desk. He doesn't have the baby. Concerned, he runs upstairs himself and checks the nursery. Where the child should have been he finds a small, white envelope containing a folded paper. Charles reads the note. The news is bad. He hides nothing from the women, "Anne, they have stolen our baby."[2]

The note, drawn out in loopy letters, reads, "Dear Sir! Have 50,000$ redy 2500$ in 20$ bills 1500$ in 10$ bills and 1000$ in 5$ bills. After 2–4 days we will inform you were to deliver the Mony. We warn you for making anyding public or for notify the Police the child is in gute care. Indication for all letters are signature and 3 holds."[3]

News of the abduction quickly spreads; the missing child is Charles Augustus Lindbergh Jr. His father, Colonel Charles Augustus Lindbergh, "Lucky Lindy," is the world's most renowned aviator. Often called the "Lone Eagle," he is considered "one of the most interesting figures in the world to-day to the general public."[4] Almost five years before the kidnapping, on May 21, 1927, Lindbergh captivated the world when he became the first person to complete a transatlantic flight from New York City to Paris. The flight captured the sentiments of the "Roaring Twenties," when everything seemed possible, and the feat was celebrated as tangible proof of the unparalleled victory of the human spirit. "For his achievement," boasted a 1927 biography, "Lindbergh had to support his purpose with unflinching courage, with great confidence, with simplicity of thought and action. . . . Added to all those qualities was the power of concentration and the qualities of a dreamer who could dream and then make his dreams come true."

The morning after the kidnapping, the news is broadcast around the world. The sorrow of the family quickly becomes one that millions of people around the world take to heart. In what would be a modern-day forensic nightmare, people flood onto the Lindbergh estate. Dr. John Grier Hibben, the president of Princeton University, drives to the Lindbergh home hours after the kidnapping is made public and offers the help of the entire student body to aid in the search.

The Lindbergh case shocks the nation, boosting national newspaper circulation by 300 percent and drawing millions of Americans to local theaters for updates. Lindbergh's fame makes his son's disappearance international news; in New York, Catholic, Jewish, and Protestant clergy hold a joint prayer service that is broadcast around the world. Every moment of the investigation and the slightest insight is reported in dozens of newspaper extra editions throughout the United States, Europe, and even South America. Journalist H. L. Mencken refers to the incident as "the greatest story since the Resurrection."[5]

Figure 3.1. Baby Charles Lindbergh Jr., a few months before his death, 1932. *Library of Congress, World-Telegram & Sun collection*

Even famously bad actors are moved by the cruelty—Al Capone denounces it as "the most outrageous thing I have ever heard of." He immediately offers a $10,000 reward (about $140,000 in current American dollars) for information leading to the child's return.

Investigators find footprints under a bedroom window and a broken three-piece wooden ladder, likely cracked during the ascent to or descent from the nursery; footprints lead from the house to tire marks—presumably a getaway car. There are no traces of blood nor any nonfamily fingerprints discovered in the nursery.

Lindbergh tells the head of the New Jersey Police, Colonel H. Norman Schwarzkopf, that he wants to negotiate with the kidnappers without interference. The Lindbergh family works with NBC radio to broadcast a message to the kidnappers. In the broadcast, the baby's parents promise to keep arrangements for the return of baby Charles confidential. The kidnappers are not impressed and they, in turn, send a furious ransom note, chastising the Lindberghs for notifying the police and publicizing the kidnapping. They bump the ransom up to $70,000 and declare they'll keep the baby until excitement dies down. The baby, they reassure the anxious parents, is in good care. Lindbergh recruits two bootleggers, Salvy Spitale and Irving Blitz, to act as intermediaries. On March 8, the Lindberghs receive a note from the kidnappers—Blitz and Spitale are not to be the intermediaries.

On the same day, a seventy-two-year-old, semi-retired educator named Dr. John Francis Condon makes a bold move. Along with millions of others, Dr. Condon is deeply disturbed by the Lindbergh kidnapping. Desperate to help, he writes a letter that is published in the *Bronx Home News*. The letter promises the kidnappers an additional $1,000 and declares that Condon himself would "go anywhere, alone, to give the kidnappers the extra money and promises never to utter his name to any person."[6] The kidnappers accept the offer.

On March 9, Condon finds a letter from the kidnappers in his mailbox. Condon, it declares, will suffice as a go-between. Condon alerts Colonel Lindbergh, who jumps at the opportunity. Lindbergh hands off the $70,000 and instructs him to have a note reading "Money is ready" published in the *New York American*. The note, Lindbergh decides, would be signed with the codename "Jafsie," derived from Condon's initials, J, F, and C. On March 11, Condon receives a phone call from the kidnappers, who direct him to stay at home each night between six and twelve for the remainder of the week.

At 8:30 on the evening of March 12, Condon's doorbell rings. He opens the door to Joseph Perrone, a taxicab driver. Perrone explains that a stranger in a brown topcoat and felt hat stopped his taxi and asked him to deliver the note to Condon's address. The letter instructs Condon to drive to a location a hundred feet from an outlying subway station near an empty hot dog stand. There he'll find a letter under a stone—and he'll need to be there in forty-five minutes. Condon arrives on time with a bodyguard, the former boxer Al Reich. They find the note. It reads, "Follow the fence from the cemetery direction to 233rd Street. I will meet you."

The elderly man heads toward the cemetery gate, courageously leaving Reich behind. It's dark out, but he spots a man in the cemetery waving a white handkerchief. In a thick accent, the man asks, "Did you gottit my note?"[7] Condon guesses that the man is Scandinavian. The man wants the money, but Condon knows better. He says, "I can't bring the money, until I see the baby."[8]

Somewhere in the dark the stranger notices that another man is standing outside the cemetery and is spooked; "It's too dangerous!" he blurts out. Condon gives chase. When he catches up, he sits the stranger down on a bench in nearby Van Cortlandt Park. Condon works to reassure him that there's nothing to fear. As the pair catches their breath, the man—

who calls himself "John"—worries aloud that he "might even burn."[9] A chill moves down Condon's back.

Condon keeps himself calm enough to ask for an explanation. "John" asks: "What if the baby is dead? Will I burn if the baby is dead?"[10] Condon asks why he has been asked to deliver the ransom if the baby is dead. "John" retrenches, "The baby is not dead."

Condon is instructed to inform Lindbergh that the baby is on a boat. John now announces that he must leave; he has stayed too long. "John" tells Condon that the head conspirator, "Number One," will be angry. "John" states that he will send Condon the baby's sleeping suit, as "a token," then disappears into the night.[11]

On March 16, Condon is delivered a package that contains baby pajamas, which Colonel Lindbergh confirms belong to his son. Five days later, Condon receives another note; the abduction, it declares proudly, was planned for over a year. On March 30, the kidnappers threaten to raise the ransom to $100,000, and a few days later, they demand the money by the upcoming Saturday. There is still no proof that the child is alive. Lindbergh wants to pay the money. He believes this is the only hope. Lindbergh gathers the ransom, helped by the IRS. They use gold notes because the nation is abandoning the gold standard within two years, and the gold notes—marked with distinctive round, yellow seals—will be easier to track. A Saturday morning ad announces the news: "Yes. Everything OK Jafsie."[12]

At 7:45 p.m. on Saturday, April 2, another taxi driver delivers Condon a letter from an unidentified man. Condon follows the letter's instructions and, accompanied by Colonel Lindbergh, discovers one last note under a stone outside a Bronx florist shop. The note instructs Condon to head toward the cemetery across the street. Lindbergh, who's carrying a gun, decides to stay behind, and Condon enters the cemetery alone. There he finds "John," who asks about the money. The ransom, Condon answers, is in the car—but he won't retrieve it until he learns Charles Jr.'s whereabouts. "John" promises to return in ten minutes with a note explaining where to find the baby, and Condon picks up the money from the car. When they meet again, Condon hands over $50,000, which he has convinced John to accept, and John gives him an envelope. With that exchange, the men part.

Back at the car, Condon and Lindbergh open the letter anxiously. The baby, the note reads, is on a boat named *Nelly*. "You will find the Boat between Horseneck Beach and gay Head near Elizabeth Island."[13] The following day there is a frantic search, with Lindbergh himself flying along the Atlantic coast, but neither the boat nor the baby are found. Lindbergh returns home, distraught and defeated.

Over a month passes until May 12, 1932, when a truck driver named William Allen stops his rig and heads into the woods off a highway near Mount Rose, New Jersey, to relieve himself. As he turns back to his waiting truck, he spots a tiny head and foot lying in the dirt. Upon slightly closer inspection Allen realizes he has come upon the remains of a partially buried baby. Horrified, Allen alerts police. The infant's head is crushed, his skull punctured, and the body damaged from exposure and decomposition. It appears from the weathered evidence that the child had been placed in a burlap sack.[14] The authorities assume that the boy had been placed in the sack when he was originally taken. While parts of the body have been eaten by animals, enough remains for the coroner to conclude that the baby died from a blow to the head.

The body is identified as that of Charles Jr. The flannel shirt stitched by Nanny Gow still covers the bones. The infant has been dead for at least two months, apparently killed the night of the kidnapping.

THE OUTRAGE

A black cloud falls over the nation. President Roosevelt makes an announcement on May 13: all investigative agencies should place themselves in the service of the State of New Jersey, and the Bureau of Investigation, soon to become the FBI, is tasked with coordinating all federal investigative units. During the period of Condon's involvement, the Bureau—headed by Director J. Edgar Hoover—had performed an auxiliary role, but Roosevelt's announcement intensifies the search for the baby's killer like nothing before.

For months, the Bureau pursues thousands of leads. Investigators dissect rumors about the "Purple Gang" of Detroit and pore over boat registers in an effort to locate the *Nelly*. They examine the records of employees working for certain cemeteries in New York City and Hopewell, New Jersey. They scrutinize other kidnapping and extortion cases for possible connection to the Lindbergh case, and they show hundreds of photographs and criminal descriptions to eyewitnesses in an attempt to identify "John."

The investigations terrify some. One woman, a waitress named Violet Sharpe who works for Mrs. Lindbergh's mother, falls under suspicion. She lies about a man she dated on the night of the kidnapping and, on June 10, 1932, kills herself with poison. Further investigation provides no indication that the woman was involved with the kidnapping. Another woman—wealthy socialite Evalyn McLean—is convinced by conman

Gaston B. Means that he has connections with the kidnappers. Means— claiming to negotiate with a man he calls "The Fox"—procures $100,000 from Mrs. McLean to pay the ransom. Eventually, Means and "The Fox," a disbarred Washington attorney named Norman T. Whitaker, are brought to justice.

The disappearance of the Lindbergh baby has brought the threat of violence into American homes. Kidnapping is not uncommon at the time, but it is considered something of an occupational hazard of certain professions: gangsters, bookies, and bootleggers. With the Great Depression hitting hard, kidnapping rings in cities like Detroit, St. Louis, and Chicago have begun to target respectable families. Many kidnappers are frighteningly well-organized professionals, selecting victims, tracking their movements, and confirming that their families can pay handsomely for their return. According to police chiefs in 501 cities, there are 279 reported kidnapping cases in 1931.

To make matters worse, in the 1930s, laws against kidnapping are not consistent. Every state has some form of anti-kidnapping legislation, with six states allowing the death penalty, but kidnapping is only a misdemeanor in New Jersey. Federal laws are also limited: it is illegal to kidnap a person to enslave them, but regular kidnapping for ransom is not a federal offense. To make matters worse, local and state law enforcement have jurisdiction only in their own states. When a kidnapper crosses state lines, police are helpless to follow. By the time officers from different states coordinate with one another, they've lost precious time, and perpetrators and witnesses are difficult to find. Of all the kidnappings that involve the police in 1931, only sixty-nine end with criminal convictions. An even smaller number are solved entirely, as many kidnappings are conducted by groups.[15]

The city of St. Louis is particularly plagued by this dynamic. As a river town, St. Louis is pressed up into the corner of Missouri with easy access to Illinois. This geo-political boundary makes thriving St. Louis a favorite stomping ground for kidnappers. Simply by crossing the Mississippi, they leave Missouri and stymie police. In 1931—a year before the Lindbergh kidnapping—the mayor, chief of police, several Chamber of Commerce officers, and other St. Louis officials assemble a committee to advocate for federal kidnapping legislation. They draft a bill that Senator Roscoe Patterson and Congressman John Cochran introduce in their respective houses. The bill calls for imprisonment or death for kidnappers who take victims across state lines. It attracts little attention, slogging unnoticed through hearings and loitering in committee discussions. All that changes when the Lindbergh baby disappears.[16]

THE REFORM

With the nation's attention captivated by this case, the Lindbergh baby kidnapping presents a unique challenge for America's evolving legal system. In truth, federal jurisdiction has been growing—albeit slowly—for many decades. Before the Civil War, dealing with crime fell exclusively to the states, but the Civil War showed the dangerous side of decentralized military and politics. In the post–Civil War era, more powers were given over to Congress. As technology and industry grew in the late 1800s, federal criminal statutes grew along with the nation.[17] But the American legal system is still set up for states to deal with most criminals, so the push for new laws giving more power to federal law enforcement officials represents an unprecedented transition. Officials begin using the Lindbergh kidnapping as a stepping-stone to increasing federal jurisdiction.

With the recovery of the baby's body, Congress moves forward with Cochran and Patterson's bill that has long sat dormant. "The Nation still mourns with the Lindbergh family in the loss of their son," says Representative Fred S. Purnell from Indiana. "Out of this tragedy, however, has come a demand for more drastic legislation with which to meet the heartless advance of those who would kidnap and kill." He hopes to enact "a bill designed to so strengthen the arm of the Federal Government as to instill a greater amount of fear into those who make up this class of criminals."[18]

New York Representative Fiorello H. La Guardia explains the necessity of such a law. "Before we had the railroads, the automobile and automobile roads, wireless, telephones, and telegraphs each State could properly take care of its own crime situation. Why? Because crime was localized and escape was slow. It was impossible in the old days to escape local detection," he explains, "but with the telephone, the radio, the automobile, and the airplane, particularly the automobile and the airplane, crime takes advantage of all available means of transportation, and not only is escape easy, but removal and disposition of loot, and the scattering of witnesses."[19]

The bills that come out of the House and Senate Judiciary Committees differ, however. The House bill stipulates the death penalty for kidnappers, though it allows for imprisonment if the jury recommends it. The Senate version makes a life sentence the harshest punishment an abductor could receive.

The bills also differ in methods of enforcement. The House bill plans for state governors and the U.S. Department of Justice to deputize state and local police as federal officials, allowing them to cross state lines in pursuit of kidnappers. The states would bear the expense instead of the federal government. The bill reflects the concerns of Attorney General

William D. Mitchell, who worries about the cost of enforcement and wants states to maintain responsibility. The Senate, on the other hand, calls for federal government to take jurisdiction.

After a hot debate involving issues of state sovereignty, the allocation of costs, and the challenge of coordinating the work of different jurisdictions,[20] Congress adopts the more federalized Senate version, and in June of 1932, President Herbert Hoover signs the bill into law.

HUNTING THE LINDBERGH KIDNAPPER

Emboldened with stronger laws, authorities continue the hunt for the Lindbergh baby's abductors. Experts determine that all the ransom notes are from the same hand. The distinct styling of the letters, particularly the capital *S*, which looks very similar to an American capital *I*, indicates that they were produced by a German national. Dr. Condon spends hours studying photos of suspects, and a sketch of "John" is created based on his and taxi-driver John Perrone's descriptions. In early 1933, the broken ladder found under the nursery window is analyzed by wood expert Arthur Koehler of the Department of Agriculture's Forest Service.

Investigators also keep their eyes open for the marked gold certificates used to pay the ransom. Beginning on August 20, 1934, and continuing through September, sixteen gold certificates are discovered. They are primarily being used at corner produce stores around Yorkville and Harlem. Teams composed of New Jersey State Police, New York City Police, and the Bureau contact banks in greater New York and Westchester County. The man passing the bills fits Condon's description of "John."

September 18 brings a breakthrough in the investigation. The assistant manager of the Corn Exchange Bank and Trust Company phones the New York City Bureau Office. A teller has encountered a ten-dollar gold certificate in a batch of money that has just been deposited. An investigation reveals that the gold certificate came from a nearby gas station. Police interview the gas station employees, and the gas station attendant who collected the note clearly remembers a man whose appearance is consistent with eyewitness descriptions gathered in the weeks before. The individual is an average-sized German in a blue Dodge, the attendant recalls. Their conversation had been unusual, "You don't see many of those anymore," the attendant had noted when given the gold certificate. "I know," the stranger answered, "I have only about one hundred left."[21] Because the conversation seemed odd, the attendant had written down the car's license plate number.

The car is registered to Richard Bruno Hauptmann, a carpenter living in the Bronx. Aged thirty-five and German born, Hauptmann is a shy man with dark hair and deep-set eyes. In July of 1923, he stowed away on a ship to New York City but was quickly arrested and deported. After another failed stowaway attempt in August, Hauptmann finally succeeded aboard another liner later that year. In 1925, he married a waitress named Anna Schoeffler, with whom he had a son. He had a criminal record, having served time for robbery. Hauptmann worked as a carpenter until 1932, but shortly after the kidnapping of Lindbergh's baby, Hauptmann quit carpentry and began to trade stocks.

At 9:00 a.m. on September 19, 1934—over two years after the abduction—Hauptmann leaves his home in the blue Dodge, with police following close behind. Within minutes, Hauptmann's car is pulled over, and after a flurry of commands, he is handcuffed. In his pocket is a twenty-dollar gold note.

That night, Joseph Perrone identifies Hauptmann as the mysterious man who'd used him to pass anonymous notes. The next day, authorities find $1,830 of the ransom money under a board in Hauptmann's garage and another $11,930 tucked in a garage window recess.

The findings are highly suspicious, but Hauptmann insists that the evidence really tells a different story. According to Hauptman, a German friend of his named Isidor Fisch left some of his possessions with Hauptmann before returning to Germany. Fisch died of tuberculosis before ever coming to collect his possessions. Hauptmann explains that when he found the gold notes among Fisch's belongings, he decided to spend the money without telling his wife.

On October 8, Hauptmann is indicted for the murder of Charles Lindbergh Jr. He pleads not guilty, and the case goes to trial on January 2, 1935, in New Jersey State Court. The prosecution's case is based entirely on circumstantial evidence, as no one directly witnessed any part of the actual crime. The most crucial testimony comes from Arthur Koehler, a wood technologist at the U.S. Forestry Service. Koehler studies the unique machining pattern on the wooden ladder leaning against the Lindbergh's home after the kidnapping and finds that a piece of wood from the ladder (dubbed "Rail 16") and a floorboard in Hauptmann's attic were sawed from a single piece of yellow pine. Furthermore, the nail holes in Rail 16 correspond in size, position, angle, and depth to nail holes in an exposed attic joist from which a floorboard is missing. Finally, the markings created by a nicked hand plane in Hauptmann's garage match the markings on the surface of Rail 16.[22] The prosecution also calls as witnesses eight handwriting experts who independently verify that Hauptmann wrote all fifteen ransom notes.

On February 13, 1935, after a six-week trial and eleven hours of deliberation, the jury convicts Hauptmann of first-degree murder. "The most brilliant performances in the witness chair should be credited to the handwriting experts and the wood specialist," one juror exclaimed after the trial. "Their testimony was a treat to the jury."[23]

Hauptmann is immediately sentenced to death. After several failed appeals, he is executed by electric chair on April 3, 1936, using the last moments of his life to plead his innocence.

Help from the IRS and federal law enforcement officials is key in solving the Lindbergh case, but federal law enforcement remains generally uninvolved in most crimes. The new Lindbergh inspired legislation only extends federal criminal law to cases of kidnapping across state lines. But another crime problem of national scope pushes the further expansion of the federalization of law enforcement.

THE TRAGEDY—DILLINGER BANK ROBBERIES

On October 12, 1933, three men in uniforms arrive at an Ohio county jail. They are from an Indiana prison and are at the jail to interview the nation's most famous prisoner. Sheriff Jess Sarber, suspicious of the men, asks for credentials. Sarber should have acted on his suspicions sooner. One of the visitors pulls out an automatic pistol and announces, "Here's our credentials."[24] Sarber reaches for his gun but not before his visitor fires. The single shot in the chest kills Sarber. Taking the keys off the corpse, the visitors lock up Sarber's wife and deputy, then take the keys to a nearby cell and greet their old friend. John Dillinger is now a free man again.

Born on June 22, 1903, young John Dillinger is raised in a middle-class Indianapolis community called Mooresville. His father is a hardworking grocer and church deacon who believes in strict discipline. As a boy, Dillinger's family always sends a neat and presentable child to school, and he takes a liking to reading. Outside of the classroom, however, the boy's true nature is revealed. Dillinger is a thrill seeker with a kleptomaniacal streak, stealing from apple orchards, strawberry patches, and chicken coops. He loves practical jokes, seeks adventure, and frequently gets himself into fights.

At eighteen, Dillinger falls in love with Frances Thornton. The two are secretly engaged, but Thornton's stepfather rebuffs the idea of marriage, declaring Dillinger not "enough of a man yet."[25] The criticism deeply wounds young Dillinger. Fleeing his romantic failure, his father, and legal woes brought on by a recent auto theft, Dillinger joins the U.S. Navy, but—loathing its disciplined lifestyle—deserts after five months. He returns to Mooresville and meets sixteen-year-old Beryl Hovious; the two marry in 1924 and move to Indianapolis. Dillinger proves to be a violent husband—he abuses Beryl, at different times locking her in a closet and holding her head underwater.

Though short on money, Dillinger spends most of his time with friends rather than at work. One of his pals, Ed Singleton, is an ex-convict and pool shark. On the evening of September 6, 1924, Singleton and Dillinger toy with the idea of robbery, over a few drinks. Dillinger, a fan of classic outlaws like Jesse James, loves the idea, and they set their sights on a local grocery.

The duo waits for the grocer, Frank Morgan, to close up shop. Singleton waits in the getaway car while Dillinger lurks nearby, clutching a handkerchief-wrapped iron bolt. When Morgan leaves the shop with the day's receipts, Dillinger clubs him on the head but can't wrestle the money from Morgan's grip. Desperate, Dillinger pulls out a revolver, but Morgan knocks it out of his hand. It goes off, but no one is shot. The panicked Singleton speeds away without Dillinger. In a comically misguided effort to cover his trail, Dillinger pops into a nearby pool room and asks if Mr. Morgan is badly hurt. No one knows what he's talking about.

Police arrest Singleton and Dillinger. Dillinger's father refuses to hire a lawyer, advising his son to plead guilty and accept his punishment. Dillinger confesses and is convicted of assault and battery, with attempt to rob and conspiracy to commit a felony. He gets two concurrent sentences, one of two-to-fourteen years and another of ten-to-twenty years, in the Indiana State Prison. Dillinger, who expected mercy, is furious. "If Singleton comes here and gets a lighter sentence than I do for this," Dillinger tells a deputy sheriff, "I'll be the meanest sonofabitch you ever saw."[26] With the benefit of good counsel, Singleton gets only two years, and Dillinger prepares to fulfill his promise.[27]

In the Indianapolis prison where he is put away, Dillinger is not without considerable talents. He is put to work in a prison shop. He is able to get his work done easily, so he takes on the work of other men. The grateful fellow inmates return the favor by teaching Dillinger about big-time crime.

Beryl, for her part, sees little to gain from waiting for her abusive, felonious husband. On June 20, 1929, two days before his twenty-sixth birthday, she divorces him. A month later, the state denies him parole. Dillinger feels wronged by the system, despite the fact that he has tried to escape on more than one occasion and has given prison guards chronic trouble. He requests a transfer to Indiana's Michigan City jail.[28]

Dillinger has told the authorities that he wants to transfer because the Michigan City baseball team is better, but his real motivation is that his new pals who have been schooling him in bank robbery have been transferred there. Dillinger is granted a transfer, but instead of joining the baseball team, he continues receiving instruction from his fellow inmates. The men are a bloody breed of bank robbers, whose names and crimes are known nationwide—Harry Pierpont, John "Red" Hamilton, Charles Makley, and Russell Clark.[29]

Dillinger's family and friends in Mooresville want him out of prison. Even Frank Morgan, Dillinger's victim, signs their petition to the parole board. On May 10, 1933, after almost nine years of incarceration, Dillinger is granted parole.

Instead of helping Dillinger reflect and turn his life around, his time in prison served as the perfect apprenticeship for bank robbery. Upon release, he returns to crime almost immediately. As the Great Depression drags into its third year, banks across the country are shutting down and foreclosing on loans, wiping out life savings and kicking people out of their homes. Americans begin to loathe banks, viewing them as corrupt and tyrannical. Dillinger publicizes himself as a modern-day Robin Hood. Targeting banks, as he portrays it, is targeting the enemy of many Americans.

On July 16, four weeks after leaving prison, Dillinger embarks on a bank-robbing spree that will make him a legend. He and other ex-convicts raid a bank in Daleville, Indiana, a town so small it lacks a police chief. They seize $3,500 before moving on to a bank in the nearby town of Montpellier, Indiana, netting $6,000. Another bank quickly follows. Given that an average annual salary for a working American is $2,000, and the unemployment rate is almost 25 percent, these are not insignificant hauls.[30]

Dillinger is known by the nickname "Jackrabbit," in recognition of his daring moves and impressive getaways. He drives the fastest cars available, and when he crosses state lines, his pursuers have no legal authority to follow. Poor communication between cities worsens the situation; officials often don't know where to start looking for suspects hours after a robbery.

Despite these challenges, the police catch up with Dillinger by September. A few days after his arrest, several of Dillinger's friends break out of the familiar Michigan City jail. Two guards are shot with guns that Dillinger arranged to have smuggled in. Harry Pierpont, John "Red" Hamilton, Charles Makley, and Russell Clark stick together after their escape. They head directly to Lima County, where Dillinger is in custody. It is now that Sheriff Sarber is shot and Dillinger is freed.

Just two days later, the Dillinger gang invades a police station in Auburn, Indiana. Dillinger handcuffs the two on-duty policemen to the window bars and takes a cache of weapons. A week later, the crew robs another station in Peru, Indiana, seizing Thompson submachine guns, pistols, ammunition, and bulletproof vests.

On the afternoon of October 23, Dillinger, Pierpont, and other gang members stroll into the Central National Bank of Green Castle, Indiana.

Figure 3.2. John Dillinger, 1932.
Library of Congress, World-Tele-
gram & Sun collection

Pierpont reveals a machine gun to the teller and announces, "This is a stick-up. Do as we tell you." Dillinger clears out the cages as Pierpont forces the cashier to open the reserve chest in the main vault. Notably, the bandits are polite; when they realize one elderly lady can't hear them, they seat her in a chair and ask her to keep still. Ten minutes later, they flee with $75,000. Indiana begins a statewide search for the Dillinger gang, even calling up the National Guard. Wisely, the Dillinger gang leaves the state, landing in Chicago. The pattern of evading arrest by leaving the state is now clearly well-established.

On November 20, they rob the American Bank and Trust in Racine, Wisconsin. A bank employee hits an alarm, and the bank is surrounded with snipers, but Dillinger and his gang—hiding behind hostages—escape with $28,000. They drive over the state boundary, going back to Chicago.

Dillinger meets Evelyn "Billie" Frechette, an attractive and lively woman of Indian and French descent. They fall in love, and the pair takes to lounging in clubs and movie theaters—a bold but intelligent hiding tactic for Dillinger, who frequently avoids police attention by playing the part of a normal civilian.

On December 14, 1933, John "Red" Hamilton murders a Chicago police detective, and the crew flees across the state line. A month later, they rob the First National Bank in East Chicago, Indiana. Police surround the bank, but Dillinger—wearing a bulletproof vest and holding a submachine gun—boldly exits. One officer, Patrick O'Malley, fires at Dillinger. Protected by his vest, Dillinger is unharmed and fires at O'Malley, killing him instantly. The gang escapes to Tucson, Arizona.

On January 23, 1934, a fire occurs in the hotel where Clark and Makley are staying. Firemen rescue their possessions, and the robbers tip them generously. The firemen, however, recognize the criminals, the local police are alerted, and all of the men are arrested. The police recover a few tommy guns, Winchester rifles mounted as machine guns, bulletproof vests, and more than $25,000 in cash. Pierpont, Makley, and Clark are sent to Ohio to stand trial for the murder of Sheriff Sarber in Lima County.

Dillinger is flown to the county jail of Crown Point, Indiana, to await trial for the murder of Patrick O'Malley. When Dillinger arrives, cameramen ask the sheriff and prosecutor to pose for photos with the fabled outlaw. Dillinger smiles for the cameras.

With more than one hundred guards stationed outside the jail, authorities brag that the prison is "escape-proof."[31] Dillinger, however, is unconvinced. He whittles himself a harmless but realistic-looking wooden gun, and on March 3, he sticks it in the back of a jail trusty (a prison inmate who works for the prison) and forces him into a jail cell. Along with the help of another inmate, Herbert Youngblood, Dillinger locks up guards, trusties, and the warden.

The pair steals weapons from a prison locker and, with a deputy sheriff in tow, head across the street to the city garage, hop in the sheriff's car, and speed off. Before long, they cross the Indiana-Illinois border en route to Chicago. After Dillinger's easy escape, the nation sees the prison authorities as increasingly foolish. People send law enforcement agencies mocking letters addressed to Clown Point, Indiana, or Wooden Gun, Indiana. Dillinger's legend continues to grow.

Driving the stolen car across state lines represents Dillinger's first federal crime, a violation of the National Motor Vehicle Theft Act. J. Edgar Hoover, director of the Bureau of Investigation, jumps at this opportunity to get involved. Dillinger's image is starting to slip from glamorous outlaw to cold-blooded killer. Hoover is eager to demonstrate the importance of the young agency to the public. He assigns the Dillinger case to the head of the Bureau's Chicago office.

Back in Chicago, Dillinger reunites with Billie Frechette, and the pair head to St. Paul, Minnesota, where Dillinger teams up with Homer Van Meter, Lester "Baby Face Nelson" Gillis, Eddie Green, Tommy Carroll, and others. Baby Face Nelson is particularly notorious, famous for taking pleasure in his murders. On March 13, the new crew hits a bank in Mason City, Minnesota, and steals $52,000.

When Dillinger returns to St. Paul, he and Billie rent an apartment, and the observant manager soon alerts a Bureau agent. The following day, an agent and a police officer knock on the door. Billie opens the door but then immediately closes it. Reinforcements swarm around the building.

Just then, Homer Van Meter enters the hall near the apartment. Investigators begin questioning him, but the robber pulls out a gun and escapes unscathed. He then forces a truck driver at gunpoint to take him to fellow robber Eddie Green's residence.

Back at the apartment, Dillinger bursts through the door with machine gun ablaze. He's wounded by return fire, but the Jackrabbit and Billie manage to evade the hunters, again. Billie and the wounded Dillinger head to his family home in Mooresville, Indiana, to recover.

Personal conflicts among the gang's members are growing. Then on April 3, Eddie Green is found by federal agents and shot repeatedly in the ensuing gun battle. He dies in the hospital a week later. Not long after the death of Green, Billie, in Chicago to visit a friend, is arrested. She's taken to St. Paul, where she is convicted of conspiracy to harbor a fugitive and is sentenced to a two-year jail term and fined $1,000. Dillinger is helpless to intervene. With Bureau agents tracking him close behind, Dillinger heads to Wisconsin. There he takes up residence in a local lodge and works toward a reunion of his gang. However, the lodge owner's wife recognizes Dillinger and is less than pleased to have the notorious criminal living under her watch, so she alerts the Bureau of Investigation.

On April 22, 1934, with armed agents all around the property, three men get in a car and begin driving away. The agents yell for the car to stop. When it doesn't, the agents open fire, killing one man and wounding the others. It soon becomes clear that the three men are innocent lodge customers; the sound of their car radio had drowned out the agents' commands.

The gunshots alert Dillinger and his gang, who are still in the lodge. They act quickly, escaping out a second-story window. The agents, failing to notice that their quarry has already left, barrage the lodge with tear gas and gunfire. The futile assault on the empty lodge serves only to give the escaping men a head start.

Agents soon realize their mistake, and within minutes hear commotion over the radio. Special Agent W. Carter Baum and another Bureau agent are sent two miles down the road to investigate. Upon arrival, the pair spot Baby Face Nelson, who is robbing three local residents. Nelson sees the agents and opens fire, killing Baum and wounding the other agent. Nelson then speeds off in their car.

After the botched operation, the young Bureau takes a beating in the press for their repeated failures to apprehend any of the gang. Newspapers demand that Hoover be replaced. Though humiliated, Hoover remains undeterred. He raises the bounty on Dillinger's head to $15,000 and assigns Special Agent Samuel A. Cowley to manage the case.

Dillinger, meanwhile, continues to see success. After stealing $17,000 from an Ohio bank, he and Van Meter again slip over the state border and hide in Chicago. As the entire nation now knows their faces, they undergo plastic surgery in an effort to disguise themselves. Dillinger has a mole removed from his eyebrows, his chin cleft reduced, and his cheeks lifted.

On June 22, 1934, Dillinger's thirty-first birthday, the Bureau names him Public Enemy Number One. Dillinger is delighted with his new title. He is happy to receive an ego boost from the Bureau. While in Chicago, Dillinger is enjoying time with his latest girlfriend, Polly Hamilton. He'd met Hamilton through a woman named Anna Sage, aka Ana Cumpănaş, a Romanian immigrant and brothel owner plagued by run-ins with the law. Threatened by deportation, Sage thinks Dillinger could be a way out of her legal troubles.

In a secret meeting with federal agents, headed by Melvin Purvis, Sage promises them Dillinger in return for a cash reward and protection from deportation. The agents hastily agree, and Sage announces that she, Hamilton, and Dillinger will be at one of two movie theaters the following evening. She promises to wear orange so she will be easy to identify (though legend will turn her into the "Woman in Red").

The following evening, July 22, 1934, Sage, Hamilton, and Dillinger enter the Biograph Theater in Chicago to see *Manhattan Melodrama*. As the movie plays, agents, led by the chief of the investigating forces of the Department of Justice in Chicago, Melvin H. Purvis, surround the theater, waiting for over two hours for the movie to finish. At 10:30 p.m., Dillinger and the two women stroll out to the sidewalk. Purvis, leaning coolly by the entrance, lights a cigar as a signal. Dillinger turns and stares at Purvis, studying him carefully before noticing the men around him. After a second of tense realization, Dillinger pulls out a gun and sprints toward a nearby alley, but the agents open fire, hitting him four times. He dies instantly. John Dillinger—"the most notorious criminal of modern times"—lies splayed on the sidewalk exposed to full public view.[32]

Even before the gangster's body can be picked up, the frenzy begins. Bystanders rip off pieces of their clothing or use their hats to mop up specks of Dillinger's blood. As the corpse is taken to the morgue, thousands trail behind, searching for a glimpse of the now dead legend. Despite the deal she made, Sage is deported.

Before Dillinger's burial, fifteen thousand spectators pass through the morgue. In time, Dillinger's body is returned to Indiana, where he is buried alongside his mother in the family plot. Visitors come year after year. For two full years, Dillinger reigned as the King of Crime. In total, he and his gang stole $300,000, escaped from jail twice, and dodged bullets like no one had before. From state to state, law enforcement scrambled to capture him, but—until betrayal by the "Woman in Red"—Dillinger outran, outshot, and outsmarted them all, searing his iconic smirk into the public imagination. The Dillinger legend thrives.

THE OUTRAGE

Dillinger isn't alone in his career as a bank robber. The 1920s and 1930s are plagued by infamous bank robbers like Bonnie and Clyde, Pretty Boy Floyd, and Baby Face Nelson, who steal ravenously, kill police and civilians, and wriggle again and again from the clutches of the law. J. Edgar Hoover coins the term "public enemies" to refer to criminals at large, crowning the worst as "Public Enemy No. 1." After Dillinger, Pretty Boy Floyd inherits the title; after Floyd's death, it's Baby Face Nelson.

For years, progress seems futile. "Crime always keeps abreast of the times," Congressman Fiorello La Guardia declares. "As mechanics improve a lock, as inventive ingenuity devises an intricate safe, the criminal keeps abreast and sometimes one step ahead. Likewise with chemistry, explosives, firearms, transportation, and communication, crime makes use of every improvement." Dillinger is no different. Like the shadowy kidnappers feared by the nation, he remains one step—and one state— ahead, leaving police in the dust.

In 1931, a team of scholars and practitioners confirms La Guardia's warnings. The group publishes the Wickersham Commission Report, which details the state of American crime on an enormous scale. The results are unambiguous: crime is rampant, and federal oversight is needed.[33] But nothing is actually done to curb the crime wave that the Wickersham Commission sees forming. By 1934, with Dillinger still on the move, people are demanding change.

THE REFORM

On February 21, 1934, Arizona senator Henry F. Ashurst answers the charge, introducing a bill to crack down on state-hopping outlaws. (Recall that Dillinger and his gang had moved to Senator Ashurst's Arizona just a few months before this.) The bill is one of several prepared by the Department of Justice, a bundle dubbed "the anti-gangster bills."[34] The bills are also backed by Attorney General Homer Cummings. In a letter to Congress, Homer acknowledges that states have traditionally been responsible for keeping crime in check, but times are now different. "The recent growth of certain types of crime has brought forcefully to our attention the fact that criminals engaged therein are not under adequate control."[35] Gangsters and robbers like the Dillinger Gang, he warns, move from state to state, taking "advantage of the limited jurisdiction possessed by State authorities in pursuing fugitive criminals, and of the want of any central coordinating agency acting on behalf of all of the states. Although the local authorities are generally honest, alert, and efficient, the territorial limitations on their jurisdiction prevent them from adequately protecting their citizens from this type of criminal."[36]

The bundle of bills is extraordinarily far-reaching. It taxes and regulates gun dealers, extends the Motor Vehicle Theft Act to cover other valuable property, and intensifies punishments for bank robbers. One bill amends the Lindbergh Act; another makes it illegal to flee a state to avoid testifying. Other proposals criminalize and protect against extortion. And so the list continues, bill after bill. Though diverse, each aims to strangle criminal activity, overwriting old rules with daring new ones.[37] Bank robbers brought the issue forward, but many types of criminals are now being targeted by the new federal laws.

One bill, the Federal Bank Robbery Act, is especially meticulous. It clarifies the crime of bank robbery and prescribes harsher punishments in extreme instances. Most importantly, bank robbery—or the "misappropriation of property under circumstances involving a danger to the person as well as a danger to property"[38]—now falls under federal jurisdiction.

On May 14, 1934, the Federal Bank Robbery Act passes, and within a month, nine more bills follow in a package nicknamed "The New Deal on Crime." The legislation is endorsed by the president and attorney general, who finger Dillinger as the prime example of its importance. As if on cue, Dillinger robs an Ohio bank, stealing $17,000.

For a nation accustomed to states as the almost exclusive law enforcement power, the new laws represent the beginning of an unprecedented transition. With the media abuzz with tales of outlaws, kidnappers, and terrible crime, federal jurisdiction continues to grow, using the New Deal on Crime as a stepping stone.

The Civil War demonstrated to all the ugly side of decentralized policing.[39] Therefore, even in an era of great distrust in the country, placing a limited number of crimes and enforcement powers into a centralized authority seemed to be necessary. Over time the gradual shift has accelerated, and federal criminal statutes continue to expand even now. The very limited number of federal statutes has grown to the point that no one actually knows the current extent of federal criminal law today.

As federal laws surged, law enforcement scrambled to keep up. The nation saw its first federal prison in 1897, and the Bureau of Investigation was created in 1909.[40] In its first ten years, the Bureau grew to over three hundred agents, with a network of offices in major cities across the nation, but with few federal crimes, the agency struggled to defend its relevance.[41]

"The lawless years," however, give the Bureau the basis on which to clearly justify its existence, and the publicity-seeking Dillinger is a major influence. The outlaw's death boosts the agency's reputation, and in 1935 the agency is renamed the "Federal Bureau of Investigation" (FBI). Shortly afterward, the National Academy is established to train its officers, and the agency constructs a forensic lab.[42] The FBI quickly becomes a powerful force in the fight "to end the 'lawless years.'"[43]

The genie has left the bottle, and the federalization of criminal law enforcement has begun. As of 2017, no one knows how many federal criminal laws there are. They are too numerous to count and are found in the documents of many agencies. The FBI's budget is $9.5 billion.[44] The agency is staffed by 35,000 agents, analysts, and other professionals. In 2012, the FBI seized $8.205 billion in assets.[45] Fear of kidnappers and deadly bank robberies began the federalization process. The terror attacks of September 11, 2001, brought a great deal of fear to the country and new powers to the FBI. Many people feel that the current powers of the FBI are simply too broad.[46]

Since the night Bessie Gow found the Lindbergh crib empty, the FBI has become a national police force that aggressively pursues cross–state border crimes. Finding the balance between safety and intrusion is a debate that continues today.

Chapter Four

1937
Sulfanilamide Crisis

Drug Safety

THE TRAGEDY

Six otherwise healthy children are treated for sore throats in Tulsa, Oklahoma, in October of 1937.[1] A few days later, they are all dead. Doctors at St. John's Hospital know that something terrible is happening, and that time is not on their side.[2] They soon come to suspect that the Elixir Sulfanilamide, a drug the children were given to treat their sore throat, is the cause.

The story of Elixir Sulfanilamide begins in the late 1800s, when the German chemical company Bayer begins investigating whether their dyes might have health benefits. In 1932, Bayer scientist Gerhard Domagk discovers something that appears to fight infections—a deep red dye that Bayer called "Prontosil." The dye does not kill bacteria in a petri dish, but given to infected mice, chickens, and dogs, it is effective in fighting bacteria. While Domagk and others at Bayer ponder what to do with this new knowledge, Domagk's six-year-old daughter punctures her finger with a needle while sewing. The open wound becomes infected, and it soon becomes clear that the girl is approaching death. With nothing to lose, Domagk injects his child with Prontosil. She turns as red as a lobster, but soon grows stronger, and the infection disappears. The red dye metabolizes out of her system, and her normal color returns. Prontosil works.

A group of French researchers solves the mystery of why the dye does not kill bacteria in a petri dish but works in living creatures. Once inside the body, Prontosil is metabolized into a number of derivatives. One of those metabolic derivatives—a chemical called "sulfanilamide"—clears

49

infection. In 1908, soon after the French discovery that sulfanilamide is the real infection-curing agent, an Austrian scientist publishes a paper detailing a process by which to synthesize sulfanilamide by itself. Bayer, for its part, is less than thrilled about the development. Sulfanilamide is cheaper and less involved to produce than Prontosil, and it has the additional bonus of not turning patients lobster red. In other words, Bayer's patent on Prontosil, obtained after years of expensive research and testing, is practically worthless.

All over the world minor cuts regularly lead to deadly infections, and now there is an answer. In 1935, President Franklin Delano Roosevelt's dying son is saved by sulfanilamide tablets at the Massachusetts General Hospital. The Roosevelt boy's story is national news, and suddenly everyone is talking about the drug.[3]

American drug companies race to manufacture sulfanilamide products. In an effort to get an edge over competitors, salesmen from the S. E. Massengill Company in Bristol, Tennessee, approach Harold Cole Watkins, the company's chief chemist and pharmacist: Could he make sulfanilamide in liquid form? Consumers are asking for a product that will be tasty enough for children to swallow and easy to administer to babies. Watkins gets to work, and quickly finds that he can dissolve sulfanilamide in diethylene glycol. Diethylene glycol tastes sweet, a bit like raspberries. Massengill tests the new mixture and finds its flavor and appearance acceptable.

What Watkins fails to realize is that diethylene glycol, usually used as antifreeze, is poisonous. But it does not cross his mind to test the mixture: in 1937, toxicity tests for new drugs are not routine in the industry, let alone mandated by law. Drug companies are not required to test whether the drugs they sell are safe. What Watkins knows is that he has tried the drug himself, and the company needs to get it on the market as fast as possible. Watkins produces 240 gallons of the drug, which the company dubs "Elixir of Sulfanilamide," at its main plant in Bristol and another branch in Kansas. It ships some 633 cases across the United States.

Patients start dying before the month ends.[4] At first, the deaths are not seen as connected. But after a string of children come to the hospital with a sore throat, are treated, then suddenly experience "stoppage of urine, severe abdominal pain, nausea, vomiting, stupor, and convulsions" and "intense and unrelenting pain," Tulsa doctors become gravely concerned.[5]

By October 10, adults with gonorrhea are exhibiting similar symptoms and dying. The only obvious connection is that all of the patients have been given Elixir of Sulfanilamide. The St. John's team sends a sample of the elixir to the American Medical Association's office in Chicago for analysis.

Figure 4.1. A bottle of sulfanilamide which was seized, 1937. *FDA collection*

On October 14, a New York doctor and a professor at Johns Hopkins University hear about the strange deaths and reach out to the Food and Drug Administration (FDA). By this point, at least a dozen people are already dead, and the elixir is still being sold all over the country. The FDA dispatches inspectors from Kansas City on an overnight drive to Tulsa. They open an investigation on October 15 and send samples of the elixir to the FDA labs. The FDA also issues a call to stop the sale of Elixir Sulfanilamide.[6]

Legally, the FDA is on thin ice if it acts to forcibly collect the toxic drug. The government's best argument is to exploit a trivial legal charge of misbranding: technically, federal regulations define an "elixir" as a product that contains alcohol, and Elixir Sulfanilamide contains none. Authorities work feverishly over the course of several days to refine their legal approach. On October 20, the U.S. attorney in Oklahoma files a lawsuit against Massengill contending that the alcohol-free mixture branded as an "elixir" is in violation of the Food and Drugs Act. Additionally, the label says the product came from Bristol, Tennessee, when in fact some had been produced in Kansas City, Missouri.[7]

No one is kidding themselves: these are rather dubious legal challenges. Drug safety laws are weak, and calls for change have been drowned out by interest like Massengill that profit from the status quo. The government makes the best case it can, given the limited legal tools it has, but ultimately the existing legal framework is not designed to accommodate the unsafe-drug lawsuit that it wants to bring.

Meanwhile, the same day the suit is filed in Oklahoma, Massengill telegrams the American Medical Association inquiring about any known antidotes for diethylene glycol. Massengill knows very little about the toxicity of the chemical, and when the AMA responds, it becomes clear that Massengill is not alone. No known antidote is available.

Scientists at the AMA dive into investigating diethylene glycol, conducting several tests on guinea pigs. Researchers also learn more about the symptoms of diethylene glycol poisoning. Victims are sick for one to three weeks, and their symptoms correspond closely to those of kidney failure.[8] Indeed, upon autopsy, doctors find kidneys swollen well beyond their normal size, choked with purple clots.[9]

While the AMA runs tests, several additional deaths are reported in East St. Louis, Illinois. Massengill is finally persuaded to send a telegram to over a thousand salesmen, druggists, and doctors asking them to return the elixir to the company. The telegram is fairly mild: it does not warn that the drug is deadly.[10]

The FDA's priority is to recover all of the elixir on the market, even if it is not within its legal purview to do so. In cooperation with state and local health officials, the FDA sends almost the entire field force of 239 inspectors and chemists out to find and recover the deadly medication. The media takes up the cry and warns citizens to stay away from Elixir Sulfanilamide. Massengill's shipping information and distribution lists, as well as records from drugstores across the country, are searched for clues.

The FDA sends inspectors to Massengill's Bristol headquarters and to the drug company's offices in New York, Kansas City, and San Francisco. The FDA instructs Massengill to send a new mass telegram, which reads: "Imperative you take up immediately all elixir sulfanilamide dispensed. Product may be dangerous to life. Return all stocks, our expense."[11]

As news about the drug spreads, doctors across the country react in horror. Dr. Archie Calhoun, who practices in Mt. Olive, Mississippi, received his first shipment of Elixir Sulfanilamide on September 27. He purchased another gallon on October 13 and gave out at least fourteen prescriptions for the elixir. Several of his patients become gravely ill and die, and Calhoun starts to feel something is not right. Finally, on October 19, Calhoun's brother, who had bought the first shipment of the elixir, receives the second telegram from Massengill. By now, four of Calhoun's patients are dead.

Calhoun is sickened to know that he has served as the last link in a supply chain of death, and he also knows that more of his patients are at risk of meeting the same fate. He drives from house to house to warn his patients through the night, struggling to remember everyone to whom he prescribed the elixir. What about the men to whom, out of sensitivity to their embarrassment, Calhoun had given the medication for the treatment of gonorrhea without a prescription? Could they be found?

While Dr. Calhoun is making his desperate rounds, Nola Penn's husband takes her to the hospital. Calhoun's warning has come too late; tonight Nola will be his fifth dead patient.[12] Calhoun also helplessly remembers that he prescribed the elixir to his best friend, Reverend Boyd, a Baptist minister, just before Boyd left town for an ecclesiastical conference. Soon Calhoun gets the devastating news: Boyd will not be coming back. It seems as though the relentless march of death is unstoppable.

Calhoun is tormented by grief and writes a letter in a New Orleans newspaper about living with the knowledge that he has played a part in these deaths. "That realization has given me such days and nights of mental and spiritual agony as I did not believe a human being could undergo and survive. I have spent hours on my knees, once I had done all any physician could do for his patients, I have known hours when death for me would be a welcome relief from this agony."[13]

The FDA's staff of 239 continues to pursue the drug. They attempt to interview each person on the company's two hundred–member sales staff so that the reps might help track down orders and doctor's samples. Finding the sales people, though, is not easy. In one case, a salesman is said to be in a Washington, D.C., hotel. When they check the hotel, the man isn't there, but he has left forwarding addresses of Jackson, Michigan, and Baltimore, Maryland. Upon investigation, it turns out the man wasn't the salesman at all, but a different person with the same name. The salesman finally turns up, after a four-day search, in University Park, Maryland. Even after they are found, many of the sales staff do not cooperate. One man refuses to give up the information until he is locked in a Texas jail.

Tracking down pharmacists, doctors, and their patients proves even more vexing. The drug can be sold over the counter, so most local pharmacists have no way of knowing to whom they sold the poisonous elixir. Doctors of the time generally keep no records, and even the limited records that are kept are often useless, looking more like cryptic allusions than medical records.[14]

Like the salesmen, doctors and druggists range widely in their level of cooperation. Some doctors are eager to help and do everything they can to recover the drug. One even postpones his wedding to help the FDA look for a young child whose family moved out to the mountains after getting a prescription for sulfanilamide. Other doctors are less helpful, caught in the fear of the personal consequences for having prescribed the elixir.

Potential liability issues also keep some pharmacists from being completely honest about their sales records. In one incident in Georgia, a pharmacist tells the FDA inspector that he returned a gallon of Elixir Sulfanilamide after he sold six ounces, and the patient who bought the six ounces is fine. Back in Bristol, FDA officials inspect the gallon container and find that twelve ounces are missing, not six. The inspector in Georgia discovers that two other people purchased the elixir and died.

In another case, a physician in South Carolina claims that he only gave the medicine to five people, and all are fine. However, someone else in town describes a lumberjack who died exhibiting the symptoms of diethylene glycol poisoning. The inspector speaks to the man's sister, who confirms that her brother had taken the medicine. She also says that they buried him with the medicine, so they exhume the body and retrieve the bottle. By the end of his investigation, the inspector discovers that three more of the doctor's patients had died after taking the drug.

Even when people hear of the warnings, they often do not follow the protocol outlined by the FDA. For example, inspectors find a woman who says she heard the warning and destroyed her bottle of Elixir Sulfanilamide. When the inspector presses her to explain what she means by "destroy,"[15] she explains that she tossed the poison out the window. The inspector finds the intact bottle in the alleyway outside the house.

Despite these enormous challenges, the FDA manages to retrieve all of the existing stock of Elixir Sulfanilamide, a total of 234 gallons and 1 pint. The rest has been ingested by patients. In the end, 107 people die, most of them children. Consumption of all 240 gallons could have led to in excess of 4,000 deaths.[16]

THE OUTRAGE

The situation provokes outrage: all of the deaths would have been prevented with even the most basic testing of the new drug before sale to the public. Giving the drug to a few mice would have demonstrated the danger of the product; even reviewing the medical literature of the time would have revealed that diethylene glycol causes kidney failure. But there was no requirement that any drug be tested before being sold. As Dr. Samuel Evan Massengill, the owner of the company, says, "My chemists and I deeply regret the fatal results, but there was no error in the manufacture of the product. We have been supplying a legitimate professional demand and not once could have foreseen the unlooked-for results. I do not feel that there was any responsibility on our part."[17]

The FDA takes Dr. Massengill to court on criminal charges. The lawyers argue that the Elixir Sulfanilamide "fell below the professed standard under which it was sold" as it was supposed to cure infections but "its principal action was that of an acute poison."[18] Massengill, after a failed demurer, pleads guilty to most of the charges and is fined $24,600. Harold Cole Watkins, the chemist who formulated the elixir, is wracked with guilt. He commits suicide before the investigation ends.

Everyone wants to know why the laws are so weak. Mrs. Maise Nidiffer, whose daughter died from the elixir, captures the nation's sentiments in a letter she writes to President Roosevelt. In it, she reminds Roosevelt that his own son had been saved by sulfanilamide and writes of her joyful daughter Joan who had listened on the radio "jumping and shouting"[19] when the president was reelected the year before. She goes on to describe how painful it was to see that same little girl with "her little body tossing to and fro and hear[ing] that little voice screaming with pain and it seems as though it would drive me insane."[20] Mrs. Nidiffer puts it plainly, "Surely we can have laws governing doctors also who will give such a medicine, not knowing what extent its danger."[21] It is now well-known that the current laws do not protect patients. Nidiffer tells the president, "I am writing you and hope that you can realize a little of what I am suffering and that you will take steps to prevent such in the future."[22] She encloses a photograph of six-year-old Joan, "the baby I grieve for day and night." She wants the president to act so that Joan's death might save other children.[23]

Mrs. Nidiffer is up against an army of powerful lobbyists from the drug industry. Theirs is a multi-billion-dollar business that employs thousands and keeps newspapers solvent with advertising. Additionally, while no one wants children poisoned, consumers across the country are still eager to buy drugs, regulated or not. Many people are certain that these nostrums improve the quality of life. There have been demands from women's activist groups and the AMA for consumer protections such as honest statements of ingredients, warning labels for hidden opiates, and risk warnings, but those voices have not been enough.

The drug industry also argues that it *is* already regulated by the FDA. But the claim is weak: the FDA started as a scientific research body in 1862, as led by Charles M. Wetherill, the first chemist of the Department of Agriculture. The FDA originally focused on agricultural research and development; it was not a law enforcement agency. In the nineteenth and early twentieth centuries, the U.S. food and drug companies have the unrestrained right to package and sell whatever they choose. Without breaking any laws, manufacturers use all sorts of chemical additives, unwholesome ingredients, and hazardous dyes. Milk isn't pasteurized, and cows don't get tested for tuberculosis. Drugs containing strong substances such as opium, heroin, cocaine, and morphine are unregulated. Ingredients are not listed on labels, and labels do not need to match what is actually in the package. There are no requirements for warning labels. Medicine peddlers sell "cure-alls" of unknown formulation that might be safe to ingest but might also be poison.[24]

THE REFORM

Alarmed by the dangers that Americans face at the grocery store or the druggist's, Dr. Harvey W. Wiley, longtime head of the Division of Chemistry at the United States Department of Agriculture, starts campaigning for regulation. In 1902, Wiley gets together a volunteer "poison squad" of young men who eat foods with certain amounts of chemical preservatives.[25] The goal of the volunteers is to establish whether these preservatives are deleterious to human health.

The experiment lasts for five years. Over this time, the men consume many risky items, including borax, salicylic acid, sulfur compounds, benzoic acid, and formaldehyde. Wiley concludes that chemical preservatives shouldn't be used unless absolutely necessary, producers should have to prove the safety of their preservatives, and labels should let consumers know what is in their food. Women's activist groups join the cause demanding "pure food."[26]

The reform movement is assisted by the publication of Upton Sinclair's novel *The Jungle*, which includes grisly descriptions of conditions at Chicago meatpacking plants (including an instance of a worker slipping into a boiling vat and being rendered into lard and packaged for sale). The wider public starts to demand change. The Wiley Act, or Pure Food and Drugs Act,[27] becomes law in 1906 along with regulations on the meat industry. The act is designed to counter food adulteration and fraudulent medicines. However, drugs are only required to meet standards of purity and strength.[28]

Then in 1912, quacks peddling fraudulent medicines catch a break when Congress alters the laws, mandating that the government prove the manufacturer *intended* to defraud its customers before it can be cited for violations. This new standard improves the chances of shady medicine men escaping the law's restrictions. As long as the sellers claim that they *believed* their drugs actually work, they are legally protected. With this burden of proof requirement, the law is rendered relatively toothless.

In 1933, FDA commissioner Walter Campbell proposes stronger food and drug laws, but the bill faces massive opposition from industry and advertising and is never enacted. Campbell reminds everyone that the sulfanilamide crisis could have been prevented with the stronger laws he proposed years earlier.[29] "It is unfortunate that under the terms of our present inadequate Federal law, the Food and Drug Administration is obliged to proceed against this product on a technical and trivial charge of misbranding," he says. "The Elixir Sulfanilamide incident emphasizes how essential it is to public welfare that the distribution of highly potent drugs should be controlled by an adequate Federal Food and Drug law."[30]

Campbell warns that "these unfortunate occurrences may be expected to continue because new and relatively untried drug preparations are being manufactured almost daily at the whim of the individual manufacturer, and the damage to public health cannot accurately be estimated. The only remedy for such a situation is the enactment by Congress of an adequate and comprehensive national Food and Drugs Act which will require that all medicines placed upon the market shall be safe to use under the directions for use."[31]

Campbell is not alone in his conviction. *Time* magazine notes that if the proposed bill had been passed during the previous congressional session, Massengill would have faced criminal prosecution for the sulfanilamide crisis. One FDA agent describes Massengill's practices as essentially "throw[ing] drugs together, and if they don't explode they are placed on sale."[32] And yet, under existing law, Massengill is only convicted of misbranding and fined several thousand dollars—a terrible injustice given that their product killed over one hundred innocent Americans.

In the shadow of the incident, there continues strong pressure to pass a new FDA bill. The *General Bulletin of Consumers' Research* expresses hope in January 1938 that "at last the public will demand of Congress that [a new law] be passed that these more than ninety innocent victims . . . shall not have died in vain."[33] The American Pharmaceutical Association, various women's groups, the AMA, and the national media all call for appropriate reforms. Two movies, *Permit to Kill* and *G-Men of Science* come out about the sulfanilamide disaster, turning the FDA inspectors into Hollywood heroes.

With the country still reeling from the sulfanilamide crisis, the 1933 bill finds new life. Legislators feel ever increasing pressure from their constituents. Many "found [their] mail heavy with demands for a new law 'so as to make impossible a repetition of the recent Sulfanilamide tragedy.'"[34] Drug companies also understand that the reforms could help them restore public confidence in their products. Change might be possible.

In December of 1937, Senator Copeland introduces what would become known as the "Sulfanilamide Bill." The bill requires proof of safety before a drug is distributed, typically by way of extensive reports filled out by packers of the drugs. The bill moves through Congress at an unprecedented pace. The Senate Commerce Committee reports the bill without amendments, hearings, or a written report in February 1938. In May, the Senate passes the bill unanimously.

On June 25, 1938, President Roosevelt signs the Federal Food, Drug, and Cosmetic Act (FDCA) into law. The new law mandates that drug companies like Massengill need scientific evidence of the safety of their products before they are able to be sold to the public. The law establishes regulations on therapeutic devices and cosmetics. Old laws permitting a person to sell any product as long as he or she personally *believed* in its curative powers are taken off the books; proof of deliberate fraud is no longer required to cite companies that make inaccurate claims about drug efficacy.

With the new law, it is also illegal to put poison in food, except in certain defined cases. Acceptable levels of permitted poisonous substances, such as pesticides, are established. The FDA is granted the authority to conduct factory inspections. Food standards are made mandatory when necessary "to promote honesty and fair dealing in the interest of consumers."[35] The law also establishes new legal avenues for redressing violations in the form of federal court injunctions. At long last, the sulfanilamide crisis has resulted in safer food, medication, and cosmetics across the country.

The issues surrounding food and drug safety were addressed with the act, and in time there is a push for further reform, but nothing much happens. In the early 1960s, Thalidomide, which is not available in the United States because the FDA is not convinced of the drug's safety, is selling well in Europe. To the great regret of many, Thalidomide proves itself to be unsafe. "Thalidomide babies" are born with flipper-like appendages or no limbs at all and typically have substantial brain damage. Worldwide, only 50 percent of infants born to mothers who took Thalidomide survive beyond a few months. Researchers find that the severity and location of the deformities is linked to how many days into the pregnancy the mother took the drug. When Thalidomide is taken on the 20th day of pregnancy it causes central brain damage. On day 21, the damage occurs to the eyes. Day 22 use would lead to damage to the ears and face. Ingestion on day 24 would impair the formation of the long bones in the arms. And the damage to the formation of the legs would occur if taken up to day 28. Thalidomide did not seem to damage the fetus if taken after 42 days gestation. A professor of pediatrics at Johns Hopkins University explains with horror that "this compound, Thalidomide, could have passed our present drug laws."[36] The reformers get the changes they have been seeking.

Further problems bring additional reform. With each reform, the scope of the FDA is expanded. The FDCA originally filled a mere fifteen pages in the *U.S. Code of Laws*, but as of 2012 the amended version occupies 504 pages.[37] While still subject to judicial as well as legislative and executive oversight, the FDA is presently responsible for regulating products in the United States that make up approximately "twenty-five cents of every dollar spent by the American consumer."[38]

BEYOND REFORM

The agency has further attempted to test its regulatory powers in response to scientific and technological advances such as human cloning experiments, bioengineered drugs, tissue engineering and regenerative medicine, pharmacogenomics, genetically modified foods, nanotechnology, and gene therapy. The efforts by the FDA to put limits on scientific exploration leads many to vehemently argue that the FDA has too much power.

Critics level three major charges against the FDA. First, some argue that politics has overtaken science as the driving factor behind many FDA decisions. Critics point to the problems with getting *Plan-B One Step*, an emergency contraceptive, to the market. Despite clear scientific studies showing the medication to be both safe and effective, the FDA kept access to the medication limited. But after a vocal group labeled the medication an abortion drug, a federal court battle ensued. In the end, Judge Edward Korman opined that the FDA was "putting politics ahead of science" and ordered the FDA to approve unrestricted sales of emergency contraceptives.[39]

Second, the FDA sometimes uses its broad regulatory authority to engage in outright censorship. Dietary supplements fall within the ambit of the FDA's regulatory reach and are prohibited from making claims that the supplements can cure or prevent diseases. This has led some to criticize the FDA for censoring truthful claims and to accuse the agency of impermissibly being in cahoots with larger drug companies.

Finally, complex pre-market procedures required to get a product to market significantly increase costs for consumers. The cost of drug development ranges from $500 million to an exorbitant $2 billion, depending on the type of therapy being tested or the developing firm, and much of that cost is a direct result of FDA regulations.[40] Critics point out that the high costs mean that fewer potentially life-enhancing drugs will be developed.[41] Economist Gary S. Becker confirms this negative effect of zealous FDA regulation.[42]

Additionally, FDA regulations often do not allow cheaper alternatives to enter the market. This was the case in 2011 with the drug Makena, already on the market to prevent premature births. The FDA granted the company producing the drug a temporary monopoly status, and the price skyrocketed from \$10 to \$1,500.[43] Cost issues that are caused by the FDA are also exacerbated by a burdensome approval system where even a "fast track" approval will take between twelve and fifteen years.

On the other hand, others say the FDA does not go far enough.[44] Most notably, the Institute of Medicine issued a \$1.8 million report in 2006 revealing overwhelming deficiencies in the FDA's procedures to ensure the safety and efficacy of drugs in the U.S. market. The researchers called for twenty-five sweeping recommendations, including more organization and transparency of FDA procedures to the general public. In response, the FDA has created a "Product Quality for the 21st Century Initiative" focusing on ensuring that quality standards do not impede innovation.[45] Additionally, FDA advisory committee meetings are scheduled regularly, allowing the general public to observe the FDA's decision-making process and outside advisors to contribute their view on improving the FDA's programs.[46]

Others point to specific areas that the FDA should more tightly regulate. The list commonly includes antibiotics in domestic animals (which contribute to the development of antibiotic-resistant bacteria strains),[47] food dyes linked to hyperactivity in children (which are already banned in nearly all European countries),[48] cloned animals sold as food,[49] and food additives—only 19 percent of which currently include toxicology information.[50]

Then-professor of administrative law and current Supreme Court justice Stephen Breyer writes in *Breaking the Vicious Circle* (1992) about the pattern of FDA reforms: risk, public response, and regulation.[51] Breyer criticizes the United States for continuously responding to largely irrational public perceptions of risks backed by nominal scientific certainty.

Some suggest a successful conclusion to the cyclical paradigms involving the FDA would require continuous system maintenance analogous to "police patrols." Advocates suggest this approach would be preferable to and more effective in ensuring pharmaceutical safety than the current system of merely waiting and responding to "fire alarms," which typically conclude with an unnecessarily large response.

Though the scope and power of the FDA continues to be debated today, it is clear that Americans are far safer than in 1937 when S. E. Massengill shipped sulfanilamide dissolved in antifreeze to doctors and pharmacists all over the country. The question today, first posed in 1962 by Senator Douglas, is this: "Can we learn from this lesson, . . . or can mankind educate itself only by disaster and tragedy?"[52]

Chapter Five

1956
NYC Mad Bomber
Criminal Profiling

THE TRAGEDY

While eating lunch at his office in the Consolidated Energy Company building, one day in 1940, an employee spots a tool box on a second-story windowsill.[1] Thinking this an odd place for such a thing, the curious employee takes a closer look. Inside he discovers a single piece of large iron pipe about four-and-a-half inches long. It is capped on both ends and wrapped in a sheet of paper. Intrigued, the man removes the pipe and unrolls the paper. Neatly printed in block letters, the note reads: "CON EDISON CROOKS, THIS IS FOR YOU. THERE IS NO SHORTAGE OF POWDER BOYS."[2]

The man realizes he is holding a bomb. He replaces the pipe in the box and alerts his supervisors. The police arrive, and the bomb squad soon follows.

The bomb is homemade, so police resort to guesswork in order to disarm it. A detective approaches the bomb listening for ticking sounds, an indicator of a timing device, but the bomb is mute. The detective dons body armor, steel-mesh gloves and shoes and a steel-plated helmet. Behind a bulletproof glass shield, he turns the bomb over with a five-foot-long gripping pole. The bomb doesn't explode; it's not motion sensitive. Armored squad members then place the pipe into a steel-cable bag. Holding it at the end of a fifteen-foot pole, they walk it out of the building and into a containment truck.

Having safely transported the device to a secluded area, they check it for fingerprints. No trace evidence of any kind is found. With the outside free of evidentiary clues, the authorities dunk it in motor oil to prevent any electrical or chemical reactions. They then take the bomb apart. Beyond the explosive material, they discover it contains a flashlight bulb, a battery, a steel spring, and a dampened throat lozenge—meant to be a timing device. Had it worked properly, the melting lozenge would have allowed the spring to release, triggering the explosive potential of the bomb. However, the bomb is poorly constructed and does not properly function. Still, the message is clear: someone wants blood from Con Ed.

Police set to work trying to identify a suspect. Clearly, the person who constructed the bomb dislikes Con Ed, but this is hardly special. Con Ed is a huge company with plenty of disgruntled workers, unhappy clients, would-be suppliers, and rival utilities. Having no meaningful way to advance the investigation, police abandon the case. The incident does not even make the newspapers.

On September 24, 1941, nearly a year later, a pipe bomb tucked inside a red wool sock is found on a road four blocks from Con Ed's headquarters. There is no note, but the proximity to Con Ed and the design of the device suggest that the same would-be bomber is again at work.

Shortly after the 1941 bomb is found, the bomber switches tactics. Now, letters start arriving at newspapers, hotels, clothiers, department stores, and Con Ed itself. The letters, postmarked from all over New York, are all about Con Ed. A few of the letters are typed, but most are handwritten in the same distinctive block printing style of the note found with the first bomb. The letters condemn the "ghoulish acts" and "dastardly deeds" of Con Ed.[3] The writer is demanding justice for himself and other people wronged by the energy company. Many of the letters threaten more bombings, and some come "with the compliments of the 'mobsters' at #4 Irving Place—for further information—see the Mayor." The letters are signed with the initials "F.P."[4]

While the letters are alarming, the nation has far more pressing issues to worry about. War rages in Europe, and on December 7, 1941, Japan launches an attack on the American naval base at Pearl Harbor. In the attack 2,300 Americans die, and President Franklin Roosevelt feels there is no longer a choice, so he calls the nation to arms.[5] America is at war.

After the attack on Pearl Harbor, the New York City bomber sends another round of letters to a seemingly random group of New York institutions, including Bloomingdales, Radio City Music Hall, the Roxy Theatre, and the Astor Hotel. While the letters continue to condemn Con Ed, the last includes a surprising message: "I WILL MAKE NO MORE BOMB UNITS FOR THE DURATION OF THE WAR—MY PATRIOTIC FEELINGS HAVE MADE ME DECIDE THIS—LATER I WILL BRING THE CON-ED TO JUSTICE—THEY WILL PAY FOR THEIR DASTARDLY DEEDS . . . F.P."[6]

The bomber stays true to his word; for the duration of the war, no bombs appear. Eventually, the war ends, and though letters crop up throughout the 1940s, there are no bombs. The memory of the bomber fades away.

At 5:25 p.m. on March 19, 1951, a bomb explodes in a cigarette sand urn outside the Oyster Bar in the Grand Central Terminal. No one is injured. The police don't immediately connect the incident to the bombs of nearly a decade ago. Three weeks later, at 6:10 p.m., a bomb explodes in a phone booth in the New York Public Library's basement. Now, people are paying attention. At the end of August, a bomb explodes at Grand Central Terminal. This is followed, within a few weeks, by a bomb that explodes in a lobby telephone booth of Con Ed's headquarters. William Schmitt, a New York City detective, comes to understand that the bombings are all connected. The notion that one man has been targeting the city for more than a decade changes everything for the police and the public. The history makes it clear this bomber is not going to go away. He needs to be stopped.

Two weeks after the bomb at the Con Ed phone booth, a large manila envelope arrives in the company's third-floor mailroom. The letter, addressed to Con Ed's personnel director, is postmarked from White Plains, New York. Upon opening the package, the director discovers a pipe bomb. The bomb squad safely removes the bomb. When the device is dismantled, it is found to contain sugar instead of gunpowder.

After a break of a few months, the bomber is back to work. On the evening of October 22, the *New York Herald Tribune*'s editor receives a handwritten, penciled letter. The letter announces a bomb in the Paramount Theatre. The bomb squad acts fast, scouring the Paramount for the bomb while 3,600 theatergoers enjoy the night unaware. And, indeed, a bomb is found, tucked in the ventilation system of the men's bathroom. The device is recovered safely, but officials are at a loss as to how to end the campaign.

The letter received by the *Tribune* does nothing to calm the growing sense of fear. The letter says that the "BOMBS WILL CONTINUE UNTIL THE CONSOLIDATED EDISON COMPANY IS BROUGHT TO JUSTICE FOR THEIR DASTARDLY ACTS AGAINST ME. I HAVE EXHAUSTED ALL OTHER MEANS. I INTEND WITH BOMBS TO CAUSE OTHERS TO CRY OUT FOR JUSTICE FOR ME."[7] The letter concludes with a menacing threat: bigger bombs are on their way.

In the first week of November 1951, police arrest fifty-six-year-old Frederick Eberhardt, a former Con Ed employee. His handwriting resembles the bomber's, and he has a grudge against the company. "This arrest is an outrage," his wife insists. "He couldn't hurt a fly."[8]

Eberhardt is sent to Bellevue Hospital for psychiatric observation, but on November 11, an anonymous caller alerts police to bombs at the Capitol Theatre and a Catholic cathedral. On November 28, a bomb explodes in a subway station at Union Square. No one is injured, and it seems the imprisoned Eberhardt is not the perpetrator.

Around Christmas, the bomber sends another letter to the *New York Herald Tribune*. "HAVE YOU NOTICED THE BOMBS IN YOUR CITY," the letter asks. "IF YOU ARE WORRIED, I AM SORRY—AND ALSO IF ANYONE IS INJURED. BUT IT CANNOT BE HELPED," the letter laments, "FOR JUSTICE WILL BE SERVED." The bomber writes that he will "PLACE MORE UNITS UNDER THEATER SEATS" and signs the note "F.P."[9]

In 1952, there are three additional bombs, with one exploding in a bus terminal telephone booth and the others detonating at the Lexington Theatre. The second of the theater bombings injures a patron, with shrapnel striking her legs and feet. The police, keen to keep the details of the bombings under wraps, say very little, and the newspapers hardly cover the case. Poor Eberhardt is finally allowed to return home on May 15, 1952.

On March 10, 1953, a bomb explodes in Radio City Music Hall, the world's largest indoor theater. Though the theater can seat thousands, the explosion injures nobody. The newspapers call the explosion a "mild 'pop,'" and the *New York Times*, quoting police, calls the bomber a "publicity seeking jerk" and a "mental case."[10]

Two weeks after the Radio City Music Hall failure, the bomber sends another letter to the *New York Herald Tribune*. The paper has offended the bomber. He now demands that the paper correct its "SLOPPY OR NO REPORTING" about the bombings. "IN THE PRESS," the letter says, "I AM CALLED A 'BAD NAME.' JUST WHAT NAME FITS YOU PEOPLE WHO DENIED ME THE PURCHASE OF 'SPACE' TO TELL MY STORY—YOU WHO ARE TOO 'YELLOW' TO PRINT THE FACTS WHICH CONCERN THE SAFETY OF SO MANY?" "I AM BEWILDERED BY YOUR ATTITUDE," the letter concludes. "I CAN ONLY RESPOND WITH MORE AND LARGER BOMBS." The return address is "CONSOLIDATED EDISON CO., 4 IRVING PLACE, NEW YORK CITY."[11]

In 1954, the bomber plants bombs in Grand Central Terminal, the 8th Avenue Port Authority Bus Terminal, and Radio City Music Hall. All three explode—the bomber's skills are improving. The explosion at Radio City Music Hall occurs when the theater is packed with 6,200 people during a Christmas-season showing of Bing Cosby's *White Christmas*. Four audience members are injured by the shrapnel. Going forward, the bombings are headlines, and in true newspaper style, the culprit now gets a nickname—he is now the "Mad Bomber."[12]

THE OUTRAGE AND THE FEAR

The bombs become increasingly dangerous, and New York becomes increasingly fearful. Soon yet another device is found at Radio City. Though authorities deactivate it safely, they conclude that this bomb had lethal potential. Newspapers seize the story, and headlines the next day are terrifying: "Radio City Bomb Found to Be Deadly," reads one, while another announces "City Hunts Mad Bomb Planter."[13]

Despite the growing fame of the "Mad Bomber," investigators still know little more than they did when the first bomb was found in 1940. They have no new leads to follow, and the materials for making the bombs are so common that it is impossible to trace their sources. "I personally have taken the watch-timing mechanism from one of the bombs this clown has made to 75 stores around Times Square," Detective Schmitt says. "Everyone stocked that watch."[14]

More bombs come in 1956. On February 21, a seventy-four-year-old porter named Lloyd Hill heads to a men's bathroom in Penn Station to unplug a toilet. While he's working, the toilet explodes, showering him with porcelain and metal. Hill survives with injuries to his head and legs. Police discover the remains of a red wool sock, a familiar marker of the bomber's handiwork. The following day, newspapers announce that the FBI will get involved in the case.

Several months later, on August 4, Rockefeller Center security guard Thomas Dorney finds a piece of pipe and takes it home. "You never know when a piece of pipe is going to come in handy," Dorney figures,[15] leaving the pipe on his kitchen table that night. At 6:00 a.m. the following morning, a sound "like two cars coming together" wakens the Dorney family. The salvage pipe explodes, destroying the Dorneys' kitchen but injuring no one.

The Mad Bomber continues to write letters. One to the *Tribune* reads: "WHILE VICTIMS GET BLASTED—THE YELLOW PRESS MAKES NO MENTION OF THESE GHOULISH ACTS—THESE BOMBINGS WILL CONTINUE UNTIL CON EDISON IS BROUGHT TO JUSTICE—MY LIFE IS DEDICATED TO THIS TASK. EXPECT NO CALLS ABOUT BOMBS IN THEATERS AS YOUR ACTIONS NO LONGER WARRANT THE EFFORT OR THE DIME—ALL MY SUFFERINGS—ALL MY FINANCIAL LOSS—WILL HAVE TO BE PAID IN FULL." The bomber innocently ends his note: "I MERELY SEEK JUSTICE."

On the evening of December 2, 1956, a bomb explodes in Brooklyn's Paramount Theatre, injuring several people. The Mad Bomber has now built and placed thirty-two separate devices across New York. The next day, Police Commissioner Stephen Patrick Kennedy calls together his 350 borough and division chiefs, representing a force of 23,000 officers. "This man is not in his right mind," Kennedy announces, and the bombings are "an outrage that cannot be tolerated." He demands that departments prioritize the case and offers an "immediate good promotion" for anyone who arrests the Mad Bomber. "I appeal to members of the public to come forward and give to the police whatever information they may have concerning this man," Kennedy tells reporters. The manhunt, he says, is the "greatest in department history," and the bomber is "our No. 1 most wanted criminal."[16]

POLICE TAKE A NEW APPROACH

Even with the full attention of authorities, there seem to be few options for how to make progress. That changes when John J. Cronin, the captain in charge of the police department's missing persons division, has an idea. Six years ago, Cronin was on a panel with a psychiatrist, Dr. James Brussel.[17] In Cronin's view, the doctor has deep insight into the workings of the criminal mind. Perhaps, Cronin thinks, the doctor could help.

Dr. Brussel, a thin, well-dressed man, is an extraordinary character. He loves parakeets, and as a hobby, he produces crossword puzzles for publication in the *New York Times*. He is so prolific that the newspaper publishes his puzzles under three different names. Brussel is also a serious writer, having published numerous psychiatry books and even a work of fiction. He studied medicine at the University of Pennsylvania and completed his residency at a New York state hospital. After the Pearl Harbor attack, he enlisted in the army and worked as an army psychiatrist. He also served as assistant director of Willard State Hospital in New York, doing criminological consulting. Eventually, he was named the assistant director of the Division of New York City Services and, in 1952, became assistant commissioner of mental hygiene for New York State. Police approach Dr. Brussel, requesting his help. He answers "No," citing his caseload of three thousand patients a year.

Dr. Brussel's curiosity, however, gets the best of him. In his free time, Dr. Brussel has been building a theory of crime analysis that he has borrowed from fiction. Brussel is an admirer of several fictional detectives, including Edgar Allan Poe's Dupin, Agatha Christy's Poirot, and Arthur Conan Doyle's Sherlock Holmes. He feels that real-life crimes can be understood by building a theory about the perpetrator based on the crime itself.[18] Dr. Brussel cannot bring himself to pass up an opportunity to test out his new theory, so in early 1956, he agrees to meet with Captain Howard Finney of the crime laboratory. Finney and his team pay Dr. Brussel a visit at his office, which is littered with towers of reports, letters, and books. The police add to the disarray by dumping all the collected evidence concerning the Mad Bomber onto Brussel's desk.

Over the course of a four-hour meeting, Brussel pores through the materials brought by the police. Noting the skilled handiwork of the bombs, the doctor suggests that the bomber has training in metalworking. Those mechanical talents, as well as the act of bombing, are "alien to the feminine personality."[19] Because the bomber's anger extends not only to Con Ed but also to newspapers, theaters, libraries, and train stations, Dr. Brussel suggests that the bomber suffers from paranoia, "a chronic disorder . . . characterized by persistent, unalterable, systematized, logically constructed delusions." This disorder can progressively worsen. "These are the people who eventually go on to become God," he says. "They feel they are omnipotent."[20]

Brussel also decides that the bomber is "middle-aged,"[21] in his late forties or older; after all, paranoia usually sets in after thirty, and the first bomb had gone off over fifteen years ago. Brussel notes that a sense of superiority is typical of a paranoiac, perhaps motivating the bomber to perfect his handiwork and even penmanship. The bomber also values himself highly. He tries to appear flawless and act in a socially proper way. He is clean shaven and fastidious. He will wear no ornaments, no jewelry, no flashy ties or clothes. "He is quiet, polite, methodical, prompt."[22]

Brussel also observes that, while most of the letters in the bomber's notes are sharp, his *W*s are curved. Brussel, a devoted Freudian, thinks the curves resemble breasts or a scrotum. "Something about sex seemed to be troubling the Bomber," he speculates. "But what?"[23] Brussel suggests that the bomber has an unresolved Oedipal complex: he wants to sleep with his mother and kill his father, which explains why he's so convinced that men of authority are "trying to deprive him of something that [is] rightfully his." The bomber—seeking "the love of his mother"—probably wants nothing to do with men or women. Brussel concludes that the bomber must be unmarried and living with "some older female relative who [reminds] him of his mother."[24]

Additionally, the bomber must either be foreign or from an immigrant community, as his letters lack "slang or American colloquialisms." Brussel figures the bomber must be a Slav because Slavs use both knives and bombs, and the bomber uses knives to slash open theater seats for his bombs. If he's a Slav, "odds are he's a Roman Catholic" and regular churchgoer. Brussel also decides that the man must suffer from chronic heart disease, as the bomber references illness in his letters, and Brussel thinks heart disease is the most likely.

As Brussel finishes talking, Captain Finney and the two officers—stunned by the onslaught of information—get up to leave. "One more thing," Brussel says, "When you catch him—and I have no doubt you will—he'll be wearing a double-breasted suit. And it will be buttoned," the doctor adds.[25]

On Christmas morning, the *New York Times* publishes Dr. Brussel's description. The bomber is a "Single man, between 40 and 50 years old, introvert. Unsocial but not anti-social. Skilled mechanic. Cunning. Neat with tools. Egotistical of mechanical skill. Contemptuous of other people. Resentful of criticism of his work but probably conceals resentment. Moral. Honest. [Not] interested in women. High School Graduate. Expert in civil or military ordnance. Religious. Might flare up violently at work when criticized. Possible motive: discharge or reprimand. Feels superior to critics. Resentment keeps growing. Present or former Consolidated Edison worker. Probably case of progressive paranoia."[26]

Seymour Berkson, the publisher of the *New York Journal-American* newspaper, calls his assistant managing editor to discuss the Mad Bomber. There is a high demand for stories about the Mad Bomber, but there is little new information to report. Instead of dully recapping what they already know, Berkson proposes that they try contacting the bomber directly.

On December 26, the newspaper publishes an open letter to the bomber on its front page. "Give yourself up," the letter reads. "For your own welfare and for that of the community, the time has come for you to reveal your identity." The bomber, it announces, would have the benefit of the American justice system, and the newspaper would even print his story, allowing him to publicize his "grievances" against the Consolidated Edison Company.[27]

Two days later, the paper receives a letter from the bomber. "WHERE WERE YOU PEOPLE WHEN I WAS ASKING FOR HELP?" it reads. "PLACING MYSELF IN CUSTODY WOULD BE STUPID—DO NOT INSULT MY INTELLIGENCE." The irate crusader tells the paper to bring Con Ed to justice and promises to hold off bombing until mid-January.[28]

On January 12, 1957, the bomber sends another letter, which reads, "I WAS INJURED ON JOB AT CONSOLIDATED EDISON PLANT— AS A RESULT I AM ADJUDGED—TOTALLY AND PERMANENTLY DISABLED—I DID NOT RECEIVE 'ANY AID'—OF ANY KIND FROM COMPANY—THAT I DID NOT PAY FOR MYSELF." He'd been unable to receive workmen's compensation, as "'SECTION 28'" requires claims to be made within a year of injury. "I DID NOT GET A SINGLE PENNY FOR A LIFETIME OF MISERY AND SUFFERING—JUST ABUSE."[29]

Through a series of public exchanges, the paper promises medical care, legal counsel, and psychiatric treatment. On January 19, the paper receives several letters. "THANKS VERY MUCH FOR YOUR EFFORT," one letter says, "THE BOMBINGS WILL NEVER BE RESUMED—COME WHAT MAY—YOU PEOPLE HAVE LET THE PEOPLE KNOW—MY

PART OF THE STORY—I CANNOT ASK FOR MUCH MORE." In the second letter, the bomber reveals that he was injured on September 5, 1931, noting that the *New York Journal-American* accomplished in three weeks what law enforcement could not in sixteen years. "YOU STOPPED THE BOMBINGS," the bomber writes, signing off "F.P."[30]

The information proves vital. Just the day before, a Con Ed employee named Alice Kelly had been combing through company documents looking for the case file of the former employee who had become the Mad Bomber. At around 4:20 p.m., she'd found a promising lead: a case marked with the words "injustice" and "permanent disability."[31] The file belongs to George P. Metesky, an employee who'd started working in 1929 and sustained an injury in a boiler room accident in 1931. He contracted tuberculosis, a bacterial condition, which Metesky believed was somehow related to the accident (but which medical science suggests is highly unlikely). Con Ed stopped paying him in 1932. Metesky had sought compensation in 1934, but to no avail. In one letter, Metesky declares that he'll seek revenge and "take justice into his own hands." Another letter described the company's "dastardly deeds."[32]

On the morning of January 20, a group of detectives knocks on the door of Metesky's house in Waterbury, Connecticut, where Metesky, the fifty-three-year-old son of Lithuanian immigrants, lives with his two older sisters. Metesky opens the door wearing pajamas, and police search the house. Metesky's room is meticulous; a religious picture hangs on one wall. They find subway tokens, flashlight bulbs, and a loaded .38 revolver in the bedroom, and in the garage, a neat workbench, toolbox, and metalworking lathe. Metesky disappears into his room to get dressed. When he emerges, he's wearing a blue pinstripe double-breasted suit, buttoned.

"Why are we here?" one detective asks Metesky. "Maybe you suspect that I'm the Mad Bomber," he responds. The detective asks what F.P. stands for. "Fair Play," Metesky answers, calmly adjusting his tie.[33]

THE REFORM

Though Brussel's successful predictions seem to approach the supernatural, criminal profiling—forming predictions about a criminal's mind and body based on crime scene evidence—isn't new. Thousands of years ago, Homer and Plato noted relationships between appearance and behavior. Books during the Spanish Inquisition described the physical traits and behaviors of witches and Satanists. In the nineteenth century, the Italian doctor Cesare Lombroso developed a theory of "born criminals." Unlike criminals driven by lunacy or opportunism, he suggested, the born criminal is "an atavistic being who reproduces in his person the ferocious

Figure 5.1. George Metesky, smiling from his jail cell, 1957. *Al Rayenna, Library of Congress, World-Telegram & Sun Collection*

instincts of primitive humanity and the inferior animals."[34] And, as Brussel himself is fully aware of, criminal profiling even pervades fiction. Sherlock Holmes and Dr. Watson, characters created by Sir Arthur Conan Doyle in the nineteenth century, use empirical methods to identify criminals.

In 1888, British police surgeon Thomas Bond attempted to use a similar method to build a profile of Jack the Ripper, a serial killer of women. Based on victims' wounds, Bond concluded that the perpetrator was a powerful, unemotional individual, "[a] man subject to periodical attacks of Homicidal and Erotic mania. The murderer in external appearance is quite likely to be a quiet and inoffensive man, probably middle-aged and neatly and respectably dressed. He would be solitary and eccentric in his habits, also most likely to be a man without regular occupation, but with a small income or pension."[35] The murderer was never found, but Bond's empirical methodology did indeed represent a solid attempt at criminal profiling.

Before 1956, American law enforcement officials had never used a formal criminal profile to aid in the apprehension of an unknown offender.

Dr. James Brussel is the first to apply psychiatric principles to a criminal case in the United States.

Though profiling does not lead directly to Metesky's arrest, it does help to focus the search. Dr. Brussel enjoys a surge of fame. In February of 1957, *Newsweek* calls Brussel's profile "amazingly accurate," and the *New York Times* praises the police for "getting a theoretical portrait of the man they were seeking.[36] "Brussel, pleased with the public recognition, reiterates that the Bomber is a "textbook case of paranoia," this despite the fact that the two have never met.[37]

Behind the scenes, however, Brussel's work is debated. Captain Finney thinks highly of Brussel, but Detective William Schmitt believes that the "word picture" drawn by the psychiatrist "could fit anyone in the world."[38] After all, some of Dr. Brussel's predictions were slightly off the mark: Metesky's background is Lithuanian, not Slavic (though Lithuania is in a heavily Slavic part of the world), and Metesky is fifty-three, slightly older than Brussel guessed. He suffers from tuberculosis, not heart disease. The profiling errors cited seem nitpicky to most; the portrait is largely accurate. Brussel's work is seen as representing an important milestone.

In the years after George Metesky's arrest, other police departments seek Brussel's help. In 1964, officials in Massachusetts ask Brussel to help catch the Boston Strangler. Brussel insists that the murders were caused by just one person, though others disagree; he's proven correct when Albert DeSalvo is arrested and found guilty. In 1968, Dr. Brussel publishes his memoir, *Casebook of a Crime Psychiatrist*, which articulates his technique—a "private blend of science, intuition, and hope"[39]—and shares the stories of his aid to law enforcement. Newspapers across the nation publish sections of the book; one FBI representative calls it "the first crude manual in criminal profiling for police use."[40] In 1969, psychiatrist Martin Schorr testifies that Sirhan Sirhan, Robert Kennedy's assassin, is a paranoid schizophrenic. Schorr presents a report buttressing his argument. Unfortunately for Schorr, the report is plagiarized straight out of Brussel's book, and his deception is uncovered. Schorr's testimony is thrown out, but sales of the *Casebook* increase.

While Brussel's ideas and reputation grow during the 1960s, others are working out different parts of the profiling puzzle. One of these people is Howard Teten, a crime analyst for the San Leandro Police Department, and later, the FBI. Teten hypothesizes a connection between a crime and the type of person likely to commit it. Teten develops careful experiments to test his theories, developing profiles for known criminals and then comparing their actual profiles.

In 1970, Teten applies his new technique to an unsolved crime for the first time. A young woman was stabbed to death in her home, and police have no suspects. After analyzing the crime scene, Teten concludes that the perpetrator is an adolescent male who stabbed the woman in a violent, emotional state, an act that was probably his first crime. Now, Teten suggests, the murderer feels guilty, and he'll confess immediately when confronted. Teten recommends that police knock on doors in nearby neighborhoods. At one house, a teenager opens the door. Before the police say anything, the teen declares, "You got me."[41]

Teten's success increases the interest felt by police departments. He works with Patrick Mullany, an FBI New York special agent with expertise in abnormal psychology, to hone his method. In 1972, the FBI academy in Quantico, Virginia, opens, and the pair starts teaching their ideas in the classroom.[42]

With Teten now part of the FBI, he and Dr. Brussel compare notes. Teten is skeptical about Brussel's Freudianism and the use of ethnicity to predict behaviors, and he believes Brussel should factor in crime-scene contamination more carefully. While the two are not in total agreement, Teten respects Brussel, calling him "an innovator" and an "individualist who was not content with the status quo."[43]

Both men prove instrumental in developing the science of criminal profiling. In the FBI, their ideas spread quickly, with students learning, and eventually applying, Teten's techniques. Though the methods are unofficial, officers frequently report that they were instrumental in solving cases, as profiles narrow the focus of searches and save time.[44] Eventually, the science is given its own name in the FBI: Criminal Investigation Analysis. Though best known for its unknown-offender profiles, the unit's tasks are diverse, including personality assessments, equivocal death analysis, investigative suggestions, interview and trial strategies, threat assessments, search warrant affidavit assistance, geographic profiling, and more. The analysts avoid direct involvement with the investigative process, but examine evidence and advise the agency.[45]

The profiling process is formulaic. First, a profiler collects information: autopsy reports, crime-scene photos, and the like, with the exception of suspect lists. The profiler then organizes and analyzes the information according to victim risk, with high-risk victims more likely to face dangerous or vulnerable situations; a prostitute, for example, faces more danger than a typical nine-to-five worker. Offenders are ranked, too. High-risk offenders commit crimes that increase their chances of being caught—for example, during daytime or with potential witnesses—while low-risk offenders carefully avoid these risks.[46] With this information, the profiler tries to reimagine the crime and pinpoint criminal motive, carefully incorporating facts about timing and location. The task isn't easy; perpetrators often manipulate crime scenes to cover their tracks.

The profiler then compares this analysis to known offender characteristics, psychological disorders, and the like to produce predictions about a criminal. The information—now a criminal profile—is sent to police, who use it to guide investigators. If new information is revealed, the profiler will reevaluate.[47]

The FBI profilers try to further their understanding of criminals by interviewing thirty-six convicted serial killers. They immediately find that serial killers are not bound by the truth: their interviews are laden with manipulation and dishonest answers. Still, the FBI determines that there is an "organized/disorganized dichotomy" in most criminals. Under this scheme, organized killers are planners who leave few clues behind at the crime scene. These killers are not insane, they are antisocial and incapable of remorse, and are fully able to distinguish right from wrong. At the other end of the continuum are the disorganized criminals. These are impulsive actors, often young and/or intoxicated. The mentally ill who commit murder usually fall within this group. Because they act without a plan, they often leave more evidence behind.

Gregg McCary, a retired FBI agent, offers this: "The basic premise is that behavior reflects personality."[48] Crimes are viewed by profilers in four steps. The *Antecedent*: what were the factors needed for the criminal to act? This is an exploration of the likely triggering conditions. Next, the *Manner*: how was the actual killing done? For example, multiple stabbings, often called "overkill," equates to rage, and these killers are generally disorganized. Third, the hows and whys of *Body Disposal* are important. Was the body moved? Was the corpse arranged after death? Did the disposal require particular skill or strength? Finally, profilers try to get a sense of likely *Postoffense Behavior*: Will the killer be interested in media reports? Will the person want to revisit the crime scene? Will the killer leave the area?[49]

With criminal profiling becoming an integral part of the FBI's work, law enforcement across the country catches on quickly, tweaking methods to suit departmental needs. Profiling goes by several names, including *criminal, psychological,* or *behavioral profiling* and *criminal investigative analysis*. No matter the name, they all strive to connect criminals with their crimes using a mix of law enforcement experience, psychology, science, and even art. Profiling narrows down suspect lists, directs investigations, aids in confessions, and helps explain the rationale for crimes.[50]

BEYOND REFORM

Criminal profiling becomes a standard and commonly used tool of crime investigators. For example, authorities use it to help understand the

Unabomber. The bomber begins sending bomb-rigged packages across the nation in 1978. A package addressed to a Northwestern University engineering professor is found in a Chicago parking lot. When someone gives the professor the package, he notes that the return address is also his own.[51] He gives the suspicious package to campus security, and it explodes when a guard opens it to investigate, causing the guard minor injuries. Another bomb activates aboard a commercial airplane, but the device malfunctions and it fills the cabin with smoke. A Northwestern student is injured in another attack, and a computer store owner in Sacramento, California, is killed when a bomb explodes outside his shop.

The Unabomber—shorthand for **Un**iversity and Airline **Bomber**—goes on a spree that spans seventeen years, killing three and injuring twenty-four. Though the FBI has 150 full-time agents working the case, investigators struggle to identify a suspect: there is little forensic evidence, and the victims appear to be unconnected. The biggest clue investigators have is the bombs' materials. Though they are too common to be tracked, most of the materials are clearly salvaged, and some are even handcrafted from wood. Some dub him the "junk bomber."

John Douglass, a detective in the FBI's Behavioral Science Unit, attempts to use this limited evidence to develop a criminal profile. He predicts that the bomber is a scruffy white male who is "highly educated, quiet, antisocial, meticulous."[52] He has connections to academia, lives or has lived in Chicago, and is avidly anti-technology, which may indicate a link between the victims. The bomber has a great deal of free time but not a lot of financial resources.

Other agents scoff at Douglass's profile. Many in the FBI believe that the Behavioral Science Unit rarely offers investigators anything of value; they view it as little more than the "BS Unit." While Douglass and his team see the Unabomber described above, traditional investigators believe he is a blue-collar airplane mechanic.[53] Douglass advocates putting all available information out to the public. To Douglass, the Unabomber is a product of rigorous university training. He would have come into contact with lots of people over the course of his life, and someone is bound to remember his unique personality.

For years, the bombings continue, and no progress is made. Then there is a breakthrough: the Unabomber demands that some of his writings be published in the national press. To compel the papers to cooperate, the Unabomber promises to blow up an airliner if they fail to print the work. *Penthouse* magazine wants the job, but the Unabomber brushes the idea aside. He wants the readers of America's biggest newspapers to hear what he has to say.

The Unabomber's enormous anti-technology manifesto appears in the *New York Times* and *The Washington Post*, along with the FBI profile. New

York City resident David Kaczynski instantly recognizes the profile and writing style as matching his brother's, Ted Kaczynski. Ted, a Chicago native, has always been quiet and unsocial, but he's highly educated, boasting an undergraduate degree from Harvard, a master's and PhD in mathematics, and experience as a mathematics professor. In 1971, Ted quit his job and moved to an isolated cabin in Montana, from which he began sending bombs. Law enforcement officials raid the ten-by-twelve cabin in 1996, arresting Kaczynski. Bombs, bomb parts, thousands of incriminating journal pages, and the original manifesto litter the floor. (Kaczynski's neighbors believed their local hermit to be B. D. Cooper, a skyjacker who had gotten away with $200,000 in ransom in 1971, equivalent to $1,180,000 in 2016.)[54]

The profile offered by Douglass had been correct. Later, when reflecting on the Unabomber investigation, he writes:

> The Bureau dropped the ball so many times. The behavioral scientists had a guy like Kaczynski pegged from the beginning, and if the Bureau had used our proactive strategies after the traditional ones had failed for so many years it might have caught the suspect ten years and three lives sooner.[55]

Many still point out that the criminal profile did not directly lead to the killer.[56] On one level, this is true: the profile of Ted Kaczynski developed by Douglass and his team did not reveal a particular suspect. And yet, when the profile was published next to his manifesto, someone who knew Kaczynski made the connection and contacted police, just as the profilers predicted.

Criminal profiling is used effectively again in Seattle in 1992 to stop a spree of arsons.[57] The first fires are reported in July in the Seattle suburbs, initially targeting churches. Before long, dumpsters, woodpiles at construction sites, and property surrounding homes, such as carports, are being set ablaze. The fires, often several in a single night, destroy millions of dollars' worth of property and injure several people. Some terrified citizens prepare to face the arsonist, arming themselves with bats or guns. Some communities set up neighborhood watches.

Then in September, the arsonist breaks into a retirement home and sets an empty bed on fire. The building goes up in flames, killing three people and causing $1 million in property damage. A task force of twenty-seven agencies is formed, and investigators decide to assemble a criminal profile. The resulting profile says that the arsonist is a white male in his twenties or thirties. He is well dressed, intelligent, articulate, and a pathological liar. Though probably a traveling salesman, he's interested in becoming a police officer or fireman. He likely has low self-esteem and deep emotional problems. The start of the arson spree, July, coincides with a traumatic event in his life. As a child, the arsonist is likely to have been cruel to animals or other children, and may have wet the bed. His experiments with arson began at an early age. The man they are seeking for the arson attacks will be preoccupied with media reports on the fires. He might, in their view, use drugs or alcohol and is probably looking to leave town.

Investigators release the profile to the public in a press conference. Ben Keller reads the description in the newspaper and immediately thinks of his brother, Paul Keller. Paul's parents read the profile and independently reach the same conclusion. His father turns Paul in.

The accuracy of the profile is astonishing. Paul, twenty-seven years old and divorced, works for his father's advertisement company as a traveling salesman. Paul has twice been rejected as a volunteer firefighter. In July, he'd had to file for bankruptcy, a traumatic and life-changing decision. Paul's emotional instability and low self-esteem had been constant in his life, despite a stable, loving family. At the age of nine, he had incinerated an empty house next to his family's home.[58] Everyone agrees that he was frequently cruel to his siblings and had been a convincing liar since childhood. Now, he drinks heavily and has often discussed leaving the state.

Paul Keller is taken into custody and interrogated carefully, with investigators drawing from the criminal profile to shape their questions. Eventually, Paul confesses to starting 76 fires causing over $30 million in property damage. He is sentenced to 99 years in prison.

Measuring the effectiveness of criminal profiles is difficult; whether or not any particular crime could have been solved without the effort requires speculation. Based on surveys, criminal profiles directly identify suspects in 17 percent of cases, but investigators claim that profiles help investigations almost 80 percent of the time. Their reasons are diverse: profiles can speed up an investigation, eliminate false leads, and provide new insights. Profiles are also useful tools for encouraging confessions, and they're frequently used to promote community involvement. Investigators report that, in a small number of cases, an inaccurate profile misled them or dragged out a search—but regardless, they feel that these are usually surmountable bumps, and profiles rarely ruin an investigation.[59] Other investigators, however, are far from convinced. Some investigators are simply skeptical; others are turned off after using them once and finding them unhelpful.[60]

Profiles are developed by different people with varied training and unequal amounts of useable information. All of these variables will contribute to the reliability of the resulting profile. Profiles of arsonists are generally successful, while certain killers are less easily profiled.[61] In many cases, the information critical to finding a specific individual comes from the family and friends of perpetrators. For example, the three components of the "Homicidal Triad"—a history of bed-wetting, animal cruelty, and starting fires—are knowable only by close family members, but the combination reflects a need for control and a desire for emotional and sexual release.[62]

Criminal profiling has also proven crucial in hostage situations. Crisis negotiation teams usually have a psychologist on hand, who aids the team before and during the crisis, assessing behaviors and profiling both hostage takers and hostages. Another team member continually gathers information for the psychologist and negotiators; the more information the team has, the higher the likelihood of a successful negotiation.[63] Relevant information can relate to the hostage taker's family, background, mental history, criminal history, relationships with the hostages, or a connection to the location. Once criminal profiles are outlined, team members can assess the danger of the situation, settle on specific negotiation tactics, and predict a perpetrator's reactions. Profiling in hostage situations can be even more accurate than in searching for the unknown criminal.[64] These teams are enormously successful: 95 percent of hostage crises are resolved without any fatalities.

Modern criminal profiling, a hybrid of law, psychology, science, and art, has come a long way since New York police detectives first sat down in Dr. Brussel's cluttered office to write a profile of the Mad Bomber. As the field matures, investigators continue to develop new techniques to make the principles of profiling more relevant and accurate. For example, new software programs use statistical analysis of crime-scene locations to determine where a suspect lives or works. The computer can, with impressive accuracy, see patterns that might elude an investigator.[65]

Today, the rate at which murders are "cleared," which is to say the killer is identified, can be alarmingly low. (In 2016, the clearance rate for murders in Chicago was about 21 percent.)[66] Highly skilled criminal profiling is not going to solve every murder, but it seems wasteful to reject any crime fighting instrument because it does not always work as well as we would wish.

Chapter Six

1957
Mafia Commission
Apalachin Meeting

*Racketeer Influenced and Corrupt
Organizations Act (RICO)*

THE CRIME

On a drizzly November afternoon of 1957, in Apalachin, New York, Sergeant Edgar Croswell peers through binoculars at a row of beautiful cars parked in a spacious driveway. His eyes linger on a Chrysler Crown Imperial, a car like none other: graceful, polished, and expensive. The wealth before Croswell makes him uneasy, as the house—made of fieldstone and nestled on a lovely rural estate—is owned by Mafia boss Joe Barbara.[1] Croswell is certain that at least one hundred of Barbara's fellow mobsters from across the nation are inside. He is witnessing—and will soon disrupt—a historic Mafia meeting.

The Mafia's journey to this moment began in 1880, when thousands of Italian immigrants began arriving in the United States. By 1920, four million have made America their new home. Italian immigrants, like many other groups, struggle to integrate into American society. They tend to settle together in urban centers, such as New York City's "Little Italy."

Italian immigrants bring many elements of Italian culture. One of those is the concept of the Mafia, which implies an attitude of defiance of authority, loyalty to family, and the settlement of disputes by vendetta or by the decree of a village headman. The Mafia as an organized criminal endeavor that evolved from bands of hired thugs brought in to enforce the will of local landowners. In time, power shifted, and the thugs outgrew their need for the landowner. Going forward, they worked for themselves.[2]

Figure 6.1.   **Cars parked on the lawn of Mafia boss Joe Barbara, 1957.** *National Crime Syndicate*

Transplanted to the United States, Mafia members and former members organize and resume the petty extortion and violence they know from Italy against their fellow Italian immigrants.[3] Italian immigrants already accept family-based crime groups as a fact of life and raise little fuss. The larger country shrugs at this arrangement, and the Mafia is allowed to quietly grow, building an organization and expanding their regional network.

All of that starts to change in 1920 when America ratifies the Eighteenth Amendment, outlawing alcohol nationwide. The Mafia, or Cosa Nostra, is perfectly positioned to manage the underground alcohol industry that booms in the age of Prohibition. The Mafia is already a tightly organized, hierarchical enterprise and is adept at coordinating operations that need to go undetected by the authorities. The Cosa Nostra quietly sets the rates for graft payments, manages the burgeoning network of shipments, and keeps their own speakeasy system running with an efficiency that other criminals cannot match. During Prohibition, the Mafia amasses unparalleled wealth and unimpeded power.

With so much money to be made, the Mafia is no longer dependent on exploiting immigrants, nor is it confined to one neighborhood of New York City. They divide the country into five strictly hierarchical "families," with each controlling a defined territory. However, in 1931, Salvator

Maranzano—a mob boss of the "old-style" Mafia tradition, which values Italian heritage and family above money—upsets the fragile balance of power when he declares himself to be the "boss of all bosses."

His primary opposition comes from Lucky (Charles) Luciano, a man who ascribes to a more modern view of the Mafia. The Luciano vision eschews notions of culture and tradition. The enterprise is not cloaked in a philosophy but rather aims to be a ruthless, efficient money-making machine. Luciano sees Maranzano and his tradition-bound way of doing business as a roadblock on the path to profits. So Luciano elects to eliminate the roadblock: his men murder Maranzano in his office, leaving his body sprawled across the floor. Luciano inherits the mantle from Maranzano, and indeed becomes the uncontested boss of bosses. Luciano is a businessman who understands that interfamily rivalries cost everyone money. He creates a commission to negotiate within the Five Families and keep disputes to a minimum.

In 1936, Luciano is convicted on charges related to prostitution and sentenced to thirty years in prison. Though Luciano is in custody, nothing about his imprisonment prevents him from remaining in control of the family. Even behind bars, Luciano continues to manage his empire. His authority extends to the prison itself, where he has a personal chef. As a side business, he also manages the prison. Various individuals and families rise and fall in power, but the focus remains largely internal. The Mafia continues to reap large profits from its criminal business model.

The Mafia avoids crimes that make headlines and keeps the killings among themselves, so American law enforcement is largely uninterested through the 1940s and 1950s. FBI director J. Edgar Hoover sees the Mafia as an unwelcome distraction, pulling investigative resources away from American's primary threat—communists.[4] Many in the government are comfortable with the idea that the secretive organization is actually just a myth.

In 1957, power struggles erupt within the Five Families, leaving two powerful bosses dead.[5] The attacks shake the larger organization. If two powerful bosses can be brought down, is anyone safe? Vito Genovese, who by now has taken over for Luciano, knows that it was a serious breach of Mafia etiquette to kill his rival bosses, knows it is up to him to bring stability to the organization. Genovese decides the path to peace is for him to consolidate his power further. On November 14, 1957, he calls a meeting of over one hundred Mafia leaders at the New York home of Joe Barbara.

The federal government is turning a blind eye to the Mafia, but Sergeant Croswell of the New York State Police has been spying on Barbara for over a decade. Barbara is the area distributor for the soda brand Canada Dry and is beloved by many community members because of his generous donations to charity. But he is also a powerful member of the Mafia. Barbara, who emigrated from Sicily in 1921, is arrested three times for separate murders in the New York City area, including that of a man stabbed twenty-two times with an icepick. There are three arrests but no convictions.

Croswell first becomes aware of Barbara in 1944 after a tense confrontation at a police station. Two years later, Barbara is convicted of illegally buying three hundred thousand pounds of sugar, a purchase obviously intended for illegal moonshining. In another incident in 1956, a man named Carmine Galante—a squat, sharp-eyed Italian American with a long arrest record—is pulled over for speeding and brought in by a New York state trooper. The case is passed to Croswell, who learns that Galante has just met with Barbara in a nearby hotel. When several of his fellow New York police officers offer Croswell a bribe to release Galante, Croswell realizes that the men have powerful connections—exactly the sort of connections sought after by leaders of the criminal underworld.

For years, Croswell has prowled around the Barbara property, visiting several times each month on his own initiative. He takes photographs, and in one incident pretends to be a magazine photographer when he is caught by Barbara. Though the evidence is sparse, Croswell is entirely convinced that Joe Barbara, aka Joe Bananas, is a high-powered member of the Mafia.

For Officer Croswell, the scores of pricey automobiles parked in Barbara's driveway confirm his suspicions. Scanning the license plates, he reads "New Jersey, Pennsylvania, New Jersey, New York, New York, Ohio, Illinois," to his state police partner, trooper Vincent Vasisko. Vasisko responds dryly, "Those aren't salesmen cars." The pair starts writing down as many plate numbers as they can, and Croswell picks up his radio. The trooper requests "assistance from all uniformed troopers in the area."[6]

Standing in the wet afternoon, Croswell's team can see more than sixty middle-aged men inside the home. The men move leisurely around the sprawling fieldstone house. As Vasiko noted, these are not salesmen from the soda company. They are all finely dressed in elegant suits with gleaming shoes. Answering Croswell's summons, seventeen officers encircle the Barbara estate; roadblocks appear at every exit.

A delivery truck driver sees the police roadblocks and gets word to the men inside the house. News of troopers gathered outside the property sets the well-tailored suits in motion. Croswell, now standing at the edge of the estate with binoculars, begins to laugh. The police have no legal access to the men while they are on private property, but as soon as they hit the road, the police can act.

The first car to pull down the drive is a handsome Lincoln convertible carrying two men. As it approaches, Croswell sets his trap. Clearly, the others are waiting and watching from the estate. Croswell allows the Lincoln to pass unchallenged. Croswell assumes this false sense of security will draw them off the property. Sure enough, they all soon begin to pile into their cars. The lot next to the garage starts to empty as cars line up and move slowly down the road, "as though in a funeral cortege."[7]

Croswell's heart jumps. There are too many of them, he thinks, as he watches the procession approach. With Vasiko down the road organizing other roadblocks, Croswell is left with only two IRS men at his side. As the parade of killers draws near, he swallows his panic and begins to stop the cars.

The first car, a Chrysler Imperial, comes to a stop. Croswell peers into the passenger window, where a squat, thick-bellied man with yellow-tinted glasses and bushy, arched brows is sitting. The driver and the three backseat passengers are silent. Croswell doesn't recognize him, but the sullen passenger is Vito Genovese.

"You've all been at Mr. Barbara's?" Croswell asks. "What were you doing there?"

"He is a very sick, the poor man," Genovese answers sadly. "We just came to wish him a speedy recovery." The men are cooperative, giving the officer their IDs and consenting to a trunk search, though Genovese politely reminds Croswell that he doesn't need to answer questions.

The pressure mounts for Croswell. More than a dozen cars now idle behind the Imperial, backed up all the way to the house. Each vehicle is filled with grim-looking men. Croswell cannot process them all. He allows them to proceed knowing that they will be picked up at other roadblocks.

To those still at Barbara's house, it becomes clear that driving out is not a good plan. A group leaves on foot, heading into the nearby woods. No one runs; in their expensive suits and elegant shoes, they trudge into the sodden grass with heads and shoulders down. The majority are heading southeast, into the thick woods blanketing the mountain nearby. Barbara's property is well groomed, cut with lovely riding trails, but all the trails lead back to the house; the men must move off trail to escape. The rain has turned the earth soft and slippery, and autumn leaves conceal obstacles. Most of the mobsters are in poor physical condition. It is not an ideal afternoon for bushwhacking.

Barbara's neighbor, a dairyman named Ray Martin, is mucking out his yard. Suddenly, two men come crashing out of the nearby woods, both dressed in suits. "Which way to Pennsylvania?" one of them asks Martin, breathless and exhausted. Another group encounters Glen Craig who is out doing chores on his farm. They want to pay the farmer for a ride to Binghamton, a nearby town. Craig agrees, but the trip is cut short by one of Croswell's roadblocks at the end of the lane. A few of the savvy guests elect to stay at Barbara's. They are not picked up—visiting a sick friend is perfectly legal.

It takes eight hours for police to gather up all the men. Those who had fled on foot are wet, cold, and miserable. By day's end, sixty men are detained, loitering in the lobby of the State Police substation on the outskirts of Binghamton. Many are caked with mud and exhausted, because, as Croswell says sarcastically, "There are no sidewalks in the woods."[8] All smell faintly of smoke, lingering from the barbeque lunch. Nobody is arrested. They are brusque but polite while being questioned. Almost all offer the same explanation for their presence at Joe Barbara's house that chilly afternoon: Joe was recovering from a heart attack, and his friends were wishing him well. No, the event wasn't planned. Yes, the number of people was only a coincidence. "I guess we just happened to have the same idea at the same time," shrugs one man, who had flown two thousand miles from Los Angeles.[9] Some of the men offer even less. "I'm not going to answer your questions," says Joe Barbara Jr. calmly.[10] He doesn't.

No illegal weapons or drugs are found. The sixty men have around $300,000 in cash on them, worth well more than $2.5 million today. Trooper Croswell has a problem. State law only permits a suspect to be held for twelve hours without an arrest. Croswell has no evidence of any crimes. Almost as soon as it starts, the gathering is over; everyone is released.[11]

THE OUTRAGE

Croswell does not manage to arrest a single mobster, but he does get the attention of officials in Washington. The Apalachin raid is too big for the federal government to ignore. FBI director Hoover, who has long denied the existence of the Mafia to the American public, is keenly embarrassed. How could a lowly state trooper find scores of Mafia men when Hoover had not located a single one? Faced with such overwhelming evidence, Hoover makes a show of the FBI's efforts to shut down the mob; for the next five years, the FBI heavily investigates organized crime. Outside of the public eye, however, Hoover drags his feet. When he learns of an FBI report on the Mafia being circulated to key government officials, for example, he orders that the report be recalled.

In 1961, Robert Kennedy is appointed U.S. attorney general and the Mafia is on his agenda. Kennedy soon discovers that "the FBI didn't know anything, really, about these people who were the major gangsters in the United States."[12] Kennedy is appalled, his charge is unambiguous: "Do something about it."[13] He beefs up the FBI's organized-crime squads and quadruples the number of attorneys in the racketeering section.

Even with the increased focus, the war on organized crime is difficult to fight. Mobsters carefully hide behind the masks of legitimate business-men, and their crimes take place in the shadows. For several years, the internal code of silence makes it nearly impossible to gain information that might lead to arrests.

All of that changes on the morning of June 22, 1962, at the U.S. peni-tentiary in Atlanta, Georgia, when an inmate—prisoner number 82811—seizes a two-foot iron pipe from a construction site, runs to a fellow inmate, and lets "him have it over the head."[14] A guard spots the attack and rushes the armed man, demanding the pipe. "There's a guy dying," the guard says frantically when the inmate refuses to surrender his make-shift weapon. The response is chilling: "Good. Let him die."[15] By the time inmate 82811, a man named Joe Valachi, stops the beating, his victim is unconscious with a fractured skull. The inmate is escorted, pipe in hand, to the associate warden's office. Valachi is in his late fifties, a squat man at only five feet, six inches tall, but he's built like a bull, with burly shoulders and cropped gray hair. The beaten inmate dies two days later.

Valachi, born in Manhattan in 1904 to Italian immigrants, is one of six surviving children out of seventeen. His father was an alcoholic who beat his wife and children frequently. "My mother always had a black eye," Valachi says.[16] Valachi, who flunked out of school and spent time in juve-nile delinquency centers, began working at a garbage dump at the age of fifteen. His father pocketed all of Valachi's earnings, so, Valachi says, "I started to steal to have a little money of my own."[17] By age eighteen, he is a member of an East Harlem burglary gang called the Minutemen, so named for their speedy crimes. He is picked up numerous times on sus-picion of burglary or larceny charges; his first conviction comes in 1923. He spends nine months in prison. Shortly after his release, he is caught again and sentenced to more than three years in prison.[18] Upon his release in 1928, Valachi becomes acquainted with the Cosa Nostra through a mob member named Dominick Petrilli; some time later, he becomes a soldier in the Reina (later Lucchese) family, and then in the Genovese family. He remains in this position for years, carrying out mob "contracts," or mur-ders. Valachi has always been rebellious; his personality does not seem well matched with a secretive criminal organization that prizes hierarchy and order. But Valachi is an effective killer. The Justice Department esti-mates that he has been involved in at least thirty-three deaths during his time with the mob.

Like most mob members, he does many things. His exploits run the gamut from loan sharking, heroin trafficking, jukebox racketeering, num-bers racketeering, gas-ration stamp racketeering, as well as involvement in the restaurant business, dress manufacturing, horse racing, and the linen supply business. In 1959, agents from the Narcotics Bureau arrest him on drug distribution charges. The following year, Valachi is sentenced to fifteen years, and then in 1962 is convicted again and sentenced to twenty-five concurrent years behind bars. His cellmate Vito Genovese is serving a fifteen-year sentence, from April 1959, for heroin trafficking. Valachi has been in prison for three years when he decides to pick up the pipe.

Valachi's explanation for the brutal murder is "I just went crazy." Everyone is suspicious that there is more to the story, but Valachi is tightlipped. "I get the feeling that Valachi . . . will never come out with a full account of the whole story," says one official.[19] For three weeks, this seems true—Valachi evades investigators' questions, and nobody knows what happened. But things change when the prosecuting attorney elects to pursue the death penalty because of the "brutality and senselessness" of the murder.[20] Valachi, desperate for a way out, contacts Robert Morgenthau, the U.S. attorney for New York, and says that he's willing to cooperate with the U.S. government.

THE VALACHI PAPERS

Morgenthau and the prosecutor are intrigued; perhaps Valachi can offer useful information about drug trafficking. Valachi negotiates a deal where, in exchange for a life sentence, he will tell the authorities everything he knows. As soon as Valachi opens up, attorneys grow wide-eyed. He paints a picture of an organization more powerful than anyone imagined—a national crime syndicate with roots in major cities across the country, employing thousands, earning billions. Henry L. Giordano, the commissioner of the Bureau of Narcotics, realizes the significance of the Valachi information.

The FBI is thrilled to hear of Valachi's willingness to talk.[21] For years, the FBI has struggled to gain credible evidence of the so-called criminal underworld demanded by Attorney General Kennedy. Valachi's cooperation promises to be a game changer.[22] James P. Flynn, a special agent with the FBI, is dispatched. Flynn is a sharp and imaginative interrogator.[23] Valachi is stubborn at first, but on September 8, things take a dramatic turn. Flynn, alone with Valachi, announces, "Joe, let's stop fooling around. You know I'm here because the Attorney General wants this information. I want to talk about the organization. . . . What's the name? Is it Mafia?" Valachi spars with him, but then Flynn says, "We know a lot more than you think. Now I'll give you the first part. You give me the rest. It's Cosa ___" "Cosa Nostra!" Valachi responds hoarsely. "So you know about it."[24] For the first time in American history, a member of the Mafia has admitted its existence.

Flynn's interrogation quickly reveals the reason for Valachi's brutal killing. Earlier in the year, Valachi explains, another Cosa Nostra member accused him of being a rat for the Federal Bureau of Narcotics. While it is true that Valachi had offered some information about drug trafficking, he never mentioned the Cosa Nostra. Regardless, the organization wants him dead. Vito Genovese—the most feared mob boss in the Cosa Nostra and now Valachi's cellmate—gives him "the kiss of death," an act that confirms Valachi's worst fears. Certain of death, Valachi begged for solitary confinement, wrote frantic letters to his wife, and tried to contact another mob boss who might help him. Nobody comes to his aid.

On June 22, Valachi takes matters into his own hands. He spots an inmate whom he believes to be Joseph "Joe Beck" DiPalermo, one of Genovese's men. He believes the man may be the one who has been tasked to kill him. "He looked just like Joe Beck," Valachi remembers, "So I said to myself, I might as well take him, too."[25] He attacks with the pipe in hand. Sometime later, Valachi learns it isn't Joe Beck whom he murdered, but another inmate, Joseph Saupp, a typical criminal serving time for mail robbery and forgery. Faced with certain death in prison at Genovese's behest and the prospect of the death penalty for his mistaken crime, Valachi feels that he has nothing to lose by cooperating.

Valachi is interviewed an average of four days a week until September 1962. The syndicate, the FBI learns, is divided into families, with each family reigning over a particular city or district. The family is strictly hierarchical, but all members must be Italian. Valachi names bosses, particularly those leading the New York families, and describes the operation of the "Commission," the Mafia's governing body, comprising nine to twelve bosses from across the country.[26] The Mafia is big, organized, and more than anything, powerful.

By early 1963, Valachi expresses an interest in testifying to the public. Attorney General Kennedy and his staff like the idea; none of Valachi's testimony conflicts with their existing information, and the public, Congress included, ought to hear it. Perhaps, they also reason, his public testimony might spark support for anticrime legislation.[27]

On September 9, Valachi is flown to Washington, D.C., to speak before an investigating committee. The testimony is broadcast across the nation.

THE REFORM

For Attorney General Kennedy, Joe Valachi provides the "biggest single intelligence breakthrough yet in combating organized crime and racketeering in the United States."[28] Valachi is the first insider to describe the Cosa Nostra to the government and the nation. Kennedy, for his part, is

a key figure in cracking down on American mobsters. The FBI is restruc-
tured to give priority to breaking organized crime. Across the country,
more than a thousand FBI agents are shuffled into trained, organized-
crime squads, led by tough supervisors, many fresh out of the Vietnam
War. Agents routinely disguise themselves as Mafia associates. Mob
members are encouraged to rat out others in the organization, enticed by
a promise that their crimes will be pardoned.[29] Government victories, including the deportation of a New Orleans mob boss and a full-court press
on a boss in Chicago, shake the criminal underworld. But the families
adapt, and with increased vigilance they continue to do business.

In 1964, Kennedy resigns from his position as attorney general to run
for a U.S. Senate seat in New York. Though he makes significant progress
in bringing pressure upon organized crime during his stint as attorney
general, the laws themselves remain a problem. At trial, prosecutors are
legally barred from introducing evidence that defendants are involved in
other crimes besides those for which they are presently being tried—in
other words, prosecutors struggle to prove a pattern of criminal activity.
There is also no law against simply being a member of a criminal organization. This is why Sergeant Edgar Croswell had no grounds to arrest
an entire houseful of mobsters in his Apalachin raid. Addressing these
problems will require new laws.

In 1965, President Johnson directs Attorney General Nicholas Katzen-
bach to head an investigation into criminal justice in the United States.[30]
Nine task forces are established, focusing on everything from crime,
courts, and juvenile delinquency to narcotics. One of the task forces—the
Task Force on Organized Crime—is headed by Charles Rogovin, chief
assistant district attorney of Philadelphia. He stations a handful of detectives away from the office to gather intelligence.

In 1967, the president's commission publishes a report on its progress
and findings. The Task Force on Organized Crime presents a bleak picture
of the power of the American Mafia: things haven't really changed. The report adds little to existing knowledge about the Mafia, helplessly restating
the claims of earlier reports: "[The] core of organized crime in the United
States consists of 24 groups operating as criminal cartels in large cities."[31]
The report also offers subtle jabs at federal reluctance to fight the Mafia,
particularly the foot dragging of Johnson and his staff. Most significantly,
though, the report recommends that federal laws be enacted that allow
"electronic eavesdropping" technologies. Johnson is hesitant, but with
pressure mounting, he agrees to back the legislative proposals. In 1968,
Johnson signs into law the Omnibus Crime Control and Safe Streets Act,
which allows the use of court-approved electronic surveillance. Though
the law is a useful tool in the fight against the Mafia, it is not enough. An
entirely new strategy is needed to truly address the problem.

In 1970, G. Robert Blakey, an attorney at the Department of Justice, sees a solution. Blakey has a background in philosophy, and he is well schooled in unions and organized crime. Ten years out of law school, Blakey drafts the Racketeer Influenced and Corrupt Organizations statute, more commonly known as RICO. Though few members of Congress actually understand what RICO does, they are eager to support a bill taking on organized crime, and the bill sails through Congress in less than a year.

Under RICO, any conduct that is not normally criminal—for example investing money in a legitimate business or purchasing securities for investment—is illegal if the money used to finance the conduct comes from a "racketeering activity." The law specifies twenty-seven federal crimes that are considered to be a racketeering activity, covering everything from duplicating passports to embezzling union funds. For the behavior to fall under RICO, it must be committed by a group with a pattern of criminality. In order to establish such a pattern, at least two crimes must be committed by the group, known as an "ongoing concern," within a span of ten years. Finally—and most crucially—RICO stipulates that *any* person who is a member of the ongoing concern can be held criminally liable for the conduct of the whole ongoing concern, whether or not they duplicated passports or embezzled money themselves.

With RICO, it is suddenly far easier for prosecutors to go after high-level mob bosses who in the past have successfully insulated themselves from criminal liability. The big men were, again, not the ones perpetrating the crimes that Valachi listed. The men actually doing the deeds were hardly more important than a particular gun or a given car. They were instruments through which the Mafia "dons" could act without getting any legal dirt on their well-polished shoes. Valachi provided authorities with a lifetime's worth of information, but at the time it mattered very little that the government knew who worked for whom. Under RICO, however, evidence of such leadership activity can be the basis for serious criminal liability.

The RICO law is meant to be broad, Blakely tells an interviewer: "We don't want one set of rules for people whose collars are blue or whose names end in vowels, and another set for those whose collars are white and have Ivy League diplomas."[32] The new laws are aimed not only at the Mafia but also at white-collar crime and corruption as a whole.[33] The goal of RICO is to make it illegal to participate in an organization involved in a pattern of racketeering. The definition of a pattern is not hard to meet: a "pattern" might consist of as few as two state and federal crimes committed in ten years, and a defendant could be convicted of both the substantive crime and a conspiracy to commit the crime. Existing statutes of limitations no longer apply.

In a radical departure from standard practice, prosecutors can cite a defendant's prior crimes to prove their involvement in a criminal organization. States can also prosecute leaders, members, and associates of criminal enterprises in combined cases, and a RICO conviction can be pursued "in any district in which such offense was begun, continued, or completed," allowing more effective enforcement.[34] RICO also comes with harsh penalties. A prosecution under RICO can result in a twenty-year sentence for *each* offense, and a life sentence for murder. Additionally, the financial sanctions for RICO offenses are permitted to be three times the amount that is permitted under normal law.

As useful as RICO is, it is also very complex. Using RICO to bring cases to trial will require a vast commitment of resources over a long period of time. This is not the way any of the players in the justice process are used to conducting business. The tried-and-true method of law enforcement is to arrest one person for one crime.[35] This new brand of crime fighting is an intellectual one. Proving links between individuals and crimes that stretch across time and geography requires a new skill set for investigators.

Blakey is eager to promote the use of the new law. In 1972, he arranges a briefing for the staff of the U.S. attorney for the Southern District of New York—a hotbed of organized crime activity—which has a long history of pursuing organized crime cases. Blakey is optimistic that the office will be thrilled about this new prosecution tool. U.S. Attorney Whitney North Seymour Jr., however, doesn't see it that way. In the middle of Blakey's presentation, Seymour ends the meeting, calling it a waste of time. RICO will not be used in the district for another decade.[36]

While Blakey struggles to convince some federal prosecutors of RICO's merits, many states embrace the idea enthusiastically. Between 1972 to 1989, thirty-three states, the Virgin Islands, and Puerto Rico work to create RICO laws for their own jurisdictions, called "little RICO" or "baby RICO" statutes. Their nicknames are deceptive: they're certainly no weaker than their federal counterparts, and many are even broader.[37] With these laws, states can pursue their own cases. Regardless, many prosecutors are still hesitant to use RICO; one study suggests that only forty-seven cases involving RICO or "little RICO" statutes are prosecuted from 1989 to 1991.

Blakey isn't discouraged. He works to push prosecutors to use the law. In the summer of 1979, Blakey hosts a series of two-week seminars on RICO at Cornell University. Neil Welch, head of the FBI's New York office, duly attends one. As Welch listens absentmindedly, his initial boredom suddenly gives way to a realization: RICO could be the tool they needed to bring down the mob families altogether. Not only is each one of their independent criminal enterprises a RICO violation, he realizes, but the family itself—in the five families together coordinating their activities, that is, Cosa Nostra itself—is a RICO violation. Following the seminar, Welch assigns a squad to each one of the five mob families of New York, with agents monitoring specific members from satellite FBI offices in each outer borough.

Initially, the squads suffer a few embarrassing setbacks. On one occasion, a group of agents can't find Staten Island, and other agents can hardly keep suspects' names straight. But the squads' effort is quickly streamlined by Jim Kallstrom, a former marine captain. He trains the team to use eavesdropping equipment on short notice and in obscure locations. When Kallstrom anticipates a run-in with mob gunmen, he recruits the FBI's "half-dollar club" for help, so named because the group's agents are rumored to be able to land six shots close enough together that all six bullet holes could be covered with a fifty-cent coin.

The mob, feeling the heat, becomes increasingly secretive. One family, the Luccheses, elects to hold their meetings in a car to avoid detection. (Of course, the car is still an elegant black Jaguar worth $120,000.) Month by month, year by year, the FBI builds their cases. They take their time; they are not looking to get the small players but rather to bring down each family for good.

Finally, in February of 1985, federal attorney and eventual mayor Rudy Giuliani drops the hammer with indictments against eleven Mafia leaders, including the heads of all five families. In November of 1986, the Mafia Commission Trial ensues, marking a long-sought victory in tackling the mob. Just as Blakely had foreseen, RICO's appearance in the courtroom leads to unprecedented success for law enforcement.[38] Now the federal government can take down the entire chain of command instead of individual low-level players.

Two cases are particularly famous. The first—nicknamed the "pizza case"—targets nineteen mobsters whose cash laundering and heroin schemes are disguised by their ownership of a number of pizza parlors.[39] One crime family is charged under RICO with drug and money laundering offenses, as well as conspiracy. Because police were unable to seize any drugs, Louis Freeh, lead prosecutor for the Southern District, relies instead on recordings from electronic eavesdropping, even having professional actors read the transcripts aloud to jurors. The Valachi testimony from the mid-1960s is introduced to inform the jury on the interconnectedness of the various players. After reviewing the 120-page indictment, 350 pages of charges, and 410 pages of charts, the jury finds all but one defendant guilty, with sentences ranging from twenty to thirty-five years.

The second major case is the Mafia Commission Trial of 1985, officially known as *United States v. Anthony Salerno, et al.* For Giuliani, it represents "an attempt . . . to dismantle a structure that has been used from the beginning of organized crime in the United States."[40] Naysayers are skeptical of the notion that it is possible to target an entire crime family, let alone five families in one trial. But Giuliani knows this is the smartest course of action.

When the case is brought to court, prosecutors start by painstakingly educating the court on the Mafia's rise from 1900 onward. This is done to establish its status as a single entity. If the prosecutors can demonstrate that the families actually represent a single ongoing concern, the case will be RICO eligible. The witnesses are the bosses of each of the families, Paul "Big Paul" Castellano, Anthony "Fat Tony" Salerno, Carmine "Junior" Persico, Anthony "Tony Ducks" Corallo, Philip "Rusty" Rastelli, and their underbosses Aniello "The Lamb" Dellacroce, Gennaro "Gerry Lang" Langella, Salvatore "Tom Mix" Santoro, Christopher "Christy Tick" Furnari, Ralph "Little Ralphie" Scopo, and Anthony "Bruno" Indelicato. The list of witnesses even includes Croswell who, twenty-nine years earlier, busted the Apalachin mobster meeting. Among all of them, they face a total of 151 charges including extortion, loansharking, gambling, labor racketeering, and murder for hire. Defense attorneys claim that membership in the Mafia is not evidence of actual criminal activity. Given their code of omertà, the Mafia leaders are hesitant to admit even their membership in the Cosa Nostra, despite the overwhelming evidence. The defendants are found guilty on all 151 counts, with all but one sentenced to one hundred years in prison, the maximum available under RICO. The verdict is upheld on appeal.

Eventually, each of the individual New York families is charged and convicted under its own RICO case. Similar trials occur across the nation, from Boston to Los Angeles. Some mobsters remain obstinate behind bars, refusing to admit guilt or even the existence of the Cosa Nostra, but their secrecy is in vain. The trials and RICO are bringing down the mob.

Decades after a 1977 *Time* magazine declared the Cosa Nostra "big, bad and booming," national news outlets now refer to the Mafia families as "melting icebergs."[41] The American Mafia, reduced to petty street crime, is no longer the money-making enterprise it once was. The cases that do attract attention, including cases of Mafia members in the police force and FBI, only reinforce the Mafia's dwindling influence and poor leadership. Bosses are no longer able to distance themselves from the deeds of their triggermen. Low-level members can no longer count on ongoing support to help them skirt the legal system. Other Mafia mainstays, such as Philadelphia, Cleveland, Boston, and Kansas City are slowly drained of mobsters. Insiders feel the loss, and an organization that had five thousand members nationwide at its height dwindles to an estimated one thousand. Fear of the mob fades with the passage of time.

With the Mafia out, other less well-organized gangs are anxious to take over, but their efforts are laughable to many ex-Mafia members. "I hear the Chinese [and] the Russians are going to move in," mobster Sammy Gravano says. "Believe me, they can't put together what took us fifty, sixty years to do."[42] Bootlegging and drug trafficking are complex businesses that require transportation knowledge, accounting skills, and innumerable other logistical talents. It is akin to building a multinational company without a single outsider finding out about it.

BEYOND REFORM

Today, the actual Mafia's influence has declined so sharply that many Americans believe the five families are extinct, and the Mafia lives on mostly in a collection of popular movies.[43] Currently, the FBI estimates that New York mobs and their New Jersey affiliates have memberships of 700 to 800. The FBI has cut back on organized crime investigations. The FBI's anti-Mafia force currently has only two units: one to handle the Bonnanos, Colombos, and Genoveses, and another for the Luccheses and Gambinos. The number of agents working on such cases in New York City has dropped from 350 in the 1990s to approximately 100 in 2005, and the NYPD has also significantly reduced the number of detectives working on organized crime. After the September 11, 2001, terrorist attacks, organized crime fell to being the FBI's sixth priority, after terrorism, espionage, cybercrime, public corruption, and civil rights protection.

A further demonstration of the Mafia's dwindling power is that omertà, the code of honor that requires members to stay quiet about the mob, is now frequently broken. As one NYPD detective says of today's Mafia members, "They're younger [now], a lot of them have young kids and they don't want to look at 25 to life."[44]

After being used to cripple the Mafia, RICO has since been used effectively to go after political corruption and white-collar criminals and other types of highly organized, sophisticated crime.[45] Such cases start to become common in the late 1970s, and by the mid-1980s, about 125 federal RICO cases are prosecuted annually. Half of the cases involve securities and commodities fraud, and many of the rest deal with organized crime involving gambling, drugs, and labor racketeering. Civil RICO cases see even more traction, with an average of 85 cases per month.

The success only grows into the 1980s and 1990s. In 1986, the President's Commission on Organized Crimes praises RICO, encouraging states to enact similar laws. The General Accounting Office offers a similar endorsement. By 1990, the U.S. federal courts prosecute approximately

996 RICO cases annually.[46] That year, 2 percent of federal offenders are convicted on charges of racketeering or continuing criminal enterprises (CCE), and 27 percent of those convictions rely on RICO. Of those sentenced to prison, 10 percent receive terms of eleven or more years—far more than those sentenced only for the underlying offenses. Most convicts are male (97 percent) and white (76 percent).

Almost two decades after the infamous Mafia Commission Trials, another high-profile RICO case emerges. Although the American Mafia is on the decline, organized crime still thrives, not as the traditional family-based structure of the Mafia but in the form of international groups made up of transnational corporations that are sometimes even partnered with foreign states' security services. The staggering internal complexity of some of these organizations is often designed with the purpose of camouflaging illegal activity. One such group is called the Bank of Credit and Commerce International (BCCI).

Despite the name, the purpose of BCCI is never banking—it is meant to be a global money-laundering scheme that accrues as much cash as possible. A 1993 Congressional Report—which reads in some sections like a movie script—unravels the tale of BCCI, saying it is "made up of multiplying layers of entities, related to one another through an impenetrable series of holding companies, affiliates, subsidiaries, banks-within-banks, insider dealings and nominee relationships."[47] The report goes on to say that BCCI "had 3,000 criminal customers and every one of those 3,000 criminal clients is a page 1 story."[48] The clients of the bank include Pablo Escobar and his Medellin drug cartel, and Panamanian general Manuel Noriega. The bank offers education on how to launder assets. The whole fraud takes more than a decade to comprehend, and several countries continue to protect BCCI the entire time, but in 1995, prosecutors take it down using RICO. Effective pursuit by BCCI investigators drains the organization's financial resources, and the leaders of BCCI eventually negotiate a plea bargain in which they plead guilty to a series of fraud and racketeering charges, including several RICO violations.

Such modern corporate crime closely mirrors the organization of Mafia crime in the past. Like the Mafia, international corporations such as this one are "armed sovereign state[s]," which operate as a "black network."[49] Similarly, organizations like BCCI use squads of thugs and intelligence operatives to carry out missions, such as scaring off competitors and keeping employees in line by way of violence, including murder. However, in some ways, the new international corporate criminal organizations are even stronger than the Mafia because they hide behind national boundaries, while simultaneously using sovereign states to do the dirty work for their personal gain.

In 2015, another major RICO case involving sports emerges when four-teen FIFA affiliates, including high-ranking officers, are indicted under RICO on forty-seven counts of "racketeering, wire fraud and money laundering conspiracies, among other offenses, in connection with the defendants' participation in a 24-year scheme to enrich themselves through the corruption of international soccer."[50] The defendants are accused of using FIFA as a front to collect bribes, perhaps even influencing the choices of Russia and Qatar as respective hosts for the 2018 and 2022 FIFA World Cups.

THE FUTURE OF THE MOB

In a world with RICO, the future of the mob is uncertain. Mobs have also changed their practices, reflecting ingenuity that the legal climate under RICO necessitates. In New York, several families today elect not to have a don. Even crew chiefs in some circles are told no more than is immediately necessary, members may not congregate in easily identifiable locations, and all conversations are conducted as if strangers are listening in. The idea is that if one crew is taken down, the entire operation will not be implicated in a RICO case. The less everyone knows, even those inside, the better off they all are.

To some extent, this has required a looser hierarchical structure, and the process is much more individualized than it once was. In general, these crime families are less territorial and operate with more collaboration than the Mafioso of the past. "As long as they [keep] earning, they are less concerned," says Inspector John Denesopolis of the New York Police Department's Organized Crime Unit.[51] The mob is humming along, but isolated individuals cannot pull off the high-volume criminality that the big families were able to manage in years past.

Some believe the mob will return to power, especially in Chicago, New York, and New Jersey. There are many people who speculate that mobsters are strategically lying low, covering their tracks and waiting to strike. "I don't know that I'd say La Cosa Nostra is what it was in its heyday," notes FBI agent Richard Frankel, "but I wouldn't say by any means it's gone away." Others believe young mobsters—who "have not been through the wars and feel they can become big shots"—are trying to rise throughout the ranks.

Another likely scenario is that the Mafia will move into the financial world, adopting the model of the corrupt business cartel. Mafiaesque groups may well have the capability to engage in all types of sharp dealings that legitimate firms partake in: threatening competitors, bribing regulators, and the like. As further evidence of their capacity to engage in such activities, in 2000, nineteen defendants from three of the five families are charged with running a "pump and dump" operation by fraudulently driving up stock prices and selling it to the general public just before the artificial price collapses.

Alternatively, the mobs could turn their mainstay cartels of business scams and drug rings over to other groups and focus their own efforts on providing support and financing for money laundering. For example, in Chicago some "mob watchers" believe one group is using professional associates with no criminal record to operate their personal enterprises with Mafia funding. These legitimate businesses then pay invoices of artificial firms to funnel money back to the Mafia. Still, critics doubt whether the current Mafia has the infrastructure, intellect, and tenacity to exploit the financial system on a large scale.

As organized crime has globalized, so too has the legal tools to fight it, RICO has inspired similar legislation in foreign countries.[52] For example, Interpol, the world's largest international police organization, provides a standardized definition of crimes inspired by RICO, although guidelines for interpretation and implementation greatly vary across jurisdictions. Canada, Australia, and New Zealand have similar systems, as does the Eurasian Organized Crime system within eastern and central European countries, Russia, and other independent states. Mexico and Colombia even have "International Cooperation" laws in place mandating authorities to cooperate with foreign officials when foreign assets are seized within their country.[53] In fact, most nations are willing to cooperate with the United States' RICO legislation if their domestic laws specified for such situations are lacking because organized crime impacts them, too. Other nations work together in this effort, culminating in treaties such as the United Nations Convention against Transnational Organized Crime and the Protocols Thereto.[54]

Sergeant Croswell would be pleased to see how America's crime-fighting tools have evolved since he interrupted Joe Barbara's meeting in 1957. The Mafia, and other organized crime, will grow more sophisticated as time goes on, and RICO laws will have to adapt to keep up.

Chapter Seven

1962
Harlem Heroin Epidemic
War on Drugs

THE TRAGEDY—REVEREND DEMPSEY

Oberia Dempsey has found his way from rural Texas to Harlem after serving in the army during World War II. By 1960, he is working as a youth minister at the Abyssinian Baptist Church, under the direction of Adam Clayton Powell Jr. By 1962, the daily contact with so many young people starts Dempsey on what will be a lifelong campaign to find real solutions to the horrors that drugs inflict on everyone's lives. Dempsey may not have been born in the area, but he makes the people of his congregation his heartfelt community.[1]

Walter Vandermeer, a twelve-year-old, lives in Dempsey's community. One Saturday night, Walter tells his mother that he is going out to the newsstand. He does not return. At 4:00 p.m. on the following day, his eighty-pound body is found locked in the bathroom of a neighboring building. Next to Walt, are a syringe, a bottle cap, and two empty glassine envelopes.[2] He died of a heroin overdose. To Dempsey, Walter is an eighty-pound example of a much larger problem. To Dempsey's way of thinking, Walter was murdered by authorities who cannot or will not do anything to stop the drug trade. By 1962, heroin has seized the neighborhood; by Dempsey's count, forty thousand dope addicts roam the streets. The pastor sees the suffering addicts, but he also sees ordinary citizens threatened by crime fueled by the insatiable need for drugs. Dempsey sees promising lives melting away with the heated crystals of heroin. He fears the community he loves is cascading into destitution and violence.[3] He decides that he will find a way to get their attention.

The pastor's concerns are well founded. In 1940, not a single child of Harlem dies from heroin or any type of drug abuse. But by the early 1960s, heroin is the number-one killer of young men in New York City, and Harlem is at the center of the heroin trade.[4] In 1969 when twelve-year-old Walter dies, he is but one of 248 deaths.[5] Ages of heroin users are dropping rapidly; in less than a decade, the average age of someone killed by heroin falls from thirty-one to twenty-three.[6] With heroin use on the rise, crime—used to fund drug habits—is becoming more prevalent. The community of Harlem is being burned at both ends: young people are dying, and public safety is threatened. "Citizens fear to venture out after dark," Dempsey says; many members of his church are too scared to attend nightly meetings. Muggers and robbers scour street corners, and the murder rate spikes 400 percent over the course of several years.[7]

New York State representative Charles Rangel surveys his constituents and finds that "there was almost unanimous consent that narcotics are our number one problem, followed by housing and lack of State and City services."[8] Reverend Edward T. Dugan, pastor of a Roman Catholic parish in Harlem, offers a survey to his eighteen hundred parishioners. The results suggest that "the average person had been held up at least once." Father Dugan attributes the area's crime to "poor junkies," calling the epidemic "a tragedy for the little people."[9] Heroin users, for the most part, are not violent criminals but, rather, turn to petty crime in order to fund their addition. Reverend E. G. Clark, pastor of Harlem's Second Friendship Baptist Church, is appalled. "Because of the circumstances," he says, "90 percent of the people refuse to come out at night."[10] Churches no longer hold evening services.

Law enforcement, meanwhile, has done nothing meaningful to address the problem. Reverend Kenneth Clark, another Harlem pastor, notices the police absence: "We've begged for patrolmen but we can't get them."[11] Another civic leader, James Lawson, says that there are 360 undercover police who work the area, 320 of whom leave by 4:00 p.m. Even when the police are around, they focus on the wrong issues: "chasing numbers writers, numbers control and small black bankers. They should be working on narcotics and protecting the individual citizen."[12]

Dempsey believes that race is a crucial factor in the authorities' lack of commitment. He sees the police as indifferent to the poor, black communities most affected by the heroin epidemic. In a city where only 14 percent of the population is African American,[13] blacks make up 39 percent of the heroin-related deaths between 1950 and 1961. By 1962, 50 percent of all newly reported addicts in New York City are black.[14] Certainly, some whites are using heroin, but their relative privilege generally keeps them out of the statistics.

The Amsterdam News sees the same problems and agrees that extraordinary harm is being done to the community. The paper offers some degree of sympathy for addicts, but non-addict dealers, motivated solely by greed, are seen as a scourge that society need not tolerate. To sell drugs simply for profit "is an act of cold calculated, pre-meditated, indiscriminate murder of our community."[15]

THE OUTRAGE

Dempsey refuses to watch from the sidelines. He works to get addicts into treatment programs. But the more energy Dempsey puts into trying to get the drug users clean, the angrier he becomes against the dealers. Dempsey grows frustrated at the community-based drug-treatment models advocated by social workers and doctors of the time. To him, these programs are guaranteed to fail. Without attacking the source of the problem, no lasting good can stem from the community's efforts.[16]

For Dempsey, the heroin epidemic—and the police apathy it reveals—is an affront to black civil rights. "There are forces still bent on keeping Afro-Americans down," he warns, and the drug game is a conspiracy to do just that.[17] Keen to fight back, Dempsey founds the Anti-Narcotics and Anti-Drug Committee of Harlem from his church, the Upper Park Avenue Baptist Church. The Anti-Drug Committee has a focus on self-advocacy and grassroots campaigns to protect young community members from the problems associated with drug addiction. That year, 1962, the committee rallies black associations, church groups, and other community organizations to protest Harlem's destructive drug problem and police ineffectiveness. Banners on Dempsey's church read: "ALL DOPE PEDDLERS AND GANGSTERS GET OUT OF HARLEM & NEW YORK CITY" and "RETURN HARLEM BACK INTO THE HANDS OF DECENT PEOPLE."[18] Increasing awareness of Harlem's plight, Dempsey calculates, is the only way to provoke an official response.

Dempsey is a talented organizer who sees the need for a multipronged approach. Everyone tells him that his efforts are failing, and that his message dangerously insinuates that devoting resources to addicts is a waste of time. This only makes Dempsey more determined, and by the mid-1960s, he resolves to adopt a more radical approach. He begins to lead the police to apartments where he claims drug dealers operate. His idea is to round up hardcore narcotics addicts and involuntarily move them to a rehabilitation camp. There they would be housed in a military-style arrangement and given fifteen dollars per month. This would accomplish several goals: crime associated with drug use would decline dramatically if users were taken off the streets, young people would be discouraged from trying heroin so as not to end up in one of Dempsey's rehabilitation camps, and addicts would receive the care they need.[19]

Dempsey is aware that his conception of the problem is not a popular one. "Sure the Civil Liberties Union and the N.A.A.C.P. would howl about violation of constitutional rights. But we've got to end this terror and restore New York to decent people. Instead of fighting all the time for civil rights we should be fighting civil wrongs."[20] To Reverend Dempsey, the question is not if civil liberties are being violated—it is a matter of whose rights should be protected. Dempsey sees a "grave unconstitutional situation that allows the addicts to harass innocent citizens and forces churches to close at night."[21] Why should the constitution protect drug-crazed thieves over regular people trying to get by?

But by 1965, no positive change has come—in fact, the problem has only gotten worse. That year, Dempsey, frustrated by the ineffectiveness of his Anti-Drug Committee, turns toward an even more militant solution, a movement that he calls "Operation Confiscation." He develops an armed vigilante group composed of two hundred community members, including seven former police officers, who "watch for [drug] pushers, summon police, and where they are not forthcoming immediately, make citizen arrests."[22] Many carry guns on patrol; Dempsey himself has a .21 revolver, earning him the nickname of "pistol packin' pastor." The group harasses dealers and encourages residents to antagonize drug pushers. For community members too nervous to confront dealers or contact police, Dempsey makes himself available.[23] The Reverend also blames local landlords, whom he calls slumlords, for refusing to install effective locks on apartment doors. This, he argues, contributes to drug dealers' success by making it easy to find places to do deals and hide out. Dempsey calls on community members to withhold rent from these slumlords.

In 1969, Dempsey petitions Robert Morgenthau, New York's U.S. attorney, for help. "If something isn't done immediately, people are going to arm themselves," he predicts. "There's going to be a lot of bloodshed."[24] Dempsey advocates stricter penalties for drugs dealers, including "death by firing squad" for anyone trafficking dope.[25] His pleas are ignored by Morgenthau. Dempsey also turns to New York governor Nelson Rockefeller, who isn't much more helpful. Rockefeller views drugs as a social, rather than criminal, problem. He's developed educational and treatment programs that look nice on paper but lack the funding and scale needed to have even a small impact. To most Americans, heroin remains a "Black problem related to poor inner-city neighborhoods."[26] Reverend Dempsey and his followers, mostly heartsick mothers, decide that they cannot rely on the outside world to help them.

As an outspoken black preacher with a gun and a message, Dempsey becomes national news. *Ebony* magazine interviews him in 1970, publish-

Figure 7.1. Reverend Oberia Dempsey was a tireless advocate, 1969. *By permission of Johnson Publishing*

ing an article entitled "Blacks Declare War on Dope." But this newfound celebrity makes him a target for retribution. After a drug gang attacks him in 1971, Dempsey uses the incident to build more support for his efforts, vocally encouraging citizens to arm themselves. Speaking to the Harlem community, Dempsey calls on them to "find the heaviest baseball bats around or any other type of weapon that's sold legally to ward off those hoodlums."[27] The people who have suffered the ravages of drugs, the parents who have lost children, and the businesses that have been ransacked all line up behind Dempsey. Whatever it takes, the drugs have to go. The mother of an eighteen-year-old Harlem girl who recently died of an overdose sums up the community's sentiment. When asked what should be done about the drug epidemic, her answer leaves little room for misinterpretation: "Kill the pushers."[28]

THE REFORM

By the 1970s, the demands are finally being heard outside of Harlem, and the national agenda, motivated by anxiety about escalating crime rates, is catching up with Harlem's antidrug leaders. Now, people far from Harlem have come to fear the counterculture movement. Once associated only with inner-city kids, drug abuse is increasing among white suburban youth. These fears are amplified by popular movies like *The French Connection* and *Panic in Needle Park*, which expose the dark world of heroin abuse and trafficking. In 1971, President Richard Nixon declares the national War on Drugs.

Finally in late 1972, Governor Rockefeller becomes convinced that progressive approaches to drug addiction have failed. To the astonishment of even his closest advisors, Rockefeller suddenly announces a new plan, this one derived from the zero-tolerance approach of Japan's war on drugs: "For drug pushing, life sentence, no parole, no probation." Rockefeller's own staff privately expresses concern that the approach is excessive, but the governor is passionate. "I have one goal and one objective," he declares, "and that is to stop the pushing of drugs and to protect the innocent victim."

With a vision of saving young lives and clearing the streets of the current crime wave, harsh laws are brought in. The new laws punish offenders severely, even those arrested for simple possession. They demand, for example, mandatory minimum sentences of fifteen years to life for possession of four ounces of narcotics—about the same as a sentence for second-degree murder. New York City residents, including Harlemites, welcome the harsh penalties; the new laws are largely unopposed in the New York Legislature.

Other states, facing similar epidemics, are quick to follow New York's lead. Laws differ state by state but all aim to protect citizens by punishing drug offenses severely. In 1978, for example, Michigan passes the "650-lifer" law, which requires judges to incarcerate drug offenders convicted of delivering more than 650 grams of narcotics for life without parole.

Before long, the wave of heroin—or at least the national new media coverage of it—begins to subside, but the national drug crisis itself does not. Inner-city heroin use is being replaced by a wider-reaching drug: cocaine.

THE TRAGEDY—LEN BIAS OVERDOSE

Cocaine gains popularity in the 1970s, and by 1986 over 20 million Americans report trying it at least once.[29] Its names—"White Cloud," "Cloud Nine," "Based-ball," and "Serpico"—are as varied as the people who use it, from middle-class teenagers to wealthy businessmen and everyone in between. Unlike heroin, cocaine is seen as cool, carrying with it an irresistible aura of drugs, sex, and money.

In June of 1986, the national cocaine epidemic leaves the shadows and becomes major news. On June 17, a young man dressed in a sharp gray suit waits nervously among a small crowd in Madison Square Garden. On the stage above them, the manager of the Boston Celtics, Arnold Jacob "Red" Auerbach, approaches the microphone, and silence blankets the arena. The NBA draft has begun.

The young man is Leonard Kevin Bias and at six feet eight and 205 pounds, Bias is unrivaled on the basketball court. In his senior year of high school, he averaged twenty-five points a game. In his first college game with the Terrapins, University of Maryland's basketball team, he scored eight points and had five rebounds, all within eighteen minutes. He earned Most Outstanding Player in the Atlantic Coast Conference Tournament as a sophomore, and as a junior won ACC Player of the Year.

Bias is ushered to a front-row seat in Madison Square Garden as the draft gets started. A grinning Auerbach surprises no one when he announces that the Celtics are taking Bias. As Bias mounts the stage, someone hands him a green Celtics hat. A photo of Bias in the hat makes it into many papers.

Bias's triumph in the draft is about more than basketball. For many people, Bias is a symbol of hope for young African Americans, particularly those hurt by poverty, prejudice, and institutional racism. Bias is an athlete and a college student, a good Christian and a good man. He represents the possibility of a better life, achieved through perseverance and grit.[30]

The next day, June 18, Bias heads to Boston and signs a deal with Reebok. Back in Maryland by nightfall, he and his friend, Brian Tribble, buy a six-pack of beer and a bottle of cognac. Some more friends join, and along with the alcohol, Bias breaks out an ounce of high-grade cocaine. Time passes in a drug-induced blur. At 6:30 a.m., Bias, seated on a bed, declares himself a "horse" (his team's nickname for him) and snorts one last line of cocaine. A few moments later, the vigorous young athlete, staggers, and collapses on the bed, where his body erupts in a violent seizure. Tribble calls 911. An ambulance gets Bias to the hospital alive, but it is too late. Len Bias is dead.

THE OUTRAGE

Bias is buried on June 23. Jesse Jackson eulogizes him, comparing him to Martin Luther King Jr., Mozart, Gandhi, and Jesus. God, he says, "sometimes uses our best to get our attention."[31] Larry Bird, a Boston Celtics star, calls Bias's death "one of the cruelest things I've ever heard."[32]

The autopsy report, however, is harsh. "LEONARD K. BIAS, a 22-year-old Black male, died as a result of cocaine intoxication, which interrupted the normal electrical control of his heartbeat, resulting in the sudden onset of seizures and cardiac arrest," it reads. "The blood cocaine level was 6.5 milligrams per liter."[33] Police discover several grams of cocaine under the seat of Bias's leased sports car.

People are at a loss, Bias was known to joke about the importance of staying clean: "I'm not taking anything to hurt this body, this physical specimen." He'd striven to be a Celtic and the Celtic's first pick, and "he accomplished those goals."[34] Adrian Branch, a teammate of Bias's, insists that Bias was "nobody's drug user."[35]

Bias's death sparks a flurry of accusations and indictments. The media scrutinize everyone involved. On July 25, a grand jury indicts Brian Tribble for possession and intent to distribute, and he surrenders to authorities on July 29. On August 26, State Attorney Arthur Marshall claims that shortly after Bias's death, Terrapin coach Charles "Lefty" Driesell told players to clear drugs out of Bias's dorm room.

Before long, Len Bias has become synonymous with a larger menace: recreational drug use. His death breathes new life into a national movement to crack down on illegal drugs. After all, if the beloved young athlete could succumb to illegal substances, then anyone could.

Adding to the fear, Bias's death in the summer of 1986 also brings awareness of a new scourge, crack cocaine. In the powdered form, cocaine has hydrochloride salt; because the substance does not occur in crack cocaine, it can be smoked. Smoking the drug delivers a larger dose that reaches the brain faster—and, some say, makes it more potent and addictive than cocaine. Another attraction of the drug is that it can be mass-produced more easily and for a lower price than powdered cocaine. Barriers to entry are few, and there is enormous money to be made for anyone, including teenagers, who wants to give it a try.

The emergence of crack intensifies the debate over drugs through the rest of 1986. Crack seeps its way into the Bias case when a *Baltimore Sun* article reports, falsely, that Bias had ingested *crack* cocaine.[36] The media elevate Bias's case to the center of the national conversation about drugs. Bias becomes, as journalist Dan Baum puts it, "the Archduke Ferdinand of the Total War on Drugs."[37] The *Washington Post* notes that the Bias affair is the ultimate parental nightmare. Bias was "an all-American kid, from a nice family, a good person from all indications, who got involved with a drug and quickly he was dead."[38] The conclusion for many is clear: drugs, especially cocaine and crack, threaten every segment of American society.[39]

Just before Bias's death, the *New York Times* publishes a big story on crack in the country, noting that the drug is flourishing in New York and devastating inner-city neighborhoods. To show how easily drugs can be obtained, about a month after Bias dies, Senator Alphonse D'Amato and Rudolph Giuliani, disguised in a Hell's Angels jacket and a faded army cap respectively, hit the streets with cameras rolling. That evening, millions of Americans watch the men purchase crack with alarming ease; that summer, newspapers across the country scrutinize the problem.

Magazines and other media also quickly snatch up the story. *Time* reports that the new drug war is "urgent and necessary."[40] *Time* puts cocaine on its cover five times in 1986; *Newsweek* does the same. In 1986 alone, national newspapers and magazines publish around a thousand stories about crack, representing what the New York Drug Enforcement Agency (DEA) calls "the hottest combat-reporting story to come along since the end of the Vietnam War."[41] Networks air seventy-four news segments that highlight the dangers of crack and cocaine, and advertisers give billions of dollars in ads and television time to the anti-drug campaign.

Legislators are influenced by the media blitz, and their rhetoric reflects it. Drugs, declares one congressman, are "the biggest threat that we have ever had to our national security." Another member of Congress is equally fervent, calling drugs "a menace draining away our economy of some \$230 billion this year, slowly rotting away the fabric of our society and seducing and killing our young."[42] (This estimate later turns out to be a fabrication.)

The media-driven frenzy does attract some scrutiny. The Nieman Foundation, which focuses on ethical journalism, publicly bemoans the one-sided approach to the drug-abuse debate. All that's heard in the news, notes curator Howard Simons, is "Drugs are bad. Period." But this critique largely falls on deaf ears. Eric E. Sterling, counsel to the House Committee on the Judiciary, notes that the media response is so enormous that it's difficult to know whether Congress is influencing television or vice versa.

The impact shows strongly in public polls. In the summer of 1986, three-fourths of Americans believe drugs are a terrible problem "for the country," but less than a third of these people believe that drugs are a problem within their communities.

THE REFORM

The intense media campaign is felt on Capitol Hill. Less than a month after Bias's death, the Crime Subcommittee puts forth antidrug legislation at the behest of House Speaker "Tip" O'Neill Jr., who represents Boston, home of the Celtics and Bias's erstwhile team. O'Neill calls an emergency meeting of the crime-related committee chairmen. "Write me some god-dam legislation," he bellows. "All anybody in Boston is talking about is Len Bias. The papers are screaming for blood. We need to get out in front of this now. This week. Today."

O'Neill is anxious to be seen as a leader on this issue, especially after President Reagan won his second term partially because of his tough stance on drugs. "The Republicans beat us to it in 1984 and I don't want that to happen again," he explains to assembled Democratic leadership, "I want dramatic new initiatives for dealing with crack and other drugs. If we can do this fast enough, we can take the issue away from the White House."[43]

The bill that lawmakers present to O'Neill is stringent. Some in Congress suggest holding defense attorneys liable as accessories for taking fees from clients who make their money from illegal activities; California representative Dan Lungren wants to target businesses that profit from "drug money" and expand the definition of "designer drug" to any "substance which has stimulant, depressant, or hallucinogenic effects on the central nervous system." Some congressmen even suggest criminalizing cornstarch, frequently mixed with cocaine. Cocaine is a huge issue in Florida and Representative Larry Smith of Florida explains, "If somebody has got 400 parts of cornstarch and one part of cocaine, it is obvious that they are intending to kill somebody."[44]

The most dramatic change that Congress considers is mandatory minimum sentencing. One congressman puts it in perspective: "It would be embarrassing if we came in and wound up being less tough when we put a bill out this fall."[45] Pennsylvania congressman George Gekas expresses his support for the death penalty for drug traffickers, though other congressmen quickly shoot down the idea. Regardless, most favor no plea bargaining, and the House—facing enormous public outcry—has little time to think logically about what is being enacted.

While the debates continue in Congress, many states take action. In August of 1986, New York's Governor Mario Cuomo introduces new state-level antidrug legislation, heightening preexisting Rockefeller-era penalties, particularly for crack. For the public, the legislation is aptly timed; "Hardly a week goes by that we don't have an anti-crack rally in the Bronx," explains District Attorney Mario Meorla.[46] Minnesota follows, passing a law that imprisons offenders for at least four years for crack possession.

The White House pays attention, too. In August, President Reagan submits a urine sample to prove he's drug free; Vice President Bush, as well as the governor and first lady of Arkansas, Bill and Hillary Clinton, follow suit.

Despite the wide support for antidrug legislation, many are skeptical of President Reagan's overambitious plan to pass a law by Thanksgiving, but the president is determined. On September 14, 1986, he and his wife appear on television, comparing the situation to the American crusade in World War II: All people must take part in the fight, "not just the boys flying the planes and driving the tanks."[47] He goes on: "We want you to help us create an outspoken intolerance for drug use" because drugs, the couple pleads, are a "cancer" whose peddlers "work every day to plot a new and better way to steal our children's lives—just as they've done by developing this new drug, crack."[48]

The next day, Reagan signs Executive Order 12564, titled Drug-Free Workplace, which orders all federal agencies to urine test workers whose roles require "a high degree of trust and confidence."[49] First-time offenders receive counseling and second-time offenders are fired. Concerns about drug impairment give way to concerns about drug use of any kind. As Reagan explains in his executive order, "Federal employees who use illegal drugs, on or off duty, tend to be less productive, less reliable and prone to greater absenteeism than their fellow employees who do not use illegal drugs."[50] The White House chief of staff reports an overwhelmingly positive public response, with analysis indicating that "never have reactions to one of the president's speeches been so favorable!"[51]

Some legislators find the new bill absurd, but no one dares to oppose it. David McCurdy of Oklahoma says the bill is "out of control . . . but of course I'm for it."[52] Representative Barney Frank of Massachusetts agrees: "I'm afraid this bill is the legislative equivalent of crack,"[53] producing a "short-term high [but] long-term damage to the system. And it's expensive to boot."[54]

The bill sails through Congress, and on October 27 President Reagan signs the Anti-Drug Abuse Act of 1986 (ADAA), formally initiating a new American War on Drugs. The ADAA enforces mandatory minimum sentencing for drug-related offences and asset forfeiture. To determine penalties for drugs, a mathematical formula is derived, based on the scientific and social research of the time. The addictiveness of all drugs and their propensity to make users violent toward others are calculated. The results are then used to determine criminal penalties for each substance. Crack cocaine, under this calculation, is deemed far more pernicious than powdered cocaine and yields a penalty that is one hundred times greater.

Federal laws with mandatory minimums have historically been used to punish the most severe of crimes, such as piracy or slave trafficking.[55] While only fifty-eight minimum-sentencing laws existed around the time of Bias's death, Congress adds twenty-nine more with the ADAA, representing a 50 percent increase in four months. Even a first offense for dealing a small quantity of drugs could prompt a ten-year sentence without parole. "If we have mandatories for a first-time offense," explains Carlton Turner, director of the Drug Abuse Policy Office, "we won't have people back out on the streets committing crime."[56]

The enormous pressure to push the ADAA through Congress leads to unanticipated challenges. The sentencing guidelines are scheduled to take effect in 1987, and it is unclear what happens to offenders in the interim. The bill also adds disarray to a federal prison system already at 150 percent capacity—a number that was exponentially escalating even before the ADAA. Also around this time, the U.S. Drug Enforcement Agency issues a report on the "distortion of the public perception of the extent of crack use," revealing that the drug is nearly nonexistent outside of New York and Los Angeles.

After the 1986 November elections, Congress quietly cuts $1 billion in funding from the $4 billion ADAA. In January of 1987, Reagan proposes cutting $913 million from public drug-education, enforcement, and prevention programs. The Pentagon terminates its drug operations in Bolivia, launched the previous year with immense support. Data now suggest that crack usage may be decreasing, but experts seem to attribute these numbers to decreasing public tolerance of drugs as the nation is swept by a moral panic concerning the use of drugs.

Some funding is cut, but legislators are keen to fulfill their promises to be tough on crime. The Anti-Drug Abuse Act of 1988 passes with a 346–11 vote in the House, and Reagan signs it into law on November 18. The law toughens many drug penalties and even adds the death penalty in some cases. It is now that the Office of National Drug Control Policy with the first ever "drug czar," responsible for American drug policy comes into being. Representative Charles Rangel, who in his younger years worked with Reverend Dempsey, says: "Now Congress and the American people will know who is in charge of dealing with the nation's drug crisis."[57]

BEYOND REFORM

The harsh penalties that are attached to crack disproportionately affect the nation's African American population. By June of 1987, reports begin to reveal this truth: in New York, "the ethnic distribution shows increasing trends among blacks and declining trends among whites and Hispanics"; in Denver, "the proportion of blacks in treatment has more than doubled"; in Los Angeles, the "death data . . . show that in 1986 blacks 'caught up with' whites for the first time."[58] These statistics will soon demonstrate a national pattern. In 1993, 88.3 percent of the mandatory crack sentences are imposed on blacks. Around the time of Len Bias's death, the percentages of white and black offenders incarcerated for drug crimes are similar in state prisons (17 percent and 15 percent, respectively). However, by 1999, 47 percent of black prisoners in Maryland are incarcerated for drug offenses; for whites, the number is 21 percent.

Over the next several years, drug use remains a national problem, but people begin to debate whether the War on Drugs is the most effective way to address it. As a result, policy starts to diverge. In 1994, New York governor George Pataki proposes reforms to soften the state's drug laws from the Rockefeller era. But that same year, Congress moves in the opposite direction with the passage of the Violent Crime Control and Law Enforcement Act (VCCLEA). The bill, promoted by President Clinton, allocates funding for one hundred thousand new police officers across the nation, permits use of the death penalty and "three strikes" rules, and provides federal funding to educate prison inmates on drug abuse.

But a gathering chorus says that the reforms have gone too far. Reverend Dempsey saw drugs eating away at his community—now many people argue that the drug laws are doing the same thing. Citizens, lawmakers, and some judges push for reform, but change comes slowly.

Beginning in the 1990s, the gears of legal reform start to turn, aiming to eliminate the discriminatory effects of the ADAA.[59] The United States Sentencing Commission finds that, while there is a difference between the effects of crack cocaine and powder cocaine, those effects are exaggerated. Several bills make their way through Congress in 2007 that retroactively reduce crack sentences.

In 2010, Congress passes the Fair Sentencing Act (FSA), softening penalties for the three thousand crack cocaine offenders sentenced each year. The act reduces the disparity between the amount of crack cocaine and the amount of powder cocaine that is necessary to trigger certain federal criminal penalties, with the weight ratio dropping from 100:1 to 18:1. The FSA also eliminates the five-year mandatory minimum sentence for possession of crack. After the FSA, the U.S. Sentencing Commission moves to alter sentencing guidelines to reflect the new ratio. Suddenly, 7,700 federal prisoners previously sentenced now receive sentence reductions. The sentence reductions average thirty-six months.[60] Discretionary prosecutorial decisions by which prosecutors decide to not pursue the toughest penalties allowed under the law also lead to lower sentences for many.

DEA reports, from 2000–2014, show that the number of teenagers using illicit drugs declines by 2.1 percent.[61] Within teenaged drug users, cocaine use is down 59 percent and crack cocaine use by 56 percent. While the U.S. justice system may be considered less unfair than before, many politicians and nonprofit organizations like Families against Mandatory Minimums argue for further reform. High on the agenda for change is completely eliminating the cocaine-crack disparity with a 1:1 sentencing ratio. They argue that this will save money for taxpayers and increase justice.

Internationally, other countries grappling with drug problems adopt radical reforms. In 2000, Portugal is faced with a massive drug problem: a full 1 percent of Portuguese citizens are active heroin addicts. After attempting to fight the epidemic with more enforcement and harsh punishments, the country moves to decriminalize all drugs. Any person can have up to a ten-day supply of any drug and not be subject to arrest. People found with drugs are issued a summons to appear before a "dissuasion panel."[62] The panel, in the vast majority of cases, does nothing. If an individual appears repeatedly, the panel will try to divert the individual into treatment.

Under the program, drug use has not substantially fallen, but HIV infections and overdose deaths have decreased dramatically.[63] Elisabete Moutinho, a clinical psychologist who hands out kits with clean needles to addicts so that they can shoot up safely on the streets of Lisbon, says: "I know that is not easy for everyone to accept. But they don't get AIDS from a dirty needle, or hepatitis. They are not beaten by gangs or arrested or put in jail. There is no police corruption, because there is nothing to get rich from. It is a program that reduces harm, and I don't see a better approach."[64]

Critics say Portugal's policy of blanket decriminalization fails users by making ongoing drug use too easy. Still others prefer to focus on the fact that the new policy makes the lives of ordinary people safer by reducing the opportunities for entrenched criminals to profit from the illegal drug trade. It shifts the focus of the criminal justice system back toward other types of crimes and reduces costs within the justice system.[65] Would Reverend Dempsey find this an acceptable compromise?

There is no easy answer. Combating drugs, like any vice, comes with an inherent challenge. Criminalizing drug use invites criminals to find a way to skirt the law and profit handsomely in the process. This facilitates organized crime and violence and means that tough laws often fail to actually impede access to drugs. Yet the social costs of drug use to individuals, families, and society are often staggering. Governments face the dilemma of either encouraging crime or allowing ongoing harm to their citizens.

The United States is probably not ready for a policy like Portugal's but attitudes about drug laws are shifting.[66] Fifty-three percent of Americans support the legalization of marijuana.[67] Sixty-three percent of Americans today want to reduce mandatory-minimum drug sentences.[68] These shifts in opinion have had an effect on policy. Since 1996, twenty-nine states and the District of Columbia have passed laws *allowing* medicinal marijuana. The laws vary from state to state. In 2017, Nevada became the fifth state to permit the recreational use of marijuana. Meanwhile, the District of Columbia's Initiative 71 allows citizens to grow and possess, but not sell, restricted amounts of marijuana. The long-term consequences of such laws will only be revealed with the passage of time. Since Colorado moved to legalize marijuana, fatal traffic accidents and homelessness have both gone up in the state.[69]

Even as states make significant shifts in their approaches to marijuana and other drugs, selling or distributing marijuana remains a federal crime, and federal agencies like the Department of Justice (DOJ) continue to enforce the Controlled Substances Act (CSA), which classifies marijuana as a Schedule I substance—that is, a substance that has a high potential for dependency and has no accepted medical use. The federal DOJ has been careful to preserve its right to challenge legalization if the state policies seem to be misguided. To date, the Supreme Court has deemed this an acceptable arrangement.[70]

America's most recent drug problem is the rampant abuse of prescription drugs. Every day, sixty Americans die from abusing legal painkillers.[71] Though these drugs are regulated by the FDA, they are deadly when abused, and they often put people on a path toward other drugs. Current research indicates that four out of five new heroin users start out by abusing prescription painkillers.[72]

Globally, the war on drugs remains daunting. In 2005, the United Nations estimated that the global illegal drug trade is worth over $320 billion; if it were a country, its economy would be among the world's top ten, positioned between Russia and Brazil.

As a nation, we have learned a lot since the body of twelve-year-old Walter was found locked in a Harlem bathroom, but clearly America's drug problem has found no resolution. New York City saw 556 heroin deaths in 2015.[73]

Chapter Eight

1964
Genovese
Murder-Witness Scandal

9-1-1 Emergency System

THE TRAGEDY

It is a rainy July night in the quiet Springfield Gardens neighborhood of Queens.[1] Fifteen-year-old Barbara Kralik returns home after an evening out with a friend and greets her grandmother, then spends the remainder of the evening relaxing with her parents and brother. One by one, each family member turns in for the night, and soon Barbara heads to bed herself.

It continues to rain as the family sleeps. In the early morning hours of July 20, 1963, a man outside wanders toward the Kraliks' home. He looks around, removes a screen from a porch window and crawls into the house. He walks past Barbara's brother and grandmother, who are both sleeping, into Barbara's room. He proceeds to sexually assault the sleeping teen, then stabs her multiple times. After he is finished, he leaves.

Barbara, a petite, popular high-schooler, is still alive when her attacker slips back into the night. She calls out and wakes her parents, who rush to her side and call an ambulance. She is taken to Queen's General Hospital, where doctors work desperately to save the teen. But Barbara's wounds are too severe—they cannot save her.[2] Before breathing her last shallow breath, Barbara does her best to give a vague description of her attacker. Investigators parse out her quiet words: Did she say, "It was dark," or was it "He was dark"? The authorities immediately suspect Alvin Mitchell, a troubled teenager who had known and visited Barbara.

Tall and slender, the nineteen-year-old Mitchell is well-known to local police. Dubbed "Monster" by his fellow gang members, Mitchell is known to have violent tendencies when drunk. He is currently awaiting a court hearing on an assault charge. Though Mitchell and his family have moved from Springfield Gardens to Astoria, another neighborhood in Queens, he often returns on weekends to see old friends.[3] Police have no trouble tracking him down.

As soon as police begin questioning Mitchell, he confesses to killing Kralik. Mitchell says he has no memory of the killing and cannot remember a single detail, but the police are certain that they have their man. An indictment follows in short order.

Months go by as detectives continue their investigation, and on February 29, 1964, Mitchell is still in custody awaiting trial. Several miles from the jail where he is being held, Annie Mae Johnson, a twenty-four-year-old housewife, is returning home in South Ozone Park, Queens. As she is about to unlock her door, a man she doesn't know meets her at her stoop. He subdues her and drags her into her own home. With no one else around, he proceeds to kill her in a rage of unspeakable violence. He repeatedly stabs Johnson with an icepick, shoots her no less than six times, and eventually sets her body on fire.[4] When Johnson is discovered, her corpse is so mutilated that police do not even realize she has been shot, and they are unable to determine whether she was raped during the gruesome killing. Investigators are at a loss; they have no idea who could have done this.

While detectives try to piece together what happened, Winston Mosely cruises around the Kew Garden neighborhood of Queens. Mosely is a married father of two who owns his own home and supports his family by working full time as a machine operator. He has been out driving for about an hour. Around 3:00 a.m. on Friday, March 13, 1964, Mosely is at a traffic light when he spots twenty-eight-year-old Catherine "Kitty" Genovese, who is driving home after a shift as bar manager at Ev's 11th Hour in Hollis, Queens.

Kitty is an independent woman from a large middle-class Catholic Italian American family. She grew up in Brooklyn. Her family moved to New Canaan, Connecticut, but she remained behind in New York. She was briefly married as a teenager, but quickly had the marriage annulled. The only thing remarkable about her past is an arrest for participating in a bookmaking operation. Now Kitty lives in an apartment with Mary Ann Zielonko, with whom she is in a happy romantic relationship, in the comfortable, middle-class neighborhood of Kew Garden.

Driving a white Corvair, Mosely follows Kitty to a parking lot near her apartment. She lives in a second floor apartment of a building with small shops on the first floor. Kitty parks her car in the Kew Gardens Long Island Railroad station parking lot and starts toward her apartment. Mosely also gets out of his car and heads for Kitty.

Figure 8.1. Kitty Genovese, 1962. *Filmrise*

Kitty becomes nervous when she notices Mosely's figure and begins to run up the street. Mosely draws a hunting knife and sprints toward her, quickly closing the gap between them. He gets close enough to grab her beneath a streetlight in front of a bookstore less than one hundred feet from her apartment door. He stabs her in the back twice. Genovese cries for help: "Oh, my God, he stabbed me! Please help me! Please help me!"[5] Several lights go on. A man in the apartment across the street opens his window and yells "Let that girl alone!" Nervous that neighbors have called police and will come out to help Genovese, Mosely leaves her and slips off into the shadows.

Amazingly, as soon as Mosely leaves, all of the neighborhood apartments go dark. No one comes out to see if Genovese is okay. The desperate Kitty, who has slipped around a corner, calls into the night: "I'm dying! I'm dying!" Mosely, back in his car just a few blocks away, calculates that no one is actually coming to Genovese's aid. Donning a Tyrolean hat as a disguise, he goes looking for her and finds her in the rear entryway of the Long Island Railroad Station. He resumes his attack, raping her and stabbing her at least a dozen times. Genovese fights back, but her efforts are in vain as Moseley flails his knife. With the new attack, Genovese begins screaming again, and neighbors' lights come on again. Mosely finally darts away, after also robbing his victim of the forty-nine dollars she had on her; the desperate Kitty crawls toward her apartment building. At 3:35 a.m., she collapses in the foyer of her apartment. At 3:50 a.m., one of Genovese's neighbors calls another neighbor named Sophie Farrar to tell her about the attack, which he has been watching through a crack in his door.

Farrar is horrified, so she hangs up and calls the police. Then the young mother leaves her apartment to go find the dying Kitty. Farrar cradles Kitty in her arms and comforts her until the police arrive. While police secure the scene and begin talking with neighbors to piece together a solid description of Mosely and the car he is driving, and ambulance arrives to take Genovese to the hospital. She dies on the way there.

Five days later, Mosley is burglarizing a home in another part of the city. A neighbor spots him loading a television from the house into his white Corvair. The neighbor approaches Mosley, who claims to be helping the family, the Bannisters, with their move. The neighbor knows the Bannisters—they are not moving. Mosely ignores the neighbor's protests and goes back to the Bannisters' place to get another load of goods. The neighbor runs and calls police. He then returns to Mosley's car, opens the hood, and removes the distributor cap. Mosely comes out of the house, loads everything into his car, and tries to make a getaway. But when he tries starting his car, he discovers that it won't start. Mosely starts walking down the street with his stolen goods.

Police soon arrive and take the unarmed burglar into custody without incident. Police begin questioning Mosely, and he freely admits to killing Kitty and offers details of the entire evening. As if that were not enough, Mosely proceeds to outline the dozens of robberies, rapes, and attempted rapes he has committed. He tells police that he killed Annie Mae Johnson—it is now that the police hear for the first time that she had been shot. One of the police officers who is listening says, "I bet you also killed that fifteen-year-old girl in Springfield Gardens in July of last year."[6] Mosely responds, "Yeah, I did that one too." Mosely recites the story of killing of Barbara Kralik. His account is full of details.

THE OUTRAGE

Ten days after Kitty is killed, Abraham Rosenthal, the new metropolitan editor of the *New York Times*, has lunch with Michael J. Murphy, New York City's police commissioner. They spend most of the meal talking about racial violence and civil rights. Toward the end of the meal, Rosenthal asks the commissioner about a recent peculiar case discussed in the tabloids. Two men confessed to the same murder, the killing of fifteen-year-old Barbara Kralik. Murphy opens up about the case and tells Rosenthal that while it is not clear who killed Kralik, one of the men, Winston Mosely, definitely killed Kitty Genovese.

"Brother, that Queens story is one for the books,"[7] Murphy tells Rosenthal in reference to the Genovese case, "38 witnesses."[8] A horrific half hour of stabbing and shrieking, and yet, nobody called the police. Rosenthal is captivated. The *Times* reported Genovese's death more than a week earlier in a brief four-paragraph article buried deep in the paper, but Rosenthal decides to revisit it. He tasks Martin Gansberg with doing a full-length story on the case.

On March 27, 1964, Gansberg's story runs on the front page of the *New York Times* under the headline: "37 Who Saw Murder Didn't Call the Police: Apathy at Stabbing of Queens Woman Shocks Inspector."[9] The article opens provocatively: "For more than half an hour 38 respectable, law-abiding citizens in Queens watched a killer stalk and stab a woman in three separate attacks in Kew Gardens."[10] Pursuing the angle of an uncaring and alienated urban population, Gansberg portrays Genovese's death as uniquely disturbing in comparison to the other six hundred–plus murders committed in New York City that year.

According to Gansberg's account, Genovese, Farrar, and another neighbor named Karl Ross are the only ones at the scene when police arrive. "Nobody else came forward," Gansberg writes. Gansberg quotes Assistant Chief Inspector Frederick M. Lussen: "As we have reconstructed the crime, the assailant had three chances to kill this woman during a 35-minute period. He returned twice to complete the job. If we had been called when he first attacked, the woman might not be dead now."[11]

So why had no one come forward? One woman says "We thought it was a lover's quarrel," while another claims "I didn't want my husband to get involved." A husband and wife put it plainly, "Frankly, we were afraid." One couple says they heard the first screams. The husband explains, "We went to the window to see what was happening, but the light from our bedroom made it difficult to see the street." His wife says she put the light out so they could see. Why didn't they call the police? "I don't know," she answers. One man says, "I was tired. I went back to bed."

Karl Ross, a drinking buddy of Kitty's girlfriend, is the only person to witness the second attack. In a drunken stupor, he hears the commotion and opens the door to see a man sinking a knife into Genovese. Ross quickly shuts the door and calls a friend in Long Island. The friend advises him to do nothing. He then calls a neighbor in the building and the neighbor tells him to come over. He climbs out his window, crawls across the roof, and makes his way into the apartment. Only once he is in the neighbor's apartment does he call the police. With the delay, Moseley fades into the darkness. When police ask Ross (identified in the article as "a neighbor of Miss Genovese") why he didn't call them immediately, he replies "I didn't want to get involved."[12] Joseph Fink, a man who works in the building across the street from Kitty's apartment, sees the first attack but goes down to the basement to nap, leaving Genovese to struggle on. The story ends on an accusatory note: "It was 4:25 AM when the ambulance arrived for the body of Miss Genovese. It drove off. 'Then,' a solemn police detective said, 'the people came out.'"[13] The message is clear: neighbors could have done more.

The article is laden with inaccuracies. Most importantly, many of the neighbors did not in fact witness the first attack. By the time they were awoken by Genovese's screams and made it to their windows to investigate, Mosely had already left. All they saw was Kitty stumbling down the road toward the side of the building and disappearing around the corner. Many of the witnesses were also old and had just woken up in the early hours of the morning. They were probably not in a state to be thinking clearly.

Still, Gansberg captures the public's attention with his portrayal of moral negligence. With his article, Genovese's murder is transformed into a story of how good people sat and watched while horrors were perpetrated before their very eyes. As the *New York Times* put it on March 28, 1964, "Does residence in a great city destroy all sense of personal responsibility for one's neighbors?"

Anxieties over the isolation of urban life, the breakdown of 1950s social norms, racial unrest, and the Kennedy assassination all contribute to the feelings stirred up by the murder. America is coming apart at the seams, and people don't care enough to call the police. New York City is destined for dark days. In the years following Kitty's death, the city descends into a period of awful crime. The *Herald Tribune* publishes a series of articles on a "City in Crisis." Reporters Jimmy Breslin and Dick Schaap detail "a great city's descent into hell." One particularly vivid depiction says "Women carry tear-gas pens in their pocket-books. Cabdrivers rest iron bars on the front seat next to them. Store owners keep billy clubs next to the cash register. And people enter parks and the subways and side streets of New York, the most important city in the world, only in fear. The fear is justified."[14]

Kitty Genovese has become a symbol of this urban horror. On October 12, 1965, mayoral candidate John Lindsay addresses a crowd of three hundred from a crude platform constructed on the spot where Mosely attacked Kitty. To the chagrin of Kitty's neighbors, Lindsay declares, "What the Kitty Genovese story tells us is that something has gone out of the heart and soul of New York." He gestures to the streetlamp nearby the site of the crime. "We will *light* this street," he announces. "Yes, New Yorkers will stand tall and proud again. But only if every citizen is willing to be his brother's keeper. And then the padlock on the front door will no longer be the symbol of New York City!"[15]

As more details of Genovese's murder emerge, it becomes clear that part of the problem is that getting in touch with police is not as easy as one might think. When Genovese is killed in 1964, if someone needs the police, an ambulance, or the fire department, they have to find the number for the station of each service that is nearest to them. Large cities like New York have dozens of departments and stations, each with unique numbers and areas of coverage. Someone who is away from home or new to the city will be unlikely to know the number for local emergency services and will have to fumble through the phone book or wait to talk to an operator first. Once you are connected to the station, you will more than likely be connected with a desk sergeant who might put you on hold if he is dealing with a previous caller or someone who has walked into the station. After you explain an emergency situation to the desk sergeant, he then will transfer you to a communications officer to take your report down again. And even then, sometimes the report is not transmitted promptly and police do not show up in time. In other words, there is no expectation or experience at this time of prompt emergency responses by police to citizen calls. Indeed, one witness swears that his father did call the police after Mosely's first attack, but no one picked up, and the call was never logged.[16]

The old system had another limitation: too many calls could clog the system, which makes it impossible for police personnel to understand what is going on and ultimately slows response time. As a result, people worried that others might already be calling; if they put in an additional call, it might only burden the lines beyond capacity.[17] This specific explanation was offered by one of the potential callers in the Genovese attack.

THE REFORM

A universal emergency number had first been suggested in 1957, when the National Association of Fire Chiefs recommended it as a more efficient way to report fires. But many thought such a system would be prohibitively expensive, and few leaders saw this as an urgent issue worth spending time and political capital on. That changed, however, with Genovese's murder. The incident convinces top law enforcement officials in New York City and elsewhere that a universal system is badly needed, and the case sparks a national conversation about how to make emergency services more responsive and effective. Under the current system, New Yorkers could dial *zero* to reach an operator and get the operator to help them determine the number for the local precinct and to connect them. But even that assisted process could take several minutes.

In 1967, President Lyndon B. Johnson's Commission on Law Enforcement and Administration of Justice recommends a single number for the entire nation to use in emergency situations. At the time, the Canadian city of Winnipeg, Manitoba, already has a central emergency number. Experiments in the United Kingdom with a national emergency telephone number had also been conducted. The commission wants each emergency service to have two phone numbers, the emergency-only number and a second number for regular business. In that way, emergency calls will automatically be prioritized over ordinary business and information calls. With the two-number model, it will no longer be the case that people getting information on how to pay a parking ticket, for example, will be prioritized over a person in dire need of an ambulance.

In November of 1967, the Federal Communications Commission meets with the American Telephone and Telegraph Company (AT&T), which has a nationwide monopoly on telephone service at the time, to determine what the national emergency number system should look like and how quickly the plan can be implemented. AT&T executives suggest that the most efficient number would be "9-1-1." The number 9-1-1 is short, easy to remember, and quick to dial. Back in 1967, rotary-dial telephones are in use. When using a rotary phone, the number *one* takes the least amount of time to dial. In addition, 9-1-1 is completely unique. There are no area codes, office numbers, or service codes that begin with those three digits. An added attraction is that this three-digit number is an easy add-on to the existing system. A few years earlier the company implemented *6-1-1* as a customer-service-request number and *4-1-1* for those seeking directory assistance. Adding a third short number, *9-1-1*, is relatively cheap and familiar to the public and implementation can begin quickly.[18]

The investment is good for the public, but it is also good for AT&T. Before 9-1-1, AT&T operators across the country deal with emergency calls on a daily basis, and each time this happens, the operator has to stop everything else he or she is doing until the caller has the help they need. This forces other callers to wait for longer periods of time and makes the system as a whole less efficient. The 9-1-1 system frees AT&T operators to focus on their normal duties 100 percent of the time, which is thought to save the company millions of dollars. Furthermore, the new nationwide emergency number is funded through a small additional charge placed on nearly everyone's phone bill, so the upgrades cost AT&T close to nothing.

After the FCC and AT&T approve the new universal emergency number, the president of the Alabama Telephone Company decides to implement the new system in Haleyville, Alabama. On February 16, 1968, the first 9-1-1 call is made by Alabama state senator Rankin Fite from the Haleyville mayor's office to the Haleyville, Alabama, Police Department, where U.S. Representative Tom Bevill answers. The use of 9-1-1 officially begins.

THE PSYCHOLOGY OF ASSISTANCE

It is unclear if a universal phone number would have made a difference for Kitty Genovese, but people have a sense that any move toward removing complexity will lead to more people receiving aid more quickly. Still, the anger and fear that emerged after Kitty Genovese's death could not be made right simply through the creation of 9-1-1. Part of what people found difficult to fathom, and remained outraged about, was how the neighbors could know what was happening to Kitty and yet none of them act. How is possible for so many people to stand by and wait for a woman to be killed?

In 1968, a pair of social scientists, Bibb Latané and John Darley, publish a monograph titled *The Unresponsive Bystander*. Latané and Darley claim that the "Threefold Cord" of "succor, warmth and mutual defense" that traditionally bound members of the same society together is falling apart. They note an increasing sentiment that "present-day society is fragmented, that compassion is disappearing, old moralities crumbling," speculating that perhaps the new age has borne a new type of apathetic, cold human they call *"Homo urbanis."*[19]

Latané and Darley run a series of experiments to see under what conditions people would take responsibility for their fellows. They set up situations in which a person is seemingly in mortal peril and provide bystanders with an opportunity to try and save them. The experiments show that a "very important factor in the amount of responsibility felt by any one bystander is the number of other people he thinks are present and available to help. The presence of others," they conclude, "serves to inhibit the impulse to help."[20]

For example, in one of their experiments, a woman takes a test subject into a room to fill out a questionnaire. She then heads behind a curtain. The test subject hears a crash and the woman calls out "Oh my God, my foot. My ankle! I can't get . . . this thing . . . off me."[21] If the test subject is the only person of the room, he or she helps the woman 70 percent of the time. When others are present (actors who pretend not to care), that number drops to a response rate of 7 percent.

In an experiment designed "to resemble Kitty Genovese's murder,"[22] researchers tell test subjects to await a person with a loudspeaker in a different room who will tell them what to do next. When the loudspeaker comes on, the person speaks as though something is wrong. "Oh. Uh, uh," the person says. "I could really use some help. If somebody would

. . . uh, I'm gonna die. Help."[23] The voice breaks off and the test subjects hear choking. There is an assistant in the hallway whom the test subjects can easily see and could notify about the instructor's distress. Whether or not the test subjects decide to help correlates with whether they think they are the only ones who heard what happened. Some test subjects are told that there are four other subjects in different rooms, some are told there is one other subject, and some are told that they themselves are the only subjects. Eighty-five percent of the last group tells the assistant something is wrong, while 62 percent of the middle group does so, and only 31 percent of the first group says anything.

The researchers posit something they call "diffusion of responsibility." If there is only one witness to another person's danger "he will feel all the guilt for not acting. If others are present, responsibility is diffused, and the finger of blame points less directly at any one person."[24] Thus, it might be that the reason some of the witnesses did nothing to help Kitty is that they assumed someone else would do it. In fact, the police investigators heard this in the witness statements: one woman prevented her husband from calling the police because she thought thirty people must have called already.

Later, Darley ran a variation on the study designed to see if it might be some sort of a character issue that compelled some to help and not others. This time, the psychologist went to a religious seminary. Young men studying to be ministers were put into situations where they ran across someone clearly in need of help. How many helped? It depended mostly on how pressed for time they felt. Men rushing off to an important class only stopped to help 10 percent of the time. The less time pressure the individual felt, the more likely they were to help. Even then, only 63 percent stopped to give aid.[25] It would seem that the people of Queens are not much different from people elsewhere.

In 1975, the idea of a single reporting phone number finds a new application—the Crime-Stoppers Hotline. Greg MacAleese, an Albuquerque, New Mexico, homicide detective notices that across the country "fear and apathy" prevent people from reaching out to authorities with information on crimes. He arranges for a television station to reenact a local murder that he is investigating and air the footage. Next he offers a reward, of $1,000, which he has the news publicize. And finally, he sets up a phone number by which people can anonymously give information to the police. By increasing awareness, paying rewards, and removing some fear by making reporting anonymous, the detective gets dramatic results. The program quickly spreads throughout the country. Crime Stoppers has become a national program with compelling statistics: 674,117 arrests, 8,577 homicides solved, $4 billion of property recovered.

9-1-1 TODAY

Ten years after the first 9-1-1 phone call, over a quarter of the country is able to dial 9-1-1 and immediately connect to emergency assistance. After twenty years, about 50 percent of the country has the system.[26] By 1999, 93 percent of the country is able to dial 9-1-1. The Wireless Communications and Public Safety Act of 1999, nicknamed the "9-1-1 Act," went into effect at this juncture.[27] The legislation was enacted with the goal that the Federal Communications Commission work to bring 9-1-1 to everyone in the nation. The act is to "promote and enhance public safety through use of 9-1-1 as the universal emergency assistance number, further deployment of wireless 9-1-1 service, support to States in upgrading 9-1-1 capabilities and related functions, encouragement of construction and operation of seamless, ubiquitous, and reliable networks for personal wireless services and for other purposes."[28]

And while some communities work to improve their 9-1-1 systems to address these challenges, some rural areas (especially in Alaska and the West) lack even basic 9-1-1. Some of these small communities with low populations cannot afford the expensive technology and professional staff to manage the center 24/7. Other communities lack street names with numbered homes, which makes it difficult for dispatchers to send emergency personnel to the right place. However, the federal government is committed to making 9-1-1 a truly universal number, and fewer and fewer communities do not have a system.

Currently 99 percent of Americans can dial 9-1-1 in emergency situations.[29] There are over 5,906 call centers that receive and assist with the emergency calls throughout the United States.[30] Each year, 9-1-1 is dialed over 240 million times.

The system is not perfect. At least a quarter of all 9-1-1 calls are pranks or from people with skewed judgment. For example, a woman in Deltona, Florida, was arrested after making four calls to 9-1-1 to complain about a nail technician who had cut her nails too short. In another case, a fifty-eight-year-old Florida woman repeatedly called 9-1-1 to summon the police in order to solicit sex.[31] The FBI has also warned of an increase in deliberate false alarms in which a false origin is displayed on calls to emergency services to send SWAT teams or heavily armed police to unsuspecting citizens' doorsteps. Voiceover IP (VoIP) has contributed greatly to the problem by making call origin more difficult to determine quickly and reliably. In California, Governor Jerry Brown signed legislation imposing liability for the full cost of these false alarms, which can reach $10,000 or more per incident. All of these inappropriate uses of the system distract dispatchers and police from serving the people who really need help.

The 9-1-1 system also struggles to keep pace with rapid technological change. The 9-1-1 system was designed for a world with landlines, and 93 percent of counties in the United States now have Enhanced 9-1-1 (e9-1-1) access, which ensures every call goes to the closest call center and that the person receiving the emergency call can see the landline phone number and the associated address.[32] But today, more than 70 percent of all calls placed to 9-1-1 are made from cell phones, and the system is sometimes dangerously incompatible with the capabilities of cell phones. Almost all 9-1-1 call centers have the technology to immediately identify wireless numbers and the location of the cell tower that is carrying the call in case they become disconnected, but most do not have the capacity to determine the caller's exact location (even though the technology to do so exists). Most 9-1-1 centers also do not support text messaging or photo and video messaging. This is significant in some remote areas where the poor cell coverage might not sustain a call but could relay a text message to a dispatcher.

In some cases, these shortcomings cost people their lives. In 2010, Shanell Anderson is delivering newspapers early in the morning when her car leaves the road and slides into a pond. Unable to escape the vehicle, Anderson calls 9-1-1. As her vehicle fills with water, she calmly gives the operator full information, including her exact location and crossroads near where she is trapped. However, the cell tower routes her call to another county's emergency response center. The distant dispatcher cannot find the streets on her maps, and the system cannot fix on the cell phone's location. The operator keeps trying, asking Anderson to repeat the information again and again. She gives the best information she can as the car continues to fill with water until Anderson is finally submerged.[33] When firefighters arrive, the vehicle is no longer visible, but resting in the bottom of the pond in eight feet of water. Anderson dies days later at a hospital.

The U.S. Department of Transportation (DOT) understands these issues and hopes to take advantage of new technology to advance the emergency-call system.[34] Their initiative will focus on being able to receive calls from various devices, use texting and images for quicker and more accurate dissemination of information, and have improved communication and coordination between call centers. The DOT named the new initiative "Next Generation 9-1-1," and they are working with providers and authorities to make this part of the emergency system.

Despite its challenges, the 9-1-1 system has proved so effective that it has spread around the globe. Most of North America uses 9-1-1, while Europe uses 1-1-2. Even developing countries like Burma, Guam, and Guyana have made a single emergency-response number a priority.[35]

Kitty Genovese's lonely death brought attention to how easy it is to do nothing. Since that day, laws, technology, and government have worked together to remove some of the barriers to action. Now it would be hard to find even a small child who does not know that help is just a phone call away.

Chapter Nine

1965
Watts Riots and Texas Sniper

SWAT and the Militarization of Police

THE TRAGEDY—WATTS RIOTS

On a steamy evening, Wednesday, August 11, 1965, Marquette and Ronald Frye are celebrating.[1] Ronald, the older of the two brothers, has just returned from military service. The brothers go out for drinks, and then head home for a meal prepared by their mother. Marquette, a twenty-one-year-old African American raised in Los Angeles, is behind the wheel of his mother's 1955 Buick, while Ronald is chatting away in the passenger seat. Marquette doesn't want to miss supper; he steps on the gas, exceeding the speed limit, and starts weaving around slower cars. Other drivers are not amused. Another motorist approaches Officer Lee Minikus of the California Highway Patrol: "See that man?" she says, pointing toward Marquette's Buick. "I think he's drunk."[2]

Minikus, a white officer dressed in black leather and a white crash helmet, starts his motorcycle and heads after the Buick. He pulls the car over at 116th Street and Avalon, two blocks from the Fryes' house.[3] Marquette hops out of the car as the officer approaches. Marquette is a careful dresser and looks sharp, dressed in "tapered, cuffless trousers and a tailored sport shirt."[4] He's friendly and happy, cracking jokes that make Minikus laugh. However, Minikus suspects that Marquette is drunk and administers a sobriety test. Marquette fails it, and the officer informs him that he'll have to be arrested. At first, Marquette's good-humored behavior persists; his antics attract people from the area, many of whom are outside to escape the heat of their homes. While Marquette chats and jokes with the growing crowd of spectators, Officer Minikus calls his partner, Bob Lewis, for help in getting a tow truck for the car and taking Marquette to jail. Meanwhile, Ronald leaves to get his mother, two blocks away.

Rena is short and brusque, and in the community is nicknamed "The Lady." She arrives to see the police preparing to tow her car. She is furious at Marquette. "I told you about drinking and driving," she scolds. With his mother fuming and two police officers attempting to arrest him, Marquette suddenly becomes belligerent. He argues with the officers, and Officer Lewis sends out a code 1199—"Officer Needs Help"—to get more backup. Marquette is defiant and declares that the police will have to kill him if they want him in jail.[5] Another policeman, Officer Bennett, pulls up. The crowd of onlookers has swelled tenfold and now numbers between 250 and 300. Bennett, trying to disperse onlookers, pushes them back with a shotgun in hand.

The dynamic begins to change. Rena does not want her car towed; Marquette does not want to be arrested; the family is arguing heatedly with police. The gathering crowd watching the situation unfold grows restless, expressing irritation over how the officers are treating the family. The situation escalates quickly when Officer Wayne Wilson arrives. He jumps out of his car and strikes Ronald Frye in the stomach and ribs with his baton. In a blur, his baton swings again, landing hard on Marquette's forehead above the eye; he strikes him a third time in the stomach. Rena, seeing her injured son, jumps on one of the officers and rips his shirt. Rena hits an officer in the groin, and then one of the officers hits her in the face.[6] Ronald gives Minikus a blow to the kidney. Another officer grabs Rena and shoves her against the car. The small woman is quickly cuffed. After some scuffling, all three Fryes—Ronald, Marquette, and Rena—are in custody. The Fryes are taken away in police cars at about 7:25 p.m..

Anger is stirring in the heat of a Los Angeles summer. It's August 1965, and racial tension is festering. Despite decades of push back, the city's black minority still faces inequality and de facto segregation and continues to be shut out of political power, struggling without success to elect African Americans to the city council or Congress. They feel voiceless and forgotten. Lately, black communities in the city have grown increasingly angry and vocal about issues such as high unemployment, substandard housing, and inadequate schools. "Don't bother to learn at school," one father tells his child. "The white folks won't let you use an education if you get it."[7] Disrespectful and abusive police make the situation worse. Los Angeles police chief William Parker is a tough man who leads a tough police force.

Watts, where the Fryes live, is a predominantly black neighborhood in South Central Los Angeles surrounded by majority-white regions.[8] The term "Watts" is used as a derogatory label, "the same way as city boys used 'country' as a term of derision," recalls writer and political activist Eldridge Cleaver.[9]

On Avalon Street, the crowd has grown to an estimated one thousand. The Frye family is no longer on the scene, but the crowd is only growing more tense. Someone spits at one of the officers, Officer Vaughn. Enraged, he and his partner wade into the crowd to find the assailant. They seize a young woman named Joyce Gaines and drag her forcefully to a police car. She's wearing a barber's smock that looks like a maternity dress. Hundreds of onlookers, believing that the woman is pregnant, are livid, and rumors spread through the crowd about the police beating a pregnant woman.[10] As the police try to leave, an angry onlooker hurls a bottle at the car. Within seconds, a shower of rocks, bricks, bottles, and other objects rains down on the police.

The officers on the scene can sense that the crowd is on the verge of running out of control. They can feel the tension in the air; escalation seems inevitable. Los Angeles police officer J. J. Fedrizzi is onsite armed with a billy club: "They wanted to hang some policemen real quick like, if they had a chance—right there."[11] He is certain that the vengeful crowd will attack an officer if he becomes too isolated. The police want to withdraw, but there is no obvious route out. Further complicating the situation is that the officers know they must leave together—as one later says, "I think it would have been too dangerous to have left two or three officers there."[12] After some maneuvering, the officers get into their cars and try to drive away. They find, however, that the vehicles cannot navigate the dense crowd without running over people who won't move. One car does a quick U-turn and heads out. The car is pursued by a break-away group. One officer remembers it like this: "The people ran into the street, started running after us—yelling, screaming. They began throwing anything they could get their hands on. Bottles and rocks were bouncing off the back."[13] At 7:40 p.m., the last police car gets away from the scene.[14] From the crowd, a teenager yells out "Burn, Baby, Burn." The phrase becomes the battle cry of the demonstrations that follow.

The police see their decision to withdraw as necessary to protect the safety of the officers but also as a means to disperse the crowd: their leaving the scene will allow tempers to cool. Unfortunately, removing the officers has exactly the opposite effect: it only emboldens the crowd. With the police gone, the crowd aggressively unleashes its rage on other passing motorists. They throw rocks and bricks, which thud against the metal and smash through the windows of passing vehicles. Families of all races are attacked. Cars are set afire. People are torn from their cars and beaten. Children are hit with stones.

The police realize they have made a miscalculation, so they return to the area with a larger force to regain control. As soon as they approach the crowd, they realize that their force of fewer than one hundred officers is still too small. They are also woefully unprepared, with no clear plan for taking on thousands of violent demonstrators. They make the mistake of fanning out, which allows the crowd to isolate individual officers and renders them powerless to control the throngs. The officers are again forced to retreat.

The police next try a strategy of containment. Barriers are erected to prevent the crowd from migrating, and the streets are closed to traffic. For a time, this tactic works. By now, several reporters from the *Los Angeles Times* have come to investigate the scene and are camping behind the barricades with police. In the last few minutes of Wednesday, August 11, the police begin to leave the area for the day. But unrest stirs once again, and they try to reenter the area. This time, several reporters elect to follow. The crowd responds virulently, and there is no question that this is now a full-blown riot. Twelve officers and the coterie of reporters are attacked, but they manage to escape mostly unharmed. The riot continues through the night, and by the time the sun mercifully rises, thirty-five people are injured and fifty vehicles have been attacked and damaged, including two fire trucks that had been sent to put out fires set by the rioters.[15] Most believe the tumultuous incident is over. But a passing youth wandering the streets in the smoky dawn is still chanting, "Burn, Baby, Burn."[16]

The following afternoon, Thursday, August 12, the leaders of the black community call a meeting for 2:00 p.m.. It is well attended by locals, curiosity seekers, and the press. The Human Relations Commission (HRC), a government-sponsored agency that works to eliminate discrimination in Los Angeles, takes on the organization of the meeting in nearby Athens Park. The HRC was founded for the specific purpose of managing race-based tensions, but even the HRC "had never imagined something of this magnitude."[17] The leaders are trying to shift the mood away from violence and toward dialogue. John Buggs, one of the organization's commissioners, makes their goal very clear at the meeting: they aim to start a "counter-rumor [that] it's all over, it's all off. Everybody stays in tonight."[18] Locals are recruited to spread the word: 100 to 150 adults and 100 youths.

Though well intentioned, Buggs and the HRC team struggle to control the agenda. A young man bounds up on stage and grabs the microphone, and with TV cameras rolling, he exclaims:

> I was down on Avalon last night, and we the Negro people have got completely fed up! They not going to fight down here no more. You know where they going? They're after the Whiteys! They going to congregate. They don't care! They going out to Inglewood, Playa del Rey, and everywhere else the white man supposed to stay. They going to do the white man tonight.[19]

Though the HRC staff begs news crews to not air the footage, it is aired on the evening news across Los Angeles. The productive, peaceful portions of the meeting do not make the broadcasts. The words of the teenager have an immediate impact. The chant of "Burn, Baby, Burn" returns to the simmering streets of Watts, and whites in the surrounding areas get in their cars and go off to buy guns.[20]

The police struggle to make a plan. An emergency control center is set up in a downtown building. From the control center, the police plan to receive reports and give orders. They're prepared to flex their muscles and are confident that they can shut down the riots.[21] An emergency perimeter is installed to contain the area of disturbance. In an effort to regain control, five hundred police officers, deputy sheriffs, and highway patrolmen are sent into the area to disperse the mobs. Thursday night brings more of everything: fires, looting, fear, assaults, and full-scale rioting.

By the early hours of Friday, the situation has grown more dangerous. Liquor stores are robbed and picked clean. A supermarket at 116th and Avalon is looted and set ablaze. White news reporters are attacked. They escape with only minor injuries, but their cars and equipment are incinerated. Rioters stone passing cars, but selectively: "The car in front of us, driven by a Negro, was not hit," explains one reporter.[22]

Despite the tense situation, Lieutenant Governor Anderson, sitting in for Governor Brown, who is vacationing in Greece, is informed at around 1:00 a.m. on Friday the 13th that police officials think the situation is under control. Los Angeles mayor Sam Yorty is briefed on the situation. "They'd all get real tired about two or three o'clock in the morning and then they'd go home and sleep till two o'clock in the afternoon," he explains.[23] At 5:09 a.m. on Friday, the police working the emergency perimeter withdraw. Just before 7:00 a.m., an intelligence officer on duty at the control center reports that the situation is "rather well in hand." Confident in his team's assessment, Anderson boards a plane and departs Los Angeles for Berkeley for an unrelated meeting at the University of California. It appears that order is finally returning.

Unfortunately, police have made another serious miscalculation. On Friday morning, thick black smoke billows up from the ruins of buildings, and trash litters the hellish scene everywhere. Instead of sleeping until mid-afternoon as Mayor Yorty predicted, a crowd of three thousand gathers during the morning of Friday, August 13, in the commercial area of Watts to loot and burn it. Cars are overturned and set on fire, and firefighters are unable to extinguish the flames as they dodge flying rocks and shots coming from the rioters working as snipers. As early afternoon arrives, ambulance drivers and firemen demand armed escorts. A pattern emerges: First, rioters pack into cars and drive around, searching for businesses: restaurants, stores, gas stations, and markets. They pull up, hop out, and break windows before speeding off in search of another target. Afterward, other cars pull up to loot the business. After taking all of the valuables, the rioters set fire to the building.

Initially, newsmen report that mobs are chaotic and confused, with "no leaders" and representing "isolated groups only,"[24] but as Friday drags on, police realize that rioters are more tactical than they originally realized. Police radio channels are interrupted periodically by messages from rioters, and some rioters have transmitter radios to monitor police calls. Youths communicate via telephone booths as well. The rioting bands seem to be tracking police movement and coordinating their vandalism.[25]

At 9:15 a.m. Police Chief William Parker and Mayor Yorty talk on the phone. They agree to bring in another player in the fight against the mobs: the California National Guard. Mayor Yorty departs for a talk in San Francisco, leaving Parker in charge.

Just before 10:00 a.m., Parker calls a meeting, attended by LAPD police officials and Colonel Quick of the California National Guard. "It looks like we are going to have to call the troops," Parker announces. "We will need a thousand men."[26] But deploying the National Guard requires approval from the acting governor, Anderson, who left just a few hours earlier in the belief that the situation was under control. When Parker finally reaches Anderson over an hour later, Anderson declines to call in the Guard.

Instead, Anderson flies back to Los Angeles from Berkeley to meet with leaders of the black community, Chief Parker, the sheriff, and the Highway Patrol commissioner. Commercial flights from nearby San Francisco to Los Angeles are fast and frequent, but Anderson decides to drive to Sacramento, where he can fly in the governor's official plane. He doesn't arrive in Los Angeles until after 3:30 p.m. With the Los Angeles sheriff vacationing in Canada and the Highway Patrol commissioner on business in Oregon, Chief Parker is on his own unless Anderson chooses to act.[27]

Governor Brown is contacted in Greece; he seems to quickly grasp what the others will not. Brown says that the National Guard *must* be called in, and a curfew should be set. With the governor's urging, Anderson announces to the press that he is calling in the National Guard, and at 5:00 p.m. he signs the official proclamation. Two hours later, 1,336 National Guard troops are assembled and en route to staging areas. By this time, entire blocks are burning, and snipers armed with rifles keep firemen at bay.

With the guardsmen not yet set up to intervene, rioters jam the streets and begin systematically burning several blocks of 103rd Street in Watts, driving off firemen with sniper fire and missiles. By late afternoon, the rioters' activity spreads to as far as fifty and sixty blocks to the north.[28]

At 6:30 p.m., the riot claims its first life. Leon Posey, a twenty-one-year-old black California native with a slight build and a goatee, is standing at a street corner on 89th and Broadway just outside a barbershop. Nearby, police struggle to gain ground against an approaching mob of rioters who hurl rocks and concrete and fire rifles at police. Police form a skirmish line and fire at rioters, but a policeman's bullet ricochets from a building, striking Posey and killing him instantly.[29] It's not long before news of Posey's death sweeps the rioting crowd. "Things were going crazy," recalls one HCR staff member.[30]

As Friday evening unfolds, it becomes obvious that the personnel on the ground are unable to suppress the riots. The lethargy of the initial response has allowed the unrest to grow and the rioters to become energized. Though hundreds of rioters are arrested,[31] law enforcement lacks adequate "mobile jail capacity" and cannot take all of the arrested rioters to jail.[32]

At 8:55 p.m., another man dies. Deputy Sheriff Ronald Ludlow is shot in the abdomen during a struggle to hold several suspects in police custody. The carnage continues. An estimated ten thousand rioters take to the streets that night, scattered in bands ranging in size from several hundred to several thousand.[33] Across the city, rioters chant "Burn, Baby, Burn!" as businesses go up in flames. During the night, rioters move west of Watts, leaving a trail of burning buildings, broken glass, and injured people.

At 10:00 p.m., the California National Guard finally moves in, more than twelve hours after Chief Parker made his request. The guardsmen are, for the most part, young, poorly trained, and undisciplined. They don't have enough radios, and their weapons are inadequate and too few. They try to sweep the streets shoulder to shoulder to clear mobs, with firefighting teams following behind. An additional 1,000 National Guard troops are stationed in the worst areas at midnight. By the end of the night, a total of 3,356 guardsmen are patrolling the streets, with 2,000 police, sheriff, and Highway Patrol officers at their sides. But there is little the undertrained and underequipped men can do. Each time officers or guardsmen clear a street and move on to another, looting and arson resume.

Trapped in the danger are the vast majority of residents in the area who are upset about the chaos and destruction being created around them. Many are stunned. "These can't be our people," one resident tells a reporter.[34] Residents, too afraid to venture from their homes, are becoming victims of food shortages, and civil rights organizations scramble to set up makeshift food distribution centers.

As dawn breaks early on Saturday, uncontained fires still burn. Tense and terrified police monitor the bands of rioters moving across the area. Police bar all whites from the neighborhood, but a few manage to slip past unmonitored police blockades to go sightseeing in the rubble-filled streets. Police continue to arrest rioters, filling local jails. They even reopen the condemned Lincoln Heights Jail, which had been closed for months. All of the law enforcement agencies struggle to communicate in any centralized way; many of the guardsmen receive their reports by listening on a radio station based in Tijuana. Law enforcement officials lack proper equipment, especially adequate firearms, and officers start reporting for duty carrying their own guns.

Desperate, Lieutenant Governor Anderson imposes a curfew. Early Saturday evening, a 46.5 square-mile area is sectioned off on a pin-up map, and the image is reproduced in newspapers and on televisions. After 8:00 p.m., reporters announce that it's a crime to be on the streets in this area. Not everyone gets the news, or chooses to comply. And several more people die as a result in clashes.

More troops are called to the area, and by the end of the day on Saturday, there are 13,900 guardsmen in Los Angeles. Though the curfew has kept large mobs off the streets, smaller bands still rove, and the looting continues. Battles between law enforcement and rioters are likened to guerrilla warfare, as rioters, often armed, appear out of nowhere, steal and fight, then disappear between buildings and down alleyways as quickly as they arrived. Police are not trained to deal with this type of criminal warfare, and by day's end, twenty people are dead and countless more are injured.

And the riots are spreading. They have grabbed the national media spotlight, and violence has taken hold in San Diego, San Bernardino, Bakersfield, the San Fernando Valley, Pasadena, and Hollywood, where dozens of African Americans are arrested for arson and property damage. Law enforcement agencies in these cities, however, are quick to smother riots, and attention remains locked on the city of Los Angeles.

Sunday arrives, and the rioting continues, but the crowds are smaller than the night before. The massive law enforcement presence finally seems to have an effect. Governor Brown, having arrived from Greece late Saturday night, is appalled by the devastation. "Here in California," he announces, "we have a wonderful working relationship [of race relations]. We got along fine until this happened."[35] Many blacks in Los Angeles adamantly disagree, but Brown's statement resonates with many of the city's white residents, who are terrified by the riots.

With the chaos giving way to order, attention is focused on stopping the fires. Troops are assigned to fire trucks when they are dispatched, and military guards are situated at fire stations across the area. Fires in businesses and private residences still continue to burn, set by elusive arsonists, but firefighters are less vulnerable to snipers and rock-throwing mobs. They now begin to make progress against the flames.[36]

Figure 9.1.   Fires burned in Watts for days, August 14, 1965. *Everett collection*

Monday morning dawns, and an eerie calm settles on the area. Ruined buildings spill rubble onto sidewalks and streets, and destroyed power poles and lines leave residents without electricity. Many businesses don't open, with owners still fearful of looting or destruction. School playgrounds are empty, and the doors of libraries, banks, and offices remain locked. Nearly fourteen thousand troops continue to patrol the area. The summer sun beats down, baking the streets and the people who walk them. Jails in the area are packed with thousands of arrested rioters. Court arraignments begin.

At 2:00 p.m., Governor Brown makes the announcement that the nation has waited anxiously to hear: "The rioting and looting has ended." Despite the good news, the announcement is met with grim silence. The cost of the riots, the city knows, has been enormous: thirty-four people are dead, over one thousand people are injured, and damages to homes and businesses are estimated at $40 million ($304 million in 2016 dollars). Citizens across the nation heard the cry of "Burn, Baby, Burn" and the fear lingers. The riot raged for six days because police lacked the equipment, training, tactics, and skill required to manage the crisis.

THE TRAGEDY—TEXAS SNIPER

Less than a year after the police embarrassment in the handling of the Watts riots, at some time during the night of July 31 and the morning of August 1, 1966, in Austin, Texas, Charles Whitman drives to his mother's house at 1212 Guadalupe Street. From all outward signs, he's a typical young man facing a bright future. As an accomplished pianist by age twelve, a former boy scout, and a former marine, Whitman is the quintessence of a law-abiding citizen. However, once he arrives at his mother's house, he suffocates his mother before stabbing her in the heart. He leaves a note beside her body that reads: "To Whom It May Concern: I have just taken my mother's life. I am very upset over having done it. However, I feel that if there is a heaven she is definitely there now. . . . Let there be no doubt in your mind that I loved this woman with all my heart. I am truly sorry that this is the only way I could see to relieve her suffering but I think it is best."[37] Whitman then drives home, about two miles distant, and kills his wife, Kathy, by stabbing her three times in the heart as she sleeps.

At 5:45 a.m., Whitman calls Kathy's supervisor at Bell System to inform him that she was ill and would not be going to work that day. He does the same for his mother. Whitman then prepares for the last part of his plan—the "actions" to which he alludes in his wife's death letter.

The next day, the low morning clouds disappear quickly and by 11:00 a.m., the air is shimmering in the heat. The buildings, Spanish-style with red terra cotta roof tiles, give the University of Texas, Austin, campus a distinctive character. Near its center stands the UT Tower, 307 feet high. The handsome tower is the school's one strong architectural feature. Tourists and students often climb up to the observation deck, on the twenty-eighth floor, to admire the view. From the unobstructed platform, viewers can see the city of Austin stretched out below them for miles.

Just before noon, Whitman gets out of his car in a parking lot just north of the tower. Dressed in blue coveralls and sneakers, he appears to be either a custodian or repairman. He is a handsome man in his twenties, muscular, tall, and well groomed, with cropped blond hair and striking blue eyes. He unloads a two-wheeled dolly from his car and stacks it with an army footlocker, a blanket-wrapped bundle, and a few miscellaneous parcels. When he finds that the elevator isn't running, he politely asks the receptionist for help. When she flips a switch to turn on the elevator, he says: "Thank you, ma'am. You don't know how happy that makes me."[38]

Whitman rides the elevator to the twenty-seventh floor. The receptionist there is Edna Townsley. Whitman lunges at her, rifle in his hand, and strikes the back of her head with the butt of the rifle. The force shatters her skull. She falls to the floor, glasses flying from her face, and her attacker deals another brutal blow above her eye, cracking her skull again. Whitman drags her behind a couch in the lobby, where she lies dying.

Before he steps back from the couch, a young couple emerges from the observation deck. Don is a UT, Austin, student, and his girlfriend, Cheryl, plans to enroll in a nearby college soon. The receptionist, they observe, isn't at her desk, but the man in coveralls stands nearby, silently watching them—a "good-looking young blond man holding guns," Cheryl remembers. "Don thought—and I know this sounds crazy—that he was there to shoot pigeons."[39] They smile at him and say hello, and the man, returns the smile and the greeting.

As the couple heads down the elevator, the Garbers, a family of six, head up. Teenagers Mike and Mark are ahead of the rest, climbing the last flight of stairs to the observation-deck reception area. Upon arriving, they find that the doorway is blocked by desks and chairs, so they peek through. In a matter of moments, four members of the family are dead. Whitman does not see the other two members of the family, who run in search of assistance.

The gunshots are heard on the floors below. On the twenty-sixth floor, a class of eight students in the classics department is surprised; one student thinks that "filing cabinets had fallen down the stairs."[40] Professor Fred Mench peeks into the stairway to investigate: "There are bodies all over,"[41] he cries. The small class calls the police and barricades the room.

In the reception area, Whitman is alone again. He unpacks his dolly, laying out an arsenal: a 6 mm Remington rifle with a 4-power scope, a 35-caliber Remington rifle, a 30-caliber carbine, a sawed-off 12-gauge shotgun, a revolver, two pistols, a hunting knife, and seven hundred rounds of ammunition.

In the open terrace below the tower, students stroll in the sunshine, oblivious to the armed man watching from above. Whitman selects the 6 mm Remington rifle; a powerful gun prized for its long-range accuracy, and adjusts the crosshairs of the scope. He takes aim.

On the terrace below, a young couple, Claire Wilson and Thomas Eckman, both eighteen years old, are walking. Claire is eight months pregnant, due to deliver a baby boy in the coming weeks. The shot from the Remington tears through her belly, ripping a hole through her stomach, colon, and uterus, killing the baby. "I felt like I'd stepped on a live wire, like I'd been electrocuted . . . like something really heavy was pressing down on me," Claire later says.[42] Claire screams and collapses on the pavement. Before Thomas can find out what is wrong, he too is shot. The bullet enters his shoulder below the neck, and his dead body falls across Claire.

Whitman selects another target. Just west of Claire stands physics professor Robert Hamilton Boyer. Dr. Boyer is on his way to meet another

Figure 9.2.   University of Texas at Austin, the tower looms above the campus, 1965.
Robert Yarnall Richie, DeGolyer Library, Southern Methodist University

professor for lunch, but the sound of gunfire causes him to stop. Boyer watches the couple fall to the ground. He turns, perhaps to duck behind the wall at the edge of the terrace, but the sniper fires again. The round enters Dr. Boyer's lower back, destroying his kidney. He falls down the steps leading to the terrace, dead almost instantly. Students duck behind the wall and scream at others to stay down, but the message comes too late for many, who are shot and left bleeding on the ground. The killing continues.

In the buildings surrounding the terrace, students in class look up from their textbooks, startled by the strange noises coming from outside. There are now six bodies in full view on the hot pavement, limbs twisted grotesquely. The university security office is flooded with frantic phone calls, and Chief Allen Hamilton knows he must act. He sends two men, Rodman and Gebert, to the tower. The unarmed officers make it to the twenty-seventh floor, but there is nothing they can do. All around the tower, dozens are now injured.

At 11:52 a.m., the Austin Police Department receives its first call. A minute later, Officer Houston McCoy hears the frantic dispatcher's voice on the police radio: help is needed at University Tower. Within seconds, he's speeding toward the campus. Upon arriving, he unlocks his shotgun and approaches the tower from the south. To the east of the tower, another officer, Billy Speed, arrives, too. Shotgun in hand, Officer Speed parks his car, eyes the tower, and sprints.

Officer McCoy passes the scene and pulls into the parking lot just north of the tower, as close to the building as his police car will allow. Gunshots echo across the campus, and puffs of smoke rise from the observation deck twenty-eight stories above. Realizing his own shotgun will be useless from that angle and distance McCoy begins searching for anyone who might own a high-powered rifle with a scope. McCoy finds a student who has such a rifle back in his apartment. McCoy and the student go to the apartment to retrieve the rifle and then stop at a hardware store to buy ammunition.

McCoy and the student enter a nearby building to return fire but McCoy has no experience with the rifle. He hands it back to the student. McCoy looks out the window. He sees Officer Billy Speed and Officer Jerry Culp huddling beneath a statue with a few terrified civilians. Officer Speed stands up momentarily, and a bullet tears through his shoulder and lodges itself in his chest. Students in a building nearby courageously sneak out to help him, tearing off pieces of their clothing to stop the bleeding. McCoy and the boy, still watching Speed from another building, glance at each other in horror. "If I see the sniper, should I kill him?" the student asks. McCoy, his eyes cold and angry, replies, "You shoot the shit out of him!"[43]

More police arrive but their department-issued weapons are useless against the sniper. Officers run home to retrieve their personal guns, primarily those designed for deer hunting. Students have started to return fire, too. They "took over Parlin Hall and were crashing around, firing guns," recalls one student, J. M. Coetzee (not the Nobel laureate who also attended university in Austin).[44] Billy Helmer, a student who was firing, explains why the return fire is important: it prevents Whitman from leaning over the tower to aim. Officers arm students and encourage them to return fire.

Officer McCoy leaves the student with a rifle to continue firing and runs to the university Police Station. A loosely organized group of officers is being mobilized to enter the tower, so McCoy joins the group. A group of men make their way to the twenty-eighth floor, and McCoy joins them.

Through the windows, the sniper's equipment is visible, scattered across the observation deck. Martinez kicks at the door leading to the deck, and the dolly, used as a barricade by the sniper, falls loudly. He strides bravely onto the observation deck, his .38-caliber revolver outstretched. Gunshots are coming from the northwest corner. Officer Martinez drops to his hands and knees and crawls toward the sound. McCoy, in an effort to support Martinez, lowers himself, walking with bent knees just behind his fellow officer. The gunman is not their only threat; they must dodge return fire from the ground. As the men work their way around the observation tower, the walls around them are repeatedly struck by stray bullets. The two men round the corner and see the gunman. Martinez fires several rounds but misses. The sniper turns wildly, but before he can level his gun, McCoy pulls the trigger of his shotgun. The sniper's eyes and nose are enveloped in a spray of buckshot. "Then it was over," Martinez recalls. "He was flat on his back, and I knew he was dead."[45] Civilian return fire continues for some time after, but at 1:24 p.m.—ninety-six minutes after he shot his first victim from the tower— the tower sniper is dead.

After the shooting, Officers Kidd and Gregory head to Whitman's home. Reporters are already gathered on the lawn, hoping to catch a glimpse of the widow. The officers knock; nobody answers. When they peer into a bedroom window, there is Kathy lying in bed, covered with a blanket. The officers cut their way through the screen. It does not take long for them to realize that she is not sleeping. The note, half typed and half handwritten, is long, and the officers are disturbed by its contents, especially the line: "Similar reasons provoked me to take my mother's life also."[46]

With the discoveries of Kathy and Margaret, two more deaths are added to the victim count. In total, sixteen people are dead, and thirty-two are injured. The police, though brave and willing to act, simply did not have the weaponry and organization needed to take on the sniper.

The autopsy of Whitman's brain reveals a glioblastoma tumor the size of a walnut. Damage to this part of the brain is known to cause wariness, fear, and rage. Whitman had sought professional help for his increasing inability to control his temper. His private journal is filled with remorse over his escalating outbursts of rage.

THE OUTRAGE

The inadequacy of the response to the Watts riots is still at the forefront of the nation's consciousness when Whitman goes on his shooting spree. A broad swath of the American public now feels vulnerable. The Watts riots increase Americans' fear of an urban, criminal minority class, but suddenly the suburbs aren't safe either. Whitman's crimes seem entirely random. Across the country, a terrifying thought materializes: *That could have happened here. Those kids could have been my kids.* "From that point on, the concept of mass murder was real," explains criminologist James Alan Fox. "It really changed Americans' feelings of safety."[47] Shaken civic leaders ask themselves if *their* police departments could handle situations like those in Watts and Austin.

LAPD Inspector Daryl Gates is no exception. Gates has been a favorite of LAPD Police Chief Parker for years, beginning in his early job as Parker's chauffeur. As he moves up the ranks, Gates blossoms into Parker's protégé, and is a key point man in the LAPD's response to the Watts riots. Throughout the violent week, Gates is horrified by the inability of law enforcement to manage the conflict. "We had no idea how to deal with this," Gates writes in his autobiography. "We were constantly ducking bottles, rocks, knives, and Molotov cocktails. . . . Guns were pointed out of second-story windows, random shots fired. . . . It was random chaos, in small disparate patches. We did not know how to handle guerrilla warfare. Rather than a single mob, we had people attacking from all directions."[48] Gates, like many, is also appalled by the University of Texas incident. Police in Austin, just as in Watts, lacked the right weaponry, the right tactics, and the right training.

For Gates, this is unacceptable: Never again, he vows, will police be caught off guard by a crisis, at least, not in *his* city. Gates is inspired by the strategy of the police department in Delano, a small town three hours north of Los Angeles. Faced with a series of labor strikes, the Delano police department, keen to prevent the strikes from becoming violent, began training individual officers in specific skills, including crowd control, sniper skills, riot response, and the use of specialized weapons. The tactic paid off, and the strikes stayed nonviolent. Perhaps, Gates thinks, the LAPD could learn a lesson.

Gates approaches the Parker administration with a radical new idea. Sending in thousands of unspecialized officers didn't work in Watts, he argues, and with civil conflict on the rise across the city, riots just like Watts could very well happen again. He proposes that the LAPD develop an elite police team trained specifically for riots, sniper incidents, and other emergencies. Soldiers in Vietnam have learned tactics to counter guerrilla-style warfare, and the LAPD could learn from this experience.

Gates's ideas are rebuffed immediately, but he doesn't abandon his vision. Gates and a few other LAPD officials begin consulting with marines stationed at the Naval Armory in Los Angeles. The group includes Sergeant John Nelson, a World War II veteran with specialized skills and an intimidating expertise in guerrilla warfare, and another tough officer named Jeff Rogers. All three men are determined to make Gates's idea a reality. They comb the police department, picking the best sharpshooters and sending them to the shooting range for training during off hours. They also bring in military personnel to teach tactics for dealing with snipers.

THE REFORM

The project is informal, but things change when Police Chief Parker dies in July of 1966. Thomas Reddin takes over the position. Soon after Reddin's term begins, a clash in the city between officers and antiwar protesters causes a public outcry. Footage from the scene, which shows officers beating protesters and onlookers and "ramming them with motorcycles,"[49] is broadcast across the country. Viewers are shocked, and Reddin responds by forming a unit called Tactical Operations Planning. The unit is designed to anticipate and respond to riots, protests, and other large-scale civil conflicts, or, as Reddin puts it succinctly, "roust anything strange that moves on the streets."[50] The unit is added to the city's Metropolitan Division, an elite team of officers with broad authority to "suppress criminal activity."[51] The addition boosts the Metro's numbers from 55 to 220 officers, and Reddin brings on a new leader: Daryl Gates.

This is the stepping-stone that Gates needs. His first task is to tackle a series of robberies on city buses. Gates requests more officers, but what the growing unit really needs is training and discipline. "Most of the divisions sent me the least desirable people they had,"[52] Gates says. Regardless, he's a driven leader, and his unit is able to dramatically reduce the bus robberies.

The next step is organization. Gates divides the unit into sixteen squads, and then combines squads into two platoons; his terminology reflects a militaristic structure, which looks nothing like the department's usual organization. Gates's vision is further solidified with the addition of the marksmen that he, Nelson, and Rogers have gathered. There are sixty of them, and all are now highly skilled and specialized. The Metro is becoming a force to be reckoned with.

Gates combines his marksmen with his best men from Tactical Operations Planning and breaks the unit into five-man teams. Each team has a leader, a marksman, an observer, a scout, and a rear guard. Two of these teams make up a squad, called D-Platoon. Gates finds this name clunky, so he proposes a new one to his deputy chief: SWAT, or Special Weapons Attack Teams. Gates's deputy doesn't like it. "There was no way, he said dismissively, he would ever use the word 'attack,'" Gates recalls.[53] "Attack" is too aggressive. After all, police don't attack—they protect. Gates likes his acronym, so he finds new words to fit: Special Weapons and Tactics.

Many of the higher-ups remain suspicious of the entire concept. "That SWAT operates like a quasi-militaristic operation offended some of the brass," he later recalls. Other officials are worried about SWAT using anything bigger than the standard department-issued weapons. "Officials balked at police using fully automatic weapons," Gates writes. "The standard cry was, 'Hey, the LAPD is supposed to be a civil police force.'"[54] But for Gates and his supporters, situations like those in Watts and Austin demand a swift, forceful response with weapons to match. "Don't throw away your guns," LAPD chief Reddin announces to colleagues, echoing Gates's sentiment. "Let us not be seduced by the naïve philosophy that foam dispensers or slippery substances can summarily pacify rioters, looters, and arsonists."[55]

In the beginning of 1968, a survey by the Associated Press reveals that in cities across America, "the police are stockpiling armored vehicles, helicopters, and high-powered rifles . . . They are preparing for summer and the riots they hope will not occur."[56] Departments purchase shotguns, sniper rifles, carbines, M-1 rifles, and gas masks. Gates's "military concept," it seems, is spreading.[57]

In 1969, a confrontation between LAPD SWAT and the Black Panthers catches the nation's eye. The Black Panther party has reached its peak, with ten thousand members in cities across the country.

In December of that year, the LAPD SWAT team targets a Black Panther building. Gates and the team have assembled building blueprints and develop a detailed plan to enter the building and capture everyone inside. As they begin the operation, history's first SWAT takeover, an unexpected dirt pile slows their surprise entrance. They're forced to enter through the front door instead of the back, and within seconds, a Black Panther lookout spots them. When they open the door, the team is greeted by gunfire, and three officers are shot (not fatally). The team retreats, and officers and Black Panther members exchange gunfire. The surrounding area is evacuated. After several hours, Gates's team is still unable to make headway with their guns. Gates decides that they need more powerful weaponry; he settles on a grenade launcher. He discovers that using a grenade launcher requires authorization from the Department of Defense, so Gates calls Mayor Yorty. Within an hour, Gates's grenade launcher request is granted. As soon as the device arrives, the Panthers wave a white flag to surrender.[58]

The team's success is a messy brand of luck; the tactics and logistics of the raid are scattered and muddled. The team overlooked obvious logistical challenges, most importantly that the back door was blocked by a pile of dirt. It also seems a bit of a miracle that nobody died, given that more than five thousand rounds of ammunition and dynamite were part of the exchange. "Oh God, we were lucky," says one SWAT officer involved in the raid. "I'm extremely proud of what we did that day. We got our targets and no one died. But oh God, were we lucky."[59]

Four years later, Gates's SWAT team is back on the front page. The Symbionese Liberation Army (SLA), a violent, radically leftist group in California, is becoming an ever growing threat. The group engages in an array of crimes, from robbery to murder. Their most famous crime is the kidnapping of Patty Hearst, the heiress to the Hearst family newspaper fortune.[60] On May 17, 1974, the LAPD locates key SLA members in a house in southeast Los Angeles. Twenty-five SWAT-team members surround the house. The SLA members are well equipped for a fight. They have six thousand rounds of ammunition, seventeen guns, and two pipe bombs. They have no intention of surrendering peacefully. The SWAT team and SLA exchange fire for nearly two hours. The building catches fire. By the time the SWAT team claims victory, two SLA women have been shot, and six other members are dead, two from gunshots and four from the fire.[61]

The shootout attracts a crowd of over ten thousand and is televised nationally. The operation's success is a boon for SWAT's popularity; after all, one of America's most feared radical groups has been neutralized, and nobody outside of the SLA was seriously injured.[62] Another successful raid reinforces public support for SWAT and eventually leads to Gates being promoted to chief of police in Los Angeles. The effect is felt beyond Los Angeles: within a year, "SWAT" has entered the American lexicon. A popular TV show called *S.W.A.T.* airs and brings with it an array of SWAT-themed merchandise for children: lunchboxes, board games, and action figures.[63]

By the mid-1970s, five hundred SWAT teams have been formed around the nation, including in smaller towns.[64] For some, the trend is worrisome; small-town SWAT members, often normal police officers who work in SWAT units part-time, are less skilled and less well trained than their large-city counterparts, whose training is rigorous and who focus on negotiation before force. SWAT was envisioned as a response unit for emergencies such as active shooters, armed robberies, and hostage situations, but as the previous chapter on the Harlem heroin epidemic shows, America is consumed by the drug problem. Police everywhere are scrambling to do their part in the War on Drugs, and police militarization is increasingly seen as an important part of that fight.

In 1981, Congress offers support for SWAT with the passage of the Military Cooperation with Civilian Law Enforcement Agencies Act. Before enactment of the law, police could receive only indirect assistance from the military, but now law enforcement has access to military intelligence, research, facilities, equipment, and even personnel. The law has an immediate effect: in 1984 alone, there are twenty thousand raids nationally, which utilize military spy planes, helicopters, high-tech weapons, and hundreds of guardsmen and law enforcement officers. Departments benefit from the raids financially, too, as property seized during raids is auctioned off, with proceeds going to the agency or police department in the investigation. Within seven years, the Justice Department's forfeiture fund increases by $617 million.

In 1986, the intersection between the War on Drugs and militarization of police becomes ever more entrenched. On April 8, the National Security Decision Directive 221 declares illegal drugs a threat to national security, calling for collaboration in the fight against illicit drug use. The secretary of defense and attorney general, it declares, should "enable U.S. military forces to support counter-narcotics efforts more actively, consistent with the maintenance of force readiness and training."[65] Money is offered to local police departments to enhance their SWAT teams and narcotic units.[66]

The incentives spur a growth in the number SWAT teams. In 1980, SWAT exists in 13.3 percent of cities with populations between 25,000 and 50,000; by 1990, that percentage reaches 52.1 percent. In that period, the average percentage of emergency situations to which SWAT teams are deployed increases from 3.7 to 10.3. Of cities with more than 50,000 people, 78 percent have SWAT teams by 1989, and 46 percent of all SWAT teams are trained by the military.[67]

By 1989, the National Guard has effectively been annexed to the police force. It boasts a budget of $40 million for antidrug operations, and the government "has redefined the Guard's mission to make activity against drugs as important as training for combat."[68] Along with highly trained units, the Guard brings an arsenal of equipment: helicopters, planes, advanced weaponry, and specialized equipment like night-vision goggles. Under a 1988 law, guardsmen are also permitted to search vehicles, buildings, or private property without a warrant. Some people are nervous about blurring the line between military and civilian policing, but critics risk biting personal attacks. As one California representative declares, "It depends which is more sacred, that line or your children's lives."[69]

The National Guard only grows more involved in policing efforts during the 1990s. In its second year of antinarcotics involvement, it's awarded $70 million for the War on Drugs; in its third year, it's awarded $237 million. In 1992, the National Guard aids in the arrest of almost 20,000 people, searches 120,000 vehicles and 1,200 private buildings, and enters private property 6,500 times.[70] "Symbolically," explains researcher Radley Balko, "the National Guard bridges the gap between cop and soldier. . . . Giving the Guard a more prominent role in the drug war not only escalates the drug fight, but it further conditions the country to the idea of using military force for domestic law enforcement."[71]

During this same period of time, however, police militarization begins to undergo some scrutiny. In 1991, after LAPD officers are acquitted of brutally beating a black man named Rodney King, angry rioters take to the streets for four days. SWAT teams are unable to regain control, and the National Guard is again deployed to return order to Los Angeles. The nation feels a surge of anti-SWAT sentiments, and Daryl Gates is forced to resign as head of the LAPD.[72]

A MATURING VIEW OF SWAT

In the wake of the Rodney King riots, some department heads seek policy changes. San Diego police chief Norm Stamper, for example, hopes to demilitarize his department and put an end to the use of military terminology in local law enforcement ranks. Another California police lieutenant argues that SWAT teams are being overused, with cities desperate to justify their investments in police militarization.[73] In Connecticut, the New Haven police chief is very public about his discomfort with the shift in attitudes about the role of police. Police, he claims, should aim to help the community, not fight a war. "The police were driven by fear and adventure," he says. "SWAT was a big part of that."[74]

Despite some scattered pushback, the integration of SWAT into American police departments continues. The Department of Justice and Department of Defense formally agree to share technology and equipment, allowing the development of high-tech grenades, sound cannons, armor, and wireless monitoring devices, bringing those technologies to American cities of all sizes.[75]

The 1990s also see an increase in veterans-turned-police. The "Troops to Cops" program offers grants to police departments that hire former armed services members, with program advocates claiming that veterans are ideal applicants. "The police department has the same command structure," explains police officer Steve Hagen. "You have to follow orders and procedures. Law enforcement, being paramilitary, fits in very well with prior military service."[76]

In 1997, a California bank robbery prompts another surge in pro-SWAT sentiment. On February 28, Larry Phillips Jr. and Emil Matasareanu, wearing ski masks and armed with rifles, handguns, an HK-91 semiautomatic rifle, and an automatic AR-15, steal $300,000 from a North Hollywood bank. When the robbers exit the bank, a flurry of frenzied gunfire erupts in a firefight with LAPD police officers surrounding the bank. The bank robbers seem immune to the police rounds because they are decked out in full-body bulletproof armor, and police weapons are inadequate to penetrate the armor. Several officers go to local gun shops to get appropriate equipment. It's not until the LAPD SWAT teams arrive that order is restored. After forty-four minutes and two thousand rounds of gunfire, both bank robbers are finally dead, but twenty others are injured, police officers and civilians alike.[77]

Millions of Americans witness the shoot-out on television. Police departments decide they won't wait for SWAT in times of crisis; instead, cops themselves must be prepared. Across the country, regular law enforcement rushes to acquire semiautomatic rifles, and paramilitary training increases dramatically.[78] With criminals now gaining equipment like that of the North Hollywood bank robbers, SWAT and the heavy-weapons approach no longer seems to be something that Americans can live without.[79]

Police militarization has continued since the 9/11 attacks in 2001. The newly formed Department of Homeland Security has distributed grants to police departments nationwide to help them prepare to counter terrorist attacks or other large-scale violence. However, the grants are used to purchase military equipment that is frequently deployed in drug raids. Before long, police forces in towns and cities alike can buy "military-grade armored vehicles, guns, armor, aircraft, and other equipment."[80] By 2011, the Department of Homeland Security has dispersed at least $34 billion in an effort to prepare local communities for terrorist attacks.

It is not possible to predict where dangerous events will occur, so SWAT seems to be needed everywhere. On the afternoon of April 15, 2013, two bombs explode near the finish line of the popular Boston Marathon, killing three people and injuring 264 others. In 108 hours, the terrorists are identified. SWAT teams are dispatched, and the perpetrators, armed and aggressive, are found in a residential neighborhood. One terrorist is killed, but his partner escapes. Soon after, the escapee is found in Watertown, Massachusetts. The North Metro SWAT unit swarms the area, eventually taking the terrorist into custody. "We're professionals," explains the unit's chief. "We're law enforcement. We're not an execution team."[81]

By 2014, 80 percent of communities with populations between 25,000 and 50,000 have SWAT teams, and the FBI has 56 teams. There are more than 80,000 SWAT raids per year. Sixty-two percent are drug related, and 79 percent are in private homes. Beyond the original role of these specialty units, responding to riots and active shooters, SWAT-type units are now used in response to many types of crimes, including those related to drugs, gambling, immigration, child pornography, and even alcohol inspections.

Federal funds are offered to police departments that prioritize drug crimes. Therefore, it is not a surprise that departments strive for more drug-related warrants, arrests, and seizures. To meet their goals, departments form thousands of drug task forces. Although the task forces are made up of local police, they often resemble SWAT teams and hence are eligible to receive federal funding. These factors—heavily armed officers, financial incentives for drug crackdowns, and variable training regimes—create the conditions for abuse.[82]

Some raids become particularly infamous; one such raid occurred in the tiny, five thousand–person town of Tulia, Texas. On July 23, 1999, a drug task force, armed and dressed in SWAT gear, raids dozens of homes, tearing people from their beds in front of television cameras. Forty-six people are arrested, forty of whom are black, but no drugs or weapons are discovered. Before long, the cases begin to fall apart: the officer who conducted the investigation, Tom Coleman, gives suspect testimony. The drug transactions that prompted the raids turn out to be fictitious, and nearly all of the defendants have alibis. Thirty-five of the people arrested are pardoned by the governor and receive a $5.9 million settlement. Coleman is convicted of aggravated perjury and sentenced to ten years' probation.[83]

Other drug raids result in tragedy. During a house raid in 2000, a SWAT team orders an eleven-year-old boy to lie facedown on the floor. An officer holds a gun to the boy's head, and although the boy follows orders, the gun goes off, killing him. No drugs or guns are found in the home.[84] In 2008, a SWAT team in Ohio opens fire in the home of a twenty-six-year-old woman, killing her and injuring her fourteen-month-old son; the team had entered to search for her boyfriend. In 2010, a SWAT team in Massachusetts raids the home of a sixty-eight-year-old man. The man complies with orders to lie on the ground, but a SWAT team member trips, discharging his gun and killing the man.

Police militarization remains a hotly debated topic. For many people, SWAT teams have expanded far beyond the purpose for which they were originally created. They argue that an increasingly militarized police force alienates police from the communities they serve, eroding public trust and undermining the peace that police aim to keep. Law enforcement should focus on efforts like community policing and recruiting more people of color, not investing in military-grade weapons.

Others are reassured by police militarization. If criminals have access to dangerous weapons, and terrorists can launch civilian attacks, then the authorities must be in a position to meet that challenge. For many, traumatic events like school shootings, public bombings, and riots prove the necessity of police militarization and police collaboration with the National Guard and other military units. They would agree that SWAT teams must be used carefully and thoughtfully, but demilitarization would simply be too risky.

It would be nice to think that the Watts riots and the University of Texas Tower sniper killings are unique events but, unfortunately, it seems more likely that such tragedies will continue to be a regular part of our future. The challenge is to be fully ready for whatever new emergencies might arise, without losing the effectiveness of everyday community policing.

Chapter Ten

1967
Calabrese Intimidation
WITSEC

THE TRAGEDY

Gerald Shur isn't used to seeing bodies. The photograph he's holding makes him nauseated. In it, a woman with a slit throat is sprawled across the floor.[1] She's sliced open from neck to navel, and her organs, pulled from her body, are arranged in a gruesome display. The woman had agreed to be an FBI informant in a case against a Mafia member. Now dead, she is being used to send a message to other witnesses: if you spill your guts to the authorities, the Mafia will actually spill your guts. This powerful rule—talk and die—is known as *omertà*.

It's October 1961, and Shur is a rookie attorney in the U.S. Department of Justice's Organized Crime and Racketeering Section in Washington, D.C. The woman's murder is hardly unique; she's the twenty-fifth government informant to die at the hands of the mob in the last five years. No witness testimony means no criminal convictions. Mafia members have stayed safe in courtrooms.

Testifying in court against a Mafia member is a death wish for a witness or their family. In 1942, for example, Carl Carramusa, a Kansas City mobster, testified against the Mafia and fled to Chicago with his family, but three years later, on his wedding anniversary, the mob caught up with him. He was shot in the face while waiting at a stoplight.[2] In 1961, another mobster, named Albert Agueci, threatened to go to authorities with information on a mob boss. Agueci's burned body was found soon after, with thirty pounds of flesh missing, teeth knocked out, arms and legs broken, hands bound with barbed wire, jaw shattered, and genitals severed and stuffed in his own mouth. He'd been tortured for days.[3]

Shur slides the photograph of the dead woman back into its file, feeling ill. "Omerta was very, very real," Shur later says, "and we had plenty of photographs of dead bodies in our files to prove it."[4] Fear is a powerful reason to avoid challenging the mob, and later that day Shur sees this fear firsthand. He receives a call from an Internal Revenue Service agent. "We got a promising lead," the agent announces.[5] The owner of a trucking company had been confronted by two men working for a mobster named John "Sonny" Franzese. "These guys tell me Sonny Franzese wants to be my new business partner," the owner tells Shur when they meet. When the owner refuses, the goons damage one of his new trucks and beat him unconscious. To save his own life, the owner is forced to sign over half his business.

"If you testify," Shur explains, "we can tie Franzese directly to extortion and send him to prison for a minimum of five to ten years." The man is flabbergasted. "The mob will kill me and my entire family if I testify," he says. "No way am I speaking out against Sonny Franzese!"[6] Despite the threat to his business, the man, like most potential witnesses, believes it too dangerous to work with the authorities.

FIRST STEPS

Shur knows that something has to change. Without a way to keep witnesses safe, the Mafia will remain untouchable. "I began writing memos telling people we needed to set up a program to protect government witnesses," Shur remembers. "I wasn't just thinking about criminals. I was thinking about honest citizens, too, people like the Long Island trucking company owner whom I'd asked to testify against Sonny Franzese."[7]

In 1964, Congress's legislative agenda is already packed full. President Johnson is working toward new civil rights legislation and conducting the Vietnam War. Wave after wave of domestic unrest keeps Washington power brokers busy. An anti-mob agency like Shur's, particularly their use of wiretaps, which keeps making the papers, is an unwelcome distraction. The Mafia only stays on the agenda because Attorney General Robert Kennedy insists that the mob is a significant problem. In an effort to get the Mafia problem off the front pages, but to satisfy Kennedy that progress is being made, a strike force with representatives from several agencies is assembled. The strike force is to focus on addressing mob activity in one place: Buffalo, New York. The Buffalo mob is headed by Stefano Magaddino, an Italian-born mob boss with near-legendary viciousness. Magaddino gave the order for the brutal torture of Albert Agueci—all in a day's work for the seasoned mobster.[8]

The strike force needs to learn about the Mafia to make progress, but no one is stepping up to provide the information. That changes when one of the Magaddino family members, Pascal "Paddy" Calabrese, announces that he is willing to talk. Calabrese, a young and violent mobster, is serving time for a bank robbery in 1964.[9] Calabrese feels betrayed by Magaddino. The rules are clear: "if a member got into trouble, the crime family was supposed to take care of his family while he was doing time in prison," explains attorney Robert Peloquin, "but Magaddino was a cheap old man."[10] Magaddino declines to care for Calabrese's girlfriend and her children. A Buffalo police sergeant, Sam Giambrone, has been providing for the family out of his own pay. The relationship is now bearing fruit for the authorities.

Calabrese, like all mobsters, is fully aware of the consequences of becoming a witness. If he's going to testify, Calabrese says, he'll need a few things in return. He wants out of jail, and he wants his girlfriend, Rochelle, and her kids to be moved out of Buffalo and provided with new identities.

The strike force agrees. On February 27, 1967, Calabrese identifies the major players in the Magaddino family and the notable crimes they have committed. He's able to strongly implicate two mobsters in particular, and the men are arrested. Meanwhile, Rochelle and her children are stashed in a temporary hiding spot, the Strategic Air Command military base in Maine.

Now Magaddino is livid; he is the one who has been betrayed. He launches a manhunt for Calabrese and his family, and it's rumored that he'll pay $100,000 to their finders. Mobsters search the city, terrorizing the couple's neighbors, friends, family, even a former barber. As Magaddino's frustration rises, strike force members start getting threatening phone calls. To increase security, strike force members begin traveling in pairs. Some agents even send their families out of town. Sergeant Giambrone, who had been supporting Calabrese's girlfriend, decides he needs to go on the offensive. He and a Bureau of Narcotics agent drive to the Magaddino family estate in Niagara Falls. Giambrone knocks on the door, and when Magaddino answers, Giambrone speaks in a language the mobster can understand: he yanks out his gun and shoves it in Magaddino's mouth. "If one more phone call comes in or anyone attempts to do harm to my family or anyone else's on the strike force," he hisses, "we are going to come back and blow your fucking head off."[11] Magaddino gets the message; the phone calls stop.

In late 1967, the two of the men fingered by Calabrese go to trial. Calabrese keeps his convincing cool under aggressive cross-examinations, and both men are found guilty and sentenced to twenty years. The strike

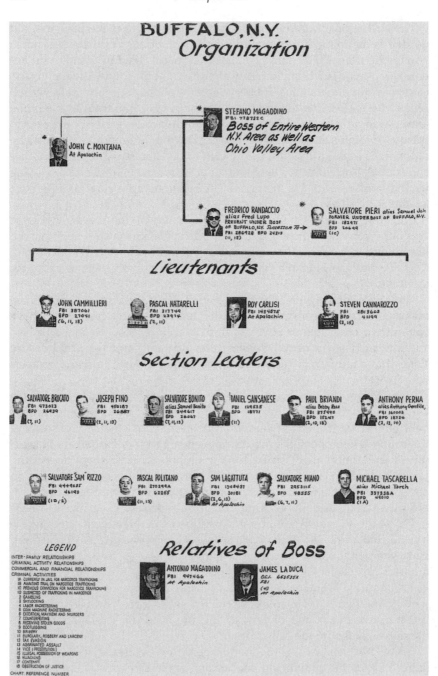

BUFFALO, N.Y.
Organization

STEFANO MAGADDINO
FBI 778722C
Boss of Entire Western N.Y. Area as well as Ohio Valley Area

JOHN C. MONTANA
At Apalachin

FREDRICO RANDACCIO
alias Fred Lupo
PRESENT UNDER BOSS
of BUFFALO, N.Y. Successor TO →
FBI 286428 BPD 24213
(11, 18)

SALVATORE PIERI alias Samuel Joh
FORMER UNDERBOSS OF BUFFALO, N.Y.
FBI 182471
BPD 20699
(16)

Lieutenants

JOHN CAMMILLIERI
FBI 387061
BPD 27041
(6, 11, 18)

PASCAL NATARELLI
FBI 317799
BPD 23974
(2, 11)

ROY CARLISI
FBI 1434575
At Apalachin

STEVEN CANNAROZZO
FBI 2813603
BPD 41199
(2, 15)

Section Leaders

SALVATORE BROCATO
FBI 473023
BPD 26439
(7, 11)

JOSEPH FINO
FBI 450187
BPD 26887
(2, 11, 13)

SALVATORE BONITO
alias Samuel Bonito
FBI 244617
BPD 26047
(7, 11, 13)

DANIEL SANSANESE
FBI 129535
BPD 18771
(11)

PAUL BRIANDI
alias Bobby Ross
FBI 375490
BPD 18247
(2, 10, 18)

ANTHONY PERNA
alias Anthony Gentile
FBI 160008
BPD 18724
(2, 13, 14)

SALVATORE "SAM" RIZZO
FBI 4449635
BPD 46198
(10/2)

PASCAL POLITANO
FBI 270299A
BPD 62265
(11, 13)

SAM LAGATTUTA
FBI 1348431
BPD 30181
(2, 6, 13)
At Apalachin

SALVATORE MIANO
FBI 2653115
BPD 48555
(6, 7, 11)

MICHAEL TASCARELLA
alias Michael Torch
FBI 357338A
BPD 49010
(1 A)

Relatives of Boss

LEGEND
INTER- FAMILY RELATIONSHIPS
CRIMINAL ACTIVITY RELATIONSHIPS
COMMERCIAL AND FINANCIAL RELATIONSHIPS
CRIMINAL ACTIVITIES
1A CURRENTLY IN JAIL FOR NARCOTICS TRAFFICKING
1B AWAITING TRIAL ON NARCOTICS TRAFFICKING
1C PREVIOUS CONVICTION FOR NARCOTICS TRAFFICKING
1D SUSPECTED OF TRAFFICKING IN NARCOTICS
2 GAMBLING
3 SKYLOCKING
4 LABOR RACKETEERING
5 COIN MACHINE RACKETEERING
6 EXTORTION, MAYHEM AND MURDERS
7 COUNTERFEITING
8 RECEIVING STOLEN GOODS
9 BOOTLEGGING
10 BRIBERY
11 BURGLARY, ROBBERY AND LARCENY
12 TAX EVASION
13 AGGRAVATED ASSAULT
14 VICE (PROSTITUTION)
15 ILLEGAL POSSESSION OF WEAPONS
16 HIJACKING
17 CONTEMPT
18 OBSTRUCTION OF JUSTICE
CHART REFERENCE NUMBER

ANTONIO MAGADDINO
FBI 942466
At Apalachin

JAMES LA DUCA
OCI 6615255
FBI
(4)
At Apalachin

Figure 10.1.   The structure of the Buffalo crime famililes, 1967. *Buffalo Police*

force is so grateful that it advocates for Calabrese's immediate parole, which the state parole board grants.

What now? The task force faces a problem. "Suddenly we had to figure out what to do with him," recalls Organized Crime and Racketeering Section (OCRS) attorney Thomas Kennelly, "and none of us had a clue."[12] As soon as he hit the streets, Magaddino's men would kill him, or worse. The strike force has to find a way to keep Calabrese and his family safe. Kennelly starts with the obvious: a name change. They choose "Angelo," and someone on the strike force convinces a reluctant priest to give the family fake baptismal certificates with their fake names. Another strike force member persuades a school superintendent to do the same with the names on the children's academic records. One of the attorneys has a brother in Michigan who runs a manufacturing plant. They arrange for Calabrese to work there. Then, the team scrapes together over a thousand dollars, mostly from their own pockets, to help Calabrese jumpstart his new life.[13]

Calabrese, unaccustomed to "normal" life, struggles to adjust, but the strike force has accomplished something that was recently too fantastical to believe: Calabrese and his family are alive. Yes, the process has been choppy; scraping together finances from officers is unsustainable, and it will be tough for families to make the transition, but it is an important victory nonetheless.

The Justice Department's problem is not unique. Around this same time, the FBI is facing a similar conundrum. Joseph "The Animal" Barboza is a seasoned contract killer with at least twenty murders under his belt. Most of Barboza's hits have been ordered by Mafia boss Raymond L. S. Patriarca, who dominates organized crime in Massachusetts, but Barboza has turned to the authorities. He had been arrested in October of 1966 on minor charges, and he expected Patriarca to post his bail, as usual. Instead, Patriarca killed three of Barboza's closest friends and put out a contract on him.

Under other circumstances, Barboza would certainly maintain omertà and keep his knowledge of Patriarca to himself. But with a contract out on his life, informing to the agents seems to be a reasonable gamble. When Barboza agrees to testify, the U.S. Marshals Service sends one of its ablest deputies to protect Barboza's family: John J. Partington, a young, sharp, and experienced officer.

Partington is struck by the difference between the hit man and his family. Twenty-something Janice Barboza is courteous, bright, and beautiful. Their daughter, Terri, is three years old and charming. "I wanted them to live as normal a life as possible while we were protecting them," Partington recalls.[14] Over the next month, he spends sixteen hours a day with them and, despite his natural hesitation, grows close to the family. "A lot of deputies didn't like protecting witnesses or their families because they considered them scum, but I didn't feel that way," he later says. "What had Barboza's little girl ever done?"[15] Terri calls him "Uncle John," and Partington does whatever he can to make their lives enjoyable. He sets up outings for Janice to the beach and a local nightclub, and he even brings his own wife, Helen, to visit with the family.[16]

Barboza, as sinister as he is, keeps his word. He provides vital information to authorities about Patriarca. In May of 1967, authorities have enough to arrest Patriarca for conspiracy to commit murder.

Patriarca announces that he will pay $300,000 to the person who kills his accuser. The FBI decides to move Barboza and his family to Thacher Island, a half-mile clump of rock off the coast of Gloucester, Massachusetts. The island houses two old lighthouses and some scattered wildlife, but no people call it home, making it perfect as a hiding place. Partington and his sixteen deputies are armed, trained, and ready to kill anyone who threatens the family. Partington catches wind that two hit men are approaching the island by yacht, so he and his men stand outside with carbines in clear view. The would-be hit men see the marshals and leave. But when a Boston newspaper runs a story with the gangster's location, Partington must scramble to transport the family out by helicopter.

As the trial date approaches, the risks increase. For Barboza to testify, he has to appear in court. The hitmen will not need to guess where their target is. Partington's biggest challenge is transporting Barboza into and out of the courthouse. On the day of Barboza's first scheduled appearance, at least five hitmen loiter outside, some with heavy weaponry. What they do not realize is that Partington had smuggled Barboza inside the courthouse three days prior. Steel plates are welded over the courthouse storeroom where Barboza is hidden to prevent bombs from being thrown in, and mobsters' attempts to get inside the courthouse are thwarted. Even when a car bomb costs Barboza's attorney his leg, the testimony continues.

Patriarca's trial is only the first step. Barboza testifies for months, shredding Patriarca's crime network. Barboza and his family remain safe. After the last trial, they're sent to Fort Knox, Tennessee. Partington is thrilled with his success. "We'd taken on the mob and we'd won," he recalls. "Trust me, there were lots of guys in the mob watching us, and the fact we'd protected Barboza and kept him alive gave them plenty to think about. We'd proved it could be done."[17]

"Protecting someone with guards, the way the government had done in the Barboza case, was expensive and dangerous," says Gerald Shur. "It also caused a witness problem in the long run."[18] Shur is certain that there is a better solution, and he's keen to see it realized. In 1966, Shur volunteers to take over the Organized Crime and Racketeering Section witnesses, and in particular, the tedious paperwork that nobody wants to do. Before long, Shur is the department's de facto witness manager. "I had been in the Justice Department long enough to realize that if I could get control of the money, by volunteering to be the person in OCRS who handled the paperwork, I could begin to establish procedures about how our witnesses would be protected."[19] He begins using money from a small department fund called Fees and Expenses for Witnesses to cover the costs of hiding witnesses. He didn't think the operation would ever be a big one; he predicted only about ten witnesses a year would need protection. In his view, the best source of safety is anonymity. "The best way to keep a witness safe was by moving him . . . to a place where no one knew who he was," Shur later recalls.[20]

THE REFORM

Finally, in early 1967, Shur's ideas are relayed to the deputy director of the President's Commission Task Force on Organized Crime, Henry Ruth Jr., who writes them up for a full panel review. By February, the final report is presented to President Johnson and includes two of Shur's recommendations: first, that local and state police departments use computer databases to track the mob, and second, that a formal witness protection program be established. "I jumped on that report," Shur later says. "It was exactly what I needed to really get the ball rolling."[21]

Shur's fledgling operation is still unrecognized by law, but regardless, witnesses, inspired by the department's success with Barboza, begin pouring in, willing to testify under the protection of authorities. The availability of witnesses accelerates the fight against organized crime, and the number of criminal cases against mobsters nearly doubles between 1968 and 1970. Relocating witnesses, Shur decides, requires at least three documents: a new birth certificate, a driver's license, and a Social Security card. Everyone in the family gets a new name, though all participants keep their original first name to prevent mistakes. For witnesses with children, school records are added to the list. Shur himself contacts state attorneys, reluctant DMV directors, and Social Security officials to pull together the documents. School records are copied with new names.[22]

Shur, for the most part, improvises as he goes along. Finding his witnesses jobs is a daunting task; many of them have never worked legitimate jobs, and their skills aren't exactly résumé friendly. "Well, they can kill, steal, embezzle, and sell drugs, and most of them are members of the Cosa Nostra," Shur says sarcastically.[23]

Without a doubt, the process is painful for witnesses and their families. Criminals are hard to sympathize with, but "what few realized was there were usually innocent people behind each of these criminals," Shur explains. "Their wives, children, parents, and other relatives all suffered.... This was a program of last resort."[24]

To make things more complicated, there is no legislation that formalizes Shur's operation. His projects are financed by the Justice Department's expert witness and witness travel fund, and his career has been consumed by the growing number of witnesses.

But in 1969, Senator John L. McClellan introduces the RICO Act, a crime bill aimed at fighting the mob. (The legislation is also discussed in the chapter "1957 Apalachin Mafia Commission Meeting—RICO.") For Shur, the most significant portion of the bill is a short section entitled "Title V: Protected Facilities for Housing Government Witnesses,"[25] which requires the federal government to "Establish residential facilities for the protection of witnesses desiring such assistance during the pendency of organized crime litigation."[26] The title encourages witness protection by any means necessary, and it gives the Department of Justice (DOJ) enormous discretion.[27] For Shur, Title V contains exactly what he needs, but he asks McClellan to add a critical line: "The Attorney General shall provide for the care and protection of witnesses in whatever manner is deemed most useful under the special circumstances of each case."[28] Simple, but powerful. On October 15, 1970, the Organized Crime Control Act is signed into law, thereby creating the Witness Protection Program (WPP) under Title V.[29]

Soon after, Shur proposes that the Marshals Service take over the responsibility of protecting witnesses. "The Marshals Service's priority would be keeping a witness alive, not rewarding him for his testimony, and this was a distinction I wanted jurors to understand," Shur explains.[30] Shur continues to oversee the program under the U.S. Marshals Service, now called the Witness Security Program, or WITSEC.[31]

In 1977, the DOJ creates the Witness Security Program Review Committee (WSPRC) to review WITSEC's effectiveness and suggest improvements. Major points of interest include parent-child relationship problems, the need to allow third parties to enforce judgments against relocated witnesses, the delivery of program services, and renewed criminal activity by relocated witnesses.

The Review Committee concludes that the interests of the general public should be given more weight. The committee recommends more controlled entry into WITSEC with stricter eligibility requirements and a program review board to advise the attorney general. In 1983, the comptroller general also recommends a better balance between the interests of the public and WITSEC participants, as well as more structured selection criteria.

After all of these refinements, the application process for WITSEC has been tightened and standardized. U.S. attorneys' offices and Organized

Crime Strike Forces across the country submit applications to the program for key witnesses in federal cases and to a lesser extent in state prosecutions. The Justice Department's Office of Enforcement Operations (OEO) makes WPP entry determinations, but the attorney general or his or her designee makes the final decision. The attorney general must consider the possibility of obtaining the testimony from another source, the importance of the testimony, recommendations by the Marshals Service, and psychological evaluations of the witness (used to determine the witness's risk to the community after relocation).

If accepted for the program, a witness's old identity is erased. Participants can choose their new names, as long as the names are ethnically compatible and aren't previously used or family names. They receive the same three key documents originally provided by Shur (birth certificate, driver's license, and Social Security card), and diplomas that correspond to their actual schooling level. The protected witness does not get a prefabbed credit history.

After this, the participant heads to a secret "safe site" and orientation center in Washington, D.C., a location with no address. Here, the participants are familiarized with their new documentation and the area they'll live in. WPP discourages participants from communicating with people from their previous life, though occasionally they may initiate, but never receive, phone calls or messages through a secure mail-forwarding system. The program provides participants with a set amount of money for necessities like rent, clothing, furniture, and vehicles.

Even when the participants are relocated, they're not alone. They receive rigorous training on how best to adapt to a new life. Over 160 witness security inspectors are situated throughout the country to protect and aid participants, and 150 deputy U.S. marshals are available for backup assistance. Seven secret safe sites, called "Protective Custody Units" (PCUs), are scattered throughout the country's major cities, intended for use when a witness needs protection during an emergency, or when the witness must make a court appearance in these cities.[32]

Jail is also made safer for incarcerated WITSEC participants. (There are a number of reasons that a WITSEC participant might be in jail; for instance, he or she may already have been convicted of a previous crime.) Each PCU has a regulated control room that monitors entries into each unit, with only select individuals allowed in. The warden of each unit determines who makes the cut. All outside vendors, clergy, Bureau of Prisons (BOP) staff, and contractors must receive preclearance from the warden. Incarcerated participants are transported from jail to court via the WITSEC Escort program, regulated by the Bureau of Prisons.[33]

BEYOND REFORM

When Shur first made his pitch for WITSEC, the government expected that the Witness Protection Program would be used for thirty to fifty people per year. But by early 1970, Shur realizes he'd underestimated the demand when an average of one mob witness a week seeks protection. It only grows after the program is formalized by statute that same year. By 1997, twenty to twenty-five witnesses are added each month. To date, over sixteen thousand witnesses and their dependents have entered the program.

The ever-growing program is not without its flaws. On the one hand, the program draws criticism for excessive expenditures and lenient witness-selection policies. Criticisms are bolstered when some participants drift back into criminal activity. In July of 1976, Benjamin Rosado, whose convictions include burglary, auto theft, armed robbery, incest, and rape, begins his life as Mr. Russo. Just two months later, in September, the federally protected witness kills Missouri police officer Fred Bergman during a robbery.

WITSEC tries to respect local law enforcement, but critics argue that "the witness protection statutes contemplate[d] only the protection of witnesses and their families—not protection of the public from the witness."[34] Some argue that local laws and law enforcement have less influence on the participants in the program than they should. Many argue that participants hide behind their new identities, able to violate child-custody and visitation agreements, commit new crimes, escape their debt obligations, and more. From 1978 to 1982, two hundred witnesses in the program are rearrested for new criminal charges, and by 1984, ten murders are committed by WITSEC participants.

On the other hand, other critics argue that the program does not do enough to protect witnesses. Because the program does not accept everyone who requests protection, 10 percent of all murders linked to organized crime from 1974 to 1978 are those of prosecution witnesses. Some individuals who come forward to authorities are not provided with security, even after prosecutors make explicit promises of support.[35] Courts determine that protected witnesses have no guaranteed right to receive program benefits promised by the government[36] and that the government's failure to protect a witness, or failure to hold a hearing on program participation, does not violate constitutional rights.[37]

Moreover, even witnesses who are accepted into the program without a hitch grow increasingly frustrated throughout the 1970s over "poorly delivered promises" and "erratic assistance."[38] Many witnesses accuse the Justice Department of failing to take even basic precautions, such as making the identity workable or removing cyber connections between the old identity and the new protected one. At least one program participant commits suicide because he does not feel safe and supported in his new life. [39]

Alarmingly, a 2008 report found dangerous gaps in protections for inmates participating in WITSEC. For one, the SENTRY database, used to store information about individuals who pose a threat to WITSEC inmates, was not being used. Researchers reviewed the case files of forty-seven WITSEC inmates and identified at least 120 fellow inmates who posed a threat to twenty-three of them. Because the Bureau of Prisons did not have identifying information that could have been obtained through the SENTRY database, the 120 inmates weren't properly flagged. The system design made it impossible for prison personnel to know if they were housing a WITSEC participant with someone who posed a threat to the witness.

Additionally, BOP employees with access to WITSEC inmates and their information don't receive up-to-date background checks, it is argued, and aren't required to sign secrecy agreements. Background checks are updated every five years, but given how sensitive the information is and how dangerous its leakage could be, it is argued by some that better oversight is required.

Despite its problems, WITSEC has still been largely successful. In twenty-six years, the DOJ has had no participant killed as a result of program involvement, and 80 percent of participants report feeling safe in the program. No WITSEC participant has ever been physically harmed while in BOP custody, and to this day, The U.S. Marshals Service boasts that no participants who adhere to their guidelines have been harmed.

Interestingly, over 97 percent of witnesses entering the program have a rich criminal history, but relocated witnesses have a significantly lower recidivism rate than the regular prison population. The U.S. Marshals Service reports, "[t]he recidivism rate for witnesses with prior criminal histories who entered the program and were later arrested and charged with crimes is less than twenty-three percent. This rate of recidivism among program participants is less than half the rate of those released from the nation's prisons." [40]

Many prosecutors see WITSEC as "the most valuable tool that they have in fighting organized crime and major criminal activity." [41] The data seem to support that belief: 89 percent of cases that utilize WITSEC end with successful convictions. Whatever its flaws, WITSEC is a powerful crime-fighting tool.

Chapter Eleven

1969
Santa Barbara Oil Spill and
Cuyahoga River Fire

Environmental Protection Agency

THE TRAGEDY—SANTA BARBARA OIL SPILL

A drilling pipe is extracted from a newly tapped oil well on the ocean floor, six miles off the coast of Santa Barbara.[1] The borehole is deep—3,500 feet to be exact. At that depth, there is a significant amount of pressure on the walls of the well. To prevent it from collapsing in on itself as the pipe is withdrawn, the crew pumps in mud from above. But somehow under the intense pressure, a bubble of natural gas ignites; causing an undersea explosion that cracks the ocean floor and pushes the mud back out of the well. Once the mud has been forced from the well, the flow does not stop; oil begins spewing into the ocean. This explosion in the Dos Cuadros Offshore Oil Fields on January 28, 1969, is the first time a well like this has ruptured, and no one quite knows what to do. A massive effort is undertaken to close the maze of cracks at the base of the well. After eleven days, crews finally inject a chemical mud that seals the cracks from which the oil is flowing. While this mud successfully seals the leaking well, the damage has been done: approximately three million gallons of oil have escaped into the ocean. Five days later on February 12, new rifts in the ocean bed are discovered.

The spill comes as a shock to Santa Barbara residents, who until now have lived in a natural paradise. To the south, the city is hugged by the Pacific Ocean, and in the north rise the Santa Ynez Mountains, green with sage scrub and coastal woodlands. The area is rich in biodiversity; birds, reptiles, deer, and coyotes call the mountains home, and the coastal waters, filled with nutrients from cold, northern currents, teem with marine life and seabirds. The blue sky and sea make it an idyllic resort town, and the city's beauty is as important for tourists as it is for residents. Home prices are high, and lots of upper-class families live in the area.

Santa Barbara's citizens always knew there was a risk that a disaster like this could happen, so for over fifteen years they fought to prevent drilling in their coastal waters. In February of 1968, they were dealt a significant blow when the federal government gave the go-ahead for oil leasing in federal waters. California state waters, meaning waters within three miles of its coast, remained free of oil rigs and drilling. But the rigs established in federal waters on the Dos Cuadros Offshore Oil Fields were still visible from the coast.

By January 1969, the new rigs are busy. On Platform A, four wells have already been drilled by Union Oil Company of California, or Unocal, and workers are finishing the fifth when the seafloor ruptures. At the company's request, the U.S. Geological Survey waived requirements for the standard well casing, which prevents oil and gas from escaping the surrounding seabed. The protective casing around the drilling hole is sixty-one feet shorter than what is federally mandated. This shortcut plays a significant role the subsequent spill.

There is no workable plan to clean up the oil, so cleanup crews resort to trial and error. Volunteers try soaking up the floating oil with straw, which is then moved to a nearby canyon. But heavy rains rinse the straw free of the oil, which allows the oil to flow right back into the ocean. Oil is scraped directly off the water's surface, and new slicks appear almost immediately. The entire Santa Barbara coastline and much of the neighboring coast is coated in thick tar-like oil that smells as pernicious as it looks. In all, some thirty to thirty-five miles of California coast becomes sodden with crude oil. Efforts to clear the beaches of contaminated sand are repeatedly frustrated because as soon as a beach is cleaned, it is quickly soiled again. The thick and heavy oil that blankets the waters silences the sound of the waves as they break.

The impact on wildlife is dramatic. Over ten thousand seabirds, dolphins, seals, and sea lions are killed. Plovers, godwits, and willets, birds that usually feed on beaches, disappear from the area and escape to clean shores. Bird species that spend time in the ocean such as grebes, cormorants, and pelicans, are not so lucky. Oil-soaked feathers lose their waterproofing, and many of the birds become susceptible to hypothermia. Birds also ingest too much oil and die. Within days of the blowout, dead and dying seabirds, their bodies drenched in oil, appear on the beaches. Rescued birds are taken to the Santa Barbara Zoo and other locations for treatment, but the survival rate is below 30 percent. The crude oil also kills many local seals. Dolphins, with their blowholes plugged by oil, suffocate, and their bodies float onto the beaches.[2]

Figure 11.1.   Many types of wildlife died in the oil spill. *Doug Steley*

Santa Barbara's seventy thousand residents are furious. A pair of local residents, one an ex-state senator and the other a corporate executive, establish a group called Get Oil Out (GOO). They draft a petition warning about the dangers of future spills and asking the state and the federal government to halt all offshore oil operations, issue no further permits, and remove the existing rigs from the Santa Barbara Channel.[3] Rallies are organized throughout the area, and one Santa Barbara high school raises money for GOO with an anti–Union Oil theater production. Artists, writers, academics, and business people jump into the fight, and GOO's petition is passed around the country.

Finally, GOO takes the petition to the White House with 110,000 signatures. President Nixon, a California native, accepts the petition and travels to California himself to visit the site. "It is sad that it was necessary that Santa Barbara should be the example that had to bring it to the attention of the American people," he laments. "What is involved is the use of our resources of the sea and of the land in a more effective way and with more concern for preserving the beauty and the natural resources that are so important to any kind of society that we want for the future. The Santa Barbara incident has frankly touched the conscience of the American people."[4]

THE TRAGEDY—CUYAHOGA RIVER FIRE

America's first major oil spill is part of a larger trend of environmental denigration. Santa Barbara residents may be rightfully shocked about the damage done to their community, but the citizens of Cleveland, Ohio, have come to yawn at oil-ridden waterways.[5] The Cuyahoga River, which winds for almost one hundred miles through northeast Ohio, is notorious for its unrivaled pollution. For decades, factories and steel mills that line the Cuyahoga have treated it as an open sewer, dumping all of their untreated industrial waste into the river. The water's surface is sludgy and dark, and animal life is nearly nonexistent. Signs dot the riverbanks: "No swimming," "No boating," "Use at your own risk." The river is so polluted, in fact, that it has caught fire twelve times since 1868. The fire of 1952 was particularly destructive, burning for three days and causing $1.8 million worth of damage (equivalent to $43 million in 2016 dollars). Since then, the City of Cleveland has kept fireboats along the river.

Around midday on June 22, 1969, the river is set ablaze again when a spark from a passing train flies into the water. The fire quickly grows and soon ignites a railroad bridge, causing at least $100,000 in damage. Fireboats make their way to the scene and use hoses to break up the burning oil slick. Within half an hour, the fire is out. The whole episode is rather minor; firefighters don't even bother calling the fire chief, and the blaze is extinguished before reporters can arrive to snap a photo. The fire doesn't make the front page of Cleveland's newspapers.

However, later in the summer, a reporter for *Time* magazine catches wind of the story and runs an article on the river fire in their August 1, 1969, issue. Without good photographs from the June fire, *Time* publishes a dramatic photo from the more destructive 1952 fire. "Some River!" the *Time* reporter writes:

> Chocolate-brown, oily, bubbling with subsurface gases, it oozes rather than flows. "Anyone who falls into the Cuyahoga does not drown," Cleveland's citizens joke grimly. "He decays." . . . The Federal Water Pollution Control Administration dryly notes: "The lower Cuyahoga has no visible signs of life, not even low forms such as leeches and sludge worms that usually thrive on wastes." It is also—literally—a fire hazard.[6]

The story captivates the nation's consciousness. Many realize that this is not a story unique to Cleveland: over one hundred years of industrialization have crippled entire regions. Lake Erie is considered a "dying lake." Biologist Charles C. Davis calls the river a "cloaca," the excretory orifice in some animal species. Across the country, other rivers have also been known to burn: Michigan's Rouge River, the Schuylkill River of

Figure 11.2. Cuyahoga River ablaze, 1952. *James Thomas, Cleveland Press Collection, courtesy of Cleveland University Library*

Philadelphia, the Buffalo River in Buffalo, and the Chicago River, as well as both Baltimore and New York harbors.

Chicago invested in a unique strategy to reduce the incidents of their river catching fire. In 1900, with a series of canals, the city reversed the flow of the Chicago River. Once the canals were completed, the river no longer flowed into Lake Michigan, which had allowed the various pollutants to linger in Chicago. Now, the river moves faster, carrying most flammable material out of town and down to the Mississippi.

Water pollution is certainly not the country's lone environmental woe. Across the country, air quality is poor: in 1948, smog in Donora, Pennsylvania, claims twenty lives and sickens an additional seven thousand. Factories pump astounding volumes of toxic pollutants into the atmosphere without regulation. Trash management across the nation basically does not exist. Barrels of toxic chemicals are simply dumped around the country without a thought.

The alarm has been sounding for years. In the early 1960s, biologist Rachel Carson receives a letter from a friend who writes that every time her Cape Cod neighborhood sprays dichloro-diphenyl-trichloroethane (DDT), local birds are found dead. The letter sets Carson on a multiyear exploration of the impact of pesticide use on the greater environment. In 1962, she publishes her findings in a bestselling book called *Silent Spring*. The book explains how DDT, which is commonly sprayed on crops as an insecticide, is actually a biocide, toxic to most animals. The chemical is retained in fat cells, and it is often passed up the food chain to birds of prey like bald eagles and even humans. *Silent Spring* stays on the *New York Times* bestseller list for eighty-six weeks.

Silent Spring touchs America in a very personal way. The book comes to the dinner table. Carson explains that pesticide use on food means that pesticides are being served with our meals. "The common salad bowl," the book informs us, "may easily present a combination of organic phosphate insecticides."[7] The environment is no longer an academic concern: if you are a tourist, a home owner, someone who eats food, drinks water, or breathes air, it is your problem.

THE OUTRAGE

With Carson's warning already in the back of America's mind, the Santa Barbara oil spill and the Cuyahoga River fire serve as a wake-up call to a nation slowly plodding toward its own destruction. Pesticide poisoning, air pollution, water pollution, industrialization, and overpopulation manifest themselves everywhere one looks. America's environmental degradation is not only damaging wildlife but also the economy, be it by driving tourists from the beaches or destroying railroad bridges or a host of other ways. Moreover, it is beginning to threaten the health and safety of humans. "Is this really sustainable?" ask many Americans. "Is anyone paying attention at all?"

The United States also faces increasing international pressure on environmental issues. In 1969, United Nations general secretary U Thant blames the United States for environmental damage and announces that humankind has ten years to save itself from catastrophe. Russell E. Train, U.S. undersecretary of Interior, is no more optimistic. "If environmental deterioration is permitted to continue and increase at present rates," he says, "[man] wouldn't stand a snowball's chance in hell."[8]

Santa Barbara residents, outraged that their concerns about oil drilling have gone unheeded, decide to act. On January 28, 1970, a year after the oil spill, a group of them produce a declaration on environmental rights. Written by University of California Santa Barbara professor of history and environmental studies Roderick Nash, the *Santa Barbara Declaration of Environmental Rights* declares that: "[a]ll people have the right to an environment capable of sustaining life and promoting happiness. . . . We need an ecological consciousness that recognizes man as member, not master, of the community of living things sharing his environment." The document ends with a call to action:

> WE PROPOSE A REVOLUTION in conduct toward an environment which is rising in revolt against us. Granted that ideas and institutions long established are not easily changed; yet today is the first day of the rest of our life on this planet. WE WILL BEGIN ANEW.[9]

The declaration garners widespread media attention, and the group vows to continue being a forceful voice for environmental issues.

Conservationists sense that momentum is swinging their way, so they seize the opportunity to bolster their support further with a brilliant tactic: fear. Conservationists use doomsday scenarios that surmise consequences far beyond the conclusions of scientific research to make the issue of import to all. *Life* magazine publishes an issue concluding:

> Before long air pollution will screen out the sun and make big cities uninhabitable, that the fragile biosphere we all live in is becoming poisonous and may cease to support life, plagues threaten, the polar icecaps may melt and inundate us, or—take your pick—a new ice age may come.[10]

THE REFORM

The mounting pressure is soon felt on Capitol Hill and in the White House. Urgency around environmental protection prompts President Nixon to establish the Environmental Quality Council, an advisory group to coordinate government response to past and future environmental problems. Shortly afterward, Congress passes the Environmental Policy Act of 1969 and creates the Council on Environmental Policy to review all federal activities relating to the environment. Then in his 1970 State of the Union Address, President Nixon makes the environment a central focus:

> The great question of the seventies is, shall we surrender to our surroundings, or shall we make our peace with nature and begin to make reparations for the damage we have done to our air, to our land, and to our water? . . . Clean air, clean water, open spaces—these should once again be the birthright of every American. If we act now, they can be.

That spring, environmental activists launch the first annual Earth Day on April 22, 1970. Students of all ages use the day to learn about the environment, and hundreds of communities across America come together to celebrate the earth and remind each other of the need to protect it. Then in July, Nixon signs another executive order, to establish the Environmental Protection Agency (EPA).[11] Decentralized efforts across departments to establish and enforce environmental protection laws will now be consolidated into the new agency.

Later that year, Congress passes the first of several major environmental laws of the 1970s: the Clean Air Act of 1970 (CAA).[12] Though many in the business community oppose the bill, citing the potential for destroying industries, strong public support is enough to push it to the president's desk. The CAA sets limits on air pollution for many chemicals across several industries and establishes standards aimed at reducing auto emissions by 90 percent. It also criminalizes violations, mandating a fine and/or imprisonment for up to five years for "knowingly" violating air pollution requirements.[13]

Congress follows two years later with another major environmental bill: the Clean Water Act of 1972 (CWA), which establishes a framework for the EPA to regulate pollutant discharges into oceans, lakes, rivers, and other bodies of water. As with the CAA, the new water regulations carry the threat of criminal prosecution.

In 1976, Congress passes a third bill, the Resource Conservation and Recovery Act (RCRA), to regulate the transportation and disposal of hazardous waste. Before the law's enactment, waste can be dumped almost indiscriminately without regard to the health of humans or the environment. This leads to messes like the Valley of the Drums, a twenty-three-acre site outside of Louisville, Kentucky that has well in excess of one hundred thousand steel drums heaped upon one another, leaking, broken, and seeping their toxic contents into the larger environment. But after the RCRA, the site is shut down, and the EPA begins a seven-year cleanup of the site in 1983.

The EPA is charged with implementing the new laws, so the agency sets to work creating an enforcement framework. In 1981, the EPA establishes the Office of Criminal Enforcement (OCE) to investigate violations of the new laws.[14] Investigators spread throughout the country into the EPA's ten regional offices and launch investigations into environmental crimes, working alongside state and local investigators.

In addition to enforcing the new laws, the EPA also ramps up enforcement of existing environmental statutes.[15] For example, the EPA brings criminal charges under the Refuse Act of 1899,[16] which criminalizes leaving "refuse" in navigable waters. Other prosecutions are brought under public-welfare offenses that impose strict liability—that is, liability even if the defendant has no knowledge of the criminal act. For example, if a fifty-five-gallon drum clearly marked "CORN SYRUP" were dumped and it is later determined that the drum contained a toxic substance like DDT, the person who did the dumping could be prosecuted even if the person honestly believed the substance was corn syrup.

As the EPA grows, the agency soon finds it can be even more effective if it works with other agencies. In 1982, the FBI agrees to help the EPA investigate environmental-crime cases, and that same year the Department of Justice establishes the Environmental Crimes Section (ECS) to aid regional U.S. attorneys in prosecuting environmental-crime cases. After that, the EPA begins referring more and more cases to the DOJ for prosecution. Then in 1987, the U.S. Customs Service agrees to help the EPA identify international environmental crime, and the EPA also develops an increasing number of informal arrangements with state and local law enforcement. The partnerships greatly expand the power of the EPA to identify violators and hold them legally accountable.

Seeing the success of the EPA in improving the environment, Congress grants full law enforcement power to the agency in 1988 to investigate environmental crimes. This allows EPA agents to execute arrest warrants, make warrantless arrests, and carry firearms.[17] Then in 1990, it strengthens the Clean Air Act with harsher penalties and adds more enforcement mechanisms for EPA use, such as blacklisting companies that violate environmental laws from receiving government contracts.[18]

With its mission well underway in the United States, the EPA expands its international outreach. In 1993, the OCE director leads a working group on environmental crime for Interpol, the international police organization. The director is later elected Interpol chairman for a group on trans-boundary waste, and is also permanent cochair of the International Chiefs of Police Standing Committee on Environmental Crime. The EPA also designs a program for environmental law enforcement chiefs from around the globe.

BEYOND REFORM

Today, the EPA continues to use its complex legal framework to ensure aggressive enforcement. The agency has doubled the number of criminal investigators since 1990 and now has representatives in almost all federal judicial districts. Almost every year, the criminal program sets a new record for number of cases, number of defendants, cumulative number of fines and years of imprisonment, number of DOJ referrals for prosecution, and the financial value of environmental-improvement projects. As of 2016, the OCE has 200 agents, 70 scientists, and 45 attorneys, all working on enforcement. That year, the agents investigate and bring charges against 184 defendants, winning convictions against about 90 percent of them that come with $207 million in fines and 93 years of incarceration.[19] While the EPA's criminal enforcement operation is effective, it pales in comparison to the agency's civil enforcement program. The EPA opens over 2,400 civil cases in 2016 and wins nearly $5.8 billion in civil and administrative penalties.[20]

Clearly, the EPA takes its enforcement power seriously and uses all available tools to pursue environmental crime. But in so doing, the agency has raised questions about whether it has too much power and sometimes goes too far in enforcing environmental regulations.

Those critical of the agency's power grow loudest during the Obama administration when the EPA issues a number of complex new environmental rules. In 2014, the EPA releases the Clean Power Plan stipulating tighter regulations for coal-burning power plants in the United States. Analysis shows that compliance costs could total $366 billion or more, leading to double-digit percentage increases in the price of electricity in most states. Then in 2015, the EPA releases the Waters of the United States Rule, a three hundred-page book ordering that all bodies of water within four thousand feet of any "traditional navigable water "are to be subject to EPA clean water regulations.[21] Republican representative Steve Scalise blasts the rule as the "EPA's attempt to redefine 'navigable waterways' to include every drainage ditch, backyard pond and puddle." He criticizes what he sees as "a radical regulatory overreach that threatens to take away the rights of property owners and will lead to costly litigation and lost jobs."[22]

Critics like Scalise often back up their claims by pointing to specific situations in which they believe the EPA has overstepped its boundaries. For example, an Ohio company called Marietta Industrial Enterprises refines medium carbon ferromanganese using a process that produces toxic fumes. Unbeknownst to company president Scott Elliot, workers sometimes turn off the fans. This is not a violation of the rules, as the employees use other containment methods. After a time, Elliot learns that the fans are being turned off and instructs the workers to turn the fans back on, which they do from that point forward. However, several years later the company is fined $50,000 and Elliott is sentenced to jail time and community service. His crime? He did not report the nonuse of the fans to the EPA. The EPA rule states that if the fans are not working properly, the company is obliged to report it. Since Elliott does not, he and his company are criminally prosecuted.[23]

Many companies also complain about the high cost of simply complying with the bureaucratic requirements of the EPA. Those costs are so high in many areas that many businesses simply find it cheaper to pay the fine instead of complying. Other businesses try to hide violations by, for example, privately dumping hazardous materials instead of paying exorbitant costs to have them disposed of at a chemical treatment plant, the very behavior the EPA's regulations seeks to prevent. And some point out that many companies ship jobs overseas to countries with laxer environmental standards to avoid the costly regulations.

Yet on the other side, some environmentalists argue that the EPA still does not go far enough. Pollutants are still discharged into major rivers like the Ohio River and the Mississippi River from industries and farm runoff full of nitrogen-based fertilizers. This causes toxic algae blooms and oxygen-depleted dead zones, including a dead zone in the Gulf of Mexico that is approximately the size of Connecticut.[24] And despite improvements in industry standards and government regulation since the Santa Barbara oil spill, environmental disasters still occur: the Deepwater Horizon spill of 2010 spewed nearly five million barrels of oil into the Gulf of Mexico, costing billions of dollars and dramatically altering the coastal ecosystem throughout the region.

Though it will probably never be possible to achieve the perfect balance between business and the environment, it is undeniable that the EPA has made a safer environment a national reality. When the EPA first assesses the Cuyahoga River in 1972, they find not a single fish between Akron and Cleveland. Instead, heavy metals like cadmium, chromium, and lead are found in concentrations as high as two hundred parts per million. In the mid-1980s, a new assessment of the same thirty-five mile stretch of river finds exactly ten fish. Not ten species—ten living fish. The pioneers include a gizzard shad with physical abnormalities, a fish known for being able to survive in heavily polluted water.

But in 2008, Ohio authorities report that the river sustains forty different species, totaling thousands of individual fish. This includes fish that require very clean water, such as trout. Heavy metal concentrations are virtually zero. Upon hearing this report, the EPA is skeptical, so they come to Ohio to check for themselves. Their investigation reaches similar conclusions: the river is indeed alive, and the fish are back.[25]

Referring to the original Cuyahoga River fire, Jane Goodman, a member of the Cleveland city council explains, "Many people see this fire as being a catalyst for the federal Clean Water Act and other environmental laws. And those laws went a long way toward bringing the river back."[26] Indeed, the river is now used for recreation by crew teams, fishermen, and boaters. Perhaps the most dramatic piece of evidence is that the river that was once a toxic joke is now the source of drinking water for the City of Cleveland.[27]

Chapter Twelve

1972
TWA Bombings
and Hijackings

Airport Security

THE TRAGEDY

At 11:30 a.m., March 9, 1972, Bette Kemmerer, the secretary to the president of Trans World Airlines (TWA), answers the phone.[1] An unidentified caller explains that there is a bomb aboard a TWA plane and that additional information can be found in a duffle bag stored in a locker at Kennedy Airport.[2] Kemmerer acts quickly to contact authorities, and TWA grounds all of its planes.

One plane, Flight 7 from Kennedy airport bound for L.A., has been in the air for just twenty minutes when the pilots are told to turn back. After the plane returns to the airport, all fifty-two of its passengers are evacuated. With passengers off, New York City police search the plane, accompanied by Brandy, a police dog. The dog stops at a black briefcase labeled "crew" in the cockpit. When the innocent-looking briefcase is opened, police discover a bomb with enough C-4 explosive to blow up the plane. The bomb's timer has twelve minutes left until detonation.

In another part of the airport, police open the locker indicated by the caller. Besides two army-style duffle bags, there is a typed note indicating that there are more bombs set to go off. The bombs will be detonated at six-hour intervals unless a $2 million ransom is paid.

TWA undertakes an intensive search of their 238 planes. They find nothing out of the ordinary on any of them, including a Boeing 707 (B-707) airplane at JFK scheduled to fly to Las Vegas in a few hours. The airline cautiously decides to move forward with the scheduled flight. The plane lands in Las Vegas early the following morning without incident.

As they are doing with all TWA flights, police search the plane again, finding nothing. Throughout the country, TWA is also putting armed guards around their planes while they are on the ground to prevent anyone from planting a bomb. While two guards monitor TWA's fleet at the Las Vegas airport, at 3:55 a.m. on March 10, the empty B-707 that had just flown in from JFK explodes on the Las Vegas tarmac. Had the plane been in the air, it seems unlikely that anyone on board would have survived.

Later the same day, a TWA flight from San Francisco lands in Seattle. The aircraft had been searched prior to departing from San Francisco just hours before. After passengers exit the plane, police search it again and uncover a bomb enclosed in a suitcase. The device, lying in the cargo hold, had made the flight with all the passengers and crew. Police successfully diffuse the bomb without incident. Someone has placed three bombs on American TWA planes; only simple luck has prevented any injuries or deaths. Though more bombs are promised, the bomber is never heard from again, and the $2 million ransom is not paid.

During the 1960s and 1970s, plane hijackings are also a routine part of the flying experience. Between 1961 and 1972, over 150 planes are hijacked in American airspace. For a time, hijackings happen almost weekly. From the perspective of criminals, hijacking is a lucrative trade: it is far less risky than bank robbery, and the financial payoff is several orders of magnitude greater. Hijacking is also not that hard: security is minimal; customers can purchase a ticket and walk directly onto a plane, and bags aren't searched, making it simple to bring weapons onto flights.

For their part, airlines see hijacking ransoms as little more than a cost of doing business. In the interest of passenger safety and mitigating the risk of mid-flight confrontations, airlines generally accommodate hijackers, and hijackers know it. Security measures like metal detectors and screeners are expensive to install and would require additional airport personnel. Moreover, airlines might risk losing business if customers were to grow frustrated by the hassle of security and choose other airlines or other means of transportation instead.

The attempted triple bombing, however, challenges that calculation. The incidents play out over several days and garner intense attention by the national media. The $2 million ransom far exceeds what is normally demanded, and paying a ransom like that could be financially crippling. The incident is not based on mere threats: there are three real bombs that could have each taken down a plane, and two of the devices were initially overlooked in the police search. The level of knowledge the attackers seem to have about the planes, as well as the logistical sophistication of the attack, leads authorities to believe the TWA incidents are the work of an insider.

Clearly, all of this is bad for TWA, but it also affects the entire airline industry. Many non-TWA flights are delayed or canceled due to various false alarms. After the attacks, passengers start canceling travel plans, and all airlines see their ticket sales drop. The whole notion of safe air travel is now suspect. Clearly the stakes have gone up.

Though the March bombings are over, airplane hijackings continue that year.[3] Extortion efforts remain frequent. Escaping criminals and political activists begin to get in on the action as well, seeking illicit transport to another country. The most common destination in the 1960s and 1970s is Cuba.

On July 5, 1972, only three months after the TWA bombings, a plane on its way to San Francisco from Sacramento is hijacked by a group of gunmen. They command the pilots to take them to the Soviet Union. FBI agents on the flight confront the gunmen, and gunfire breaks out. Two hijackers and one passenger are killed, and other civilians are injured. Although people have been injured by domestic hijackings in the past, the incident marks the first fatality. Four months later, four fugitives kill a ticket agent and hijack a plane in Houston, Texas. They force the pilots to fly the Boeing 727 to Cuba, and the hijacking fugitives escape successfully.

Two weeks later, on November 10, three more criminals hijack a Southern Airways DC-9 in Birmingham, Alabama. They threaten to crash the plane, which is carrying thirty-four people, into a nuclear reactor if the pilots don't follow orders. They order the plane to stop in Mississippi, Ohio, Ontario, Kentucky, Tennessee, Cuba, and two cities in Florida. The hijackers use the stops to pick up supplies, including guns and grenades, and refuel the plane. Afterward, the hijackers demand $10 million from officials, alcohol, and, strangely, Kentucky Fried Chicken. In Tennessee, FBI agents deliver the food and what the hijackers believe is $10 million (in reality, $2 million).

The hijackers have the plane flown to Havana, Cuba, on the assumption that Fidel Castro will welcome them. Castro, however, refuses the fugitives. They consider going to Algeria, but instead go to Orlando, Florida, due to insufficient fuel. There, FBI agents shoot out the plane's tires in an attempt to ground the aircraft. Panicking, the hijackers shoot the copilot in the arm and force the pilot to take off again. After a total of thirty hours and four thousand miles of travel, the plane lands again in Havana, where the hijackers are arrested at gunpoint. They spend eight years in a Cuban jail. Upon release, they are extradited to the United States and sentenced to twenty-five years in prison.

NATIONAL OUTRAGE AND REFORM

The bombings and hijackings of 1972 unsettle the nation, and many Americans ask the same question: Why are armed criminals repeatedly allowed to seize control of civilian aircraft? The terrifying threat of the TWA bombs, the wild rides to Cuba and elsewhere, and the increasing number of injuries and deaths that result from hijackings show that something must done about airplane security.

The federal government is ahead of the airline industry in understanding the threat. In an odd coincidence, just hours before Bette Kemmerer of TWA receives the bomb threat, President Nixon signed a directive ordering air carriers and commercial aircraft operators to submit written security programs to the FAA. The programs, to be immediately implemented, must include a mandatory screening system that has already been requested of airlines by the FAA. The system seeks to prevent unauthorized bags from entering aircraft, which the FAA hopes will deter people from smuggling weapons on planes and catch those who do. Considering the recent events, airlines are in no position to argue.

A list of security measures for the airlines is soon approved by a cabinet-level task force, created by President Nixon and the transportation secretary, John A. Volpe. The measures are remarkably comprehensive. One expands the FAA Security Task Force, which will ensure protocol implementation and investigate improvements. Another approves the deployment of sky marshals, both on flights and at posts throughout major airports. The task force also increases funding for development of technologies that detect weapons and explosives, as well as training for more dogs for use in weapons detection and emergency situations. The task force expedites the process for prosecuting hijacking suspects, a decision that officials also hope will deter criminals. Finally, the group makes it illegal to pay ransoms to hijackers.

Before the year is out, the FAA approves new protocols for luggage and scanning. By January 5, 1973, all U.S. air carriers must have a functioning system to scan people and carry-on bags before boarding. All passengers will now be searched via metal detectors, pat downs, and even physical searches. Air carriers must guarantee that all carry-on luggage contains no weapons, and any passengers who refuse searches will not be allowed to board the flight. In addition, every U.S. air carrier is required to have law enforcement in the boarding and screening areas. To crack down on hijackers seeking asylum in Cuba, the United States and Cuba, in a rare show of cooperation, sign a bilateral treaty in February of 1973 in which Cuba agrees to prosecute or extradite hijackers. The treaty strips criminals of the option of escaping to Cuba.

The security measures have an immediate result; hijacking rates plummet. On August 5, 1974, the Anti-Hijacking Act of 1974 is signed to deter hijackers further. The act codifies the FAA's rule that all passengers and carry-on luggage in the nation must be screened before boarding. Moreover, the act declares that hijackers will face a mandatory minimum sentence of twenty years in prison.

The following day, a bomb explodes in the lobby of the Los Angeles Airport. The blast propels glass and concrete through the crowd, killing two people and injuring seventeen. FBI officials believe the bomber had intended to board a plane with it, but had changed his or her mind in light of the increased security measures.[4]

In 1972, there were eight hijackings of U.S. planes. In 1973, there are none. In 1974, there is one hijacking attempt by Samuel Byck, who attempts to seize a plane and fly it into the White House to kill President Nixon. He kills a security guard and shoots the pilots before the plane even leaves the ground. However, Byck does not know how to fly the plane and assigns the task of doing so to a random passenger. The commotion is overheard, and shots are fired from the runway, wounding Byck. Eventually he kills himself in the cabin as police close in. The year 1974 eventually draws to a close with no successful hijackings. Despite fears that the new security measures will discourage customers from flying, commercial airline transport continues to grow.

TWA FLIGHT 847 HIJACKING

The airline-security reforms work well for flights within the United States, but they do not apply to international flights. With ever-increasing international travel, the limits of current American measures become obvious. On June 14, 1985, TWA Flight 847 is headed from Athens to Rome when it is hijacked.[5] The flight is carrying almost 140 passengers, about 100 of whom are American. TWA Flight 847 had taken off from Cairo and was supposed to end up in San Diego, with scheduled stops in Athens, Rome, Boston, and Los Angeles.

Not long after takeoff, at 10:10 a.m., two men who had smuggled a pistol and two grenades through the airport security take control of the plane. Their primary purpose is to seek the release of the seven hundred Muslims currently in Israeli custody. They force the plane to land in Beirut, Lebanon, to refuel. The air traffic controllers in Beirut refuse permission for the craft to land. To reinforce their point, trucks and buses are moved onto the tarmac to block the runway. Pilot John Testrake begs the controllers to change their minds, explaining that the hijacker "has pulled a hand-grenade pin and is ready to blow up the aircraft if he has to. We must, I repeat, we must land at Beirut. We must land at Beirut. No alternative. . . . They are beating the passengers. They are threatening to kill the passengers. We want fuel now. Immediately. Five minutes at most, or he is going to kill the passengers."[6] The controllers are adamant until one of the hijackers grabs the radio and says, "We are suicide terrorists! If you don't let us land, we will crash the plane into your control tower, or fly it to Baabda and crash into the Presidential Palace!"[7] The runway is immediately cleared for landing. On the ground, the hijackers call for passengers with Israeli passports, but when this elicits no response, they turn their attention to the U.S. Navy construction divers on board.

After the hijackers' multiple threats to kill all the passengers, the plane is refueled, and leaves for Algiers, Algeria. Once in Algeria, twenty passengers, mostly women and children, are released, and the plane returns to Beirut. The hijackers beat passengers throughout the flight and threaten to kill everyone on board. At the second stop in Beirut, they shoot and kill Robert Stethem, an American navy officer. They dump his body onto the tarmac.

The hijackers force the plane to make another trip to Algiers and return to Beirut for a third time. Along the way, about one hundred of the passengers are released and ten to thirteen more hijackers join the mission. Now only about thirty-two men are left on board as hostages. When the passengers are released, the hijackers insist that, in return, Shiite Muslims be released from detainment. After three days, the hostages are removed from the plane and held captive in Beirut by the Hezbollah. President Reagan and his national security team negotiate with the hijackers, and as a diplomatic maneuver, the president suspends air travel between the United States and Lebanon while the hostages are being held in Beirut.

President Reagan and his national security team finally secure the release of the last hostages on June 30, sixteen days after the initial hijacking. The captives are collected in a local schoolyard to meet with international journalists and then driven to Syria by the International Red Cross. From Damascus, they board a U.S. Air Force cargo plane and fly to West Germany, where they are met by Vice President George H. W. Bush, for medical examinations. After a short stop, they fly home to Andrews Air Force Base. Soon afterward, Israel releases several dozen Shia prisoners, although it claims the release is unrelated to the hijacking. The hijackers are not immediately punished. Two years later, however, one is arrested while attempting to board a plane with explosives.

INTERNATIONAL FLIGHT REFORMS

The drama of TWA Flight 847 leaves the nation with an important realization: regardless of domestic security measures, the United States is vulnerable abroad. The country struggles to respond to the crisis because the flight, though carrying mostly Americans on an American aircraft, was international, and the hijacking occurred abroad. This renders American agencies less capable of responding effectively. Unless other countries follow similar security measures, they will be continuing risks to flights originating outside the United States.

At the end of June, President Reagan directs the secretary of transportation to consider ways to expand FAA programs to U.S. air carriers with flights abroad. The Athens airport is specifically singled out as having insufficient security. Travelers are warned that they should use precautions when flying to and from the Greek airport. Now the secretary of transportation strongly encourages the International Civil Aviation Organization to require enhanced security.

On May 15, 1985, the Senate, by a vote of 75 to 19, passes the International Security and Development Cooperation Act after just two days of debate, with the recent events still lingering on their minds. Despite a number of disagreements over linguistic issues and the scope of the act, the bill moves quickly through the House, and on August 8, 1985, President Reagan signs it into law. The act concerns a variety of other issues, including military support to foreign nations, how to fight terrorism, and the ongoing War on Drugs. In Title V, however, the act looks at the weaknesses laid bare by the hijacking of Flight 847. The Federal Air Marshal Program is expanded so that armed agents will be able to ride on international flights. The Federal Air Marshals become a permanent part of the Federal Aviation Administration workforce for all flights of U.S. air carriers. The act also provides that airports around the world are now subject to rigorous assessment; if security measures don't meet standards, the secretary of transportation will label the airport inappropriate for travel. That labeling will be made public and posted in American airports to deter travel to or through those sites. Further, if the secretary of transportation finds that aircraft and the lives of passengers are in immediate danger if they travel to or from a particular foreign airport, the secretary is required to suspend all services between the United States and the foreign airport. If the secretary of state and the secretary of transportation determine that the airport has improved their security measures appropriately, they can lift the ban. The act takes a large step toward safer international travel. Foreign airports are now heavily incentivized to improve safety procedures because failure to do so will directly impact their business.

The law is used in 1993, when the FAA exercises its authority to ban travel from the Murtala Mohammed International Airport in Lagos, Nigeria. The FAA had posted warnings about the dangers of the airport for years: there was a hijacking, immigration officers stamp passports upon payment of bribes, taxiing planes are forced to stop while thieves rob the cargo hold, and security is arbitrary at best. When the situation did not improve, it became the first and only airport with an absolute prohibition of flights into the United States. In 1999, six years into the international

Figure 12.1.   The cockpit of the jet that exploded over Lockerbie, Scotland, 1988.
Alamay photo

ban, Nigeria, among other measures, begins a policy of shooting on sight anyone found in secure areas of the airport who do not belong there. By 2001, full international flying privileges are restored. The security demanded by the United States makes American citizens safer, but it also makes the airports of the world safer for everyone.

However, the act does not stop all terrorism on airlines. On December 21, 1988, Pan Am Flight 103 takes off from Heathrow Airport in London, heading to John F. Kennedy Airport in New York City.[8] Its passengers represent over twenty countries, but most, about 189, are American. Around 7:00 p.m., shortly after takeoff, the airplane explodes over Lockerbie, Scotland. A bomb detonates near the left wing and tears the plane apart, scattering wreckage across Lockerbie. All 259 passengers and crew members, as well as eleven people on the ground, are killed, and twenty-one houses are destroyed.

The ensuing investigation reveals that an agent of the Libyan leader Muammar al-Qaddafi had hidden a bomb inside a radio cassette player, which was tucked in an unaccompanied suitcase on the plane. After years of international negotiations, one Libyan man, Abdelbaset Ali Mohmed al-Megrahi, is convicted of 270 counts of murder. He is sentenced to life in prison.

In response, heightened security measures are implemented at European and Middle Eastern airports, requiring that checked bags be x-rayed or searched and that every bag be matched to a passenger. Pan Am, for its part, faces a host of lawsuits for violating security rules, and ultimately the airline goes bankrupt as a result of the litigation. Other carriers get the message: violating security rules is no longer good business. The attack also leads to the creation of the Aviation Security Advisory Committee, which serves as an advisory body for the TSA (Transportation Security Administration).

The security implementations that followed the 1972 TWA bombings, the 1985 Beirut hostage crisis, and the 1988 Pan Am bombing dramatically reduced aircraft bombings and hijackings, and for years air travel remained safe. Hijacking no longer presented an easy and profitable crime. As we will see in a later chapter, the attacks of September 11, 2001, will lead to further changes in airline and airport security, but it is the TWA bombings that started the airline security reforms that we have today.

Chapter Thirteen

1980
Killing of Cari Lightner

Drunk Driving

THE TRAGEDY

It is a bright spring morning on May 3, 1980, and thirteen-year-old Cari Lightner is dressed in her bright-orange softball uniform. Cari and her sister have just finished taking their softball team pictures in Fair Oaks, California. Cari is heading to the church carnival, so she joins a friend and they begin walking down the road. The neighborhood is quiet, and the girls' laughter fills the street. Without warning, a car veers off the road and hits Cari. She is thrown into the air, landing in the middle of the road 125 feet from where she was struck. Cari's friend stands frozen in shock. A nearby postman does his best to revive Cari, but within an hour, Cari is dead. In fact, her internal injuries are so catastrophic that none of her organs can be donated.[1]

Cari, a pretty girl with brown hair and freckles, is known for her quick humor and athleticism. She is involved in sports, school, and church and loves hanging out with her friends. Her younger brother Travis is doing pretty much the same thing with his weekend; he is playing kickball in the street with pals from the neighborhood. Their mother, Candace, is running errands with a friend. It is a normal day for the busy and happy family.

When Cari's mother, Candace, arrives back home from shopping, her father and ex-husband Steve are waiting in the driveway. She assumes that Steve is here to pick up the kids for the weekend. She climbs out of the car, and accepts her father's unexpectedly warm embrace. "We've lost Cari," Steve quietly says. Candace nervously reassures them that Cari is

Figure 13.1.   Cari Lightner, hours before her death, 1980. *MADD*

probably at a neighbor's house. "She's dead," Steve says, his voice shaking. "She was hit by a car and she is dead."[2]

Clarence Busch, another Fair Oaks resident, works locally as a quality control technician and machinist. Outside of work, he spends most of his free time drinking. He has at least eight convictions for alcohol-related offences on his record. On May 1, 1980, two days before Cari's death, Busch drives drunk, hits someone's car, and speeds off. No one is injured, but Busch is arrested and his car impounded. Busch spends less than forty-eight hours in jail before he is released on bail. The May 1 incident is his fourth drunk-driving offense, but he retains a valid driver's license.

Almost as soon as he is out of jail, Busch takes his wife's car to a bar, where he drinks through the rest of the day and into the night. The drunken Busch finally heads home the next morning, on May 3. He turns down a small, tree-lined street in Fair Oaks. In a roadside bike lane, two girls are walking with their backs to Busch's approaching car. Busch hits Cari, and in a drunken confusion does not stop. When he arrives home, he stumbles into his room and tells his wife, Sharleen, to stay away from the car. Then Busch falls into bed and goes to sleep.

Over the weekend, Sharleen notices that her husband is behaving oddly. Suspicious, Sharleen seeks out a highway patrol officer and asks if anything bad has happened recently. The officer tells Sharleen about Cari being killed by a hit-and-run driver. Horrified, Sharleen tells police that her husband might be the culprit. When Busch is arrested, he admits he'd been drinking but claims to remember nothing from the night of Cari's death. Soon afterward, he confesses that he knows he killed Cari.

Police inform Cari's mother, Candace, that the driver has been caught, but they do not mention his history of alcohol use. She has no idea that Busch was driving drunk when he hit Cari. Later that week, she finds that out when she approaches a few police officers at the site where Cari died. Candace has been given few details about what happened, but she feigns knowledge, hoping to trick the officers into sharing more information with her. It works, and the police reveal not only that Busch had been drunk but also that the incident represented his fifth drunk-driving offense in four years. Shocked, Candace asks about Busch's punishment. She's told she'll be lucky "if this guy gets any jail time, much less prison."[3]

Busch is convicted of vehicular manslaughter. The maximum sentence Busch could have received is three years in jail, but the judge sentences him to two years, citing Busch's impaired judgment on account of the alcohol. Candace's grief over losing her daughter turns to fury at the unjust penalty her killer receives. For Candace, two years isn't long enough. "Death caused by drunk drivers," she insists, "are not really accidents. Drinkers are making choices."[4] Candace decides that something needs to change.

THE OUTRAGE

Candace quits her job as a real estate agent and, using her savings and an insurance settlement from Cari's death, founds the organization Mothers Against Drunk Driving, or MADD, to increase the public attention on drunk-driving issues. Cari's bedroom serves as MADD's first office. Candace is ready to commit her all to this cause, but she is up against significant obstacles: she has no experience in advocacy or lobbying, and drunk driving is, at best, a minor issue in 1980. DUI bills in California, and in every other state, fail consistently. It is common for judges, just like the one who reduced Busch's charge for his most recent DUI, to effectively reward drivers for being drunk when they hit someone.

These political challenges reflect the social consensus of the time: most Americans don't view drunk driving as morally reprehensible. Many Americans drink, and many more Americans drive, and people understand that at some point, you will want to head home after a night out drinking. People also understand that once a person is drunk, they are not totally in control of themselves the way they are when sober, but few see that impairment as a crime. Candace Lightner, however, is determined to tear the blameless skin off of this behavior.[5]

First, Lightner sets out to understand why drunk-driving laws are so lax. Like most states, by the 1920s, California has laws on the books that address driving drunk. What actually constitutes an infraction is fairly vague, the charge is a misdemeanor, and penalties are slight. In 1935, the state adds a felony charge in cases where an impaired driver causes bodily injury.[6]

By the 1960s, police have the technology to determine blood alcohol content (BAC). California becomes one of many states that adopt a standard whereby a BAC of .10 percent is considered to be over the legal limit. However, .10 percent is not a binding number. An individual can claim that even though their alcohol level might be .10 percent, or even higher, they personally are able to function safely.[7] If the judge agrees, there is no conviction.

In 1966, the federal government standardizes the legal BAC limit at .10 percent and requires states to do the same, lest they forfeit their federal highway dollars. The new rules require that each state set a BAC of no greater than .10 percent. The rules also stipulate that states adopt legal doctrines of implied consent, meaning that by driving on a public road, every driver gives consent for a blood-alcohol-content test. If someone is stopped by the police and refuses the test, then he or she is presumed guilty.[8] This same type of implied-consent standard is used at airports, giving the authority to go through personal possessions or even the messages on a cell phone. In 1969, California adopts the measures necessary to comply with the new federal standards. But more than a decade later, the seemingly tough rules have done little to change the culture.

Lightner seeks to make that change. In September of 1980, four months after Cari's death, after MADD is incorporated, her organization offers counseling to victims and victims' families. The organization's larger goal is to spur legislative change that will enhance penalties for drunk driving. The organization struggles at first; when MADD starts lobbying for bills with mandatory sentences and stricter drunk-driving laws, the group is largely ignored. Candace is even thrown out of one California legislator's office. Regardless, Candace remains vocal, and ordinary people begin to listen to her message.

Later that fall, news of another drunk-driving tragedy brings MADD to the East Coast. On the morning of November 10, 1979, Maryland resident Cindi Lamb is driving to the grocery store with her six-month-old daughter, Laura, in the backseat.[9] As she crests a hill, an oncoming car going 125 miles per hour swerves into her lane. The cars smash into each other, and Cindi suffers a crushed sternum, fourteen broken bones, a cracked hip, and a four-inch head wound. Laura fares far worse. Her car seat is snapped in two and she is sent flying out of the vehicle. The baby survives, but three vertebrae are broken, and she is paralyzed from the neck down, becoming the nation's youngest quadriplegic. The driver who hit their car is passed out drunk; it is his fifth drunk-driving offense. A local newspaper runs a detailed account of the crash and the struggle to keep the baby alive. A television station picks up the story and produces a five-part series on the issue of drunk driving.

Laura had been a vigorous baby, now she is breathing through a tracheotomy tube, and her body is plagued by seizures. Sickened by what drunk driving has done to their daughter, Cindi Lamb and her husband begin the Laura Lamb Crusade. Unlike Lightner, the Lambs have a legislator who is listening: their congressman, Michael Barnes.

Across the country, Candace Lightner hears of Lamb's effort. The two groups meet, and they agree to merge into a single organization. In October, not quite a year after Cari's death, the two women host MADD's first national press conference on Capitol Hill in Washington, D.C. The event electrifies the movement for stronger drunk-driving laws. "You could literally feel things change at that moment," says Chuck Hurley, MADD's chief executive officer. "On that day, public tolerance of drunk driving changed forever."[10]

The press conference brings MADD into the spotlight. The Lambs bring their paralyzed daughter Laura, and Candace defiantly shows photographs of Cari. Images from the press conference make it to television and are in newspapers around the nation. Horrified by their tragic stories, thousands of American parents rally around MADD's cause. Shortly after the Capitol Hill press conference, over one hundred people march at the White House. By the end of 1980, MADD has twenty-four chapters scattered in California, Maryland, Virginia, and Pennsylvania.

Cari Lightner's death becomes a story about a national problem, a problem that is very real. In the ten years before Cari's death, an average of twenty-five thousand Americans died annually from drunk-driving incidents, and most Americans know of someone who has been injured or killed in such an incident.

Prior to MADD, the only strong voice for federal change is the National Highway Traffic Safety Administration (NHTSA), established in 1966. The NHTSA funded research relating to DUIs and highway accidents, supported the development of breath-test devices, and released "Don't Drink and Drive" public service announcements. In the 1970s, the government developed Alcohol Safety Action Programs (ASAPs), which sought to prevent drunk driving with improved counseling and education for drunk drivers and better public awareness about the issue. But none of this had a measureable impact, so funding was directed elsewhere.[11] "Alcohol was involved in nearly 60 percent of fatal crashes and we were banging our heads against the wall," remembers Jim Fell, who works for the National Highway Traffic Safety Administration. "Then, all of a sudden, a woman named [Candace] Lightner came along, kicking and screaming about her daughter who had been killed."[12]

MADD, and their intimate approach, changes the equation. MADD insists that drunk driving be treated not as an unfortunate reality but as an irresponsible, condemnable, and, most importantly, punishable behavior. Lightner points out to all who will listen that drunk driving "is the only socially acceptable form of homicide."[13] "We saw that MADD was really getting the public's attention," explains NHTSA representative Jim Fell. "With our research bolstering their cause, we realized they had the emotional appeal we were lacking."[14] The NHTSA backs MADD as soon as it's formed, providing statistics for MADD's public outreach. The two groups join forces; the NHTSA works with Lightner and Lamb to host press events. In 1981, NHTSA awards a grant of $60,000 to MADD to help start new chapters across the nation.

THE REFORM

In 1981, MADD achieves their first legislative victory. California passes a law imposing a minimum fine of $375 and a mandatory prison term of up to four years for repeat drunk-driving offenders. It's the toughest drunk-driving law in any state. The law also changes the drunk-driving offense definition from "driving under the influence" to "driving with a blood alcohol concentration of .10 percent or greater."[15] The shift is crucial; now, drunk driving can be measured quantitatively, and a driver's drunkenness cannot be disputed in court.

By 1982, less than two years after MADD's founding, one hundred MADD chapters exist around the country, with more forming daily. Forty-one states establish task forces and commissions to assess the state's drunk-driving problem and propose solutions.[16] By 1983, 129 new anti-drunk-driving laws have passed around the nation. MADD keeps the issue fresh by focusing on victims and their families. They reach out to support them and offer them a way to channel their pain and anger into positive change. MADD provides them with a platform to tell their story and, in so doing, keeps the issue of drunk driving ever present in the public mind.

MADD chapters use several strategies to go after what they view as a system that is too soft on offenders. One of their favorite stratagems is to cast a watchful eye on judges' decisions in drunk-driving cases. Organization volunteers start attending drunk-driving trials to evaluate judges and prosecutors, earning the nickname "Court Watchers." MADD's presence in courtrooms has a real impact: Court Watchers increase the chances that a judge will find the defendant guilty, that a judge will impose harsher punishments, and that a driver will plead guilty.

MADD also continues to hone its advocacy efforts, and in early 1982, MADD wins an important victory at the national level when Congress passes a bill to award extra highway funds to states taking steps to reduce drunk driving. Congress also urges President Reagan to establish the Presidential Commission on Drunk Driving. In April, President Reagan obliges, appointing Lightner to the commission and insisting that MADD actively participate. The commission's twenty-eight members are tasked with determining better ways to increase public awareness of drunk driving and public support for anti-drunk-driving laws. In addition, the commission seeks to "persuade States and communities to attack the drunk-driving problem in a more organized and systematic manner" and "accept and use the latest techniques and methods to solve the problem."[17]

The commission's final report proposes a three-part solution that includes better education, additional legislation, as well as improved enforcement programs. "Drunk driving is a national menace, a national tragedy, and a national disgrace," says President Reagan. "It is my fervent hope that this report will receive the attention it deserves, and that it will speed the adoption of whatever measures are appropriate to remove this hazard from our national life."[18]

Included in the report is a recommendation to deny highway funds to states that refuse to elevate the drinking age to twenty-one, a shift that MADD has supported since its inception. In partnership with the NHTSA, MADD comes armed with the research to back up their position. Inconsistent state drinking ages, MADD claims, make fighting drunk driving difficult and lead to more drunk-driving deaths. For example, New Jersey has a drinking age of twenty-one, so eighteen-year-olds often drive to neighboring states to drink. Then they drive back home to New Jersey after they are drunk.

Many groups, including the alcohol and hospitality industries, oppose raising the drinking age. President Reagan doesn't initially support the change, either, maintaining that states should have the right to determine the drinking age on their own. But when MADD offers compelling research that states with drinking ages under twenty-one see more alcohol-related teen car crashes, Reagan changes his mind. Congress passes the Uniform Drinking Age Act to raise the drinking age to twenty-one across the country, and on July 17, 1984, President Reagan signs the bill into law. In a show of gratitude and joy, Lightner herself pins a MADD button on Reagan's jacket. By the end of the year, MADD has 330 chapters in forty-seven states.

While Cari's death has inspired her mother to launch a national campaign and landed her in the Oval Office with the president, the reform momentum has not done much to alter the system's tolerance of Clarence Busch. Busch is released for good behavior after serving nine months of his two-year sentence for killing Cari. Seven months after his release, Busch lies to obtain a Wisconsin driver's license. Police in California discover he has violated his parole and arrest him again; he is sentenced to ten more months in prison. He is released on parole in February of 1983. Busch drifts between jail, work camps, and halfway houses. In February of 1985, he moves to Citrus Heights, California. He is granted a temporary driver's license by California. On the night of April 17, 1985, his most recent jail term having ended two weeks earlier, he is out drinking in Sacramento.[19] His 1980 Chevy Citation makes an illegal left turn at a red light and smashes into a car driven by nineteen-year-old Carrie Sinnott. Carrie survives with minor injuries, but her car is destroyed. Busch smells of alcohol and slurs his speech. He fails a sobriety test. His blood alcohol content is .20 percent, two times California's legal limit. He is arrested yet again.

Lightner is horrified that Busch was permitted to drive again so quickly after his release. When the court date arrives, she decides to watch the trial. "I still felt the anger and hatred," she remembers, "and when I saw him in the courtroom, it was in many ways like déjà vu."[20] Lightner, furious that Busch was behind the wheel legally, believes he should face serious jail time and shouldn't be permitted to drive again.

But even after the legislative gains spearheaded by MADD, a drunk driver in California involved in a crash that doesn't kill or seriously injure anyone is often convicted of no more than a misdemeanor and serves a maximum sentence of one year in prison. Even if the prosecutors pursue a felony charge, the maximum sentence is three years.

Busch's lawyer argues that Busch should be sent to a state rehabilitation center for his alcoholism, but the court sentences him to three years for drunk driving and one year for parole violations. Though Candace had wanted more, the sentence is a victory; before MADD, Busch might have been driving the very next day. After his release from prison, Busch continues to drink and drive. He is subsequently convicted of yet another DUI in Wisconsin, and he is fined $583, and his driver's license is suspended for nine months.[21]

MADD continues their aggressive legislative efforts throughout the 1990s, and in 1995, the group launches a five-year campaign called "20 by 2000," which seeks to reduce alcohol-related traffic fatalities by 20 percent by the year 2000. This initiative identifies five target areas: youth issues, enforcement of laws, sanctions, self-sufficiency, and responsible marketing and service. It focuses MADD's advocacy efforts on addressing each of them.

As part of their agenda, MADD pushes for "Zero Tolerance" laws for drivers under twenty-one.[22] These plans stipulate that anyone under twenty-one who drives with any amount of alcohol in their system faces a drunk-driving charge. Proponents point to evidence suggesting that people under twenty-one are far more likely to combine drinking and driving and that they are more likely to get into a car accident after a few drinks. MADD wins a national victory on "Zero Tolerance" in the first year of their "20 by 2000" campaign with the passage of the National Highway System Designation Act. The act declares that if states fail to pass Zero Tolerance legislation for underage drinkers, then highway funding will be withheld. By 1998, every state has enacted some form of the law: twelve states and the District of Columbia set the BAC limit for those under 21 at .00 percent, two states at .01 percent, and thirty-six states at .02 percent.[23]

MADD also launches "Youth Movement" to focus on the dangers of alcohol use by youth. As part of the initiative, MADD holds a national youth summit in 1997 in Washington, D.C. Representing every congressional district in the nation, 435 young people attend the summit to brainstorm solutions to underage drinking and meet with senators. That same year, MADD reaches its larger goal of the "20 by 2000" of reducing alcohol-related traffic fatalities by 20 percent three years early.

These successes only embolden MADD and other anti-drunk-driving advocates. MADD turns its attention to lowering the allowable blood alcohol level for of-age drivers from .10 percent to .08 percent. The organization presents evidence showing a BAC of .08 percent can render someone significantly impaired. They also publicize a 1996 study by prominent public health expert Ralph Hingson predicting that the adoption of a nationwide standard of .08 percent BAC would result in five hundred fewer alcohol-related deaths per year. Hingson dedicates the study to the president of MADD, Millie Webb. In 1971, a drunk driver with a BAC of .08 percent hit Webb and her four-year old daughter, Lori. Webb survived, but Lori, who suffered burns on 75 percent of her body, died two weeks later.[24] Stories like Webb's and studies such as Hingson's form the backbone of MADD's most recent initiative.

Critics argue that the law would impact "social drinkers" instead of "problem drinkers," the latter group being at a higher risk of causing drunk-driving accidents.[25] Moreover, they argue, lowering the legal driving BAC is a slippery slope, and .08 percent might be lowered even further. Supporters of the measure retort that that would not necessarily be bad, because the U.S. legal driving BAC is remarkably high compared to other countries. Sweden's and Poland's legal limits are .02 percent, Germany's and Italy's are .05 percent, and the Czech Republic's and Brazil's are 0.0 percent.[26] By 1998, ten states—Kansas, North Carolina, Florida, New Hampshire, New Mexico, Virginia, Alabama, Hawaii, Idaho, and Illinois—have adopted the .08 percent BAC standard for drunk driving.[27] In 2000, MADD wins another national victory when President Clinton signs a law requiring states to set the legal BAC limit for driving at .08 percent by 2004 if they are to continue receiving federal highway grants. By July of 2004, all fifty states and the District of Columbia have adopted the .08 percent standard. Webb, like many of the law's supporters, is relieved: "I felt that my daughter had not died in vain."[28]

In 2006, MADD launches another initiative called the Campaign to Eliminate Drunk Driving. This initiative seeks to support law enforcement and take advantage of ever-improving technology to prevent drunk drivers from getting behind the wheel. In particular, MADD pushes states to use ignition interlock technology to prevent drunk driving. These devices are installed in a car and require a driver to blow a sober sample into a tube before their car can start. If the sample reads too high, the ignition simply will not engage. Ignition interlocks have been shown to reduce rearrests (recidivism) for driving under the influence by nearly 70 percent while they are installed (though recidivism rates jump back to that of normal offenders as soon as the system is removed).[29] Today, every state has some form of an ignition interlock law, and twenty-four states require or encourage the use of an ignition interlock for every drunk-driving offender.

Throughout this time, MADD and other anti-drunk-driving advocates have pushed for accountability for drunk-driving deaths beyond the conduct of the driver. In 1984, the New Jersey Supreme Court rules that those who serve liquor can be held liable, in both criminal and civil cases, for the harms that come about as a result of alcohol consumption.[30] Over the next two decades, other states follow the lead of New Jersey. Forty-three states and the District of Columbia now have "dram shop laws," which hold establishments like bars or restaurants accountable for some actions by its intoxicated customers. The laws vary widely by state, but many of them make it illegal for establishments to encourage intoxication, to serve too many drinks within a short time, to not make nonalcoholic drinks available, to serve underage customers or fail to request proof of a customer's age before serving alcohol, to serve someone after closing time, or to serve over-alcoholic drinks. While the laws' opponents argue that drunk drivers should be the sole parties responsible for their actions, supporters say that the laws decrease illegal and excessive drinking.

In a 2009 Montana case, Travis Vandersloot finishes his shift at Pick's Bowling Center, but sticks around as a customer to have a few drinks. His friend and coworker Nathan Hale is tending bar, and in the next three-and-a-half hours, Vandersloot is served at least thirteen drinks, most of them by Hale. Vandersloot leaves the bowling alley in his car at about 2:20 a.m., and, on his way home, runs his vehicle headlong into that of Montana Highway Patrol trooper Michael Haynes. Both Haynes and Vandersloot die in the crash. Vandersloot's blood alcohol level registers 0.18 percent, more than twice the legal limit.[31] Hale is tried and convicted of serving drinks after hours and is sentenced to four months in prison, two hundred hours of community service, and a fine.

Another attempt to hold younger drinkers themselves accountable are the social-host laws, which apply to drinking in noncommercial settings. The laws make it possible to hold the host of a noncommercial gathering, such as a house party, criminally liable for overserving adults, allowing a drunken guest to drive away, or serving alcohol to minors. For supporters of social-host laws, the more people who can be held responsible, the more likely people will disallow drunk driving. While only ten states have social-host laws against overserving adults, thirty-three states have a social-host law against serving minors.

When strictly enforced, social-host laws have tough consequences, some would argue too tough. For example, Nick Spencer's parents offer to host a party after his baseball team wins the state championships in the spring of 2010. The rules are clear: no alcohol and no drugs. The Spencers monitor the kids as they arrive at the party, checking for alcohol. When some uninvited guests start showing up at about 10:30 p.m., the police arrive. Barry Spencer, Nick's father, asks that the police help monitor the kids coming in. The police watch for a time but they soon leave when they see no evidence of illegal drinking. Soon after police leave, the party of fifty invited guests is crashed by an additional fifty teenaged partiers, some of whom have brought alcohol. The parents seize and dispose of several bottles of liquor, but they do not end the party. Around 11:00 p.m., a driver leaving the party is pulled over by the police. The driver is sober but his underage passenger is drunk. The passenger tells the police that she has been drinking at the Spencer party. Police return to the Spencer home, shut down the party, and arrest the Spencers. Their case goes to trial, but the jury is unable to reach a verdict. Rather than face a retrial, the

Spencers pay $17,000 in fines and restitution, write a letter of apology for the local newspaper, and serve one hundred hours of community service each to avoid jail.[32] This is a sharp contrast to the $583 fine Clarence Busch received for his sixth drunk-driving conviction.

The anti-drunk-driving movement spurred by MADD's creation in 1980 has had an enormous impact. While sentencing varies based on BAC levels, past drunk-driving convictions, the individual state, and culpability at the time of the crash, penalties have increased significantly. Today, a drunk driver in California can be sentenced to ten years in prison for killing someone, while a similar person in North Dakota can receive life in prison. In Tennessee, someone can receive sixty years, and in Nebraska fifty years.

More dramatically, drinking-related accidents and traffic deaths have decreased significantly in the last thirty-five years. Every year from 1980 to 1997 sees a decrease in alcohol-related fatalities; during that period, total alcohol-related traffic fatalities drop by almost 40 percent, saving 8,400 lives per year.[33]

The rate of fatalities stagnates after 1997; annual alcohol-related traffic fatalities hover in the thirteen thousands. MADD's goal of fatality reduction remains frustratingly elusive but legislative gains that they fight for, such as the .08 percent BAC and Zero Tolerance laws, gradually make their way into law, and alcohol-related traffic fatalities again begin to fall, in 2008 dropping to 11,773. Fatalities for people between the ages of sixteen and twenty drop even further. In the 1970s, 67 percent of all traffic deaths for people between sixteen and twenty were alcohol related; today only 37 percent involve alcohol. The Department of Transportation estimates that the higher drinking age alone saves over one thousand people annually.

BEYOND REFORM

The progress has not come without controversy. MADD tends to consider drunk drivers criminals, best controlled by prison sentences and license suspensions. And license suspensions and revocations have become standard as a result of MADD's advocacy. In forty-two states, a driver who submits a sample with a BAC above .08 percent or refuses to submit to a BAC test loses their license on the spot. States vary in their rules about the length of the suspensions. In Kansas, first-time offenders lose their license for thirty days, but in Georgia, a driver can lose their license for a year. Nationwide, the average suspension is for ninety days. Supporters argue that these sanctions are an effective deterrent and have dramatically decreased the number of drunk drivers. They emphasize that the laws must be strong for first-time offenders, as a first arrest is not likely to be a first occurrence: the average drunk driver has gotten behind the wheel drunk eighty times before their first arrest.

But some civil rights advocates argue that license revocation is too great a punishment, as the suspension often prevents people from getting to and from work, and even a month-long suspension might cost someone their job, especially lower-income and minority offenders. They argue that losing the capacity to earn a living is a disproportionate sanction, especially for a first offense. Furthermore, many repeat drunk drivers suffer from alcoholism, which many consider a debilitating disease, a disease that warrants treatment rather than incarceration. MADD does not give those addicted to alcohol a second chance. Whether rehabilitation or retribution should be prioritized remains a major source of contention.

Other critics fear that all these penalties have paved the way for neo-prohibitionism. As more and more laws are adopted to penalize drunk drivers, alcohol-serving establishments, and even private parties, many fear the rules will only serve to drive alcohol consumption underground and encourage people to take unnecessary risks to hide behavior that is otherwise legal. For example, MADD and several other advocacy groups have pushed to lower the legal driving BAC to .05 percent. They say the threat is real: several studies have shown that with a BAC of .05 percent, the relative risk of being in a crash is 38 percent higher than at a BAC of 0.00 percent. Critics, however, contend that this targets average social drinkers, rather than "problem drinkers." Sarah Longwell, managing director of American Beverage Institute, captures the industry's sentiments: "This recommendation is ludicrous. Moving from 0.08 to 0.05 would criminalize perfectly responsible behavior."

Additionally, some MADD advocates have taken other controversial positions: for example, MADD has also expressed skepticism of medical amnesty policies that many universities and several states have adopted that prevent young people from being cited for underage drinking if they call 9-1-1 when someone they know needs medical attention because they have had too much to drink.[34] Many believe these policies, while imperfect, save lives by ensuring that people will call for help when it is needed.

Other anti-drunk-driving advocates believe drunk drivers who cause an accident in which another person dies ought to be held liable for murder. But others point out that there is an enormous difference between intentionally killing another person, murder, and only creating a risk that unfortunately comes about in another person's death, manslaughter. To treat drunk driving as murder is to fail to recognize that, while very serious, it is still less blameworthy than intentionally causing a death. Still, supporters of the drunk-driving-is-murder position argue that it is a sober person who always makes the decision to start drinking, so the law can appropriately hold people accountable for knowingly engaging in activity that endangers others. On the other hand, starting to drink is perfectly legal, so it would be highly inappropriate to use it as the basis for murder liability. While state laws vary, at least four states do treat drunk-driving fatalities as murder.

Finally, critics point out the unfairness and ineffectiveness of targeting only alcohol. Many people drive under the influence of marijuana and other drugs, whether legal or illegal, but police procedures are designed to focus only on alcohol use. Alcohol and marijuana use create different kinds of driver impairments, both of which are highly dangerous when one is operating an automobile on a public highway. However, currently available tests look only to the kind of impairment caused by alcohol, not that caused by marijuana. While MADD and similar organizations have shaped today's anti-drunk-driving legislation, drugs, especially marijuana, represent somewhat uncharted territory.

As America continues to wrestle with these questions, it is clear the problem has not disappeared. Statistically, twenty-seven people are killed by a drunk driver every day; in 2012 alone, two hundred children were killed. Of the 1.4 million DUI arrests each year, one-third of drivers are repeat offenders. Today, alcohol-related crashes cost taxpayers over $100 billion.[35]

Still, we have come a long way. With expanded drunk-driving laws and increased public awareness, drunk driving has become a social taboo, and fatalities from alcohol-related accidents continue to fall. Cari Lightner's mother can feel comfort in the fact that her daughter's death continues to save lives every day.

Chapter Fourteen

1981
Reagan
Assassination Attempt

Insanity Defense

THE TRAGEDY

At 2:25 p.m. on March 30, 1981, President Ronald Reagan has just finished speaking to a group of labor leaders at the Hilton Hotel in Washington, D.C. After shaking hands with everyone one last time, the president and his entourage walk out of the hotel to his motorcade. He takes a moment to greet the crowd of reporters and supporters gathered outside. As he is about to enter the presidential limousine, he turns to give the crowd one last wave. Six shots ring out.

White House press secretary James Brady is shot in the head, local policeman Thomas Delahanty in the back, secret service agent Tim McCarthy in the abdomen, and President Reagan seems to have been grazed by a bullet that ricochets off the car. Alfred Antenucci, a labor official, is near the shooter and hits him in the head, dragging him down to the ground. Agent Dennis McCarthy dives on top, and within seconds the shooter is swarmed and taken into custody. On his person are several books, including a copy of *The Catcher in the Rye*.

Secret Service agent Jerry Parr directs the motorcade back to the White House instead of an unsecured hospital, but soon Reagan begins to cough up bright red blood, so the motorcade heads to George Washington University Hospital. It turns out that the president has a bullet lodged in his lung. Nonetheless, he is able to exit the limo on his own, smiling at onlookers. Once inside the hospital, however, his knees buckle and he collapses on the floor. Surgeons rush him into the operating room to remove the bullet, which is less than an inch from his heart. The surgery

197

is successful, and after two weeks of recovery Reagan is able to leave the hospital. The others injured are not so lucky. Press Secretary Brady survives, but the bullet to his neck has left his speech impaired and caused partial paralysis that will put him in a wheelchair for the rest of his life. The bullet that strikes Officer Delahanty hits his neck and ricochets off his spinal cord. As a result, he suffers from permanent nerve damage to his left arm. McCarthy's bulletproof gear protected him from what would have otherwise been catastrophic injuries.

While President Reagan regains his strength, the shocked nation tries to piece together why someone would attempt to assassinate the president.

The shooter turns out to be twenty-six-year-old John Hinckley Jr. He was born into a well-to-do family in Ardmore, Oklahoma, in 1955.[1] Hinckley has a stable childhood until he is in junior high, when the family moves to Texas and Hinckley becomes quiet and withdrawn. In 1973, he enrolls at Texas Tech in Lubbock, where he completes his first year. The next year he gets his own place and attends school less and less frequently, and dreams of making it big as a politician or a musician. As his dreams grow larger, John's thoughts become increasingly detached from reality. He spends most of his day sitting alone in his apartment.

In the spring of 1976, he sells his car and uses the money to move to Hollywood, California, where he plans to become a famous musician. He sends a letter home to his parents on Mother's Day. "I hope this card finds you both well and in good spirits, despite your impossible younger son," he writes. He tells them where he is and explains that he is "within easy walking distance of about 30 of the most famous music publishers in the world. I'm trying to sell some of my songs."[2] A month later, he writes again: "For the past 2 1/2 weeks I have literally been without food, shelter and clothing. On May 14, someone broke into my room and stole almost all of my possessions." His parents send him money.

Several weeks later, he writes a letter questioning whether he has "any sanity left." He also complains about "Blacks, Mexicans, Chinese and God knows what else." Hinckley writes of a contact at United Artists who has encouraged him to form a duo. In August, he tells his parents about a girlfriend named Lynn Collins and says he has been asked to do a "professional demo" at a studio. The girlfriend and professional success all turn out to be complete fantasies. Around this time, Hinckley watches Martin Scorsese's film *Taxi Driver* for the first time. In the film, actor Robert De Niro plays a depressed taxicab driver who attempts to assassinate a presidential candidate and rescue a teen prostitute, played by Jodie Foster, from her pimp. Dejected and disgusted with "the entire weird, phony, impersonal Hollywood scene," Hinckley soon returns to his parents' home in Colorado.[3]

Figure 14.1. John Hinckley, mug shot, 1981. *District of Columbia Police*

The young man who returns home is "thin, agitated, and nervous," according to his parents.[4] During the winter in Colorado, Hinckley works at a series of low-paying jobs. Using the money he earns, he purchases his first gun, a .38 pistol from a local pawnshop. He expresses his racial hatred more and more often. Hinckley starts to educate himself about the American Nazis.

In August of 1979, he starts to publish his own newsletter for an organization he has invented called the "American Front." He intends the American Front to be "a viable alternative to the minority-kissing Republican and Democrat Parties" and as "a Party for the proud White conservative who would rather wear coats and ties instead of swastikas and sheets."[5] He places himself in the role of national director and fabricates a list of members from thirty-seven different states.

Hinckley is experiencing minor physical ailments, including a sore throat, eye problems, and lightheadedness. His doctors prescribe medications for his physical and mental issues, including an antidepressant called Surmontil and Valium. After starting on the medications, he purchases several additional guns. Having watched *Taxi Driver* over and over, he also now develops an obsession for the young movie star Jodie Foster.

In September 1980, he and his parents decide that Hinckley will enroll in writing classes at Yale. Although he doesn't tell his parents, his real reason for wanting to go to Yale is that Foster is an undergraduate studying literature there. He travels from Denver to New Haven on September 17 and gets a room in the Sheraton Park Plaza. On September 20, he talks to Foster on the phone and tapes the conversation. He talks to her again two days later. She makes it very clear that she is not interested in any type of relationship with Hinckley. Repeatedly rejected, Hinckley becomes increasingly depressed: "I keep getting hit over the head by reality," he writes to his sister, "It doesn't feel very good."[6]

Hinckley buys three thousand dollars' worth of traveler's checks and uses them to travel around the country. On September 28, he flies to Ohio, where President Jimmy Carter is set to give a speech. Hinckley brings guns because he wants to assassinate the president, but at the last minute he has a change of heart, stashing the guns in a locker and shaking hands with Carter instead.

He continues his cross-country travels, writing letters to Foster and greeting Carter again, and is arrested briefly on misdemeanor charges for bringing his weapons through an airport. After he overdoses on antidepressants, Hinckley begins meeting with a psychiatrist, Dr. John J. Hopper. On Election Day, November 4, 1980, Hinckley tells Hopper, "I have two obsessions in life now: writing, and the person we discussed on Nov. 4," Jodie Foster. "I care about nothing else!" he insists.[7] At the end of the month, Hinckley sends an anonymous letter to the FBI warning them about a plot to kidnap Jodie Foster. "No ransom. She's being taken for romantic reasons," he writes, "This is no joke!"[8] On November 30, Hinckley tells his mother he is going to Texas, but flies to Washington instead. There, he hangs around outside the Blair House where President-elect Ronald Reagan is being briefed. He sees Reagan several times, and on one occasion, Hinckley is carrying a gun.

The following month, Hinckley is deeply affected by the assassination of John Lennon by Mark David Chapman. Chapman writes afterward, "My wish is for all of you to someday read 'The Catcher in the Rye.' All of my efforts will now be devoted toward this goal, for this extraordinary book holds many answers." Hinckley writes an essay in response, saying "Guns are neat little things, aren't they? They can kill extraordinary people with very little effort." The essay concludes in utter despair: "The dream died. I died. You died. Everyone died. America died. The world died. The universe died."[9]

Hinckley remains true to his quest for Foster, writing her letters, slipping poems and messages under her door, calling her, and traveling to New Haven to be near her. He continues to fly around the country, regularly stopping in Denver for his appointments with Dr. Hopper. The day after Reagan's inauguration, he buys a .38, the same type of gun Chapman used to kill Lennon. In February, back in New York, he sleeps with four prostitutes, three of them in their teens, like Foster's character in *Taxi Driver*.

Hinckley continues to travel until March 5, 1981, when he runs out of money and returns home. His parents do not see their home as a solution for their son, so they give him $210 and tell him to find a way to support himself. He sells several of his guns, and boards a Greyhound bus for Washington, D.C. He arrives in Washington on March 29 and settles into a hotel. The next morning, after a poor night's sleep and a quick breakfast, he picks up a copy of *The Washington Star* and notices the president's schedule for the day. His mind begins to race, so he takes more Valium. Shortly after lunch, he puts his .22 pistol into his jacket pocket and writes a letter to Jodie Foster, which reads:

> There is definitely a possibility that I will be killed in my attempt to get Reagan. . . . At least you know that I'll always love you. Jodie, I would abandon the idea of getting Reagan in a second if I could only win your heart and live out the rest of my life with you, whether it be in total obscurity or whatever.
>
> I will admit to you that the reason I'm going ahead with this attempt now is because I cannot wait any longer to impress you. I've got to do something now to make you understand, in no uncertain terms, that I'm doing all of this for your sake! . . . Jodie, I'm asking you to please look into your heart

and at least give the chance, with this historical deed, to gain your love and respect.[10]

As soon as he is done writing, he takes a cab to the Washington Hilton where President Reagan will be speaking to representatives of the American Federation of Labor and Congress of Industrial Organizations (AFL-CIO). On this particular day, the Secret Service does not ask the president to wear a bulletproof vest since his only public exposure would be the walk from the hotel to the limousine. It turns out to be the one day the president will need one.

THE OUTRAGE

The shooting is caught on film by the big-three television networks and broadcast across the country almost instantly. The nation is shocked; communities across America cancel major events to hold prayer services for the president. For millions of Americans, the shooting brings back painful memories of the assassinations that took the Kennedy brothers, Martin Luther King Jr., and Malcom X.

The trial of John W. Hinckley Jr. begins a year after the attempted assassination. The legal wrangling is not about whether he pulled the trigger; the trial is to establish whether Hinckley was so mentally ill and that his mental illness has such an impact that he ought not to be held criminally responsible for his actions. The primary legal issue is whether he qualifies for an insanity defense.

Criminal law generally assumes that people have free will and are responsible for the decisions that they make. Even if it is clear that Hinckley pulled the trigger intending to kill the president, he may be excused from all criminal liability if he satisfies the requirements of the insanity defense. Each of the fifty states and the District of Columbia has its own insanity defense formulation. In the District of Columbia, where Hinckley's case is tried, the law governing the insanity defense was set down in the case of *United States v. Brawner*, in which the court adopted the insanity test recommended in the American Law Institute's (ALI) Model Penal Code §4.01(1). (The ALI is essentially the national academy for law in the United States.)

Under the ALI test, a defendant is entitled to an insanity defense "if at the time of [the offense] as a result of mental disease or defect he lacks substantial capacity either to appreciate the criminality of his conduct or to conform his conduct to the requirements of the law." Under this formulation of the defense, Hinckley can get an insanity defense if he committed the offense either because of (1) a serious *cognitive dysfunction*—"he lacks substantial capacity to appreciate the criminality of his conduct"—or (2) a serious *control dysfunction*—"he lacks substantial capacity to conform his conduct to the requirements of law."

In the District of Columbia, the burden of proof is on the prosecution to prove beyond a reasonable doubt that Hinckley was *not insane* when he pulled the trigger. That is, the District of Columbia law assumes that Hinckley is insane and is entitled to an insanity defense unless the prosecution can prove otherwise beyond a reasonable doubt.

During the trial, numerous psychiatric reports portray Hinckley as sufficiently mentally ill to qualify for the defense. Dr. William T. Carpenter, who tested Hinckley, states:

> In my own opinion, I reach the conclusion that he did have a substantial incapacity at that time. The basis for that view deals, of course, with the whole background of psychotic development of his illness that I have described. . . . [B]y the time March 30th had arrived he was so dominated, in my opinion, by the inner state that he had developed over a period of time that his actions and the requirement for his actions were so extensively determined by this inner state that he was, in my opinion, not able to [conform] his conduct to the outside requirements, the legal requirements or social requirements of conduct."

In other words, Hinckley's claimed insanity defense relies upon the second fork, the control dysfunction, rather than the first fork, the cognitive dysfunction. He may have known that what he was doing was criminal but, he claims, "lacked substantial capacity to conform his conduct to the requirements of law."

On June 21, 1982, after much deliberation, the jury returns a verdict of "not guilty by reason of insanity" (NGRI). An NGRI verdict means the defendant is typically remanded to authorities for evaluation, supervision, and treatment. For Hinckley, this means temporary confinement to St. Elizabeth's Hospital in Washington, D.C. for authorities to determine whether he can be civilly detained longer term because he presents a danger.

Many Americans are shocked.[11] ABC News releases a poll the following day, showing that 83 percent of those polled think that in this case "justice was not done."[12] Different journalists reflect the public's outrage by calling the verdict a "travesty of justice" that "did violence to common sense."[13] Major news stations interview the public, finding harsh negative reactions in the days after the trial, such as on the *Phil Donahue Show*. Others write letters to the presiding judge, Judge Barrington Parker, voicing their disdain for the result.

The vast majority of lay people polled say that if they were on the jury, Hinckley surely would have been convicted. The press is not shy about seeking out the jurors and asking them to explain their decision. Lawrence Coffey, the jury foreman, states that "the prosecution's evidence was not strong enough."[14] Another juror, George Blyther, defends his position by reminding the public that "we weren't lawmakers. We had to give a judgment back the way it was given to us. The evidence being what it was, we were required to send John back insane."[15] Remember that the burden of proof was on the prosecution, to disprove Hinckley's insanity beyond a reasonable doubt. If the jurors believed that Hinckley probably was not entitled to an insanity defense but that he might be—that is, there is a possibility that he might qualify for the defense—then their oath as jurors required them to return a verdict of NGRI because there does exist some reasonable doubt as to Hinckley being fully sane.

Lawmakers themselves express their disdain for the verdict and the law under which it was rendered. Senator Strom Thurmond criticizes the insanity defense for "exonerat[ing] a defendant who obviously planned and knew exactly what he was doing."[16] Senator Dan Quayle similarly implores that this insanity defense must be removed from the books as it merely "pamper[s] criminals," and affords them the luxury of killing "with impunity."[17] Something must be done about these laws.

THE REFORM

Less than one month after the jury's verdict, Congress holds hearings to review the existing insanity defense. Congress introduces twenty-six different pieces of legislation to amend or abolish the existing defense. The new proposals attempt to create stricter federal standards to avoid a perceived injustice, such as Hinckley's, in the future.[18] However, other legal and psychiatric professionals at the time urge Congress to modify rather than abolish the insanity defense.

While these debates continue, the Fifth Circuit Court of Appeals moves federal law toward a stricter standard for NGRI in a ruling that accepts the removal of the volitional prong. Hinckley's case pushes the Circuit Court to decide in *United States v. Lyons* that its earlier acceptance of the ALI Model Penal Code definition of insanity had been "premature." It goes on to state that the volitional prong should not be accepted as a part of the insanity defense because it cannot be supported by the "current medical and scientific knowledge."

Later that year, the congressional debate about reforming the insanity defense culminates in the Insanity Defense Reform Act of 1984 (IDRA).[19] The act is meant to counter the problems with the insanity defense that were raised by the Hinckley trial. The legislation moves the federal law to a stricter version of the ALI test, which says "that at the time of the commission of the acts constituting the offense, the defendant, as a result of mental disease or defect, was unable to appreciate the nature and quality or the wrongfulness of his acts." The new formulation, like the Fifth Circuit decision in *Lyons*, drops the control prong out as a possible basis for an insanity defense. It more closely resembles the traditional M'Naghten standard, which again says that "at the time of committing the act, the accused was laboring under such a defect of reason, from disease of the mind, as not to know the nature and quality of the act he was doing or, if he did know it, that he did not know what he was doing was wrong."[20]

While the new federal formulation drops the control prong altogether, it does not completely revert to the old M'Naghten standard. Instead, it retains one aspect of the Model Penal Code's cognitive dysfunction prong: federal law still contains the Model Penal Code's "appreciates" language rather than M'Naghten's "know" language. This allows the cognitive dysfunction prong to be somewhat broader in providing a defense. Unlike the M'Naghten test, the new federal cognitive prong allows defendants to argue that while they "knew" that their conduct was criminal in a purely technical sense, they did not fully "appreciate" its criminality. Nonetheless, by dropping the control prong altogether, the federal insanity defense has been dramatically reduced in breadth.

The federal legislative reform also fixes the burden-of-proof problem. The burden of proof in federal cases is shifted to the defendants to prove their eligible for an insanity defense by clear and convincing evidence. The new insanity provision reads:

> It is an affirmative defense to a prosecution under any Federal statute that, at the time of the commission of the acts constituting the offense, the defendant, as a result of a severe mental disease or defect, was unable to appreciate the nature and quality or the wrongfulness of his acts. Mental disease or defect does not otherwise constitute a defense. The defendant has the burden of proving the defense of insanity by clear and convincing evidence.[21]

Additional administrative hurdles are put in place by the IDRA. For example, expert psychiatric testimony is severely limited, and stricter procedures governing hospitalization commitment and the release of defendants who receive insanity acquittals are mandated.

While the much stricter insanity defense mollifies an angry public, some critics worry that the reform unreasonably excludes whole categories of mentally ill individuals. There is a sense by many that the one outrageous outcome of the Hinckley case will swing the pendulum too far in the other direction and result in systematic injustice for other defendants reasonably claiming the insanity defense. The *New York Times* fears the fallout:

> "[W]rong verdicts are always possible. We should not respond by abandoning a defense that justice requires. A sensible test for legal insanity, fairly applied, can help prevent the concept of the responsible person from disappearing, either because the law naïvely accepts a cacophony of untestable excuses, or because cynical legislators overreact by permitting the conviction and punishment of blameless defendants.[22]

Many argue that the federal reforms are misguided and go too far. All that is needed, they argue, is getting rid of the peculiar District of Columbia rule that put the burden of disproving insanity on the prosecution beyond a reasonable doubt. That change alone would have avoided the insanity verdict in the Hinckley case. Going further to drop the control prong altogether, as the federal legislation does, undermines the criminal law's commitment to protecting from criminal liability morally blameless offenders. There will be many cases in which the criminal offender knows his or her conduct is criminal and wrong but is literally psychologically compelled to commit the offense. Even the English common law recognized such cases of "irresistible impulse" as deserving an insanity defense.

Some mental health advocates, sensing that current public sentiment is not on their side, go on the offensive on the insanity defense. The Mental Health Association of America strongly calls on "states [to] provide a full insanity defense. When defendants' mental illnesses prevent them from understanding the wrongfulness of the act or prevent them from controlling their behavior, they should be acquitted by reason of insanity. Criminal liability in these instances is neither appropriate nor effective."[23] Further, those "acquitted because of a finding of insanity should be treated in an appropriate clinical setting. The purpose of this treatment should be rehabilitative, not punitive."[24] They argue that eliminating the insanity defense and incarcerating mentally ill offenders has strongly and negatively increased our already high prison population, and puts these individuals in a position much more likely to reoffend upon release because prison does not help rehabilitate them. But the cries of mental health professionals generally go unheeded.

In the aftermath of the Hinckley insanity acquittal, thirty-three states narrow their NGRI defense in some way.[25] Many states shift the burden of proof to the defendant and increase the standard of proof required in order to make it increasingly difficult for a defendant to sustain an insanity plea. The states commonly follow the federal trajectory by moving further away from the more progressive ALI standard and closer toward the older, more restrictive M'Naghten standard. Now, more than half of the jurisdictions in the United States have no laws-of-control prong in their insanity defense.[26]

Some states have gone further. Six have eliminated the insanity defense altogether: Idaho, Kansas, Montana, Nevada, North Dakota, and Utah. In these states, mental illness may still be introduced as evidence to negate or disprove culpability required for proof of an offense. The American Bar Association comes out strongly against these efforts, declaring:

> This approach, which would permit evidence of mental conditions on the requisite mental element of the crime but eliminate nonresponsibility as an independent, exculpatory doctrine, has been proposed in several bills in Congress and adopted in Montana, Idaho and Utah. The ABA has rejected it out of hand. Such a jarring reversal of hundreds of years of moral and legal history would constitute an unfortunate and unwarranted overreaction to the Hinckley verdict.[27]

Three states have gone even further: Louisiana, Mississippi, and Washington have tried to disallow *any* evidence regarding mental illness to be submitted for any reason, but such laws are often found to be unconstitutional.[28]

As standards for the insanity defense have tightened, the correctional system is now grappling with what to do with "insane offenders," or people with severe mental illness that are found guilty and put in prison. The case of Andrea Yates, a Texas woman who stood trial for drowning her five children one by one in a bathtub, illustrates the difficulties of dealing with these offenders.[29] Yates's lawyers argue that she has severe mental illness, by showing that she had attempted suicide twice, was diagnosed with psychosis, and was previously hospitalized four times for psychiatric care. Nonetheless, by the existing legal statutes, Yates is found guilty after a mere thirty-five minutes of jury deliberation. The 2002 case receives much publicity for allowing this very disturbed individual to be found guilty of murder.[30] Yates's case is not unique. In 2014, estimates suggest that 20 percent of inmates in jail and another 15 percent of inmates in state prisons are mentally ill. In fact, there are ten times as many people suffering from mental illness in the correctional system than are in mental-health facilities. Congress recognizes the problem and in 2016 passes the Comprehensive Justice and Mental Health Act. The act provides "millions of dollars for state and local governments to design new and innovative approaches to reduce the number of people with mental illness in jail."[31]

The United States Supreme Court has never directly addressed the issue of minimum requirements of the Constitution in regard to the insanity defense. However, many point to dicta, or indirect statements, made in cases related to the issue. For example, in *Foucha v. Lousiana* (1992),

Justice Anthony Kennedy says, "States are free to recognize and define the insanity defense as they see fit."[32] Justice O'Connor seemingly concurs. Most recently, the court declines to rule on the constitutionality of "abolition statutes" in *Montana v. Cowan* in 1994. Some read this as suggesting that the court has implicitly approved of states abolishing all insanity defenses, but most note that a court denying to hear a case has no legal precedential value.

It is unclear whether abolition of the insanity defense actually results in enhanced public safety. As mental-health-law expert David B. Wexler observes, those receiving *not guilty by reason of insanity* verdicts have "had an easier route into and a more difficult route out of the institutions than have their civilly committed counterparts."[33] Ordinary people may believe that the mentally ill are escaping punishment, but research shows that NGRI acquittees are actually confined as long (in New Jersey, Arizona, Wisconsin, and Washington) or *longer* (in California, New York, the District of Columbia, Colorado, and Connecticut) than defendants convicted on equivalent charges who have been determined to be sane. Contrary to public perception, the recidivism rate for NGRI acquittees is no greater than that of "normal" felons. Interestingly, after these reforms, there is no significant change in the number of insanity acquittals, even though that is the explicit attempt of these legislative efforts.[34]

Debate about the insanity defense also sparked discussion about the validity of psychological evaluations in the judicial system. Some legal experts argue that within the fields of psychology and psychiatry "concepts of mental abnormality remain fluid and imprecise, and most academic commentary within the last 10 years continues to question the scientific basis for assessment of volitional (control) incapacity."[35] Other skeptics argue that mental-health concepts are simply not developed enough to be applied in the legal system. *Washington Post* columnist George Will expresses the widely shared views of the time, "Psychiatry as practiced by some of today's itinerant experts-for-hire is this century's alchemy. No, that is unfair to alchemists, who were confused but honest. Some of today's rent-a-psychiatry is charlatanism laced with cynicism."[36]

The American Psychiatric Association reminds critics like Will that psychiatrists have the ability to speak to a patient's *psychological* capacity, but not to how a patient's psychological state relates to legal concepts like insanity. That, after all, is the job of lawyers and judges. Similar arguments stress the important difference between a "mental disease or defect," which is solely a legal concept used in insanity defenses, and a "mental disorder," which is a medical concept drawn from clinical criteria in the *Diagnostic and Statistical Manual* of the American Psychiatric Association.

Medical professionals may competently testify to and apply the latter with confidence, but not the former.

BEYOND REFORM

After his insanity acquittal, Hinckley spends the next three decades civilly committed in a secure mental-health facility. For years, he continues to threaten Jodie Foster from his mental-hospital bed. He also continues to implore doctors to allow him outside of the four walls of the mental institution, even if for just a few hours.

In 2005, a judge rules that Hinckley may slowly begin to take walks outside and relearn rudimentary domestic and personal skills, such as taking out the garbage and cooking. In 2016, doctors declare that Hinckley is in full remission. After consultation with mental-health professionals, the court finds that the sixty-one-year-old is no longer a danger to the public, and he is released. He moves to Virginia and lives with his ninety-year-old mother.

Americans struggle to understand the practical implications of an offender getting an insanity defense. In surveys gauging public reaction following the Hinckley trial, approximately 80.9 percent of respondents know that a NGRI verdict means Hinckley will be sent to a mental hospital, at least initially. Many assume the verdict is equal to a standard acquittal. In fact, as with Hinckley, an NGRI verdict typically means evaluation, supervision, and required treatment for one's mental disability.

Even today, many people still hold the memory of John Hinckley and have strong negative feelings regarding the insanity defense, viewing it as a loophole that lets guilty offenders walk free. But many of people's beliefs are based on false information. There is a popular belief that the insanity defense is overused, and that dangerous individuals like Hinckley are easily freed.[37] One study finds that ordinary people estimate that 38 percent of all defendants get an insanity defense. In reality, the insanity defense is typically raised in less than 1 percent of all felony cases. Across the states, the percentage of cases in which an insanity plea is entered ranges from .29 percent to 1.73 percent, with an average of .85 percent of felony indictments. Even when it is raised, it is only successful about 15 to 25 percent of the time.

In sum, empirical information suggests the insanity defense in its many formulations is not abused today. We have nothing to lose by keeping it, but by abolishing it, we risk undermining the moral credibility of the law. We know from empirical studies that ordinary people feel strongly that criminal law should punish those who are shown to be morally blameworthy but should protect from criminal liability those who are not.

And while politicians and media outlets have helped to give the insanity defense a bad name, the empirical studies confirm that ordinary people feel strongly that offenders who are not morally responsible for their conduct ought to be protected from criminal liability.[38] Finding the balance between doing justice, public safety, and the rights of the individual will not come easily or without mistakes, but upholding the credibility of the law and ensuring the protection of all citizens depends on it.

Chapter Fifteen

1983
Beirut Barracks Bombing
Internationalization of the FBI

THE TRAGEDY

In the predawn hours of the morning of October 23, 1983, the soldiers in the Marine Amphibious Unit (MAU) are sleeping in barracks. It's a Sunday, so the marines are permitted an extra hour of sleep. Lance Corporal Eddie DiFranco stands at his post in the parking lot outside the Battalion Landing Team (BLT) headquarters in Beirut, Lebanon.[1] At 5:00 a.m., a yellow Mercedes stake-bed truck pulls into the parking lot, drives around, and then leaves. Around an hour later, Lance Corporal John Berthiaume watches a white Mercedes drive down the airport highway nearby the headquarters. The driver stretches out of the window of the vehicle and snaps pictures of the building.

At 6:00 a.m., the battalion sergeant of the guard, Sergeant Stephen Russell, is on duty at the south entry to the BLT building's entrance hall. He is a twenty-eight-year-old, short mustachioed man who joined the marines right out of high school in 1974. After a five-year interlude working in a car factory, he rejoined the "Few and the Proud" and became a squad leader of an antitank missile unit.

Sergeant Russell is posted in a plywood booth with a wall of sandbags on the parking lot side. Russell finds pleasure in "a typical Beirut morning, the sunrise is bright and beautiful."[2] He chats briefly with Berthiaume, who stops by to return his night vision goggles and mentions seeing the photos taken.

A little after 6:20 a.m., Russell hears "a sort of popping or crackling sound from the direction of the parking lot."[3] As the sound grows louder,

Russell turns to see a yellow Mercedes truck pulling through the gate dividing the public parking lot from the marine headquarters.

DiFranco, who is on duty by the parking lot, is momentarily shocked. He looks at the dark bearded driver and begins to load his M-16. To enhance their image as peacekeepers, marines are not permitted to have their weapons ready to fire. In the few seconds that it takes to load and aim, DiFranco loses his opportunity for a clean shot. The truck enters the compound.

Sergeant Russell bolts up as the truck advances toward him. He sprints across the atrium toward the back door screaming "HIT THE DECK!" The sergeant bursts through the back door and commands a nearby marine to "Get down!" The soldier ducks behind a concrete wall and Russell finds his way into a parking lot between the headquarters and the garbage dump to the north. He looks behind him in time to see the truck smash his plywood guard shack. The shack explodes "like a huge wave of water rushing into the lobby, filling every space."[4] He runs for about thirty more feet before turning around again. The truck comes to a stop in the lobby, right in the center of the barracks where hundreds of American service-men are sleeping. Russell sees that the windshield and driver's side cab roof are banged up. The driver does not stir.

At 6:22 a.m., the truck explodes. From afar, Russell sees "a bright orange-yellow flash at the grill of the truck" and then "a wave of intense heat and a powerful concussion" rushes over him. The bomb is made up of some twelve thousand pounds of explosives wrapped in containers filled with combustible gas; it is the largest nonnuclear explosion since World War II. The explosion is so powerful that it lifts the four-story steel and concrete building into the air, cutting through the massive steel-reinforced sup-port columns. The building collapses on itself in a flaming sea of gas, and percussive shock radiates outward. The fireball goes downward through the basement floor, leaving a thirty-nine-by-twenty-nine-foot crater. The explosion and ensuing building collapse kills 241 American soldiers. The marines lose 220 men, 18 from the navy die, along with 3 members of the army and 1 Lebanese (the custodian). Another thirteen marines die later from injuries. The death toll is the highest in U.S. Marine Corps history since D-Day on Iwo Jima.

The story of how 241 American soldiers die on October 23, 1983, starts decades earlier in 1948, when Zionists finally realize their dream of de-claring the official Jewish state of Israel, the creation of which is urged and approved by the United Nations. Immediately after Israel comes into being, the Arab states launch an offensive against the nascent state, confident that they can crush it before Israel fully establishes itself. Israel, however, surprises everyone when it decisively wins the year-long war. Instead of ousting Israel, the war only reinforces and expands their ter-

Figure 15.1. The rubble of the barracks following the Oct. 23, 1983, bombing. *PJF Military Collection / Alamy Stock Photo*

ritorial claims to the area. Suddenly, nearly five hundred thousand Palestinians become stateless refugees.

Palestinians are angry, but they are powerless to do anything about their plight. In 1964, Palestinian leaders found the Palestinian Liberation Organization with the support of Arab states (most notably Egypt) to bolster the cause of Palestinian nationalism. The purpose of the PLO is "liberating Palestine" from rule by Israel and the return of Palestinian refugees.[5]

In 1967, Israel's Arab neighbors again take up arms to eliminate Israel. The result for the Arabs is even more devastating than last time: Israel routs the combined Arab forces after only six days. Though eight hundred Israelis die, close to twenty thousand citizens of the various Arab nations are killed, and Israel again expands its territory in Palestine.[6] This second overwhelming defeat creates a new wave of refugees and deals a serious blow to the Palestinian cause and Arab nationalism more generally. Some Palestinians respond to this by turning to radicalism. Fatah, a radical subgroup within the PLO, grows in popularity. In 1968, the larger PLO amends its charter to call for "Palestinian-initiated 'armed struggle' against Israel as the main vehicle for the liberation of Palestine."[7] "Armed struggle" against Israel comes to include airplane hijackings, bombings carried out against non-Israeli targets, the attack on the Israeli Olympic team at the Munich Olympics in 1972, and a variety of other forms of terrorist acts.

After being expelled from Jordan in 1971, the PLO takes refuge in Lebanon. Led by Yasser Arafat, they establish an autonomous entity in the middle of Lebanon, destabilizing the country and contributing to the civil war in 1975.

On the sixth of June, 1982, after an assassination attempt on Israeli ambassador Shlomo Argov by Fatah, the Israeli Defense Force (IDF) invades southern Lebanon. Israeli troops march on Lebanon's capital, Beirut, where there is a large PLO presence. The Israelis lay siege to West Beirut, and on June 14, Maronite Christian militia units, the Lebanese forces from East Beirut, join up with the IDF. The Israelis have supported the Lebanese forces both financially and militarily for years. The Christians oppose both the PLO and the Syrian forces that have invaded their country. The Lebanese forces are happy to have Israel's military clear the highway between Beirut and Damascus.

On July 2, 1982, the IDF installs a military blockade around Beirut—cutting off food, water, and oil from the city, and also bombing West Beirut—in an effort to force the PLO out, which is successful. With the PLO out, Lebanese president Bachir Gemayel calls on the UN to demand that all the warring parties leave his country. The UN, in turn, asks President Reagan to send troops to Lebanon.

This request sparks intense debate within the U.S. government. The National Security Agency and the State Department believe that sending troops will stabilize Lebanon and strengthen U.S. interests in the region. But the Joint Chiefs of Staff and other military officials are unanimously opposed as they feel the mission is poorly defined with no clear path to resolving an already degenerating situation. Reagan decides to send troops, and they arrive in Lebanon on August 25. Peace is quickly established, and before the end of the month, the Americans are off Lebanese soil and back aboard their ships. According to marine commander James Meade, the marines came to the area to "establish an environment which will permit the Lebanese Armed Forces to carry out their responsibilities in the Beirut area."[8]

On September 14, President Bachir Gemayel is assassinated by a Syrian nationalist. The killing prompts an attack on a Syrian refugee camp by persons loyal to the dead president. Chaos returns to the country. The dead president's brother, Amine Gemayel, takes control. On September 29, eighteen hundred American marines return to Lebanon. This time, President Reagan says that the troops are there to "facilitate the restoration of the sovereignty and authority of the Lebanese Government over the Beirut area. In no case will our troops stay longer than 30 days."[9]

Gemayel is determined to turn the page on the months of violence that has plagued Beirut. The next day, September 30, Gemayel reopens the Beirut International Airport. The milestone is celebrated as a symbol of peace and reunification of East and West Beirut. The president speaks, declaring "a reunification of the hearts" and calling the airport a symbol of hope for all of Lebanon. The first flight touches down, arriving from Larnaca, Cyprus. Beirut is now a single city again, and a functioning airport is visible proof to the world.

Yet as the president gives his speech, there is an explosion. Marine corporal David L. Reagan, twenty-one years old, of Chesapeake, Virginia, is killed. Three other marines are wounded. The official account is that an undetected mine killed the marine, but many feel that this is no accident.

Despite the assurances of a month-long engagement, the international peacekeeping mission of which the United States is part quietly goes on for months. The marines move into a four-story concrete building at the airport. This location puts some space between the Israeli troops to the south and the Shiite neighborhoods in the north. The building originally housed Lebanon's Aviation Administration Bureau. During more recent times, it was occupied by the PLO, the Syrians, and the Israelis, who used it as a field hospital over the summer.

The foreign forces are peacekeepers, so they go unarmed. Colonel Mead decides that for the marines to effectively achieve their objectives, they will need to make their presence very obvious. He orders his soldiers to hoist the U.S. flag everywhere, on their conveyances and fortifications. They stitch American-flag patches onto their uniforms and patrol the surrounding Shiite-populated areas.

The Lebanese Army becomes viable, a key goal of the International force. Yet outside Beirut, the country is mired in conflict. Different Muslim factions fight for control of Tripoli, Lebanon's second largest city. Christians and the Druze religious sect continue to clash. Israeli troops on the Sidon road face frequent ambushes. The international force works hard, but peace is not taking root.

By March of 1983, local resentment of the peacekeepers is building. Some Muslims resent the U.S. support of President Gemayel and see the rebuilding of the National Army as strengthening the Christian Phalange party. Extremists cannot take command of the region while the peacekeepers are in place. As a result, there are increasing attacks against the multinational peacekeeping forces. Five marines patrolling the Shiite neighborhood of Ouzai are wounded by a grenade. Italian and French forces face similar attacks. On April 18, at around 1:00 in the afternoon, a truck enters the U.S. Embassy compound and explodes, causing a third of the building to collapse. More than sixty people die, seventeen of whom are American citizens.

The situation in Lebanon continues to deteriorate. Druze fight the Lebanese forces for the town of Bhamdun and the National Army tries to extend control over Shiite areas in Beirut, only to find themselves repelled by the Shiite Amal militia. On September 4, the IDF withdraws, and fighting expands into the hills surrounding Beirut. The Lebanese forces falter without Israeli support. Palestinian and Druze fighters shell Beirut. The multinational peacekeeping force comes under heavy fire. By September 6, four marines and sixteen French soldiers are dead.

The U.S. military assistance to the Lebanese government confirms its partisan status in the eyes of the Moslem and Druze militants. The concerned marines beef up security, and the *New Jersey*, a battleship, arrives in Beirut from Nicaragua toward the end of September. From September's end until October 22, the marines are embroiled in near constant conflict, facing fire almost every day.

The next day, October 22, 1983, the truck bomb drives into the American barracks and kills 241 soldiers.

Several minutes after the blast that flattens the marine barracks, a pickup truck carrying a bomb drives toward the nine-story French paratrooper headquarters in Ramlet el-Baida, a waterside section of West Beirut. French soldiers see the truck coming and fire at the driver. The truck grinds to a stop around forty-five feet from the building. Not quite a minute passes before the bomb detonates. The building collapses, and fifty-eight soldiers are killed. Many others are wounded.

The attacks are engineered by Imad Fayez Mugniyah, a member of the Lebanese militant Shiite organization Hezbollah, which was formed by a number of Muslim clerics then financially supported by the Islamic Republic of Iran. A native son of Lebanon, Mugniyah got his start as a member of the Force 17, Yasser Arafat's personal bodyguard.

Not fully trusting the young Hezbollah, Iranian officials send their own agents to Beirut to carry out Mugniyah's planned attack against the French paratroopers and the American marines. In Beirut, the Iranians prepare the bombs and an Iranian man named Ismail Ascari drives the stake-bed truck into the BLT building.

THE OUTRAGE

In the wake of the bombings, Americans want answers. A bipartisan House subcommittee led by Representative Bill Nichols (D-AL), is established to investigate the incident. The inquiry is launched at the beginning of November, and soon the panel issues a report blaming the gruesome failure to prevent the attack on "very serious errors in judgment" on the part of field officers and their commanders.[10] The committee concludes that the peacekeeping mission was destined for failure from the beginning. Among other problems, the marines were not sufficiently trained, security was too lax, and the marine headquarters was not laid out with adequate protection against car bombs. Some members of Congress claim that the marine commanders (both in Beirut and higher up on the chain of command) are at fault because they "didn't review the Marines' posture and failed to exercise sufficient oversight."[11] Additionally, critics also claim that the marines had a lot of information about potential attacks, but the commanders failed to employ anyone able to interpret the intelligence.

The committee also recommends that Reagan reconsider the marines' mission in Lebanon. The report says that the "policy making authority" in the U.S. capital "must also be held to account" for pursuing a strategy that made it impossible to take appropriate precautions.[12] One committee member, Representative Larry J. Hopkins, reminds everyone that "the people in the Mideast have been fighting since the days of Abraham. Asking our Marines to stop the fighting there is like trying to change the course of Niagara Falls with a bucket."[13] He also claims that America's shift in policy is partly to blame: "When we started firing in support of the Lebanese armed forces, we were no longer neutral."[14]

On April 26, 1984, President Reagan addresses Congress about the threat of terrorism. In his speech, he explains:

> In the past fifteen years, terrorism has become a frightening challenge to the tranquility and political stability of our friends and allies. During the past decade alone, there have been almost 6,500 terrorist incidents. Over 3,500 people have been killed in these incidents, and more than 7,600 people have been wounded. American citizens have been the victims of more than 2,500 terrorist incidents.[15]

Reagan talks of the growing fear of "state terrorism" as opposed to traditional attacks. Foreign states increasingly train, finance, and support the terrorist groups acting in the name of the state. In order to combat these new threats, the United States needs to leverage its diplomatic tools and call on other states to help in the fight against these state terrorists.

At the same time that Reagan appeals to Congress, the media is focusing on international terrorist attacks.[16] These attacks take up the majority of newspaper print and broadcast time in television and radio. The attention from the media is so widespread that in some cases, critics say that the media has begun to serve as a platform for terrorists to present their ideas. From airplane hijackings, to hostage situations, to the Beirut bombings, the American public is growing more and more terrified. American citizens no longer feel safe abroad. American travel to western Europe and the Middle East drops significantly.

THE REFORM

After the attack in Beirut, it is clear that Congress needs to act. In 1984, Congress passes a massive piece of anticrime legislation entitled the "Comprehensive Crime Control Act."[17] While the wide-ranging bill addresses a host of domestic-crime issues, Title 18 of the act grants the FBI jurisdiction over any hostage situation in which the victim or the perpetrator is an American or which the United States is a target of the hostage takers' demands. The hostage taker need not touch American soil for the FBI to take on the case—foreign terrorists can no longer avoid FBI involvement simply by committing their crimes in other countries.

The FBI is eager to demonstrate its new power. In 1985, the FBI gets its chance when a Royal Jordanian airliner is hijacked. No one is injured in the hijacking; however, seventy passengers are taken hostage, and the hijackers force the crew to take the plane and terrorists to Cyprus, Sicily, and Beirut. As the crisis is being resolved, the plane is blown up and the terrorists flee the scene. There are four Americans among the hostages.

Behind the shield of the Comprehensive Crime Control Act of 1984, as soon as the Americans are taken hostage, the FBI has jurisdiction. Officials identify one of the terrorists as Fawaz Yunis, who lives in still-chaotic Lebanon. Lebanon does not have much in the way of a functioning legal system at the time. And, there is no treaty between Lebanon and the United States that will give officials quick access to Yunis. Instead, the FBI sets up a classic sting operation to catch the hijacker. On September 13, 1987, Yunis and his brother board an eighty-foot sailing yacht to meet a drug dealer. Instead of drug dealers, Yunis is met by undercover FBI agents. As soon he steps onto the deck of the ship in international waters, Yunis is arrested, read his rights, and interrogated. Yunis confesses to his involvement in the 1985 hijacking.

This is the first time a suspected international terrorist is arrested and apprehended overseas. He is immediately brought to the United States to stand trial. Yunis is tried, convicted and sentenced in U.S. court. The federal judge holds, for the first time, that the United States has the right to arrest someone involved in a hijacking that involves American hostages. In his decision, the judge says:

> Not only is the United States acting on behalf of the world community to punish alleged offenders of crimes that threaten the very foundations of world order, but the United States has its own interest in protecting its nationals.[18]

Attorney General Edwin Meese promises that this will be far from the last international arrest. As long as terrorists are endangering U.S. citizens, U.S. law enforcement will exercise its authority abroad. Attorney General Meese explains:

> As we have said many times, acts of terrorism are criminal acts, pure and simple. The world must deal with them as criminal acts, and utilize the rule of law in order to combat this very serious threat to the lives and well-being of citizens of every country.[19]

While the legislation goes a long way in expanding the powers of the U.S. government in fighting international crime, none of the legislation would have helped the sleeping marines. However, the same year of the hijacking in 1985, Congress authorizes the United States to exchange cash for information. Now U.S. operatives can pay informants for information about potential terrorist attacks. Such capability could have made a difference in Beirut. President Reagan also works with other nations to craft bilateral agreements on punishing terrorists and even executing terrorists found guilty of attacking diplomats.

Then in 1986, Congress expands U.S. jurisdiction further. Instead of making the location of the crime or the nationality of the perpetrator the basis for criminal prosecution—known as "active personality theory"—the new legislation uses "passive personality theory," stipulating that any homicide, attempted homicide, or even conspiracy to commit homicide against an American can give United States jurisdiction under outlined circumstances. Congress also addresses additional legal gaps in prosecuting crimes against Americans abroad, such as crimes against international shipping, or piracy, and in increased safety for diplomatic personnel. Around this same time, Congress also passes the airport-security laws (see chapter 12 on the TWA bombings) that aim to increase luggage screening, control access to terminals, and strengthen passport controls in foreign airports.

In 1989, the FBI gains the authority to arrest terrorists, drug traffickers, and other fugitives abroad after a ruling by the Justice Department's Office of Legal Counsel. Traditionally, the United States has adhered to a policy that requires the consent of the country in which the individual sought by American authorities is currently located to arrest them. The Department of Justice further declares that the president can direct the FBI to initiate investigations abroad and arrest individuals if the FBI finds they are in violation of international law.

While the powers are quite broad on paper, in reality the United States largely continues to follow international norms in the name of the cooperation that is so vital to fighting terrorism. For example, Mohammed Ali Hammadi took part in a 1985 hijacking of a plane bound for San Diego, California. Several years after the hijacking, Hammadi is arrested in Germany while attempting to smuggle liquid explosives.[20] Despite repeated U.S. requests, Germany is unwilling to extradite the killer. Though the American government wants Hammadi to serve a longer sentence than the nineteen-year sentence given by the German court, the United States knows it must respect the German legal system so that the United States and Germany can remain united in the ongoing fight against terrorism.

The FBI also introduces an official international program that enables the FBI to have full-time liaisons living in foreign countries.[21] The agents abroad, dubbed "Legal Attachés," live among their foreign counterparts so they can be at hand when the need arises. The program enhances all nations' ability to combat international terrorism, organized crime, cyber-crime, and general crime. Legal Attaché offices are established through agreements with host countries. Many countries have welcomed the FBI through this program, and there are currently over two hundred countries, territories, and islands with Legal Attaché officers.

The FBI also provides intense training to international law enforcement officers. The range of skills offered with this training includes negotiation techniques, investigation techniques, evidence gathering, strengthening working relationships, stopping terrorism, and weapons use. Training academies now are in place all over the world including Budapest, Hungary, Bangkok, Thailand, and Gaborone, Botswana. These relationships make it easier for the FBI to work in foreign countries and put foreign officers in a position to aid U.S. investigations. They also make other countries better equipped to uncover, prosecute, and deter international terrorism, making the world safer for everyone.

The FBI's expanded international powers have garnered real results.[22] For example, in 1998, the U.S. embassies in Kenya and Tanzania are bombed within minutes of each other in one of the first major attacks orchestrated by Osama bin Laden. The attack is in retaliation for American military presence in Saudi Arabia. In the Kenya attack, 224 people are killed, including 12 Americans. Those killed are mostly locals because the security guard on duty refused to allow the bomber's truck to enter the embassy's underground parking garage. In the Tanzania attack, 11 locals are killed.

Besides elevating bin Laden to the status of the world's most dangerous man, the bombings serve as an important test case for trying international crimes in an American court. The court upholds the validity of the 1985 and 1986 additions to the U.S. criminal code, even though no part of the attack was planned or executed in America. The court rules that as long as the conspiracy was formulated against United States citizens, the defendants can be held accountable in U.S. court. In 2001, four of the bombing defendants are sentenced to life in prison without parole after being convicted on over two hundred counts. More conspirators are eventually tried and convicted.

The United States government also successfully prosecutes Richard Reid, who in 2001 boards an American Airlines flight in Paris wearing shoes with explosives inside.[23] Fortunately, Reid does not successfully detonate his shoe bomb and is arrested as soon as the plane lands in Boston. Reid pleads guilty to terrorism and attempted homicide in federal court. He is sentenced to life in prison plus 110 years. Before the laws creating United States jurisdiction for terrorist attacks on airplanes, this case would have been more difficult to prosecute.

The embassy bombers and the shoe bomber are only two of many examples in which the United States has successfully used international jurisdiction to bring international terrorists to justice. In 1996, FBI director Louis Freeh submits a proposal to the Senate and House judiciary committees for further expansion of the scope of the FBI's powers, doubling the number of offices abroad and the number of special agents. To Freeh, the goal is to prevent the infiltration of "foreign criminals originating in partial or complete sanctuaries abroad and using their beyond-the-border advantages to carry out terrorism, drug trafficking, and other violent crimes while they also rob American pockets by vast, complex economic crimes."[24] The proposal succeeds and Congress enacts the necessary legislation to further broaden the powers of the FBI abroad.

However, the expanding jurisdiction of the FBI and the U.S. involvement in international terrorism has drawn criticism. Some experts, along with other nations, argue that the United States has gone too far. They say that the notion of passive personality theory makes it too easy for U.S. enforcement to brandish its weapons throughout the world. Some even say that the plan is a sort of bureaucratic empire building. Its workings have the potential to undermine operations led by the Central Intelligence Agency and the Drug Enforcement Agency among many others. Unless communications between the agencies are completely solid, there are bound to be conflicting interests. Further, some claim that the expansion of FBI jurisdiction has the potential to cause diplomatic tensions as the move may be interpreted as an infringement on the foreign state's sovereignty. With advancing technology like drones that make it easier for the United States to spy and to strike throughout the world, the debate over the increase international powers of federal law enforcement is certain to rage on for decades to come.

Chapter Sixteen

1983
Thurman Beatings
Domestic Violence

THE TRAGEDY

L ate one night, Tracey wakes up to someone's hands crushing her throat.[1] She gasps and struggles, then looks up, making out the figure of her boyfriend, Charles Thurman (whom everyone calls "Buck"). His face is cold and blank as he kneels over her, and his breath reeks of alcohol. With great effort, she kicks him with enough force to make him release his hold. Had she not, she is certain "he would have killed me."[2]

This is not the first time Buck has assaulted Tracey. She first meets him in 1979, when she is eighteen. Her mother had just died of lung cancer, so Tracey drops out of high school and leaves her hometown of Torrington, Connecticut, for St. Petersburg, Florida, where she finds work as a hotel maid. There she meets Buck, a handsome seventeen-year-old who works in construction. Tracey and Thurman develop a strong attraction to one another, and within two weeks the couple is living together.[3] With no other ties, Tracey begins to follow Thurman's construction crew from state to state. But developing friendships is hardly possible when she moves so often, so aside from Buck, Tracey has few friends. According to Tracey, Buck makes her "feel so secure. Because I didn't have anyone else."[4]

However, Tracey begins to discover that Buck has a dark side. During arguments, he physically fights with Tracey. At first, she says, "I just slapped him back, and that was the end of it."[5] But Buck soon escalates the intensity of his assaults, and Tracey grows fearful. When she becomes pregnant with their son, C.J., she flees from Buck and returns to Connecticut. Buck follows Tracey, and with seemingly great sincerity, begs for forgiveness. Tracey—reluctant at first—eventually gives in. "I didn't want to raise a child by myself,"[6] she says. With a baby on the way, the couple marries and returns to their nomadic life.

Despite his pledges to change, Buck's mood swings only grow ever more erratic. His physical assaults against his young wife become more frequent and more violent. Tracey leaves Buck two more times, but Buck always returns with promises to change that go unfulfilled. It becomes a vicious cycle.

But with the terror of almost being strangled to death by Buck in the middle of the night, Tracey realizes getting away from Buck is a matter of life or death. So in October of 1982, she flees to Torrington with baby C.J. Again, Buck tracks her down and begs for forgiveness. But this time his powers of persuasion fail; Tracey is staying in Torrington to chart a new course without him. Buck does not take the decision well. He quits his construction job and settles in Torrington, too, working as a counterman and short-order cook at Skie's Diner.

His life seems to center around tormenting Tracey. He often calls her twenty-five times in a single day, pleading to see her. He drives by her home. He openly—and frequently—tells others at work that he hopes to kill his wife. He even says this to officers of the Torrington Police Department, who frequent the diner and have come to like the new cook. Buck's animosity toward his wife is known to all. Tracey is afraid.

On October 22, 1982, Tracey—who is staying with her friends Judy Bentley and Richard St. Hilaire—hears a knock. She opens the door to find Buck standing on the porch. She refuses to let him inside, so Buck lunges, grabbing Tracey's throat. Tracey manages to break free, then she runs inside and calls police. The police arrive and they remove Buck, but within thirty minutes he is pounding at the door again. Tracey and her friends barricade the door. The police do nothing this time, but Bentley and St. Hilaire, as owners of the property, insist on filing a formal complaint against Buck and request help to keep Buck off of their property.

On November 1, Buck returns to the apartment. This time he gets past the threshold. Once inside, Buck grabs the baby and flees the apartment. According to the formal complaint filed that day with police, Buck announces to Tracey: "If we can't bring up the baby together, no one will do it."[7] Buck tells Tracey that if she calls the police, he will kill her. Tracey ignores the threat and contacts authorities. She makes it clear to the police that she is serious about her commitment to end the terror, saying "I want my husband arrested for threatening me and the baby. I will go to court."[8]

The police get baby C.J. back to his mother and consider the incident resolved. The court record indicates that no further action is taken. On

November 3, she calls the police again to report Buck for making threatening phone calls. The police record the call in the official log.

On November 5, Tracey takes a call from the city's family relations office. Buck has come to the office seeking visitation rights, and the office wants Tracey to come in so they can hear Tracey's perspective before making a decision. Tracey drives to the office, which is located on the second floor of a municipal building above the police station. After the interview, she gets in her car, and she sees Buck in the parking lot of the police station. Buck maneuvers his car to block Tracey from leaving the parking lot. With Tracey penned in, he exits his own vehicle and smashes Tracey's windshield with his fist. He yells out, "I will get you, and when I do, I will really hurt you." Many people, including several police officers, witness the incident, but no one makes any attempt to intervene or to assist Tracey. As soon as Buck leaves, Tracey files a complaint. Buck is arrested on a breach of peace charge.

Five days later, on November 10, Buck is convicted for his attack in the parking lot. He is given a six-month suspended sentence, meaning he does not have to serve jail time. The probation order requires that Buck leave his wife alone, stay off the property where Tracey is still living with friends, leave the area, and return to Virginia to live with his father.

Buck adheres to his probation for less than two months. On January 1, 1983, Tracey looks out of the apartment window and sees Buck standing under a streetlight. She immediately calls the police. By the time they arrive, Buck has left. Tracey reminds them of the court order, and they leave without taking any action. The January 1 Torrington police log notes, "Matter resolved for time being, no formal complaint made."

Buck resumes his pattern of threatening phone calls, so Tracey duly informs the police. Tracey wants to believe that Buck's parole violations will lead to his arrest, but the police never seem to act. Convinced that the police won't help her, Tracey begins to feel isolated and afraid.

Between January 1 and May 4 of 1983, Tracey and her friends call the Torrington Police Department numerous times and beseech them to act. They want Buck arrested, both for his violent threats and his violation of probation. But the police make no effort to arrest, or even confront, Buck. On May 4, Tracey and her friend Bentley report that Buck is threatening to shoot them. Tracey demands an arrest, but the officer refuses to take the complaint, telling Tracey to return in three weeks when someone in the police department might look into it.

Tracey does not give up. On May 6, she files an application for a restraining order against Buck in the Litchfield Superior Court. She receives an ex parte restraining order the same day, forbidding Buck from assaulting, threatening, and harassing her. She begins divorce proceedings.

On May 25, with the divorce pending, Buck informs Tracey that he intends to kill her when the divorce is final. Again, Tracey calls the police and files a complaint. By this time, Tracey is confined to her apartment due to fear. She calls the police and requests an escort to the police station so she can file a request for an arrest warrant. The officers tell Tracey that she'll have to wait until after the Memorial Day weekend.

Memorial Day passes, and on May 31, she goes to the station only to be told that the only officer who can help is on vacation. Later that day, Tracey speaks with her brother-in-law, Joseph Kocsis, about the department's dismissive attitude. Furious, Kocsis calls the department to protest its inaction; the police assure him that Buck will be arrested on June 8, 1983—an option that has never been offered to Tracey.

On June 5, Buck appears outside of Tracey's window again. When he starts to shout at her, she calls the police, reminding them of Buck's probation conditions and the new restraining order. The officers ignore Tracey's request for an arrest; their log reads, "no formal complaint." June 8 comes and goes; Buck remains free.

On June 10, Tracey hears Buck shouting outside her apartment again. The police have ignored her request for protection for nine months; she is certain that will not change today. Her fear is that Buck will come into the apartment and that she will be unable to protect the baby or herself.[9] Without a better option, she calls police and begs them to enforce the restraining orders, to take note of her formal complaints—to do *anything*.

Twenty-five minutes after Tracey makes the call, Officer Frederick Petrovits, who's patrolling the area, arrives. Petrovits, however, stays in his patrol car and parks across the street to observe. Police have previously used the fact that they have not witnessed an assault as an excuse to do nothing when Tracey calls. With police on site, Tracey decides to venture outside. She calculates that Buck might give her a punch in the gut, which might incline the police to act.

Unfortunately, Tracey gravely miscalculates the force Buck will wield: as soon as she steps outside to reason with her screaming husband, Buck pulls out a knife. Tracey runs, but Buck is much faster. He catches Tracey in the backyard of the apartment, where he grabs her and throws her violently to the ground. In clear view of nearby neighbors, Buck stabs Tracey thirteen times in her chest, neck, throat, and face. The knife punctures her esophagus, leaving three gaping holes.[10] Petrovits, sensing commotion, gets out of the squad car and goes to the backyard to investigate.

Petrovits sees Buck, now with a bloodied knife, standing over Tracey's body. Petrovits approaches Buck and takes the knife from him, but doesn't arrest him or ask his name. The officer later claims that he had not personally seen the assault, so he did not know what had happened. As Petrovits explains it, "He could have stabbed a chicken. He could have stabbed a dog."[11] Of course, there is no animal carcass nearby, and Petrovits had witnessed the man pull the knife and chase Tracey.

Tracey faces catastrophic blood loss as she lies on the lawn, but nobody helps her. Buck continues to walk around the premises freely. Buck again approaches his wife, who appears to be dead, and kicks her in the head. Petrovits "see[s] his foot going down on her head,"[12] but does nothing besides watch. This final blow damages Tracey's spinal cord. Buck then runs into the apartment, emerges holding C.J., and shouts, "I killed your f—ing mother." With that, he drops C.J. on Tracey's body. With Petrovits still standing by, Buck kicks Tracey's head again.

Three additional officers arrive on scene, but they make no attempt to arrest or restrain Buck, who continues to move around the premises and yell at Tracey. It is fifty minutes before the police, now seeing Tracey's bloodied body, calls for medical attention, and an ambulance arrives. During these fifty minutes, Buck is still around the premises, with the police officers showing no sign of restraint. When Tracey is loaded onto a stretcher, Buck—emboldened by police inaction—tries to climb into the ambulance to attack Tracey again. Finally, Buck is arrested.[13]

Despite the severe injuries and the delay in receiving medical care, Tracey survives the attack. She's hospitalized for seven months, and after her discharge, is wheelchair bound for another eight months. The blow to her head results in permanent nerve damage, causing paralysis on the

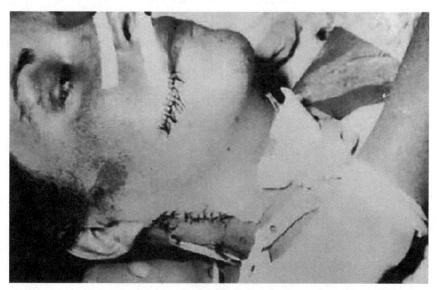

Figure 16.1.   Tracey Thurman, in the hospital after the last attack, 1983. *Torrington Police*

left side of her body. "On my left side," she says, "from my elbow down to my fingertips and from my knee down to my toes, there's not much feeling. My right leg has more feeling than my left leg, but it's physically weaker. So I don't trust it. It's like I don't know when I'm stepping."[14] She walks with a noticeable limp and has a deep scar that spans her face from ear to ear. She's unable to do simple tasks like clip her nails, change linens, dry her hair, or pick up her son.

Though C.J. is not injured, the attack leaves him with deep emotional trauma. When Tracey is reunited with her son, the boy spits at her and demands that his real mother come back. The woman before him bears little resemblance to the mother he had known. Ambulance sirens send him into a panic. "He'll ask whoever he's with, 'Is my mommy all right?'" Tracey recalls.[15]

In 1985, after her hospitalization and recovery, Tracey brings the first civil lawsuit in the country under 42 U.S.C. § 1983, "Civil Action for Deprivation of Rights," against the City of Torrington, twenty-nine individual officers, and the Torrington Police Department for damages.[16] The federal legislation of 42 U.S.C. § 1983 begins:

> Every person who, under color of any statute, ordinance, regulation, custom, or usage, of any State or Territory or the District of Columbia, subjects, or causes to be subjected, any citizen of the United States or other person within the jurisdiction thereof to the deprivation of any rights, privileges, or immunities secured by the Constitution and laws, shall be liable to the party injured in an action at law.[17]

In the suit, Tracey alleges that the police ignored her complaints for eight months, a disregard that reflected their callously indifferent approach to family violence, and thus violated her constitutional right to equal protection. Simply because she is legally married to Buck, the police have allowed the ongoing abuse to continue. Tracey believes that if she and Buck were strangers, the police would have acted. Because 95 percent of domestic-violence victims are women, sex discrimination quickly becomes a focal point of the controversy.

The City of Torrington puts up a fierce legal battle against the suit. Among other objections, the lawyers for Torrington claim that the legislation is only available to redress racial discrimination. The department's lawyers also argue that third-party liability—liability for those who don't directly commit the offense—would be disastrous for any police department.

Moreover, they argue that Tracey isn't a victim but rather a manipulator who called the police at even the slightest confrontation in order to strengthen her hand when she filed for divorce. "Tracey was not a battered woman," says the department's attorney. "Most of those incidents weren't physical confrontations. They were only phone calls. She was setting [Buck] up for the divorce proceedings, building a record against him."[18]

The jury does not buy the argument. In an unprecedented decision, the jury finds the city and police officers guilty, faulting twenty-four officers—40 percent of the police force—for ignoring Tracey's repeated pleas for assistance. Tracey is awarded $2.3 million in damages.

To Tracey's lawyer, Burton Weinstein, the problem is entirely with the police. "If cops choose not to take something seriously, then law is, in effect, repealed at their whim."[19] But police do not see it that way; even after the trial concluded, the police officers maintain that they followed procedure and did nothing wrong. After the judgment is announced, Tracey's lawyers begin proceedings to place liens on the officer's homes so as to satisfy the judgment and ensure Tracey's damages are paid. In the end, Tracey agrees to a smaller settlement of $1.9 million, allowing the officers to keep their homes. Alarmed at the outcome of the case, insurance companies now press municipalities to train their officers in how to respond appropriately to domestic-violence situations.

On August 12, 1987, Buck is convicted of first-degree assault and sentenced to twenty years in prison. Even so, he continues to threaten Tracey's life while he is incarcerated. Still, his ongoing threats do not prevent him from being released on parole in 1991, eight years into his sentence.

THE OUTRAGE

Tracey's story sparks national controversy surrounding police involvement in domestic violence and larger concerns with gender equality.[20] She testifies before the Senate Judiciary Committee while they debate federal legislation to address violence against women. She also appears on nationally televised programs like "Today" and "20/20," and in 1989, producer Dick Clark releases a movie about Tracey's story called *A Cry for Help: The Tracey Thurman Story*. The movie airs at the beginning of National Domestic Violence Awareness Month. The actress Nancy McKeon plays Tracey. "People are going to watch it and see parts of their own lives in it," McKeon says.[21] The film also prompts public scrutiny of the Torrington Police Department. As now-Chief Robert Milano states, the film provokes "nationwide indignation" toward their department and colors the officers as "uncaring brutes."[22]

Tracey's civil lawsuit also fuels the movement to increase arrests for domestic violence and to undermine assumptions that domestic disputes are less serious than disputes between strangers. Weinstein, Tracey's attorney, files twenty more lawsuits against local municipalities and police departments that fail to properly address domestic-violence allegations. Meanwhile, advocates grow more vocal about the criminal justice system's institutional indifference toward abused wives. In 1986, for example, a New York task force issues a report on women in the courts, finding that "victims' access to the courts is limited by their being dissuaded by law enforcement officials and court personnel from proceeding in criminal and family courts and by having their claims trivialized or ignored."[23]

Other cases also bring attention to domestic violence and the challenges women face in bringing charges. In March of 1983, Cheryl Araujo of New Bedford, Massachusetts, puts her two daughters to sleep, then leaves the house to buy cigarettes. When her usual spot is closed, she makes a stop at Big Dan's tavern. There, two men approach her, asking her to leave with them. When she refuses, a third man grabs her from behind, throwing her onto the bar's pool table. There, she is stripped and gang raped. Patrons on the sidelines watch, some even laughing. No one intervenes. After the rapes, Araujo manages to fight off her attackers and runs half naked into the street. Three college students passing by come upon her and drive her to the hospital. Her attackers are found guilty of aggravated rape. The harshest punishment imposed is a six-and-a-half-year prison sentence.[24] None of the bystanders who cheered or did nothing are held criminally liable.

In February of 1985, Charlotte Fedders is in court testifying before a judge during divorce proceedings with her husband John Fedders, a powerful Washington lawyer who directs enforcement operations at the Security and Exchange Commission. During the testimony, she details eight incidences of assault by her husband of sixteen years. Her most graphic testimony includes a beating while she is pregnant in which her husband screams that he does not care if he kills the baby. Her husband denies none of the claims but says that his wife is at least partly to blame because she withheld emotional support while he was struggling with his professional life. The judge agrees. The proceedings do not cause much official notice until a *Wall Street Journal* reporter slips into the courtroom to hear the recounting of the abuse. The *Journal* runs an article the following day detailing Fedders's double life as a Washington powerbroker and a wife-beating husband. It sparks public outcry, and the following day he resigns from his post at the SEC. He is not charged, however, and he retains his right to practice law. When his ex-wife writes a book about the years of abuse, Fedders is granted 25 percent of the royalties by the judge as part of the marriage settlement.[25]

In 1987, a Chinese immigrant named Dong Lu Chen bludgeons his wife, Jian Wan Chen, with a hammer eight times to the head, causing five skull fractures and eventually death.[26] During the trial, he contends that according to his culture, it was his responsibility to kill her after her confession to adultery. The jury takes this into consideration, along with Chen's lack of a police record, display of apparent remorse, meek behavior in his time awaiting trial in jail, and the unlikelihood of another crime. After deliberation, Chen is convicted of manslaughter and sentenced to five years of probation.

These and a series of other cases show the systems' apparent indifference to domestic violence and serve to incense the public further: Why should a gang rapist receive such a light sentence? How could a man, immigrant or not, receive nothing more than probation for beating his wife to death? Why should a husband get royalties from his wife's book recounting her abuse at his hands? As the outrage boils up, something needs to be done.

THE REFORM

Tracey Thurman's assault, followed by other cases like those of Cheryl Araujo, Charlotte Fedders, and Jian Wan Chen, propel domestic violence to the forefront of the public mind. Unlike efforts of the 1960s that led to the creation of the victim-shelter system, the efforts of the 1980s emphasize the need for legal reform.

Practical experience and research demonstrate to authorities that arresting perpetrators deters future violence more effectively than simply giving a warning. By 1989, four years after Tracey wins her suit in Torrington, 84 percent of U.S. police departments have adopted vigorous arrest policies for domestic-violence batterers. In a similar vein, many prosecutors adopt "no-drop" policies by which they refuse to drop charges on domestic-violence cases even in situations in which the victim requests that the charge not be pursued. The idea is to protect the victim and deprive the batterer of the power to compel the victim to drop charges. As more cases are brought forward, district attorneys and judges begin to take victim complaints more seriously.

Many states make it easier for victims to obtain restraining orders. By 1990, victims may obtain emergency protection orders outside of normal court hours in twenty-three states. Many states allow (and in some cases require) courts to issue restraining orders before the batterer is released on bail, and thirty-six states require restraining orders to be submitted to a national registry so they can be enforced even if the victim is in another state. There are even states that give cell phones to victims so that they can more readily summon police.

States also respond to research concluding that court-ordered couples' counseling is ineffective. The Coalition to End Domestic Violence and Sexual Assault calls for courts to eliminate the use of couples counseling in domestic-violence cases, even when the woman seeks it. Some states, such as New York and California, move to legally prohibit the use of couples counseling when one partner is charged with a domestic-violence crime.

The increased awareness of the domestic-violence problem brings on a wave of research. Among the work is that of educational psychologist Lenore Walker, drawing on theories of learned helplessness, who develops the concept of the "battered woman syndrome" (BWS). BWS "refers to a pattern of responses and perceptions presumed to be characteristic of women who have been subjected to continuous physical abuse by their mate." The syndrome is recognized as a type of post-traumatic stress disorder by the American Psychiatric Association. In the states that permit its use in the courtroom, it becomes an important part of the legal analysis when a battered woman claims self-defense when she attacks her abuser.

As knowledge of domestic-violence issues increases, some states enact comprehensive legislation that addresses the entire range of issues. In 1986, Connecticut becomes the first state to adopt a comprehensive law, the Connecticut Family Violence Prevention and Response Act (CFVPRA). Nicknamed "The Tracey Thurman Law," it defines family violence, guides officials in handling family-violence cases, requires the Connecticut Justice Department to maintain family-violence intervention units throughout the state, and compels officers to arrest alleged offenders if probable cause of abuse exists, regardless of whether a victim seeks to press charges.[27]

When Pennsylvania passes a similar law, it adds a provision that allows police officers to arrest batterers without witnessing the domestic violence firsthand. Illinois, a state notorious for its poor domestic-abuse responses, improves its statutes the same year. The Illinois Domestic Violence Act covers not only abuse by a live-in husband or boyfriend but also abuse by the father of a woman's child and by a man the woman used to live with. In California, domestic-violence protection is extended to a same-sex battering case.

As part of the comprehensive approach, many states set up special court systems to handle intimate-abuse crimes together with related criminal or family matters. Such systems provide litigants with specialized advocates, judges, and court personnel who work exclusively on domestic-violence disputes.

At the federal level, U.S. surgeon general C. Everett Koop declares that domestic violence is a public health issue that cannot be dealt with by the police alone.[28] Koop reminds the nation that domestic violence is the leading cause of injuries to women aged fifteen to forty-four; it is more common than automobile accidents, muggings, and cancer deaths combined. A year after Tracey is attacked, Congress enacts the Family Violence Prevention and Services Act, which provides grants for shelters, counseling, and support services for victims of domestic violence and their families.

In 1994, Congress takes a step further with the Violence Against Women Act (VAWA). The act intensifies federal penalties for domestic violence within federal jurisdiction, provides funding for domestic-violence shelters, increases the number of police officers and prosecutors devoted to eradicating violence against women, and forms the Violence Against Women Office in the U.S. Department of Justice.[29]

While the research helps to better understand the psychology of domestic violence and inform effective policy deterrents, it also makes evident the limitations of some of the strategies being used to address domestic violence. A 2001 report by the National Institute of Justice concludes that among some groups, women who report violations of restraining orders to courts are significantly more likely to die. A follow-up study in 2002 finds that, while there are overall declines in violence against women who visit rural shelters, shelters do not reduce the risk of violence in the long term.[30] In fact, the data suggest that a woman's risk of being killed by her abuser increases by 75 percent when she tries to leave.[31] Recall that it was when Tracey Thurman sought to leave that her husband's violence dramatically escalated. Despite the protection that the laws seek to provide, severing ties with an abuser remains a dangerous business.

Some organizations establish batterer intervention programs, akin to Alcoholics Anonymous, which try to socialize offenders into more acceptable strategies to deal with frustrations that might otherwise lead to assaults. However, the Department of Justice finds that not a single batterer intervention program effectively reduces domestic violence and, in fact, some programs are actually correlated with increased abuse.[32]

DOMESTIC VIOLENCE TODAY

While the situation has clearly improved, there are plenty of cases that show that victims still have reasons for concern. In 2009, for example, a Texas woman named Deanna Cook is a victim of ongoing domestic abuse at the hands of her former husband Delveccio Patrick.[33] She has called 9-1-1 on numerous occasions, she has filed complaints, she has moved her residence, and still she lives in fear. On August 17, she calls 9-1-1 after Patrick begins assaulting her. The call records her screaming, gurgling, and begging her attacker to stop. In the background, a man growls, "I'll kill you. I'll kill you. I'll kill you."[34] The police come to the door, but when no one answers, they leave. Several days later, authorities find Cook dead in her bathtub.

While there continue to be tragic cases like Deanna Cook's, victims of domestic violence today do have far more options for support and legal recourse than they had at Tracey Thurman's time in 1983. The effect has been significant. Between 1994 and 2010, the overall rate of intimate-partner violence has declined from 9.8 victimizations per 1,000 persons to 3.6.[35] Between 1976 and 2010, the homicide rate between intimate partners in the United States has fallen from about 1.36 per 100,000 people to 0.48.[36]

While the intimate homicide rate has dropped, it is still a huge number. Between 2001 and 2012, at least 11,766 women have been killed by domestic violence—almost twice the number of American soldiers who died on the battlefield during the same period.[37] The reality remains that victims are still hesitant to report domestic violence to law enforcement. Only one-fourth of women who experience physical assault call the police, and just 20 percent of women who are injured by a violent partner seek medical treatment.[38] The majority of women who don't call seem to believe that police won't believe their accounts, and 32 percent don't want the police or court system involved. Of women who do call the police, 99.7 percent don't believe the police can solve long term the domestic-violence problem.[39]

Finding meaningful ways for the criminal law and social interventions to protect the vulnerable is an ongoing quest. As a society, we may not have found a magic formula that keeps partners safe, but things have improved. Authorities are now compelled by law to intervene. The law no longer accepts that an assault behind closed doors is not a crime. Abuse is not a private matter; it is a criminal offense.

Chapter Seventeen

1986
Leicestershire Murders

DNA

THE TRAGEDY

On a frosty November morning, a hospital worker crosses a farm field on his way to work.[1] He stays on the walking path, known locally as Black Pad. Just before he gets to the hospital campus, he spots something disturbing in the meadow grass. By a clump of trees, lying motionless, is a girl naked from the waist down. The startled worker rushes to the nearby road and flags down a car. The passerby is an ambulance driver who also works at the hospital; he follows the man back into the field to investigate. As they approach the copse of trees, the first man asks hopefully: "Is it a dummy?"[2] As the driver approaches the body, he notes a pile of clothes tossed a few feet away. The two men look down at the teenager, who has dried blood under her nose and chin. Her neck is deeply bruised and her swollen tongue protrudes from her clenched teeth. The driver checks for a pulse, but both men know that she is past saving.

On the previous evening, November 21, 1983, fifteen-year-old Lynda Mann bundles up to walk over to a friend's house. When she does not return home, her parents call the police. The Manns know their daughter to be a responsible hardworking girl. Lynda, her stepfather, Eddie, explains, is "always home by ha' past nine. . . . Unless we know, she's always here!"[3] The police, who have experience in such matters, do not share their confidence. Teens commonly stay out past their parents' curfews, even in the sleepy village of Narborough, England.

Once the horrible discovery of the body is made the next day, it is immediately clear that the ice-glazed body found among the trees is Lynda

235

Mann. The postmortem reveals that she had been dragged some distance. The lack of defensive wounds and her unbroken fingernails suggest that, if she struggled, it wasn't for long. Dried fluid believed to be semen mats her pubic hair. Clear evidence of rape marks the corpse. The cause of death is strangulation.

Lynda's death is Narborough's first-ever murder, and investigators press for any type of lead. They begin by analyzing the semen on Lynda's body. A lab analysis of the semen sample has a strong PGM+1 enzyme reaction. Phosphoglucomutase, or PGM, is a genetic marker for a particular protein enzyme and is found throughout the body, including in sperm. There are many types and subtypes of PGM, each of which occurs in a different percentage of the population. Additionally, the sperm of some men contains information about their blood type. Men whose sperm contains blood type indicators are referred to forensically to as "secretors." The other portion of the population is labeled "non-secretors." The man whose sperm is found on Lynda has both a PGM+1 and is a secretor of the A blood group substance. The pattern matches one in ten of the men in England. No blood test will enable the authorities to identify the murderer, but the testing will be a powerful tool in narrowing the pool of potential suspects.

Lead investigator Derek Pearce, believing that Lynda may have known her killer and following "a timeworn police procedure of looking from the inside out,"[4] starts by taking a blood sample from Lynda's stepfather Eddie Eastwood. Eastwood is by all accounts a loving parent to the girl, and the tests clear him. Once Eastwood's blood test and alibi rule him out, the police have no obvious paths for further inquiry.

Life in the village becomes shadowed with fear. Without a clear path to follow, the police do their best to solve the case. They take thousands of statements from anyone with information, some pertaining to a "spiky-haired youth," others to "a running man"—or several men—thought to be near the scene of the murder on November 21.[5] During the investigation, 150 blood samples are taken from local men, but the tests yield nothing. The murder investigation squad, 150 strong at the height of the investigation, dwindles. By the following August, the investigation ends.

Months go by with no new leads in the case, and the town slowly settles back into normal life. Then on July 31, 1986, a little less than three years after Lynda's death, that peace is shattered again.

On the warm and damp summer afternoon, fifteen-year-old Dawn Ashworth finishes her shift in the town's news agent's shop. Dawn goes home, and a few hours later, leaves to have tea with friends in Narborough. It is an easy walk on the path known as Ten Pound Lane, a shortcut between her own village and Narborough. Since the murder of Lynda Mann, her father, Robin, has forbidden his daughter to use that path. "She was aware there was a killer about," he says. "She was well acquainted with the Lynda Mann case."[6] But this is not a dark winter night but rather a bright, beautiful, summer day, so Dawn elects to use the shortcut. By 7:00 p.m., Dawn hasn't returned home, and her parents begin to worry. At 9:40 p.m., they call the police.

The following day, tracker dogs and local police begin the hunt. The police try to reassure the family, but the fate of Lynda Mann hangs ever present on everyone's mind. Two days later, on Saturday, August 2, a police sergeant spots a denim jacket off the main road. Later that day, in a grassy field off Ten Pound Lane, Dawn's body is found, deliberately hidden under foliage.

THE OUTRAGE

There is no escaping the similarities between the two killings. Just as with Lynda Mann, Dawn is found naked from the waist down. Her face is swollen and her body is covered with abrasions. Lacerations across her face and many of the bruises on her body occurred before her death, but other marks were caused postmortem by the effort to hide the body. The pathologist finds evidence of a vicious rape, and as with Lynda, her death is determined to be the result of "manual strangulation."[7] Also as with Lynda, real clues are scarce. The police reach out to the community; headlines beg for leads, and an enormous reward is offered for information.

Four different witnesses recall seeing a motorbike ridden by someone wearing a "red crash helmet," near where the body was found. One of the witnesses reports seeing a motorcyclist "riding up and down, very slowly, past the Ashworth house."[8] In the small village, this information is enough to narrow down the potential list of suspects to a single individual: seventeen-year-old Richard Buckland. Buckland works as a kitchen porter at the hospital near the footpath. On August 1, the day before Dawn's body was found, Buckland has a conversation with a police officer that suggests he has seen the body, but his comment is discounted as being too random to be of interest, in part because he is seen as simply an odd person around town. Furthermore, twelve hours before the first clue, the jacket, was located, Buckland had shared with another hospital employee that Dawn was dead and that her body had been recovered. Another individual also tells the police that Buckland had told him about the recovery of Dawn's body. The witness is certain Buckland had said that Dawn had been found and that she was found dead. He also knows she was strangled.

On the morning of August 8, Buckland is arrested in his home "on suspicion of being concerned in the death of Dawn Ashworth."[9] During his first interview at the police station, Buckland confirms that he had known Dawn and that he saw her while he was riding on July 31 but didn't stop because his motorbike needed repairing. A few minutes later, his story changes; police demand Buckland be straight with them. Buckland produces another account of the events. This time he says that he stopped that day "to see if the oil were coming out" under his bike when he saw Dawn.[10] He explains to authorities that in fact he had walked with her for a time, on that evening, but then turned back to his bike and left. He says he did nothing to harm her. And yet, he clearly had information about Dawn and her death that others did not. Police challenge Buckland on this, and his story changes again.

Buckland's interactions with the police become increasingly bizarre. He tells the police that he has never had sex. This is followed by a description of an ongoing sexual relationship between himself and a particular girl. The story of the relationship is followed by an explanation that in fact "nobody liked him, especially girls."[11] Buckland then reiterates that he has never had sex with a woman.

The interview is going nowhere, so a break is called. At 4:06 p.m., when the interview resumes, things change dramatically. Buckland is back to a version of events that have him walking on the path with Dawn. He admits to walking with Dawn up the path, and when he is pressed for details, he says, "I probably went really mad, and I don't know it!"[12]

By evening, Richard Buckland confesses to the rape and murder of Dawn Ashworth: "Then she were lying there still. I just pressed really hard on her mouth with me hand over her nose and her mouth. She suffocated. That's all in my memory. I couldn't leave her where she was so I hid her."[13] The police breathe a sigh of relief; the murderer is in police custody, and a full confession is recorded.

The teenager insists he had nothing to do with Lynda's death earlier. With all the similarities between the two murders, the police scoff at the idea that *another* local killer is responsible. The tests on the sperm samples collected from the two girls both show the same unusual typing of the biological evidence. Still, they send blood samples from Buckland to a lab for analysis. To the authorities' surprise, his biological samples do not match the profile of the sample found on Lynda Mann's or Dawn Ashworth's body.

Of course, the science is pretty new, and there is a chance that something went wrong at the lab. The possibility of a lab error is enough to keep Buckland in custody. For the police and public, all that remains to "tidy up" the case. Officers return to their normal activities, and Ten Pound Lane is cleared of debris.[14]

Still, the police need to move past Buckland's denials of his involvement in Lynda Mann's earlier death. While police ponder how to prove

Buckland's guilt in the earlier death, Dr. Alex Jeffreys is working in his lab at Leicester University, just a few miles down the road.[15] Dr. Jeffreys has developed a method by which the structure of an individual's DNA can be seen and compared to the DNA of any other individual. For years, he and his small staff have been looking for unique variations in human DNA. The goal is to identify specific areas of DNA that tend to have the most genetic variation from person to person, then find a way to map those differences visually. "Intuitively, it seemed that regions of tandemly repeated DNA would be open to mutation processes," he recalls. "They could be highly variable, informative genetic markers."[16] The year after Lynda's death, Jeffreys and his team achieve success. They produce x-ray films of DNA profiles. The films, etched with dark and light bands, reflect a pattern unique to each individual. Jeffreys has invented genetic fingerprinting.

At this point, it is still unclear what practical applications this discovery might have. Jeffreys's wife is the first to come up with some workable ideas: it could be used in paternity tests and to confirm proper artificial inseminations, to determine if newborn twins are identical, or to ensure that endangered animals don't dangerously interbreed. Perhaps most compellingly, though, is its potential impact on forensic analysis.

Jeffreys first uses his visual representation of individual DNA to conclusively prove parentage in an immigration case. In the aftermath of that success, Jeffreys gives a public lecture on the case and the DNA representation process generally. He suggests that the same process might one day be used to help solve crimes. The audience is amused; most of the scientists listening think the idea is too far-fetched. A story on the lecture finds its way into the local news, which investigators read with intrigue.

The police approach Jeffreys and ask him for help in solving their homicide cases. For his part, Jeffreys is excited to prove the validity of his work and to aid in the case. He tests samples from Lynda and from Buckland. They do not match. The samples are retested. Again no match is found. A third test gives the same results.

Jeffreys requests a semen sample from Dawn Ashworth's body. Frustratingly, the film used to capture the DNA fingerprinting takes time to develop, but Jeffreys cannot believe his eyes when the results come in. He calls the investigators from his lab in the middle of the night. After a "nail-biting week," Jeffreys tells them he has both good and bad news. The bad news is that Jeffreys has destroyed their entire case: "Not only is your man innocent in the Mann case, he isn't even the man who killed Dawn Ashworth!"[17] An assembly of officials, including Chief Superintendent David Baker, rushes to Jeffreys's laboratory. The results are unmistakable. A dumbfounded Baker asks what the good news is. Jeffreys says he is confident that one man raped and murdered both girls, and while that man is still at large, they only need to find one man, not two. Instead of solving a second murder, the police are now back to square one on both murders. One senior inspector put it like this, "One minute we got the guy and the next we've got Jack shit."[18]

Buckland is released. It turns out that Buckland's involvement is limited to having discovered the body before the police did. Instead of reporting the corpse, he had inspected it and kept the information to himself. Nonetheless, his parents are called upon to explain their son and his disturbing sexual behaviors. "They questioned him for fifteen hours," his father says, "and although I believe they followed procedure, he was bound to be confused after all that time and just said the things they wanted to hear."[19] Richard Buckland, who already faces social isolation, is forced to spend his time at home; his parents fear that their son might be the victim of some misguided vigilante action even after his exoneration.

Fear seeps back into the community; everyone understands that the murderer is probably among them. The reward for finding the killer is raised to twenty thousand pounds. A fifty-man squad is gathered to "end it once and for all."[20] Some of the police superiors remain convinced of Richard Buckland's guilt; one of the squad members later admits that their job was to scrape up enough evidence to convict him, "genetic fingerprinting or no."[21]

Under this dubious charge, the search resumes. Eighteen hundred tips from community members, previously ignored, are now read and reread. The local population is quite small, but it seems that everyone has something to say about the murders, a sighting to describe, a neighbor to accuse. Among the nearly two thousand tips, not a single one is of use. Police are undeterred. In late December, the chief superintendent formulates a radical plan to generate a usable lead. On January 2, 1987, the newspaper headlines make an announcement: "Blood Tests for 2,000 in Killer Hunt."[22] All males from Narborough, Littlethorpe, and Enderby between seventeen and thirty-four years old are asked to voluntarily submit DNA samples. Residents are tested first, and after that, any man known to have worked in or visited the area is asked to submit samples.

The well-coordinated operation is serious business. Male residents receive a letter that specifies a specific testing session they are to attend. The stations have both day and evening sessions. Teams of doctors and police are present at all collection sessions. Many people are skeptical. After all, the tests are voluntary, and what murderer would willingly submit his blood for testing? In some sense, that was the point: of those contacted, 90 percent of the men do as the authorities ask. Police turn their interest on the remaining 10 percent.[23] "We just hoped," said one investigator, "that it might somehow flush him out."[24]

Local lingo terms the sample collections as "the bloodings." Each man is interviewed and identified. The interview includes questions about his whereabouts during the murders. Next he fills out a form, receives a registration, an ID sheet, and then submits biological samples. The individual then signs his forms. If his samples show that the man belongs to the same enzyme group as the murderer (about 10 percent of the population), then his sample is sent to the lab to undergo Jeffreys's genetic-fingerprinting analysis.[25]

Various men are suspected and then cleared; months pass with no answers. Jeffreys's tiny laboratory, desperately overwhelmed, starts freezing blood and asks the blooding squad to stop sending samples unless it is "high priority."[26] By May, 3,653 men have submitted samples; 2,000 have been eliminated, and more than 1,000 are waiting to be analyzed. The target group is again expanded, and another 1,000 men are asked to participate. The number of officers on the murder squad is reduced. By July, only sixteen remain.[27] As Chief Superintendent Baker admits during a news story, "We have not got that vital piece of information which allows us to put the jigsaw together completely."[28]

Police remain confident that as more men get tested, the killer, if he is in fact local, will find it harder to hide. Time is probably on their side. If nothing else, Jeffreys's tests keep people talking. As Baker tells the interviewers, "Somebody's bound to say something to someone in an unguarded moment. Now that's the kind of information we need."[29]

As if on cue, the following day a group of coworkers sit in a Leicester pub chatting over cobs (a local type of cheese and meat roll). They are on lunch break from Hampshires, a nearby bakery where they work. The subject of the conversation is Colin Pitchfork, another employee.

Pitchfork is a quiet man, large built and Leicester born. Colin is a skilled and well-respected cake decorator, keen on starting his own business. He is also a constant source of workplace gossip. From a young age, Colin gets in trouble for flashing. "I used to like to show it," he says. "I started going out on the streets to do it. I started showing it to strange girls."[30] He had worked at Hampshires for several years when he met Carole, a plump, friendly girl. They married in the summer of 1979.

However, eight years and two children later, the marriage seems to be in trouble. Colin has recently had an affair with a young bakery employee, called "Browneyes." Browneyes torments Pitchfork's wife with updates on her husband's extramarital activities, ringing up a devastated Carole and describing her romance with Colin in graphic detail. Browneyes becomes pregnant, but the baby is stillborn. Colin is heartbroken; he reconciles with his wife, and they agree to give their marriage another try.

That afternoon in the pub, the group puzzles over Pitchfork's affair and chats about the stillborn daughter. One of the employees, Ian Kelly, blurts out, "Colin had me take the blood test for him."[31] Ian casually shrugs off follow-up questions, heading off to get another pint of ale. Another man at the table offers that Pitchfork had offered to pay him two hundred quid to take his place at the bloodings. When asked to explain why, Pitchfork told his friend that he was afraid of the police.

A hushed discomfort settles on the group. The bakery shop manager, who is part of the group, is "deeply disturbed" by Kelly's revelation.[32] After lunch, she tries to get the others to address the issue. But Pitchfork, while odd, is one of them; no one wants to talk about it.

Alone in her angst, she stews uncomfortably for six weeks about going to the police. She does not want to implicate Kelly in taking the test for Pitchfork, which may be a crime, and possibly wrongly suggest that Pitchfork is a killer. But the possibility that Pitchfork *is* the killer is too much to bear. On September 17, 1987, she calls the investigative team. That night, excited members of the squad can hardly sleep.

On Saturday, they arrest Ian Kelly. Kelly wants to protect himself and his friend Pitchfork, so he flatly denies having stood in for him for the blood test. But in fairly short order, it becomes clear that the police know more than he thought and are not backing down. Kelly is not looking for trouble, so he admits that he lied and that he submitted a sample as Colin Pitchfork.

Kelly explains that when the program was first announced in January, Pitchfork approached him and claimed that he had already taken the test for someone else: "See, this other bloke, he had a spot of trouble from flashing and doing robberies when he were young. Scared they'd try to put it on him because of that record, so he talked *me* into it."[33] Kelly sees the problem: if Pitchfork gives a second sample under his real name, the police will catch him for lying about the first sample. Kelly evidently believed the tale; he goes to the bloodings as Colin Pitchfork. He signs Pitchfork's name at the bottom of the interview form.

Kelly's version of the events is enough to convince the police. They check the signature in Kelly's passport against the signature on the interview form. The handwriting styles clearly match. By evening, Pitchfork is arrested in his home for the murder of Dawn Ashworth. He is calm, even resigned, and asks to speak to his wife. They stand in the kitchen while an officer looks on. Colin tells his wife that he is being arrested for "them murders," and after a terse exchange, his wife asks, "Did you do it?" He doesn't respond. She repeats the question several times. With the police standing next to him, Pitchfork finally answers "Yes."[34] She attacks her husband, and in her fury misses, only to strike the arresting officer.

Figure 17.1.   Colin Pitchfork on his wedding day, 1981. *Neville Chadwick*

The investigation, which "bloodies" 4,583 men before they find the answer, is the first of its kind, a veritable "genetic manhunt."[35] Pitchfork confesses freely, and his DNA sample matches the sample found on the girls perfectly. With the murderer in custody, the investigation ends, one year after Dawn's murder and four years after Lynda's. Colin Pitchfork is the first murderer to be caught using the power of genetic fingerprinting. The DNA evidence is not introduced in court since Pitchfork confesses, but Pitchfork confesses only because of the DNA testing.

THE REFORM

After the initial success in the Pitchfork case, DNA testing is used in other cases of serial murder. In March of 1987, a serial rapist is attacking women in their homes in Orange County, Florida. Police have a few clues: fingerprints are found on a second-floor window at one of the victim's homes. At another site, police find a few hairs. Vague descriptions are offered by a few witnesses. Police lack hard evidence, but it appears to investigators that the two cases are linked.

Soon after, a woman calls police to report a prowler trying to break into her home. The police arrive in time to pick up Tommie Lee Andrews. Police discover that his fingerprints match those taken from the second-story window of the other victim.

Jeffrey Ashton, an assistant attorney for the state of Florida prosecuting the case, sees an advertisement for a DNA-based paternity test in a magazine, one of the first commercial applications of Dr. Jeffreys's work. Ashton contacts the company: Is it possible, he wonders, to apply this DNA testing to identify the man responsible for the attack? The company says that DNA testing works; it matters not how you apply the results.[36] Andrews's DNA profile matches that of the attacker in the previous two cases, and on that evidence, he is convicted of the rapes and sentenced to sixty-two years in prison. He is released from prison in 2012 after serving about a third of his original sentence, after which he is civilly committed to a facility for violent sexual offenders.

In the same year, four women, including a fifteen-year-old, are found brutally raped and murdered in Richmond, Virginia.[37] All the women are found naked or nearly naked in their bedrooms, their hands and necks bound, killed by strangulation. Semen samples from the crime scenes match DNA samples of a man named Timothy Wilson Spencer, and scientific experts present a stunning statistic to the jury: the chances that someone other than Spencer had left semen at the crimes are less than 1 in 700 million.

The defense is helpless to respond convincingly; the only attack defense attorneys are able to offer is that the newness of DNA typing should lead the court to "hold off until another day any decision."[38] Spencer is convicted and sentenced to death, becoming the first man condemned to die because of DNA evidence. "It was a landmark case because prior to that, none of us really knew much about DNA and we didn't know whether . . .

a jury would be able to understand that sufficiently to convict someone of something as serious as capital murder," recalls attorney Helen Fahey, who won the conviction for Spencer's first killing.[39] But the jury over-whelmingly understood; DNA evidence had decided a murderer's fate. In 1994, Spencer is executed.

Following Spencer's conviction in 1988, investigators begin examining evidence from past cases in an effort to connect Spencer to other crimes. They discover that his DNA profile matches evidence found on the body of Carol Hamm, who'd been raped and strangled in her Arlington home in 1984. Sadly, another man, David Vasquez, has already been convicted for the crime. He has served four years of a thirty-five year sentence. Vasquez, who is mentally impaired, confessed to the crime. In 1989, Vasquez is pardoned and released from prison, becoming the first American to be exonerated by DNA evidence.[40]

The Virginia public sees the power of DNA typing. Lawmakers recognize the value of Jeffreys's revolutionary new technique, and in 1989, the state decides to make a bold move. It proposes the creation of a DNA databank and passes legislation requiring convicted felons to submit DNA samples for inclusion in the new databank. Only a few months after Virginia announces the database, six inmates at a Virginia state prison challenge the new legislation. They view the database as a serious violation of their right to privacy and therefore of their constitutional rights. In 1992, the United States Court of Appeals for the Fourth Circuit upholds the constitutionality of Virginia's database, ruling that the new legislation does not violate individual rights.[41]

The idea of the database catches the attention of dozens of other states, which immediately pursue similar legislation.[42] Within nine years, every state has laws requiring DNA samples to be recorded for at least some criminals. All fifty states demand DNA samples from sex offenders, and many states, such as Virginia, the pioneer, collect DNA from all convicted felons. Eleven states—Alaska, Arizona, California, Kansas, Louisiana, Minnesota, New Mexico, North Dakota, Tennessee, Texas, and Virginia—allow for involuntary DNA collection from individuals arrested for a crime. In another variation, eight states—Alabama, Arizona, Florida, Kansas, Louisiana, Minnesota, New Jersey, and Wisconsin—apply the DNA collection rules to juveniles. As the crime-control power of the database is revealed, many states further expand their own laws pertaining to the collection of DNA. [43]

Initially, states only have access to their own databases, but in November 1997, enterprising Florida investigators reach outside the state to check the databases of nearby states. Florida's DNA database reveals that four rapes had been committed by the same person.[44] The crimes were brutal, with the perpetrator often breaking into homes and beating victims. "We knew this guy was going to strike again," recalls Lieutenant Jim Schultz, head of a Florida detective division.[45] Investigators are anxious to catch him. The lab combs through the state database in search of a match, but find nothing. The Florida officials are not content to wait and see. The police contact officials in Virginia and Georgia, requesting that their respective state databases be searched for the Florida rapist.

Within a day, Virginia's state forensic lab calls Florida officials: a match has been found. Thirty-one-year-old Mark Daigle had spent time in a Virginia prison on a burglary conviction, and as a result, submitted a blood sample to Virginia's DNA database. On a November night at 1:00 a.m., police roust the sleeping Daigle, who resides in Florida and works as an air-conditioning repairman. He is arrested and charged with rape.

Investigators are thrilled about Daigle's capture, but the discovery also highlights the serious shortcoming of state access to only state-based DNA databases. If Daigle had committed burglary in Florida rather than Virginia, his DNA wouldn't have been collected for Florida's DNA database; if Daigle had committed burglary in Washington or North Carolina, then Florida wouldn't be permitted to use those states' databases. It was sheer luck that Daigle had a record in one of the two states Florida officials contacted. Imagine the power of searching all fifty state databases simultaneously. Paul Ferrara, director of Virginia's laboratory, says that Daigle's case "clearly demonstrates the (potential) power of a national DNA databank."[46]

Fortunately, the federal government is committed to such a program. Three years earlier, in 1994, Congress passed the DNA Identification Act. The legislation charged the FBI with developing an integrated database called the Combined DNA Index System (CODIS).[47] Careful standards are put in place: all DNA laboratories that are federally funded or contribute information to CODIS use software designed for CODIS and must adhere to strict testing standards.

CODIS is cautiously introduced in 1997, the same year of the Daigle case. Georgia and Florida are selected to be the first test states. Using complex technology and the lessons learned by individual states, the FBI successfully links their DNA databases. The network soon expands to include all fifty states, the District of Columbia, Puerto Rico, and the United States military. There is no doubt that the system works. "You just send your data up and it's searched automatically," explains David Coffman, Florida's DNA database administrator.[48] Today, CODIS assists in more than 3,500 investigations each month, and as of April 2017, CODIS has produced over 373,099 hits assisting in more than 358,069 investigations.[49]

Unsurprisingly, not everyone is thrilled by the governments' access to such information. DNA databases are a new and intimidating prospect, and many people are concerned about privacy violations. "People hear government, DNA, computers, FBI, and they get wary," explains Stephen Niezgoda, CODIS program director. "I understand that. But the system is built to maintain privacy."[50] Ferrarra notes that a DNA match is commonly grounds only for another blood draw, not an arrest.

BEYOND REFORM

Most concerning, though, is the potential for improper or botched DNA extraction or analysis. In early trials, defense attorneys simply do not have the know-how to attack DNA matching results in court. But attorneys Barry Scheck and Peter Neufeld decide to educate themselves on the intricacies of DNA science. In 1988, the pair defends a client who is accused of murdering a woman and her two-year-old daughter. The attorneys convincingly argue to the judge that the DNA samples have been handled and analyzed poorly. The judge knows DNA typing is a reliable science, but he acknowledges that DNA typing has to be done with rigorous methodology. In the case before him, the judge decides those standards have not been met and deems the DNA record inadmissible. (In time, the client confesses and is found guilty.) This is the first time DNA typing is challenged in open court, and soon defense attorneys learn how to challenge DNA evidence.

In 1994, Scheck and Neufeld attack DNA evidence in court again in the highly publicized O.J. Simpson double-murder case.[51] Simpson is accused of murdering his ex-wife Nicole Brown Simpson and her friend Ronald Lyle Goldman. The trial lasts eight months, and the evidence against Simpson is overwhelming. DNA tests on blood samples taken at the scene of the crime link Simpson to the murders, there is a bloody glove found at Simpson's home, and there is blood found on socks in his bedroom and in his white Bronco. Although the use of DNA is fairly new in criminal cases, the prosecution is confident that the power of DNA typing will win the case. However, the jury acquits Simpson.

The defense points out that the glove he is wearing does not fit and infamously proclaims "if it doesn't fit, you must acquit." But the defense is also able to show that DNA collected at the scene has been improperly handled, permitting cross-contamination by the lab. The defense also claims that the evidence may have been planted. The defense attorneys successfully convince the jury that the DNA findings may be wrong. The prosecution is not able to explain the science clearly enough to remove all reasonable doubt.

Forensic scientists have attempted to meet such criticisms by developing new techniques that bring greater reliability to DNA forensics. While large blood samples used to be required, reliable results can now be obtained with a mere speck of blood, or simply a smear of saliva or other biological samples, through a process called Polymerase Chain Reaction. Further innovation has dramatically reduced the time required for the analysis. What used to take more than a week can now be done in less than a few hours.

Because of the success of DNA analysis and the CODIS database, use of this powerful investigative tool has accelerated. In 2000, Congress passes the DNA Analysis Backlog Elimination Act of 2000, also called the "DNA Act." In addition to providing funding that will clear the backlog of DNA analysis cases, the DNA Act codifies the use of CODIS to allow states and the District of Columbia to collect and analyze DNA and contribute to CODIS for the FBI's use. Before the statute, the FBI was legally permitted to create CODIS but was not allowed to collect DNA samples from people convicted of federal felonies.

The act requires that "the Director of the Bureau of Prisons shall collect a DNA sample from each individual in the custody of the Bureau of Prisons who is, or has been, convicted of a qualifying Federal offense."[52] In addition to including federal offenses in CODIS, the act offers grants to states that collect and analyze DNA for state offenses to include in CODIS. There are also grants offered for collecting DNA samples at crime scenes without any suspects. Finally, the DNA Act makes it a misdemeanor to refuse to cooperate with DNA collection and authorizes the use of force for DNA collection.

For some people, the DNA Act raises some questions of privacy and concerns about felons' rights. This question comes to a head when Thomas Kincade, a navy seaman convicted of armed robbery and on parole after serving his sentence, is asked by his parole officer for a blood test in compliance with the DNA Act. Kincade refuses, so he is arrested and sentenced to more time in prison. Kincade responds by filing a lawsuit arguing that the DNA Act is a violation of the Fourth Amendment. In 2004, the Ninth Circuit Court of Appeals, in a six-to-five decision, holds that forcing parolees to provide DNA is not a violation of the Fourth Amendment and that the use of CODIS is constitutional. The court balances the competing interests and concludes that the benefits of CODIS and the DNA Act are more compelling than the parolee's DNA privacy. Much of the debate compares the taking of DNA to fingerprinting criminals, which is allowed under the Fourth Amendment, calling DNA the "genetic fingerprint." The majority views DNA testing as minimally intrusive. The dissenting opinion expresses fear of a slippery slope where soon everyone could be forced to give their DNA, and as more technology develops, it will be more difficult to draw a line for Fourth Amendment rights.[53]

Less than five years later, the taking of DNA from criminals comes into question again. In 2009, Maryland's DNA law is updated to include not just convicted felons but all individuals arrested for violent crimes and burglaries, regardless of whether they are ultimately convicted or not.[54] One of the people affected by the provision is Alonzo Jay King Jr., who is arrested in 2009 for threatening a group of people with a shotgun. Before his conviction, a cheek swab of King's DNA is taken and tested according to Maryland's DNA Collection Act.

Soon afterward, police discover King's DNA matches evidence from an unsolved case in which a man with a concealed face broke into a women's home with a gun and raped her. Although the police never identified the rapist, they did collect some of his DNA and logged it in Maryland's database. When police collect King's DNA at the time of his arrest and log it into the database, they discover the match. King is subsequently put on trial for the rape, and the court allows the DNA evidence to be used against him. As a result of the evidence, King is convicted of first-degree rape and sentenced to life in prison.

On appeal, King argues that Maryland's DNA Collection Act is unconstitutional because it is an unreasonable search and seizure under the Fourth Amendment. In 2013, the Supreme Court holds that the search is reasonable and therefore constitutional. The cheek-swab DNA test is conducted for a legitimate state interest. The court says that it is important to know the dangerousness of an individual in setting conditions for bail, for example. The dissent, penned by Justice Antonin Scalia, joined by Justices Ruth Bader Ginsburg, Sonia Sotomayor, and Elena Kagan, on the other hand, argue that under the Fourth Amendment, it is unconstitutional to search someone for evidence if there is no reason to believe they are guilty of a crime.

Despite the challenges, the collection, testing, and use of DNA have become vital tools for solving crimes. In the beginning, there were fewer testable markers, gene variations by which people could be distinguished. DNA testing, therefore, could exclude people from being the perpetrator, but it often could not be used to assign guilt to a specific individual. But since DNA processing techniques have improved, and many more testable markers are available, it is possible to conclusively demonstrate that a sample belongs to one particular individual to the exclusion of all others. In addition, new technology makes it possible for regions of DNA to be amplified, similar to the natural process of DNA copying that occurs in a cell. As a result, today technicians only need minute amounts of DNA for accurate testing. A single drop of saliva that found its way onto the steering wheel of a car has been sufficient to convict a man of murder.

The advances in DNA testing have allowed prosecutors to reopen "cold cases" in which biological samples were collected but, because of the

limited sophistication of testing at the time, police were unable to identify a suspect or to gain a conviction. But when these cases are reopened
today and clear evidence of guilt is available from today's more advanced
analysis, prosecution and conviction for the offense is sometimes barred
by the statute of limitations, no matter how overwhelmingly clear the evidence of guilt of the offender. Some wonder, if reliable DNA evidence is
available, why should a rapist be allowed to go free simply because some
arbitrary amount of time has elapsed? The situation has prompted a trend
among many states to lengthen the limitation period for criminal prosecution or to create a variety of exceptions to their statute limitations. A
different kind of workaround was pioneered in 1999 by Wisconsin, where
prosecutors with a clear DNA profile, for which they had not yet found
the person to match, issued an arrest warrant for the person, identifying
the person in the warrant only as "John Doe" having a DNA profile as
described. The issuing of the warrant has the legal effect of stopping the
clock for the purposes of the statute of limitations.

DNA, WRONGFUL CONVICTIONS, AND THE CSI EFFECT

Today, DNA typing is regularly used to convict criminals, but it is also
regularly used to overturn the convictions of innocent inmates. Indeed,
had it not been for DNA evidence in the Leicestershire murders, police
would have stopped looking for the perpetrator after Richard Buckland
confessed. He would have most likely been convicted, and Colin Pitchfork would have gone free. Unfortunately, wrongful convictions have
regularly occurred in the criminal justice system for a variety of reasons,
including faulty evidence, false confessions, dishonesty in the justice
system, and the fallibility of witnesses. Analysis of the data shows, for
example, that mistaken eyewitness identification accounts for 70 percent
of erroneous convictions.[55] Once the truth-telling power of DNA was
proven, the chances of reducing the rate of wrongful convictions were
significantly improved.

One organization that has pioneered using DNA evidence to exonerate
innocent people in the United States is The Innocence Project, started in
1992 at the Cardozo School of Law and eventually growing into an independent nonprofit organization. The group is a "a national litigation and
public policy organization dedicated to exonerating wrongfully convicted
people through DNA testing and reforming the criminal justice system to
prevent future injustice."[56] The Innocence Project only takes cases from
inmates directly. Every year, the project receives over three thousand
first-time requests from prisoners seeking assistance. The group then

looks into the details of each case in an effort to determine which cases would potentially allow DNA testing to prove innocence.

One of the most consequential cases taken by the Innocence Project is the case of Kennedy Brewer. In 1992, Gloria Jackson's three-year-old daughter is abducted, raped, and murdered. The body is found two days later at a creek close to the Jackson house. Jackson's boyfriend Brewer is arrested, as he was home babysitting that evening, and there is no sign of forced entry. A semen sample is found on the victim's body, but given the state of DNA testing at the time, it is too small for forensic testing. Bite marks are found on the baby's body and an expert, who had previously been suspended from the American Board of Forensic Odontology, says that the marks are definitely from Brewer's top two teeth. His testimony is allowed at trial.

The defense brings a founding member of the American Board of Forensic Odontology to the stand who argues that the bite marks are from an insect, and that a human could not make such marks with just his two front teeth. Nonetheless, Brewer is convicted of sexual battery and capital murder and sentenced to death.

In 2001, the recovered semen from the three-year-old's body is tested using more advanced DNA testing. The results do not match Brewer, his friends, or his relatives. A judge exonerates Brewer, but prosecutors vow to retry him, so he is moved to pretrial detention for another five years. Brewer is finally released in 2007. The Innocence Project, with assistance from the attorney general, is soon able to find the real murderer.

Since its founding twenty-five years ago, the Innocence Project has helped 349 people be found innocent and freed.[57] In nearly half the cases, the actual perpetrator has subsequently been convicted.[58] (The Innocence Project receives 6,000 to 8,000 requests a year,[59] which suggests total requests of something like 175,000. The 349 exonerations, then, suggest that the wrongful conviction rate that they had exposed is approximately .002 percent of those claiming innocence.) The Innocence Project, and other similar groups, demonstrate the power of DNA typing to correct past wrongs and bring the right people to justice.

With the ever-expanding use of DNA to uncover the truth about real-world crimes, Hollywood producers have also made a discovery of their own: using fancy technology to catch an elusive bad guy makes great entertainment. One of the most successful Hollywood endeavors is *Crime Scene Investigation*, or *CSI*, a television franchise that began in 2000 (just as the DNA Act was being passed.) Each episode begins with a horrible death; the rest of the episode follows a team of fictional forensic scientists as they work to collect evidence, pursue leads, and eventually apprehend the criminal. Shows like *CSI* captivate the nation, showcasing DNA-based crime solving in the new "genetic age."[60] The show is so popular that it has three successful spinoffs, including *CSI: Miami, CSI: New York,* and *CSI: Cyber*. By 2006, seventy million people have watched one of the shows in the CSI franchise.

While forensic dramas like *CSI* and others have made people more aware and interested in the use of DNA for crime solving, it has also led to what is sometimes referred to as the "CSI effect," as discussed in the chapter "1915 Chloroform Killer—Medical Examiners."

Regular people, who eventually end up on juries, come to believe that real-life investigations work similarly to those portrayed by Hollywood. Even though people understand that TV shows are not reality, exposure to the shows still leads to misunderstandings. Juries expect overwhelming and compelling DNA evidence—often based on technology that does not actually exist—and will conclude that anything less suggests a problem case. In addition, jurors sometimes assume that every case will have fingerprints and/or usable DNA. Prosecutors argue that as a result of the "CSI effect" guilty criminals are being set free.

For example, prosecutors believed they had a strong case against actor Robert Blake, who was on trial for murdering his wife Bonnie Lee Bakely on May 4, 2001. She is shot in the head while sitting in Blake's vehicle. Blake has no alibi and has a strong motive to leave the marriage and there is a credible witness who testifies that Blake tried to hire a hit man to kill his wife. However, there is no DNA evidence, and the jury acquits Blake. Prosecutors blame the acquittal on the CSI effect. The jury wants blood, or gunshot residue, or maybe a convenient DNA match. The district attorney is sure that Blake is guilty and believes that prior to the build-up of unreasonable expectations, Blake would have been easily convicted.[61] According to many prosecutors, Blake's case is not unique. They say it is increasingly difficult to get a conviction because jurors expect scientific evidence in every issue.

The night he called the investigators of the Leicestershire murders to tell them of the results of the DNA analysis in the Dawn Ashworth case, Dr. Jeffreys forever changed the way police investigate crime. DNA evidence has made investigations more exacting, scientific, and accurate, but it also continues to raise questions about privacy, the rights of felons, and the standard of proof required for a conviction. As DNA and other forensic technologies inevitably continue to improve, our legal system must be prepared to adjust to a new world of crime investigation and adjudication.

Chapter Eighteen

1989
Schaeffer Stalking Murder

Stalking Offense

THE TRAGEDY—SCHAEFFER MURDER

Robert Bardo is living in Tucson, Arizona.[1] Bardo is the youngest of seven siblings and the son of a former air force officer. He exhibits abnormal behavior throughout his childhood. At age thirteen, for example, he steals $140 from his mother's purse and uses it to purchase a bus ticket to Maine in hopes of encountering Samantha Smith, the child famous for sending a letter to Mikhail Gorbachev.

Bardo is a straight-A student. However, his academic abilities can do nothing to mask his complete lack of social skills. Bardo avoids interaction with the faculty and his fellow students. He makes an exception for one of his teachers, to whom he writes threatening letters, often three times a day, in which he explains that it is his duty to kill her and others. Each letter is signed either "Scarface," "Dirty Harry Callahan," or "James Bond." When the school reaches out to his parents, the Bardos deny any suggestion that their son may be in need of psychiatric help. When he changes schools, he moves his letter-writing target to a new teacher. Bardo sends his English teacher a ten-page letter detailing his plan to commit suicide. His parents again deny the notion that their son has emotional problems, but they place him in foster care. Foster care does not improve Bardo's mental health. During his abbreviated school career, he is hospitalized twice, during which he is diagnosed as "severely emotionally handicapped."[2]

In 1985, his parents take him out of the hospital; Bardo returns home and drops out of high school. At sixteen years old, he lands a job as a janitor in a local Jack in the Box restaurant. When he is not working, he watches television. In particular, he is a great fan of the sitcom *My Sister Sam*, starring Rebecca Schaeffer.

Bardo begins to write letters to Schaeffer. Schaeffer, as is the case with many celebrities, has contracted out the job of responding to fan mail. The service writes a letter to Bardo, which is designed to appear as though Schaeffer herself wrote it. The reply says that the letter from Bardo is the most beautiful letter she has ever received; the writer has even includes drawings of a peace sign and a heart. The kind response is very meaningful to Bardo; he writes in his diary, "When I think of her, I would like to become famous to impress her."[3] After receiving the letter, he builds a shrine dedicated to her in his bedroom. With his obsession reinforced by her letter, Bardo travels to the Burbank studio in California in June of 1987, where *My Sister Sam* is being produced. He brings a teddy bear and a bouquet of roses for the actress; however, Warner Brothers security does not let him past the front gate. He goes home and his adoration for the actress begins to become tainted. He feels that she is becoming too full of herself. Seeing her going in the wrong direction bothers Bardo, and a month later he is back at the studio gates. This time there are no roses, but he is armed with a knife. Bardo feels that it is duty to deflate Schaeffer's ego. Again, the security guards prevent him from entering the studio.

Shortly after the incident, Bardo returns to Tucson, his attention having shifted to others; pop singers Debbie Gibson and Tiffany Darwish capture his imagination. In 1988, Bardo travels to New York City in an unsuccessful attempt to find Gibson. Since he is in the city, he also visits the archway of the Dakota where former Beatle member John Lennon was fatally shot just eight years prior by crazed-fan Mark Chapman.

In mid-1989, Hollywood releases *Scenes from the Class Struggle in Beverly Hills*, which stars Schaeffer. In one scene, the actress is in bed with an actor. Bardo is enraged to see her becoming just "another Hollywood whore."[4] Gibson and Darwish are forgotten, his attention is now purely devoted to Schaeffer.

Following his denouncement of Schaeffer as a whore, Bardo, who is now nineteen years old, takes his obsession to a new level. He bombards her with a proliferation of love letters, begins a collection of videos of all her TV shows, and plasters his room with posters of the actress. One day, he stumbles across a *People* magazine article. The article tells the story of Arthur Jackson, an obsessed fan, and how he had contrived to get the home address of actress Theresa Saldana. Jackson had tricked the young woman's mother into providing the address by pretending he wanted to hire her for a movie. Jackson got to Saldana's home easily, once he had the address. With clear intent to kill her, Jackson attacked. Saldana was

Figure 18.1. Rebecca Schaeffer, publicity headshot, 1986. *Creative Commons*

stabbed but survived the attack. Bardo now sees a way around the studio's security.

On July 17, 1989, Bardo calls the office of Schaeffer's agent. Posing as someone in the film industry trying to hire Schaeffer, he asks for her address. The agent declines to provide the address. Bardo moves to an even easier plan; he hires a private detective. For $250, the detective simply fills out a form at the DMV office, declaring who he is, what person he wants the information on, the reason, and how he intends to use it. Without any further questions, the detective gets Schaeffer's home address and passes it on to Bardo.

Armed with the address, Bardo sets the rest of his plan into motion. He writes to his sister, telling her "I have an obsession with the unobtainable and I have to eliminate [something] that I cannot attain."[5] He gets his older brother, Edgar, to buy him a gun. Bardo also adds one more item to his collection of Schaeffer fan gear that is arrayed around his room: a diagram of her body with spots marked where he intends to shoot her.

Boarding a bus, he leaves his home in Arizona for his mission in Hollywood. The next day, Bardo arrives in Schaeffer's neighborhood. For the trip, he is carrying a single bag, which contains the gun, a letter to Schaeffer, a U2 tape, and a copy of *The Catcher in the Rye*, the same book John Hinckley Jr. was carrying at the time of his assassination attempt on then-president Ronald Reagan. The U2 tape is included because the song "Exit" tells him of his destiny, with the lyrics: "He put his hands in the pocket. His finger on the steel. The pistol weighed heavy." He has chosen to use hollow-point cartridges, designed to inflict greater damage to a target upon impact.

Clad in a yellow polo shirt, Bardo locates Schaeffer's home. But he does not go in yet. Instead, he wanders aimlessly around the neighborhood, stopping random pedestrians to confirm that the apartment is indeed the actress's. Finally, he rings the buzzer to her unit. Because the intercom is broken Schaeffer must come downstairs and open the glass security door to find out what the man wants. Bardo hands her the letter in his bag. The two speak about a response that Bardo had once received to one of his fan letters. Schaeffer is polite but suspicious. She wants to know how he found her address. Wrapping up the conversation quickly, she says, "Please take care. . . . I appreciate you coming, but please don't return."[6] Schaeffer shakes his hand and Bardo walks away.

Their first physical interaction is, however, too short for Bardo. As he walks away, he remembers the CD he meant to give her and decides to return. Before going back, he stops at a local diner where he eats onion rings and cheesecake. After about an hour, he returns to the apartment complex and rings the bell once again. Schaeffer, who is preparing for her audition for the film *The Godfather Part III*, answers the door again. Caught by surprise, the actress answers the door in her bathrobe. She recognizes Bardo. "You came to my door again. . . . Hurry up, I don't have much time."[7] Bardo is insulted, remarking that this is a "very callous thing to say to a fan." He reaches in his bag, pulls out the gun, and fires. The bullet hits Schaeffer's heart. Bardo stands for a moment and thinks about what to do next. "Should I blow my head off and fall on her?"[8] After a second's hesitation, he turns and flees through the nearby alley.

Schaeffer lives long enough to scream and ask "Why?" A man living across the street, Richard Goldman, hears the commotion and rushes over to find Schaeffer barely alive.[9] The twenty-one-year-old actress is rushed to Cedars-Sinai Medical Center. This is the same hospital that saved Saldana after her stabbing, but the hollow point bullets have done their work, and Schaeffer soon dies.

Bardo walks from the apartment complex without anyone stopping him. He is soon on a bus back to Tucson. The day after the murder, a number of motorists in Tucson call 9-1-1 to report a man in yellow wandering among the cars on Interstate 10. When questioned by an officer, Bardo confesses to the killing. He is arrested and extradited to California, where he is held in Los Angeles for trial.

The case is heard by Judge Dino Fulgoni in a bench trial. Throughout the court proceedings, Bardo offers no denial of facts presented by the prosecution. He says, "I was a fan of hers and I may have carried it too far. . . . If I had one wish where if it was to ever come true it would be for Rebecca Schaeffer to be alive today."[10] The defense uses his history of mental illness to establish that the actions are the result of insanity, insisting that, instead of prison, Bardo should be institutionalized. Nevertheless, in October of 1991, Bardo is convicted of first-degree murder and subsequently sentenced to life in prison without the possibility of parole.

THE OUTRAGE

At the time of her death, Schaeffer is rising in fame. She is on the cover of *Seventeen* magazine, a popular magazine with a readership of teenagers. Her sitcom *My Sister Sam* reaches the top twenty-five in TV shows. Her sudden death triggers a national outrage. As had been the case with Theresa Saldana, Schaeffer was already known to the public. The media attention due to her celebrity leads to a rapid escalation of outrage at her killing. With all media outlets talking about the murder, Bardo is seen as the monster that killed a virtuous and pure girl, whom Schaeffer portrays on screen. The innocence and helplessness of the victim leaves the audience angry and confused. Memories of Saldana's attack also surface; what everyone thought to be a one-time incident has happened again. There is a general feeling that nothing like this should ever be allowed to happen again. The public now demands intervention to restore security and justice. Schaeffer's death now sparks a nationwide movement to institute changes to the way the legal system addresses the issue of stalkers.

As people begin talking about celebrity stalking, the evidence quickly demonstrates that this is not a celebrity-unique issue. Across the country, ordinary people are also victims of stalking. The year of Schaeffer's death, five women in Orange County are killed in a six-week period on different occasions by either former spouses or boyfriends who would certainly qualify as stalkers. In one case, Hossein Ghaffari drives his vehicle into his target's car, pours flammable liquid on her, and lights her on fire, where she burns to death inside her car. Ghaffari had dated the woman ten years earlier and had stalked her continuously for the next decade. When he learned she was to be married, he immolated her.

Schaeffer's death and those in Orange County reinforce the urgency of the issue. Advocacy organizations spring up across the nation to lobby for a law on stalking. Director Brad Siberling, Schaeffer's boyfriend at the time of her death, releases *Moonlight Mile*, a film loosely based on Schaeffer's situation, which further increases awareness of stalking and harassment.

Hollywood has a unique power to package a message. The psychological thriller *Fatal Attraction* had been released in 1987 and had done well. Now with the death of Schaeffer, the movie becomes another source of fear. The film follows a married man who has a weekend affair with a woman. The woman grows obsessed with the man. She continues to follow and harass him, despite his moving to another city. Eventually, the obsessed woman finds the man, and a violent scene ensues. A multitude of news articles are now published that compare the fictional film to real-world cases.[11]

Media sources writing about Schaeffer are able to publish plenty of other past stalking cases involving celebrities, such as David Letterman and Michael J. Fox. Compilations of the cases by the media show the American people that the stalking incidents are a consistent pattern across the country.

THE REFORM

In 1989, criminal law contains no offense that specifically prohibits stalking. Assault is a crime, so if a stalker crosses the line and actually harms their victim, the law can act. The same is true of trespass, if a stalker trespasses, and the victim is able to get the police to take it seriously enough, a formal complaint can be lodged. Laws such as those seem to leave the victim few options.

Civil remedies at the time include restraining orders and lawsuits for civil wrongs such as invasion of privacy or intentional infliction of emotional distress. But these civil remedies require a victim to have the financial resources to bring the legal actions. And they do very little to increase the safety of the person being stalked. Every victim in the Orange County killings had a restraining order against her attacker. It is hard to imagine that any administrative order would have made a dent in Ghaffari's obsession.

In the wake of the focused media attention and public outrage following the star's death, California legislators begin to draft bills targeting stalking. As the legislators take up the issue, a wave of victims and their advocates are inspired to come forward. When the legislators start to listen the stories are chilling. Kathleen Baty, wife a former NFL player Greg Baty, testifies before the state Senate of her own stalker, Lawrence Stagner, who followed her for eight years.[12] It isn't until May of 1990, when he shows up at her home with a buck knife and a semiautomatic rifle and attempts to abduct her, that he is arrested. He pleads guilty to a charge of attempted kidnapping and receives a sentence of eight years and ten months in prison. (He serves four years, and within a few weeks of being released is stalking her again. But now, legislation is in place, and he is returned to prison.)

California enacts the first anti-stalking law under the lead of State Senator Edward Royce. The legislation provides a possible stalking conviction for a person who:

willfully, maliciously, and repeatedly follows or harasses another person *and* who makes a credible threat with the intent to place that person in reasonable fear of death or great bodily injury.

The law makes stalking punishable by up to one year in jail and/or a $1,000 fine. For the purpose of clarification, "harasses" is defined as a:

knowing and willful course of conduct directed at a specific person which seriously alarms, annoys, or harasses the person, and which serves no legitimate purpose. The course of conduct must be such as would cause a reasonable person to suffer substantial emotional distress, and must actually cause substantial emotional distress to the person.

In this case, the "course of conduct" is a "pattern of conduct composed of a series of acts over a period of time, however short, evidencing a continuity of purpose." The idea of a "credible threat" is said to be one with the

intent and the apparent ability to carry out the threat so as to cause the person who is the target of the threat to reasonably fear for his or her safety. The threat must be against the life of, or a threat to cause great bodily injury to, [the] person.[13]

In addition to making stalking a criminal offense, California tightens privacy laws. After all, the lack of sufficient privacy measures enabled Jackson and Bardo to get their hands on their victims' addresses and phone numbers. If Bardo did not get Schaeffer's address from the DMV, perhaps she might still be alive. In 1991, California governor George Deukmejian signs into law the Driver's Privacy Protection Act, which prohibits the disclosure of personal information without the consent of the person to whom the information pertains. This rule is formulated to keep private information out of reach of potential harassers and attackers.

Many other states also follow suit, using the laws developed in California as a model for their own. State Representative Dianne Byrum of Michigan explains her own motivation for introducing an anti-stalking law on January 30, 1992, saying, "In the most tragic case, the young actress Rebecca Schaeffer was brutally killed by a man who stalked her across the country."[14] Schaeffer's murder causes a great awakening across the nation. Between 1992 and 1993, forty-eight other states pass their own form of anti-stalking laws.

Many states follow the California law, but many others depart from the California model in one way or another. For example, the California law requires that a stalker follow a victim *and* have intent to cause fear. Stalking laws adopted in Washington and Michigan allow intent to be presumed based on the perpetrator's behavior. If the perpetrator knows that he or she has scared the target, that is sufficient cause be arrested on charges of stalking, regardless of what the intent may have been. In Illinois, Ohio, Iowa, and Massachusetts, the anti-stalking laws include a section that sets a lower limit on bail for the stalker. In fact, Illinois purports to deny bail for such an offense before trial. Though Massachusetts does not go as far as Illinois in denying an accused stalker bail, it does limit the accused's pretrial activity. Further, Florida and Ohio enact legislation that allows police officers to arrest without a warrant anyone they believe to be a stalker. In Ohio, a simple written statement by the victim is deemed sufficient proof for an arrest. Massachusetts, in addition to the limit on bail, sets a mandatory minimum sentence for convicted stalkers, which is not subject to reductions in sentences, suspensions, or possibilities of parole.

In the wide variation in stalking laws across states, some statutes are more restrictive. In West Virginia, the accused stalker must have lived with or must have an intimate relationship with the victim. Under this definition, celebrity-obsessed fans would not be considered stalkers. Exceptions to the stalking laws are made in Washington, Delaware, and Tennessee for private detectives, who are allowed to conduct surveillance, even if such surveillance resembles stalker-type behavior. In Nebraska and North Carolina, the law requires previous actions by the victim for following to constitute stalking. That is, the victim must have made previous attempts to stop the stalker from his or her activity, such as obtaining a temporary restraining order.

With all the evidence pointing to the need of an anti-stalking law, in October of 1993, the National Institute of Justice launches a project to develop a model anti-stalking code for the states. Strong activity at the state level soon leads to federal action. Both the U.S. House and Senate draft their own versions of a federal anti-stalking law. The primary differences between the two are in the definitions of stalking and penalties for stalkers. The House version defines a stalker as someone who repeatedly follows or harasses a victim and makes a credible threat toward the victim, but the Senate bill only requires that a stalker harasses a victim and makes a credible threat. Simply following someone is not enough to constitute a stalking offense in either version of the bill. The Senate bill also lists harsher penalties for violations of the stalking laws. In 1994, Congress passes the Violence Against Women Act (also discussed in the chapter "1983 Thurman Beatings—Domestic Violence"), which combines the two bills, though resembling the Senate version more.[15] The bill also applies the offense to both men and women, despite the name of the act.

Stalking is a shadowy offense; without clear borders, it is hard to construct meaningful legislation. The stalking laws inspired by Schaeffer's death would have done nothing to protect her. Furthermore, the stalkers in Orange County threatened their victims, but it is not clear whether the murders were carried out maliciously with the intent of posing a threat to the victims' lives or to cause great bodily injury, as the law requires. The possibility of the stalking taking place out of overzealous love, rather than an actual intent to harm the subject, also means that stalking charges might not be possible. In fact, neither Bardo nor the murderers in Orange County would have been guilty of stalking charges.

In response to these shortcomings, California legislators amend their first anti-stalking law four times in the span of five years. The definition of stalking is refined. The credible-threat language is modified so that the victim must only show a "reasonable fear for his or her safety or the safety of his or her immediate relatives."[16]

BEYOND REFORM

A particular problem for effectively dealing with stalkers is the fact they come in several different forms; each type has a somewhat different perspective on the situation and a different motivation for the stalking. Many are mentally or emotionally unbalanced.

One stalker profile is that of delusional erotomania. Erotomania is a persistent "erotic delusion that one is loved by another,"[17] regardless of whether that other knows of the person's existence. Saldana's attacker, Jackson, seems to have had erotomania because he believes that he and Saldana love each other, and he attacks so that they can be in perfect union.

Another stalker profile is borderline erotomania, which is characterized by knowledge that the other individual does not reciprocate the person's feelings, as opposed to delusional erotomania, in which there is a belief that the intense feelings are mutual. Borderline erotomanics, unlike delusional ones, also tend to have had previous interaction with the victim, however trivial. Bardo fits this profile; the fan letters were enough to convince him of his love for her.

A third type of stalker is a "former intimate," referring to a former intimate partner, such as a romantic partner or spouse, though these types of stalkers tend to exhibit characteristics of disorders that are medically diagnosable, such as personality disorders or mood disorders. Some of these symptoms include low self-esteem, low occupational status, and a history of physical-abuse victimization. Hossein Ghaffari, from Orange County, fits this profile. These people's obsessions are triggered by their former partners moving on.

Finally, the fourth type of stalker is the sociopathic one, who does not seek any real intimate relationship with their victim, but rather arbitrarily chooses their target. Constructing a stalking offense that would capture all of these different types of stalkers may not be possible.

Part of the special challenge in drafting stalking statutes is that they tend to approach, or cross, the line of what the Constitution permits the government to do in restricting a person's freedom of movement.

By January 1996, just six years after the first anti-stalking law was instituted, the Justice Department identifies fifty-three causes of constitutional concerns in stalking statutes in nineteen states. Most of these challenges to the laws stem from the overly broad and vague language. Many of the existing laws are already criticized as an overreach of the governments' power and an infringement of civil rights. In Florida and Illinois, for example, the presumption of intent, denial of bail, and arrest without warrant present constitutional concerns in violation of the Bill of Rights.

Obsessed fans professing their love can also cause celebrities emotional distress, especially if the language is strong and emotional. However, to see those as stalking offenses also comes into direct conflict with the First Amendment, allowing for freedom of speech. The line between self-expression and threatening language can be thin. The vague terms employed in many of the laws are also signs of concern. Based on due process, a law is void if its prohibitions are not clearly defined. However, much of the language in anti-stalking laws is sufficiently broad as to be open to interpretation, and thus not providing a clear fixed meaning.

Another challenge to stalking-offense drafters is the advance of technology. Physically stalking one's victim is now made easier by way of new devices that allow one to stay far from sight, yet keep a close eye on the victim. The digitalization of mass information also presents a new concern in terms of stalking. With cyber-stalking growing more and more prevalent, information about one's personal life is at anyone's disposal. A home address can be looked up online. Also, through various encryption methods and software, stalkers are increasingly able to send threatening messages to their victim over the multitude of social media platforms under the veil of anonymity.

As of 2013, all fifty states and the District of Columbia have some form of anti-stalking legislation. Within the fifty-two American criminal codes, there is a great deal of diversity as to what qualifies as stalking. Refining the laws requires criminal code drafters to balance constitutional limitations on governmental intrusion in the lives of individuals with the array of means by which a stalker might imagine to inflict physical, and emotional, damage on their victims.

Chapter Nineteen

1993
Polly Klaas Abduction

Three-Strikes Sentencing

THE TRAGEDY

In 1967, Richard Davis will turn thirteen, but early in the year, before that day arrives, he is arrested for his first burglary.[1] His arrest record continues to grow. Shortly after his seventeenth birthday, Davis is involved in a motorcycle theft. Davis has now been convicted on four separate occasions but has never done real time in jail. The judge gives Davis the choice of joining the army or being sent to the California Youth Authority. All over the country 162,746 men are drafted in 1971 and Davis elects to serve with them.[2] The army needs men, but not Davis. He is discharged after a year. His service record shows multiple instances of discipline for going AWOL, fighting, failure to report, and morphine use. In his own view, the army was a time of discovery. Stationed in Europe, he finds cheap drugs: "I start getting loaded like a motherfucker—hash, coke, opium, and shooting morphine."[3]

In October of 1973, Davis is arrested for the fourth time since leaving the army. The arrest is for a stack of traffic violations. By now he has a bigger problem; his La Honda, California, neighbors are worked up about the ongoing burglaries that Davis is committing. While the police may not to have the evidence they need to arrest Davis, to his neighbors there is no doubt. Davis's probation officer feels that for his own safety Davis must be put in jail. He receives a six-month sentence and three years of probation.

May of 1974 brings Davis back into court. The proceedings are suspended when he voluntarily enters a ninety-day residential alcohol-treatment program. Davis enters the program one day and leaves the next.

By fall, Davis is back in jail, but he is permitted to leave to attend an alcohol-treatment program. While in jail, he has conspired with some fellow inmates to use his access to the greater world to obtain drugs. They give him money and he gives them the slip. He does not return to jail. Evidently, the authorities do not know how to find the missing prisoner, but the cheated inmates do. Upon their release from jail a few months later, the men hunt down Davis and shoot him. He survives the attack only to be returned to prison. The fact that he turns in the men who shot him and tells authorities everything he knows about them makes his return to jail dangerous, so he is placed in protective custody.

His original sentence is for a year. During those 365 days, Davis is involved in a prison drug deal, steals money from other inmates, is shot, escapes from custody, returns to prison, is released only to be arrested again in March, April, July, and August. In August of 1975, after a burglary and grand-theft conviction, it is decided that his parole should be revoked. He is also given a sentence of six months to fifteen years. He serves one year.

Upon release in late summer of 1976, Davis embarks on a more violent path. As twenty-six-year-old Francis Mays gets off a commuter train, Davis grabs her and forces her into her car. After driving to a remote spot, before he can rape her, Mays grabs the blade of Davis's knife and escapes with Davis chasing right behind her. Mays flags down a passing car driven by Jim Wentz, an off-duty police officer. Wentz cuffs Davis on the spot and takes him into custody.

Davis tells the authorities that he was hearing voices that instructed him to rape Mays, and then he stages a suicide attempt. The authorities react as Davis assumes they will: he is sent to the Napa State Hospital. After eight days at the hospital, he walks out.

Once free, he does not hesitate to get back on his violent track. That night, he breaks into a home and attacks Marjorie Mitchell with a fire poker. He is unable to establish control and she is screaming, so he moves on. Next he kidnaps Hazel Frost as she is getting into her car. Frost too resists. When Davis attempts to bind her, she rolls out of the car, grabs her own gun, which is hidden under the seat, and shoots at Davis. She does not hit him but Davis flees. Davis now breaks into the home of Josephine Krieger, steals what he wants, then lies in wait. Josephine returns to find her house ransacked. Davis intends to kidnap and rape her. He hides in the bushes with a shotgun and a pair of knives, waiting to see if anyone else is coming home. The police respond to Josephine's call about the break-in. Davis tells the police that his intent was to tie the residents up and steal their car. Davis is again taken into custody.

In less than five years he is back on the streets and his pattern of victimization continues: home invasions, a couple of bank robberies, assaults, kidnapping, and a variety of other crimes. He is returned to prison in 1985. While in prison Davis learns metalworking and is a good prisoner. He is free again in June of 1993.

Davis settles at a homeless shelter in San Mateo. He doesn't find full-time work, but for months, he makes his meetings at the parole office, passes his drug tests, and follows the rules. "He was unremarkable," says one shelter official; another says he "did everything he was supposed to do."[4] Davis earns the right to travel. On September 23, 1993, Davis is given permission to go out of town to visit his sister in Ukiah, a city north of San Mateo. On the way, he passes through Petaluma. He returns to San Mateo, as instructed, three days later.

Davis returns to Petaluma on October 1. Petaluma is a beautiful, docile city known for its historic buildings and riverside marina. Flanked by green hills and rolling oak woodlands, the city is a popular tourist destination. It's no surprise, then, that Davis stands out. He is seen there "loitering around Walnut Park and Wickersham Park."[5] He is now thirty-nine years old, large and loud. Tattoos cover his arms, and his salt-and-pepper hair and beard are disheveled. He's the sort of man that just seeing him inspires fear.

Polly Klaas, who is twelve, lives with her mother just across the street from Wickersham Park. Polly is a cheerful girl, known for her infectious laugh and sense of humor. Something of a musician, Polly is an accomplished pianist and clarinet player who loves being on stage.

Polly is hosting a sleepover with two of her classmates, Kate and Gillian. When Kate's mother leaves after dropping off her daughter, she notices a bearded, dark-featured man on the sidewalk, carrying a bag or a box. He seems disoriented, but she doesn't think much of it.

It's the first day of October 1993; as part of the fun, the girls walk a few blocks to the nearby convenience store for Popsicles. They pass the park as they come and go to the store but are safely home before long. With Halloween on their minds, they play dress-up, donning heavy makeup and silly clothes. At 10:00 p.m., Polly's mother, reminds them not to stay up too late and heads to bed with Polly's sister, Annie. The girls move on to board games, and the night starts to wind down.

The girls are getting sleepy; Polly hops up to fetch the sleeping bags. She opens her bedroom door only to find a stranger blocking her exit. He is menacing, muscular, and clothed in black. As he comes into the room he brings a fog of unpleasant smells. He reeks of alcohol, old sweat, and smoke. He is armed with a knife.

The man enters the room and takes command: "Don't scream or I'll slit your throats."[6] He forces the girls to lie face down on the floor and tells them to look away from him. The overnight guests wonder if this man is a friend of Polly's family. Is it a prank of sorts? The man demands to know where the valuables are. He reassures them that he is "only doing this for the money."[7] How much of value could a twelve-year-old have? Polly begs the intruder not to hurt her sleeping family. She offers up what she has and directs him to her jewelry box where all her money is kept.

Davis's control begins to ebb. He had come in calmly but grows frantic as the minutes pass. He ties the children up with cords and clothing collected from Polly's floor. The girls are gagged and he covers their heads with pillowcases. No one believes this is a prank any more.

Davis tells the girls that he is taking Polly to help him locate other valuables in the home. He reassures them that Polly will return shortly. Gillian and Kate are instructed to count to one thousand. Polly, who is sobbing uncontrollably, leaves with the intruder. From beginning to end, the encounter lasts about ten minutes.

Kate and Gillian struggle free of their bonds and rush to wake Polly's mother. Polly is gone. Polly's mother, Eve Nichol, calls 9-1-1. It's 11:00 p.m. when the police begin to mobilize.

Not long afterward, twenty miles to the north, a local resident named Dana Jaffe comes home from an evening out. She and her twelve-year-old daughter live on a beautiful, green hillside in Sonoma County, at the end of a private road lined with "No Trespassing" signs. Shannon Lynch has been babysitting. Lynch leaves the Jaffe home at about 11:15 p.m. Before reaching the road, Lynch spots a Ford Pinto stuck in a ditch. A large man, dressed in black, is inspecting the rear bumper. Lynch stops her car and the man approaches. Lynch rolls down the window a bit but does not get out. The man is dirty with leaves in his hair, he smells terrible, and his shirt is inside out. "I'm stuck. I need some rope,"[8] he tells Lynch. Lynch confronts him about his trespassing. The man, pressing his hands against her window, tells her to get out the car and demands to know what's at the end of the road. Lynch is afraid. She warns him that the people who live there will call the police. The man continues to insist that she get out of her car; instead Lynch speeds off. Finding a pay phone, she calls Jaffe and warns her about the man. Jaffe takes the warning seriously and decides that she and her daughter need to leave. They pass the white Ford Pinto, but they do not see anyone. Jaffe calls the police to report the incident.

Jaffe leads two officers to the Pinto. Polly's kidnapping has not been broadcast to the Sonoma police, so the officers have no knowledge of the abduction. When they arrive, the man is leaning calmly against his car, smoking a cigarette. His sweaty clothes and hair are covered with leaves and twigs, and the smell of alcohol lingers. As the officers approach, the dirty man says: "What the fuck are you doing here?"[9]

When confronted with the trespassing issue, he claims he was passing through on his way toward Redwood Valley when he decided to pull off for some sightseeing. They do not delve into the story, but they do run a license plate check. He checks out, but they realize they have incorrectly entered his plate number. For a simple trespass, they decide it's not worth running another check. They search the car and spot unopened beer cans and two bags of torn clothing. Finding no probable cause on which to make an arrest, they help free the man's car.

With that, Richard Allen Davis disappears into the darkness. He continues to meet his parole obligations in San Mateo.

THE OUTRAGE

Polly Klaas's widely publicized abduction shocks and terrifies the nation. The FBI alone puts seventy-five agents on the case. Thousands of tips are followed up on, but two months pass with no useful leads. Families across America, sharing the agony felt by Polly's family, wait for news about the stolen girl. "I have a daughter out there—without shoes," her mother cries, a desperate plea that echoes in the hearts of mothers around the world.[10] Polly's father, Marc Klaas, says, "It's the most desperate time any parent can experience. Getting up and not knowing."[11] He stops working and drops thirty pounds as the wait drags on.

After Thanksgiving, Dana Jaffe is walking her property when she finds "a pair of child-sized knitted tights that are knotted at the knee, an adult-sized dark sweatshirt, and a knotted piece of white silky cloth shaped like a hood."[12] Jaffe calls the sheriff's office, and the following day, she and Deputy Sheriff Mike McManus search the area again. They find an unrolled condom, a torn condom wrapper, tape, a beer bottle, a six-pack holder, and matches. McManus collects everything except the condom and places it in a box. An FBI team recovers the condom and takes photographs. The white cloth matches cloth found in Polly's room.

Jaffe reminds the officers of the strange man who'd gotten his car stuck off her driveway on the night of October 1. McManus finds the case record, which reveals Davis's name and criminal record. Davis, it seems, has been in violation of his parole starting in mid-November. He is no longer returning to the shelter in San Mateo. His parole officer tells the police that Davis is probably in Ukiah with family. Using the parole violation, police arrest Davis in his sister's home on November 30.

On December 2, while Davis is still in custody, it is determined that a palm print recovered from Polly's bedroom is Davis's. Davis is told of the match. He tells the police: "I fucked up big time." Polly, he says, is dead.

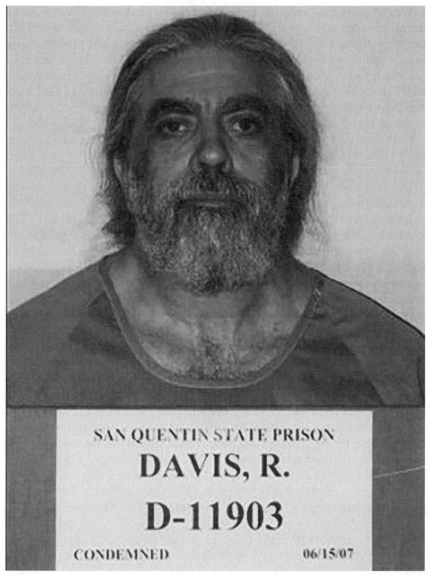

Figure 19.1.   Richard Allan Davis, while in prison, 2007. *California Prisons*

Davis gives a version of the events. He claims that he is foggy on the facts. Drunk and high at the time of the kidnapping, he recalls breaking into a house, tying up the girls, and driving away. He says he realizes Polly is in the car only when she whimpers that her hands are going numb from her bindings. Panicked and confused, he gets lost, getting his car stuck off Jaffe's driveway. He claims that he left Polly on an embankment while he worked on his car. After the encounter with police, he says he drove around for a while before returning to pick her up. In an effort to avoid prison, he strangled her with a piece of cloth and then cinched a cord around her throat "just to make sure."[13]

After a two-hour interrogation, Davis leads police officers to Polly. Her body is recovered only one hundred feet from a highway, partially hidden under plywood and thorny underbrush. Animals have long since found her; her organs are gone, and much of her body is skeletonized. Her skull lies nearby. A nightgown is draped over her, and her arms are folded on her lap. Forensic analysis of her underwear reveals the possible presence of semen. When confronted about the semen on her underwear, Davis says, "not in her though."[14] At the end of the interrogation, he adds nervously, "I have to see what comes out of forensic—hope nothing comes up. Hope nothing's in there."[15] Davis is worried about his safety if he is imprisoned for child rape.

Polly's parents are informed soon after her body is found; officers can only look on as they weep helplessly. A wave of shock washes over parents everywhere.[16] *People* magazine calls her "America's Child," and *Newsweek* writes an article titled "The Sad Case of Polly Klass." For Polly's funeral, President Clinton sends a message of sympathy.

On June 18, 1996, Richard Allen Davis is convicted of ten felony counts, including the kidnapping and murder of Polly Klaas and a "lewd act" attempted on a child.[17] Davis is caught by cameras gesturing obscenely at the courtroom, raising his middle fingers on both hands.

September 26, 1996, is the last day of the trial. Davis, permitted to give a final statement, jolts spectators when he says, "The main reason I know that I did not attempt any lewd act that night was because of a statement the young girl made to me when walking her up the embankment: 'Just don't do me like my dad.'"[18] Shocked gasps fill the courtroom, and Polly's father yells and makes a lunge at Davis before being restrained and led out. Richard Allen Davis is sentenced to death. Davis smirks, as the judge announces the death penalty; he says: "Mr. Davis, this is always a traumatic and emotional decision for a judge. You've made it very easy today by your conduct."[19]

Despite Richard Allen Davis's death sentence, his face, an image of terror, haunts California's public. People demand answers to a frighteningly simple question: Why was Davis on the streets that evening in October of 1993? How could such a dangerous predator be allowed the freedom to hunt for his next victim? Could there be more of them?

For one man, Polly's death and the widespread anger that it prompts represents an opportunity. Mike Reynolds, a short, pudgy man in his mid-forties, follows the Polly Klaas case carefully. A California native, Reynolds has lived a quiet, steady life. He and his wife, Sharon, had settled in Fresno to raise their three children: Kimber, Christopher, and Michael. He is the primary care giver and builds a photography career that allows him to put his kids at the center of his life.

In 1992, a year before Polly's abduction and murder, his only daughter, Kimber, a slim, pretty blonde, eighteen-year-old is home from college. She and a friend have just left Planet Hollywood after meeting for dinner.[20] As she stands by her car, getting ready to leave, a motorcycle carrying two men pulls alongside her. The woman is trapped between her car and the men on the motorcycle. One of the men tries to grab her purse. When she does not yield quickly enough, the rider produces a revolver, places it near her ear, and pulls the trigger. Kimber Reynolds dies in a hospital twenty-six hours later. The perpetrator, a meth addict named Joe Davis, is shot in a police confrontation shortly after. As with Richard Allen Davis, Joe Davis has an extensive arrest record and was on parole when he murdered Kimber.

For Mike Reynolds the police shooting of Joe Davis is a rare sort of justice. "Think about it," he says. "Somebody kills your daughter, and forty-eight hours later, the cops shoot *him*. Usually there's a trial three years later, and if you're lucky, the killer gets a death sentence that's never carried out."[21] (Richard Davis killed Polly in 1993. He was sentenced to die in 1996. He remains alive today, twenty-five years later.) Reynolds has long been cynical about the criminal justice system. But it is the murder of his daughter that pushes him toward activism. "At some point, somebody had to do something to keep this from happening again," he says.[22] The law, in his view is fundamentally flawed, and it must change.

THE REFORM

A little over a month after Kimber's death, Reynolds and a handful of politically powerful community members meet in Reynolds's backyard and draft a bill designed to put repeat offenders behind bars. Reynolds's bill is a sweeping, ambitious criminal statute that would crack down on the state's repeat offenders like no other piece of legislation had before. They settled on a memorable name for the bill: "Three Strikes and You're Out!"[23]

Reynolds and his team present the bill to state assemblyman Bill Jones, a rugged middle-aged man with strong anticrime message. Jones agrees to sponsor the bill, and another Fresno assemblyman, Democrat Jim Costa, soon joins the fight. As the bill makes its way through the various parties, it gains some powerful advocates. Soon afterward, the bill receives a blessing from California's attorney general, Dan Lungren. Most significantly, the bill catches the attention of George Deukmejian. Deukmejian has been the state's attorney general and its governor. Deukmejian was elected attorney general in 1978, in part because of his advocacy for harsher sentencing, a legislative change favored by the Californian public. California is experiencing a skyrocketing crime rate during the social turmoil of the 1960s and 1970s.

Even with strong advocates, Reynolds's bill struggles to make headway. The state assembly's Public Safety Committee will only allow the bill onto the assembly floor with enormous modifications—modifications, Reynolds realizes angrily, that transform it into "nothing more than the old habitual-offender law" that is already in place.[24] Reynolds's push back gets the bill voted off the agenda. It seems to die without ever being discussed.

In the meantime, in 1993, Washington is the first state to enact a modern habitual-offender law, which provides that someone convicted of a third serious felony will be sentenced to life in prison without possibility of parole. Moreover, repeat offenders will no longer be released from prison unless they meet specific guidelines. First, they must be deemed to no longer be a threat to society. Next, they must be at least sixty years old. And finally, the governor must decide to grant the individual a pardon or clemency. Washington's three-strikes statute applies only to criminals convicted of three serious felonies as an adult, such as rape, robbery, child molestation, aggravated assault, or murder, but not nonviolent burglaries. It also has a "wash-out" provision that allows certain felonies to be removed after five or ten years with no convictions.[25]

After the death of Polly Klaas in 1993, Reynolds's bill is resurrected. Reynolds, like the rest of California, is grief stricken at Polly's death. It seems very clear to him that, had the state acted to keep Davis behind bars, Polly would be alive. Polly died because the people who had the power to change the system elected not to do so, but Reynolds also sees a silver lining in the brutal murder. This is just the kind of case that his struggling three-strikes law needs to gain public support. As the public's outrage over the crime rises, Reynolds predicts that his bill will gain enough momentum to change the law.

He predicts correctly. As news of Polly's death floods the state, tens of thousands of calls flood the three-strikes committee's 800 number. The Petaluma Search Center, which had previously led the effort to find Polly, is transformed into a political headquarters to distribute petitions. People drive dozens of miles to sign. Polly Klaas becomes the face of the three-strikes campaign. The bill is renamed Proposition 164. Polly's father, Marc, campaigns for the bill, announcing to impassioned audiences across the state that he will not "let [his] daughter's death be in vain."[26]

Joe Klaas, Polly's grandfather, however, is suspicious. The older man digs deeper into the details of Reynolds's bill. He understands that there are implications far beyond those being debated. The proposed bill will not stop at long sentences for hardened murderers and pedophiles, as the bill's advocates publicize. The bill mandates that after a third strike conviction, for a list of forty crimes, a defendant must receive twenty-five years to life, with twenty-five years being the minimum spent behind bars. Most striking to Joe Klaas are the crimes included in the bill. While serious crimes like murder, rape, and armed robbery are included, other far less severe crimes are also, including residential burglary. "Residential burglary runs the gamut from breaking into someone's bedroom in the middle of the night and raping his watch dog," says one San Diego public defender bitterly, "to someone walking into your open attached garage and taking a ninety-eight-cent screwdriver."[27] Residential burglaries, unlike other serious crimes, are considered nonviolent, and it's certainly not as serious as, say, child molestation or murder.

Joe Klaas worries more as his understanding grows. Under the California law put in place during Deukmejian's time, prosecutors are allowed to bump a misdemeanor charge to a felony charge if a similar crime had been committed previously. These later crimes are termed "wobblers" as they can go either way. In the aggregate, the combination means a history of misdemeanors could represent a three-strikes conviction and life in prison.

Joe Klaas discusses his discoveries with his son, and Marc is shocked. He now tours the state opposing the bill, pointing out its hidden truths. As he says coldly to one audience, "I've had my stereo stolen and I've had my daughter murdered, and I know the difference,"[28] but the genie is already out of the bottle, and people are too wrought up to process the subtleties.

Marc's prior support for the bill has resonated with Californians everywhere. The bill is reintroduced in March of 1994. Elections are in November, and no politician dares to challenge Reynolds, at the risk of being labeled soft on crime. Public fear of crime has exploded, enhanced by several highly publicized cases. (The most publicized is certainly the murder of Marc's own daughter.) On a sunny day in March, Governor Wilson signs Proposition 184 into law. That November, 72 percent of voters in the state cast a ballot favoring the proposition.

In 1996, the California Supreme Court makes a modification to the law. The *Romero* ruling, as it's called, allows judges to eliminate strikes at their own discretion.[29] Public defenders are thrilled, as are many judges who feel that the three-strikes law is unjust and are glad to reclaim authority. Regardless, nearly one-half of defendants serving life sentences under the three-strike statute committed only nonviolent offenses—a percentage that remains about the same before and after *Romero*. Further, the California Supreme Court later places limits on when judges can eliminate strikes, requiring them to consider certain factors.[30]

The law is tough, representing the harshest repeat-offender legislation in the nation. Only nine hours after the law is enacted in March, a homeless schizophrenic named Lester Wallace is arrested for attempting to steal a car radio. With two nonviolent burglaries already on his record, he is sentenced to twenty-five years to life. Less than a year later, a thirty-three-year-old man, working a steady job and involved in a happy relationship, his early arrest record long behind him, is sentenced to life in prison for attempting to steal a pair of white socks worth $2.50.[31] Johnny Quirino shoplifts razor blades and receives twenty-five years to life; Arthur Fernandez aids in the theft of baby formula and Tylenol and receives the same.[32] While the cases shock some, most California residents believe the three-strikes law represents an important step toward securing public safety.

Marc Klaas begins the KlaasKids Foundation, an organization dedicated to preventing crimes against children. Occasionally, grateful citizens stop him on the street to thank him for helping with the passage of California's three-strikes law. Sometimes he corrects them, asserting that he *opposed* the law; other times, he says hopelessly, he doesn't even bother.

California's three-strikes law is enacted less than a year after Washington's but it's far more influential and controversial, setting the stage for similar legislative movements across the country. Some experts believe that the spread of three-strikes and other anticrime movements, even if short-lived campaigns, "have widespread appeal to a disenchanted public who, through the media, have perceived the criminal justice system as overly lenient and incapable of protecting them from violent offenders."[33]

The campaign spreads rapidly; in 1994, President Bill Clinton's State of the Union speech receives a standing ovation when he endorses three-strikes as a federal sentencing policy. By 1996, less than three years after Polly's murder, twenty-four states and the federal government have enacted three-strikes laws, even using California's catchy "three strikes, you're out" phrase.[34]

BEYOND REFORM

Today, twenty-eight states and the federal government have stringent habitual-offender statutes that assign enhanced sentences to certain groups of offenders. The most recent three-strikes law was passed by Massachusetts in 2012. Because three-strikes laws are facing criticism nationally, supporters in Massachusetts struggled for eleven years to pass their bill. When, in 1999, twenty-seven-year-old schoolteacher Melissa Gosule is kidnapped, raped, and murdered by a paroled offender with twenty-seven previous convictions, resistance to the bill begins to erode. The final push comes in 2010 when a seventy-four-times convicted felon on parole kills a veteran police officer, John Maguire.[35] Dominic Cinelli, Maguire's killer, had been imprisoned for shooting a security guard during an armed robbery. Cinelli's prior crimes included armed robberies and assaults. He was sentenced to three life terms for shooting the guard. In prison, he was a chronic disciplinary problem, and he escaped twice. Despite all of these warnings, the parole board in November 2008 releases him again. To the people of Massachusetts, the deaths of Gosule and Maguire are proof that the system is broken, and the laws need to change. A three-strikes statute is finally enacted.

Each state constructs a unique, though similar, version of the law. All states include violent felonies, such as rape, assault, and murder, as crimes that qualify as strikes. Some states go further and also include nonviolent crimes, such as using or selling drugs, treason, petty theft, and bribery. States also differ on the number of prior offenses—"strikes"—required to be "out." Many states have followed California's lead in establishing a three-strikes system, including Colorado, Connecticut, Delaware, Illinois, Indiana, Louisiana, New Jersey, New Mexico, North Carolina, Pennsylvania, Texas, Virginia, Washington, West Virginia, and Wisconsin. In some states, including Georgia and Montana, sentencing is increased after two strikes. Maryland and Florida have elected formulations that require four strikes. The length of time for imprisonment varies, too. Eleven states mandate life sentences *without* possibility of parole, and three states—California, New Mexico, and Colorado—mandate life sentences *with* the possibility of parole, though only after twenty-five, thirty, and forty years of incarceration respectively. The remaining states leave the sentencing to the court's discretion or use different sentencing ranges for different crimes. For example, Louisiana's habitual-offender statute requires anyone convicted of three felonies—any kind of felony, including nonviolent ones—be sentenced under a mandatory minimum of thirteen years and four months.[36]

Several states have either neutered or un-enacted their three-strike laws. Several states rarely sentence offenders under their three-strike provisions; Pennsylvania, for example, has used its three-strikes law only a handful of times. In several states, there are ongoing campaigns to repeal the three-strike laws. Prominent figures that previously supported the laws, including President Bill Clinton, have now renounced them. In 2016, Delaware significantly scaled back its three-strikes law, which previously had been one of the harshest in the nation. In spite of opposition, however, three-strikes laws have mostly remained intact in most states.[37]

Have the three-strikes laws been effective? The results are mixed, and people on both sides have arguments in support of their view. Supporters of the laws argue that they have successfully incapacitated dangerous criminals and deterred others. California's attorney general Dan Lungren claims that California's crime rate dropped 26.9 percent in four years, attributing the drop largely to the three-strikes law. Between 1996 and 2003, the number of people sentenced under the California three-strikes law decreased every year, leading supporters of the law to claim that the law was successfully taking dangerous people off the street.[38] In *Ewing v. California*, the Supreme Court case in which the constitutionality of the three-strikes law was challenged, Justice O'Connor notes that more parolees are leaving California than are entering it, possibly because they fear the consequences of offending again under the three-strikes law.[39]

However, the causes for the decrease in crime rates are not clear. During the same time period, New York saw the nation's largest decrease in crime rates, though it had no three-strikes law at the time. Moreover, crime rates were already declining before the three-strikes law was passed. The rate of decline was almost exactly the same before and after the enactment of three-strikes laws, suggesting that the three-strikes laws were less impactful than believed. "Were 'three strikes' the cause of a significant part of the decline," explains scholar Michael Vitiello, "the rate of decline should have increased after its passage. Instead, the rate of decline remained constant, suggesting that the causes of the decline that were operating prior to the passage of the law continued to be the primary reason for the drop in crime rates."[40]

There are also arguments that most manipulations of specific criminal laws are not likely to have a significant deterrent effect. In order for a legal statute to have a deterrent effect, three prerequisites are necessary. First, the criminal has to be aware of the law. Second, the criminal has to be a rational calculator, able and willing to weigh the "benefits" of committing another crime versus the costs imposed by the three-strikes threat. Third, the criminal's calculations must reach the "correct" conclusion, that it's not worth it to commit another crime. All three of these prerequisites, especially in combination, are dubious.[41] Further, even if three-strikes statutes had some deterrent effect, one has to worry that the bad reputation that they give the criminal justice system by giving wildly excessive punishment in some cases tends to undermine the system's moral credibility, which reduces people's inclination to defer to it.[42]

Many argue that some three-strikes laws are unjust, that they go too far. In 1988, for example, a nineteen-year-old Californian named Shane Taylor burglarized two empty residences in two weeks. He used no weapons, and nobody was injured. The only item reported missing was a checkbook, which police quickly recovered. When Taylor was released from prison, he got married, found a stable job, and had a daughter. Eight years later, Taylor was caught with ten dollars' worth of methamphetamine and was convicted of simple possession. The conviction represented Taylor's third strike, and he received twenty-five years to life. Had Taylor not burglarized ten years prior, he likely would have received probation and drug counseling.[43] Today, Taylor, a model inmate, remains incarcerated. Even Judge Howard Broadman, who sentenced Taylor and considers himself tough on crime, regrets it. He says, "I'm sorry. I'm really sorry."[44]

Similar cases have occurred under the three-strikes laws of other states. For example, in Louisiana, the mandatory thirteen-years-and-four-months sentence was applied against a man convicted of possessing marijuana three times.[45] In South Carolina, Anthony Jackson received a life sentence after he stole a wallet from a hotel room; because he had two prior burglary convictions, he received a mandatory sentence under South Carolina's three-strikes laws. Robert Book received a life sentence under the federal three-strikes law for three nonviolent drug crimes involving cocaine. Cases like these have the potential to damage the criminal law's moral credibility, thereby undermining its effectiveness.

California has reformed its three-strikes law since its initial enactment in 1994, particularly after California citizens caught wind of a series of cases of three-strikes convictions for petty crimes, like that of a homeless man sentenced to twenty-five years to life for attempting to steal a car radio. In November of 2012, 68.6 percent of California citizens voted to pass Proposition 36, the Three Strikes Reform Act. The act eliminates life sentences for third strikes that are nonviolent and nonserious crimes. If the prior conviction is child molestation, rape, or murder, however, the criminal will still receive a life sentence for the third strike.[46] The law also authorizes almost three thousand prisoners serving life sentences for nonviolent third strikes to petition for reduced terms. The law doesn't affect sentencing for any violent, serious crimes, some nonserious nonviolent sex and drug offenses, or crimes involving firearm possession. Less than a year after Proposition 36 is approved, more than a thousand prisoners are released and two thousand more become eligible for release. One of the prisoners released is Shane Taylor, who'd spent over fifteen years in prison for his possession of ten dollars' worth of methamphetamine.

Chapter Twenty

2001
9/11 Attacks

War on Terror

THE TRAGEDY

American Airlines Flight 11 out of Boston, Massachusetts, is heading for Los Angeles with eighty-one passengers and eleven crew members. The plane departs one minute late, leaving the ground at almost exactly 8:00 a.m. Fifteen minutes later, Mohammed Atta, along with four accomplices, begins to attack passengers with box cutters, knives, and mace. The men breach the cockpit door by force. Atta, a thirty-three-year-old Egyptian, enters the cockpit and stabs Captain John Ogonowski. Before dying, the captain turns on the radio, allowing air traffic controllers to monitor the conversation in the cockpit. Atta, who has training as a pilot, takes over flying the aircraft.[1]

Flight attendant Madeline Sweeney, who is huddled in a back corner of the plane, is able to get in touch with the airline's operations center. At around 8:44, she says, "Something is wrong. We are in a rapid descent. We are all over the place." The operations center asks what she sees. "I see water. I see buildings. We are flying low. We are flying very, very low. We are flying way too low. Oh my God we are flying way too low. Oh my god!"[2] At 8:46 the fuel-laden Boeing 767 is flown into the North Tower of the World Trade Center.

More destruction is already in motion. At about 9:00 a.m., Peter Hanson, who is on board United Airlines flight 175, with his wife and daughter, calls his father, "It's getting bad, Dad," he says "A stewardess was stabbed. They seem to have knives and Mace. They said they have a bomb. Passengers are throwing up and getting sick. The plane is making

Figure 20.1. Twin Towers burning, 2001. *Beth Dixson*

jerky movements. I don't think the pilot is flying the plane. I think we are going down. I think they intend to go to Chicago or someplace and fly into a building. Don't worry, Dad. If it happens, it'll be very fast. My God, my God." Eighteen minutes after American Flight 11 strikes the North Tower, United Flight 175 is flown into the South Tower of the World Trade Center. The plane explodes. The Twin Towers are aflame.

At 9:17, the Federal Aviation Administration shuts down all New York City area airports and, at 9:21, the Port Authority of New York and New Jersey closes all bridges and tunnels in the area. By 9:30, President George W. Bush, speaking from Sarasota, Florida, says that the country has suffered an "apparent terrorist attack." "Terrorism against our nation will not stand," President Bush declares. He asks the country to join him in a moment of silence and prays that "God bless the victims, their families, and America."[3] At 9:37, American Airlines Flight 77, a Washington, D.C., flight that had departed for Los Angeles, hits the Pentagon. A column of smoke rises into the air.

At 9:42, for the first time in history, all ordinary air traffic over the United States is halted under directives from the FAA. No further planes are allowed to take off anywhere in the country, and planes already in the air are ordered to land as quickly as possible. A couple of minutes later, the White House is evacuated. Within fifteen minutes, President

Bush leaves Florida and is on a plane and in the air. He is not going to Washington, D.C., where many federal buildings are being evacuated but instead is headed for a military base in Louisiana.

Standing in the streets, gazing upward, thousands of New Yorkers bear witness as smoke billows from the buildings into the amazingly blue sky. Many have camcorders out, capturing the gruesome scene unfolding in front of them. People trapped in the burning buildings are forced out by the flames. They jump, their bodies falling from the smoking towers and bursting on the street below. At 9:59 the South Tower collapses. The crowd moans and cries. "Oh my God!" someone yells. "Holy shit! The whole building collapsed. The whole building collapsed," he cries in anguished disbelief. A great cloud of dust rises with the smoke.[4]

Planes all over the nation begin to land at the closest airport. The FAA discovers that it does not know where seven airborne craft are. Of the seven, three have crashed into the three buildings. Three others have been missed in the confusion and will land safely. The last plane, United Airlines Flight 93 departed from Newark, New Jersey, just before American Flight 11 crashed. United Flight 93 has been hijacked by Atta's confederates, who have turned off the plane's transponder, making it invisible to the FAA. But the passengers have been following the morning's events and know of the attacks on the World Trade Center. They learn that their plane is to be flown into the U.S. Capitol. The Flight 93 passengers decide to fight back.

The captain of Flight 93 has been wounded. He refuses to cooperate with the hijackers in flying the aircraft and surreptitiously sets the radios so that ground control can hear the events in the cockpit. The passengers attack the terrorists in their section of the plane, then storm the cockpit. At 10:07, the passengers overwhelm the terrorists, but in the melee, the plane crashes in an open field in Somerset County, Pennsylvania, just twenty minutes flying time from the Capitol. Everyone on board is killed, but no one on the ground is injured.

At 10:10, part of the Pentagon collapses from the earlier airplane strike. The FAA redirects all transatlantic flights heading toward the United States to Canada. At 10:28, half an hour after the South Tower, the North Tower collapses from the top down. Smoke and dust fill the air again.

Throughout the day, official updates are made public; people stare at their televisions. Newscasters continuously speculate about what is happening and who is behind it. Asked how many are dead, Mayor Rudi Giuliani of New York City answers: "More than any of us can bear."[5] By afternoon, missile destroyers are sent by the navy to Washington and New York. The buildings surrounding the World Trade Center and the Pentagon continue to smolder. Around 5:20 p.m., the forty-seven-story Building 7 of the World Trade Center complex collapses.

THE PATH TO THE 9/11 ATTACKS

As the world begins to process the shock and horror of what will be forever known as the *9/11 attacks*, many begin to ask, Who could have committed such an appalling act of terror, and how they could have done so undetected? Intelligence officials begin to piece together the attack; they soon focus their attention on a radical Islamic extremist named Osama bin Laden. Osama bin Muhammad bin Awad bin Laden was born in Riyadh, Saudi Arabia, on March 10, 1957, the seventeenth child of a wealthy construction tycoon. In 1979, Osama bin Laden graduates from King Abdul Aziz University in Jiddah. That same year, the Soviet Union invades Afghanistan. The newly minted civil engineer leaves Saudi Arabia to join the Afghan resistance, the mujahedeen. Between 1980 and 1986, bin Laden provides the mujahedeen with logistical and humanitarian support from the Pakistani border. Between 1986 and 1989, he fights in several major battles against the Soviets, serving as a guerrilla commander. He fights at the Battle of Jalalabad, the battle that forces the Soviets to withdraw from Afghanistan. The weapons used by the mujahedeen are all supplied by America.

In August of 1988, bin Laden and fourteen associates hold a meeting at which they decide to establish an organization called "al-Qaeda," to be headquartered in a western suburb of the Pakistani city Peshawar. Al-Qaeda, a rather nondescript name, is the Arabic word for "the base." Bin Laden claims the name refers to the training base set up by Abu-Ubaydah al-Banshiri to train youths to fight the Soviets. The secretary recording the minutes of the meeting writes that "The mentioned Al-Qaeda is basically an organized Islamic faction; its goal is to lift the word of God, to make His religion victorious."[6] The resultant group is small, consisting of fifteen members, with nine of the fifteen on the leading council.

Al-Qaeda is differentiated from other militant groups by its internationalism. The founders want to unite the divergent militants fighting in tribally oriented Afghanistan and to turn their focus to larger goals. They seek to overcome the parochialism of Islamic radicals in many countries, who until then focused on "liberating" their own nations from "despotic, hypocrite, apostate rulers." They plan to pursue two mutually reinforcing strategies. First, they plan to fight irregular wars using guerrilla warfare against the "enemies of Islam," and second, they plan to engage in spectacular acts of violent terrorism that will help rally Muslims and provoke a mass uprising.[7]

In 1990, bin Laden returns to Saudi Arabia. He offers to raise an international militia army to defend Saudi Arabia against an invasion by Saddam Hussein, but the Saudi royal family rejects his offer. Bin Laden opposes the Saudi alliance with the United States, and as a result is confined to the city of Jiddah. Realizing he will be unable to develop his radical goals in Saudi Arabia, bin Laden moves to Khartoum, Sudan. Sudan, ruled by the Islamist Hassan ul-Turabi, is admitting Muslims into the country without visas, as a show of solidarity with its Islamic brethren. The no-visa policy attracts many radicalized veterans of the Afghan war who now find that they are unwelcome in their native countries. The radicalized immigrant population in Khartoum feeds even greater fervor among the men. The 1993 bombing of the World Trade Center directed by Pakistani native Ramzi Yousef captures the interest of many of the militants.

In 1996, Sudan comes to realize that the former militants are exploiting its no-visa policy, and they are not good for Sudan. The government works to expel a large number of the radicals, including bin Laden. He leaves for Afghanistan. It is now that al-Qaeda begins to develop "the base" envisioned by the men eight years earlier. Bin Laden and Ayman Mohammed Rabie al-Zawahiri take control of dozens of training camps and facilities, which allows them to train volunteers for their various projects. They also start reaching out to militant organizations around the Islamic world, offering help in exchange for some loyalty. Though many groups insist on maintaining their independence, bin Laden and al-Zawahiri begin to develop a network.

On August 23, 1996, bin Laden releases a Declaration of Jihad, delineating al-Qaeda's goals: the expulsion of U.S. troops from Saudi Arabia, the overthrow of the Saudi government, and the liberation of Islamic holy sites. He also pledges his support to Islamic revolutionary movements around the world. He insists that using terror against America as long as it retains troops in Saudi Arabia is "a legitimate right and a moral obligation." Addressing U.S. defense secretary William Perry, bin Laden emphasizes the depths of his militants' dedication: "These youths love death as you love life."[8]

In February 1998, bin Laden releases a joint statement with several other jihadist groups under the banner "World Islamic Front," saying that Muslims should kill Americans, even civilians, wherever they can. On August 7, 1998, al-Qaeda militants detonate bombs in the U.S. embassies in Kenya and Tanzania; 224 people are killed and over 4,500 are injured. Americans make up a tiny fraction of those harmed; the majority are ordinary Kenyans.

Alec Station is a subunit of the CIA's Counterterrorist Center dedicated to keeping an eye on bin Laden and al Qaeda. Based near Washington, D.C., it is officially opened in January 1996 as a cooperative venture between the CIA, FBI, NSA, DIA, and other players in the intelligence community. In 1996, Daniel Coleman, an FBI agent, is sent to Alec Station to see if there is any reason for the FBI to open up an investigation on bin Laden. To begin building its case, former FBI agent Coleman, now among one of twelve staff members of the station, shows bin Laden's August 1996 Declaration of Jihad fatwa to the U.S. Attorney's Office for the Southern District of New York and asks them if they can open a criminal file. The lawyers are unsure. The fatwa is disturbing, but it isn't clearly a crime. They settle on a seditious conspiracy statute from the time of the Civil War that makes it a crime to incite violence and try to overthrow the government. Coleman opens the file.

Several months later, Coleman interviews a Sudanese informant named Jamal al-Fadl, who claims to have worked with bin Laden when the latter was in Sudan. Al-Fadl's interview is the first time American investigators learn about the existence of al-Qaeda. The Sudanese informer details the training camps and sleeper cells. He warns that bin Laden wants to get his hands on chemical and nuclear weapons. He claims that al-Qaeda was behind a 1992 bombing in Yemen, and that it trained the militants who shot down American helicopters in Somalia that same year.

Coleman brings the testimony to the attention of the FBI, but his colleagues are dismissive. They don't trust al-Fadl and don't know how to verify his allegations. Because he is at Alec Station, Coleman's superiors ignore his calls and seem to forget about him. Coleman spends the next year and half carrying on a lonely investigation of bin Laden. He manages to draw a map of al-Qaeda's extensive network, covering the Middle East, Europe, Africa, and Central Asia, and he discovers that many al-Qaeda associates have ties to the United States. Al-Qaeda is still relatively small, but it has plenty of resources, and its members are fanatically dedicated to the destruction of America. Perhaps most terrifying, no one in the United States seems to be taking al-Qaeda seriously. To most intelligence officials, al-Qaeda doesn't seem like a real threat. What can a bunch of Afghani cave dwellers really do against the United States of America?

Al-Qaeda has set itself a mission and dreams big. The idea for the September 11 attacks originates with Khaled Sheikh Mohammed, a Kuwait-born Pakistani militant who sought out bin Laden after he was kicked out of Sudan and settled in Afghanistan. Mohammed suggests hijacking dozens of planes and using them to attack American targets. After initial hesitation, bin Laden embraces the idea and convinces al-Qaeda leadership to accept the plan in the spring of 1999. Al-Qaeda selects volunteers for the plan from various training camps. Most come from al-Farooq, a camp near Kandahar, the second largest city in Afghanistan. Al-Farooq has many of the more westernized, cosmopolitan militants. Many people in the camp speak English. This makes the camp the ideal place to assemble jihadists who can evade detection in the United States.

Mohammed Atta is chosen as operational commander. Atta is a thirty-three-year-old Egyptian raised in a modern Muslim household that allowed his older sisters to become academics. He originally traveled to

Germany in 1992 to get a master's in architecture. While studying in Germany, Atta traveled frequently and became involved with fundamentalist groups in Egypt. He started to live an observant Islamic lifestyle, which included attending mosque at El-Aksa, in Hamburg. Before graduating in 1999, Atta took time off from school to undergo training in an Afghani camp.

Two terror cells form the basis of the planned attack. The "Hamburg Group," led by Atta, recruits members from the worshippers at Al-Quds mosque in Hamburg, which, like many mosques in the capitols of Europe, enlists young Muslims with radical leanings in the mission of Global Jihad. The nuclear cell of the Hamburg Group consists of six members, three of whom will pilot hijacked planes. The other three members act as logistical collaborators. The second terror cell, the "Saudi Group," consists of sixteen members (fifteen of Saudi Arabian origin). They train separately from the Hamburg Group. Except for the pilot Hani Hanjur, they will serve as bodyguards for the hijacking pilots. They are all between the ages of twenty and twenty-nine. Not all members are aware that they are participating in a suicide mission. Financing for the conspirators is provided by Al Khazawi, a Saudi citizen and al-Qaeda's senior financial director. Money to cover the conspirators' cost of living and their preparations for the attack is transferred from banks in the Persian Gulf and Pakistan.

In the summer of 2001, the hijacking teams arrive in America. The intended pilots take flying lessons. At the end of August, Atta signals that the attacks will commence the second week of September. Bin Laden tells his retinue to go into hiding, and the al-Qaeda training camps are evacuated.

Immediately after the attacks, intelligence agencies from across the globe work feverishly to determine who is responsible. Even before the third plane hit the Pentagon, Richard Clarke, the White House counterterrorism coordinator, tells the national security advisor Condoleezza Rice and Vice President Dick Cheney that the attack is being carried out by al-Qaeda. By early afternoon, individuals known to have connections to Osama bin Laden are found on the passenger lists of the hijacked planes. Stephen Lander, head of the British security service MI5, and John Scarlett, chairman of the Joint Intelligence Committee (a government body that gathers intelligence from various British agencies and consolidates it for decision makers), tell Prime Minister Tony Blair that al-Qaeda is the only organization that could have executed such an attack.

THE OUTRAGE

The human cost of 9/11 is staggering. The actual number of deaths from September 11, 2001, is 2,977 people, with many more injured. The dead come from sixty different countries and represent almost every world religion. Aside from the fifty-five servicemen and women who die at the Pentagon, all the victims are civilians. Ordinary people, bankers, executives, cooks, custodians, tourists, entrepreneurs, and many others die suddenly in a horrific way while going about their everyday lives. The youngest victim is Christine Hanson from Groton, Massachusetts. Two years old, Christine is going to Disneyland with her parents when their plane crashes into the South Tower. Robert Grant Norton, the day's oldest victim, is eighty-five. He and his wife are headed to San Francisco for their son's wedding when Mohammed Atta takes control of the aircraft.

Tens of thousands of others who don't die also suffer. Between the psychological trauma wrought on the survivors, the families torn apart, and responders whose health is devastated by the fumes and dust of the fallen buildings, the attacks claim more victims. More than twenty thousand people suffer physical injuries.[9]

The financial cost of the attacks is also immense.[10] The loss of four civilian aircrafts costs $385 million. The destruction of the World Trade Center buildings costs from $3 to $4.5 billion. The damage to the Pentagon costs another billion dollars. With the damaged property, 83,000 jobs are lost, costing $17 billion in wages. The insurance industry loses $40 billion, and the loss of air traffic revenue costs another $10 billion. The fall of global markets results in an indeterminable loss. Including the monetary value of the lost lives, the damage to property, lost production of goods and provision of services, and the stock market hit, the cost of the attacks comes close to $2 trillion.

On September 12, 2001, the prominent astrophysicist and cosmologist Neil deGrasse Tyson, whose home is just four blocks away from the World Trade Center and who observed the collapse of both towers, writes an e-mail recounting the "indelible images of horror" he witnessed the previous morning. Based on what he saw, he assumes that no one in the buildings could have survived and that all of the first responders must have been wiped out by the buildings' collapse. "It is more spectacularly tragic than the Titanic, the Hindenburg, Oklahoma City, car bombs, and airplane hijackings," he writes, "How naïve I was to believe that the world is fundamentally different from that of our ancestors, whose lives were changed by bearing witness to the 20th century's vilest acts of war."[11]

As footage of the burning towers circulates, horror sweeps the globe. "We are all traumatized by this terrible tragedy," announces Secretary General Kofi Annan. Queen Elizabeth is struck by "growing disbelief and total shock." The French newspaper *Le Monde* proclaims poignantly, "we are all Americans now." German chancellor Gerhard Schroeder calls the attacks "a declaration of war against the civilized world,"[12] and Russian president Vladimir Putin condemns the "barbaric acts," berating Prime Minister Blair, President Bush, and others for ignoring his warnings about rising fundamentalism.[13] Israeli prime minister Ariel Sharon declares a day of national mourning and encourages the world to be vigilant in the fight against terrorism.

Within twenty-four hours of the attack, NATO unanimously invokes Article Five of the North Atlantic Treaty, which identifies an attack on any member of NATO as an attack on all members. Diplomats call for the U.N. Security Council to sanction any governments or organizations involved in the strikes, and government buildings and tall structures around the world are evacuated. Intelligence agencies are abuzz with information about sleeper cells and possible terrorist machinations. The CIA warns President Bush that there might be al-Qaeda agents in the United States planning attacks with biological, chemical, or nuclear weapons.

Fear also seeps deeply into the United States populace. Civilians demand answers to a frightening set of questions: How could a network of Afghani militants cause so much harm? What went wrong? The spotlight turns on American intelligence agencies. Historically, they've focused on preventing domestic terrorism committed by U.S. citizens and attacks against American foreign interests by citizens of other countries. But 9/11 is a new animal entirely: a domestic attack launched by foreigners, the nation's Achilles heel. The attack, people realize, is a tragic failure of America's intelligence organizations.

Since bin Laden's 1998 bombing, U.S. policy makers have known him to be a threat, but they were unsure of how to respond. With a legal framework that is fuzzy at best, what steps can they take to preempt an Islamic militant conspiracy? Can the United States use military force to quash a terrorist plot within the United States? Does the government have legal authority to assassinate bin Laden after the 1998 attack, despite the limited evidence for his responsibility?

But laws aren't the only tools the United States lacks. The nation is well equipped to fight conventional enemies—state militaries, soldiers, and the like—but al-Qaeda is both nebulous and unfamiliar. With the potential to kill thousands, with methods that are unpredictable, shaped by sporadic guerrilla fighters and terrorist cells, how was al-Qaeda to be fought? It has no buildings or territories to seize. For a military accustomed to battlefields and firefights, al-Qaeda's irregular warfare is alien. It's no surprise, then, that America's response to the 1998 bombings is ineffective, netting the death of a few militants unconnected to al-Qaeda and the destruction of a factory for veterinary antibiotics.

Worse, the CIA lacks a human presence in Middle Eastern countries, and its connections with locals are weak. Intelligence agencies increasingly have come to rely on intercepted communication instead of intelligence gathered on the ground, and the CIA agents who *are* on the ground often live in diplomatic compounds, don't speak the local language, and struggle to connect to natives. The agency has traditionally hired upper-crust Americans with impressive diplomas rather than skilled operators in touch with the local culture. The agencies have few Arabists and virtually no one fluent in the languages of Afghanistan and Pakistan. At the time of the 9/11 attacks, our allies are seemingly no better prepared. MI6, the CIA's counterpart in the United Kingdom, has no Pashto speakers on its staff. The CIA has some connections with tribes in Afghanistan but none in the inner circles connected to bin Laden.

Information from Persian Gulf countries is no better. Jordan, Egypt, and Algeria, keen to prove their stability, are motivated to gloss over the threat of militant fundamentalists. India, meanwhile, tries to convince the United States that bin Laden is hiding in Kashmir, a region that Pakistan and India have scuffled over for decades, with the hopes that the United States will attempt a political attack on Pakistan.

Interagency communication within the United States is riddled with problems, too, as various intelligence agencies do not know what information to share. In 1995, fears of constitutional violations led the Justice Department and the FBI to curb the flow of intelligence between them—a set of restrictions aptly called "The Wall." The Wall is applied excessively and incorrectly, and the effects are damaging. FBI agents keep information from each other and from criminal investigators; critical information about 9/11 terrorists is never shared with the right people who can piece it together.

Aside from the communication issues, it is also clear that the White House failed to take seriously recent reports of bin Laden's threats. Prior to 9/11, CIA intelligence suggested that terrorists might be planning an attack overseas to show their global reach, and in early August, President Bush is told that bin Laden plans to attack the United States, possibly through a hijacking. Regardless, a meeting to discuss the threat is postponed until September 4.[14]

There are also serious problems in airline security. On the morning of September 11, the airline's automatic screening system identifies half of the hijackers as potentially high-risk passengers, including Atta. The men are flagged for further inspection; without FBI intelligence, the system has no way of recognizing them as potential al-Qaeda affiliates. The only precaution the airlines can take is to keep the men's checked luggage off the plane until the men board. If indeed a bomb is ticking in a suitcase, they reason, nobody would be crazy enough to set it off after they board. The hijackers and their carry-ons are not searched.[15]

THE REFORM

With the nation grieving, Congress reacts swiftly to the attacks. On September 14, Congress passes the Authorization of Use of Military Force, which stipulates that "the President is authorized to use all necessary and appropriate force against those nations, organizations, or persons he determines planned, authorized, committed, or aided the terrorist attacks that occurred on September 11, 2001 . . . to prevent any future acts of international terrorism."[16] Within a month, the FBI and immigration authorities arrest or detain almost fifteen hundred people. The process by which these people are selected and the identity of the detainees are kept secret to preserve national security. In November, secret military tribunals for noncitizen terrorists are enacted by military order. The Department of Justice heads the trials and decides punishments, though the constitutionality of its role is unclear.

Within a few short years, more than 130 pieces of legislation are introduced in response to 9/11, 48 of which are signed into law. This legislation touches on a large mix of issues: border security, health issues of personnel who worked at Ground Zero, educational funding for soldiers, and rules to compel the State Department and Immigration to share visa and immigrant data with each other. President Bush also establishes the Department of Homeland Security, intended to protect the United States from terrorist attacks, as well as manmade and natural accidents.

One act in particular, The USA PATRIOT Act, an acronym for the bulky "Uniting and Strengthening America by Providing Appropriate Tools Required to Intercept and Obstruct Terrorism" Act, becomes the lightning rod for attention. The Patriot Act is first proposed on September 19. The legislation is made up of bills previously proposed by Presidents Reagan, Bush, and Clinton, but Congress, concerned about constitutional violations, had refused to pass them.

But in the months following 9/11, constitutional and privacy concerns are outweighed by the imperative of ensuring national security. The Patriot Act, comprising 342 pages, 161 sections, and 10 titles, aims to crack down on terrorism by strengthening domestic security, border regulations, and intelligence operations. None of the titles attract more attention than Title II, "Surveillance Procedures." Title II allows the FBI to intercept all forms of communication, including phone, e-mail, and cable connections. Legal authorities for wiretapping, surveillance, and search warrants are expanded dramatically. Title II also alters the Foreign Surveillance Intelligence Act (FISA), allowing the government to gather information from both U.S. and non-U.S. citizens. The changes make FISA's authority very broad. Title II also attempts to break down The Wall by allowing federal government branches to share information without court orders.[17]

While the nation is focused on responding to the 9/11 attacks, America faces another smaller attack just a week later, when letters containing anthrax are mailed to several media companies, including the *New York Post* and the *National Inquirer* on September 18, 2001. The first victim, photojournalist Robert Stevens, dies on October 5, and four other deaths follow. On October 15, the Senate majority leader receives a letter containing anthrax; soon afterward, the chairman of the Senate Judiciary Committee receives the same. There is strong belief that this is a second attack by Al Qaeda, this time against Congress and members of the media.[18] (Though it is later found that these attacks were most likely carried out by an American government biologist named Edwards Ivins.)

The anthrax attacks give the Patriot Act a final boost of public support, and few members of Congress dare vote against it. "Our war on terror begins with al Qaeda, but it does not end there," announced President Bush to Congress. "It will not end until every terrorist group of global reach has been found, stopped and defeated."[19] Attorney General John Ashcroft also supports the act: "I think it's time for us to be productive on behalf of the American people," he says. "Talk won't prevent terrorism. It's time to get off our duffs and do what's right."[20]

On October 24, the House passes the bill on a vote of 357 to 66. The next day, the bill passes in the Senate with 98 votes for and 1 against.[21] On October 26, 2001, President Bush signs the bill into law. "Today, we take an essential step in defeating terrorism," he says, "while protecting the constitutional rights of all Americans."[22]

BEYOND REFORM

And yet, concerns persist. Some worry that the act is too broad and gives federal investigators too much power; others argue that it hasn't been sufficiently debated. As such, many of the provisions are written to expire, or "sunset," after a few years, which will force legislators to revisit them. Four years later, Congress passes the USA PATRIOT Act Improvement and Reauthorization Act of 2005. Fourteen of the sixteen sunset provisions are made permanent, and two are reauthorized as sunset provisions, due to expire in another four years. Additional provisions are added; including judicial review for powerful search warrants called "National Security Letters" and standardized penalties for terrorist attacks.

With the gears of the Patriot Act in motion, Washington turns its attention to another security threat: airplane and travel safety. In November of 2001, the Aviation and Transportation Act is signed into law, establishing the Transportation Security Administration, or TSA. Prior to the passage of the legislation, security is run by each airline, which is responsible for operating the screening checkpoint, which is contracted out to a number of private companies. Now under the control of the government, airport security under the TSA is run by the Department of Homeland Security. The agency overhauls security protocol across the country.[23]

To minimize the chance of information reaching terrorists, the impact of the Patriot Act and related legislation is kept out of the public eye. When the FBI requests information (via a National Security Letter, for instance) from third parties, for example, the FBI can prohibit the cooperating source from telling others about the request.[24] In addition, the Foreign Intelligence Surveillance Court (FISA Court), which grants requests for surveillance court orders, meets secretly and conceals orders from surveillance targets and the public. Military actions, interrogations, and sentencing are also kept under wraps.

Beginning in June 2013, a young, disenchanted NSA contractor named Edward Snowden begins leaking tens of thousands of classified intelligence documents to the media. The revelations from the leak reverberate around the world. The information details U.S. surveillance across the globe. People learn that the NSA, under the authority of the new legislation, has been accessing servers of at least nine major Internet companies, including Google and Facebook. The companies are required to comply, even installing "backdoors" into their servers and computer systems so that the NSA is able to bypass encryptions.[25] Additionally, the FISA Court has authorized government access to information from Verizon's call records, including phone numbers, caller location, and length of calls, though not the conversations themselves.[26]

Snowden's leaks reveal that American citizens aren't the only subjects of NSA intelligence surveillance. At least 35 and possibly up to 122 world leaders had their phones monitored, including Brazil's president, Mexico's president, the French Foreign Ministry, and several more. Angela Merkel, the German chancellor whose private cell phone was monitored, vocalizes her shock. "We need to have trust in our allies and partners, and this must now be established once again," she explains at the EU Summit. "I repeat that spying among friends is not at all acceptable against anyone, and that goes for every citizen in Germany."[27]

In the summer of 2015, several remaining sunset provisions of the Patriot Act are set to expire. With the Snowden leaks still dominating dialogue, Congress decides not to extend the provisions. Section 215, which allows the government to collect unlimited phone records, financial data, and Internet records, expires and is not renewed. Congress also terminates the "lone wolf" provision, which targets suspected individuals instead of groups, and the "roving wiretap" provision, which monitors people regardless of device.

Today, the PATRIOT Act and other post-9/11 policies remain conten-
tious. Critics argue that intelligence operations target particular religions
and ideologies, thus violating First Amendment rights. Others worry that
the new surge in surveillance undervalues privacy concerns. On the other
hand, supporters of the new legislation argue that limiting the effectiveness of the intelligence agencies only invites tragedy and heartbreak.
Those concerned with civil liberties ought to focus on the civil liberties of
the tens of thousands of people who can be killed or injured in the next
9/11-type attacks.

The attacks of 9/11 remain the deadliest terrorist attacks in recorded
history. They shook the world and wounded the psyche of an entire nation. However, the legislation that followed has had a more ambiguous
impact. It has certainly inconvenienced millions of American travelers
and given the government greater power to monitor its citizens. But has
it saved lives and deterred another major attack? Possibly, but who can
know? The Patriot Act and other post-9/11 changes serve as reminders
that balancing citizens' civil rights and national security is difficult, and
with the threat of terrorism making headlines around the globe, the debate isn't likely to end soon.

Chapter Twenty-One

2001
Enron Scandal
Financial Crimes

THE TRAGEDY—ENRON

The natural gas industry does not generally garner a great deal of public attention.[1] But in 1985, businessman Kenneth Lay begins down a path filled with twists and turns that will thrust the energy industry into the national spotlight. Lay facilitates the merger of two natural gas companies, one based in Omaha, Nebraska and the other based in Houston, Texas, to form a new company, eventually called Enron.

In 1990, Enron hires Jeffery Skilling, a somewhat abrasive and ambitious consultant who has a novel idea: Enron should be more than a producer of natural gas. In Skilling's view, the prospects for the company will improve mightily if the company also becomes an options-trading entity. In his first year at Enron, Skilling hires Andrew Fastow to work with him in Enron's finance arm.

Natural gas is a commodity just like wheat or corn, Skilling reasons, and therefore Enron could trade gas just like any other commodity. One of the ways other commodities are traded is in futures, so Enron could make a great deal of money by trading in futures and options without the expense that it takes to produce more product. Skilling compares natural gas to cows, explaining, "A cow doesn't just have one kind of meat; it has all different meats, from sirloin to hamburger. And people are willing to pay different prices for the part that they want. In the same way, you could divide a gas contract into many different parts and sell them to people with different needs."[2] The idea to trade natural gas contracts creates a new market, a market in which Enron is easily the largest player, expanding to handle complex trades in derivatives of natural gas products. Skilling becomes president and chief operating officer in 1996. Enron is on *Fortune*'s U.S. "Most Innovative" list for several years in a row. In 2000, it reaches number seven on the Fortune 500 list. In February of 2001, CEO Kenneth Lay steps aside, and Jeff Skilling takes the helm as CEO of Enron.

Skilling propels Enron to the top; with thirty-six thousand miles of pipeline, it is soon the largest provider of natural gas in the United States. Additionally, the company handles the largest portfolio of natural gas risk management contracts in the world and is renowned for its original trading products.

In the 1990s, Skilling and other Enron executives deliver handsome profits. They set their aspirations high, hoping to turn Enron into the world's largest company. The corporation promises investors 15 percent growth every year. Among all industrial concerns, including energy companies, a growth rate of around 3 percent is seen as respectable.[3] Still, Enron somehow manages to blow their 15 percent annual growth target out of the water. For four years in a row, the company expands at a rate of 65 percent. The money that fuels the growth is reported to come from futures trading and not the sale of physical commodities.

Anyone with a casual knowledge of commodity trading knows that something must be amiss: no company wins their bets on future prices all the time. Indeed, it turns out that when Enron's trading strategies fail to produce the desired results, they simply use accounting tricks to make the trading losses disappear. This type of accounting is sometimes rather innocently referred to as "window dressing tactics."[4] The basic scheme is to delay posting losses, speed up revenues, and manipulate values of some of its assets. While not exactly pristine from a moral standpoint, these practices do not so clearly violate the letter of the Generally Accepted Accounting Practices, a set of standards American companies use to write financial statements. Accounting practices need to be flexible enough for many types of industries to use them while being sufficiently constraining so that the results are meaningful to outside reviewers. But as the losses add up at Enron, the company charges its bookkeepers to exercise ever-increasing creativity at the end of each quarter in order to hide losses and exaggerate profits.

In the late 1990s, Skilling expands Enron into electrical power and broadband. In Skilling's world scheme, he will transform these markets with the same type of creative trading he successfully brought to the natural gas market. The flaw in the new plan is that Enron has a real advantage in the gas market: it is a major producer. That advantage does not exist in other markets. This big expansion brings big problems, and Enron managers come under ever greater pressure to create profits.

Some industry insiders openly wonder whether Enron is manipulating its earnings. A Morgan Stanley analyst writes, "one of the biggest concerns consistently voiced about Enron is the complexity of its operations and how these interrelationships affect the quality of its earnings."[5] Most people, though, are far too impressed with Enron's spectacular profits to question the corporation's operation.

By midyear in 2000, the losses are becoming very serious. Enron executives, however, intend to report another year of 65 percent growth. To make massive losses appear as profits, CFO Andrew Fastow has Enron use a method of recording called "mark-market accounting." The practice is a proper system of accounting for companies that trade in securities. When using mark-market accounting, an item is accounted for based on its current market value (what it is worth now) instead of its book value (how much it was purchased for).

In the securities industry, this is a logical accounting system because the price of securities fluctuates. Enron, however, applies the method to all kinds of assets. For instance, building a power plant requires an enormous capital investment. Therefore, most companies write construction off as a loss at first. Enron, however, elects to post a profit of all the money that the plant will make in the future and put the cost of construction in an off-the-books corporation that they do not report as part of Enron. Suddenly the power plant costs nothing to build and immediately brings in decades' worth of revenue.[6]

With full approval from his bosses, Fastow dreams up a web of off-the-balance-sheet companies and creates painfully complicated financial arrangements for each one. At first, the entities push the bounds of what is legal. Soon, however, they go over the line entirely. The on-paper companies are useful for two reasons. First, they hide debt. Enron's balance sheets show a debt of $0; in reality, the company is $30 billion underwater. Second, they are very profitable for the Enron executives selected to be put on the books as executives of these companies. They suck real money out of Enron by tens of millions. The trick works well, and by 2001, Enron has constructed hundreds of special-purpose entities to hide its ever growing debt.[7]

In the spring of 2001, on April 17, Enron reports its first-quarter earnings to investors. To the delight of the corporation's executives, Enron reports that it has made $425 million in the first quarter. The corporation organizes a conference call with Wall Street analysts, excited to trumpet the good news. As the analysts wait on the line, they hear music playing in the background. Presently, an operator announces that Skilling is on the line. He's calling from Enron headquarters in Houston. "I hope you all heard that music that was on," Skilling says cheerfully, "We're all dancing here. It's pretty good stuff."[8] Skilling spends the next fifteen minutes or so detailing Enron's performance. "So in conclusion, first-quarter results were great." He finishes, "We are very optimistic about our new businesses and are confident that our record of growth is sustainable for many years to come."[9]

Skilling stays on the line to handle analysts' queries. During the well-attended conference call, Richard Grubman from Highfields Capital Management, a man who stands to profit if Enron's stock falls, asks why Enron does not release a balance sheet listing its assets and liabilities along with its profits. Skilling replies that this is not Enron's policy, but Grubman is unsatisfied: "You're the only financial institution that can't produce a balance sheet or a cash flow statement with their earnings." There is a pause on Skilling's end. Everyone waits, and then he replies: "Well thank you very much, we appreciate it. Asshole." Grubman is being disparaged for requesting very basic information about the company's reported earnings. The question lingers in the minds of many: where did the $425 million earnings come from? Outsiders' confidence in Enron begins to crack.

By the middle of 2001, Enron executives know the company is in trouble. But instead of trying to turn the company around, they continue to personally feed off Enron's private partnerships, and later that year twenty-four Enron execs and board members sell their own Enron stock worth over a billion dollars. But publicly, Enron's corporate leadership continues to insist that all is well.

In August of 2001, Skilling suddenly resigns as CEO, citing his desire to spend more time with his family. The company stock that was selling for ninety dollars a share a year ago is now selling at forty-two dollars. Ken Lay, the original CEO of Enron, steps back into his old job, maintaining that the company is strong. Not long after arriving back at the helm, Lay receives a one-page, unsigned letter from a concerned employee. The letter details problems with Enron's partnership that the author worries will cause financial catastrophe within a year. "I am incredibly nervous that we will implode in a wave of accounting scandals," the letter says. "Skilling is resigning for 'personal reasons,' but I think he wasn't having fun, looked down the road and knew this stuff was unfixable and would rather abandon ship now than resign in shame in two years."[10]

The author of the letter is Sherron S. Watkins, an accountant who was fired the previous spring and then rehired in June. Watkins reveals herself, and Lay agrees to meet with her. Lay hires the law firm Vinson & Elkins to launch an investigation. Lawyers interview Fastow and several people involved in Fastow's transactions. On September 21, the law firm tells Lay that everything seems fine with what Fastow is doing. Still, Lay sells millions of dollars of his own Enron stock after he hears the report. Vinson & Elkins promises a full written report in a few weeks.

Five days after his personal stock sell-off, Lay informs employees that "our financial liquidity has never been stronger."[11] This is painfully false. By September, the stock is selling at just under thirty dollars per share, and other executives start to sell their stakes in the company. However, the company bars its employees, other than the top executives, from selling their Enron shares, which for most employees make up their retirement savings. The top executives explain their decision by claiming that the company is in the process of switching retirement-plan administrators.

In the weeks following the Vinson & Elkins investigation, Enron's auditors from the Arthur Andersen accounting firm discover that they accidently reported that Enron had $1.2 billion in assets that did not actually exist. Correcting the mistake will force Enron to report a loss of a billion dollars. Lay decides to end some of Fastow's off-the-books partnerships. Ending the partnerships means the company will need to report losses that they have been hiding from investors, which means the company is now admitting to an additional loss of $591 million. But, the bad news is still coming. On October 16, Enron releases its previous quarter earnings; Enron reports a third quarter loss of $618 million. The stock value continues to slip.

From there, the trouble only mounts. By the time employees are allowed to sell their stock on November 19, the stock has plummeted from ninety dollars a share to only nine dollars a share. On November 30, the stock is selling for twenty-six cents a share. Thousands of people lose their jobs and their savings. Enron declares bankruptcy on December 2, 2001. Still, the team from Enron that comes to New York to file the bankruptcy

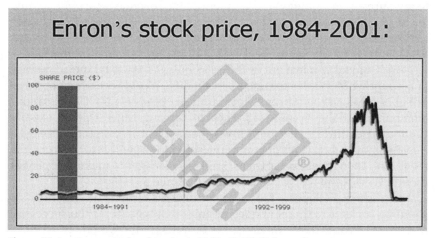

Figure 21.1.   Enron stock value chart, 2001. *Public information*

flies in on the $45 million corporate jet and stays at the upscale Four Seasons Hotel.

Unfortunately, Enron is far from alone in their financial folly.

THE TRAGEDY—WORLDCOM AND OTHERS

Bernie Ebbers has worked in a diverse array of jobs in his life. He's been a milkman, bartender, car salesman, motel manager, high school basketball coach, and most recently cofounder and CEO of WorldCom, a massive telecommunications company. Ebbers is a pious Christian, starting every board and shareholders' meeting with a prayer. A Canadian cowboy of sorts, in alligator boots, Ebbers is a bit of a corporate wonder. Under his leadership, the telecommunications giant WorldCom's stock value increases 7,000 percent in the 1990s.[12] WorldCom takes over MCI, a competitor, in 1997, and as the millennium draws to a close, it has twenty million customers and sixty thousand employees around the world.

As with Enron, WorldCom's success is shakier than the public picture represents. Ebbers acquires a plethora of other companies, and often WorldCom can't integrate the new companies into its existing corporate structure particularly well. The company develops a reputation for poor customer service, in large part due to subpar management. With many unsolved issues brewing at WorldCom, the fast-acting Ebbers tries to take over Sprint, another telecommunications rival, in October of 1999, announcing his plans to purchase the company for $129 billion. This move does not make a great deal of sense as Internet growth is fading and telecommunications companies' stock is generally spiraling earthward. Due to advances in technology and regulation, the revenue is just not coming in. In one year, the cost of a long-distance phone call goes from fifteen to two cents per minute. WorldCom is drowning, and things get worse. Regulators block the Sprint deal, and WorldCom's stock plummets.

WorldCom takes a leaf out of Enron's book and starts taking advantage of accounting loopholes to hide its instability. WorldCom, though, is not as subtle or clever as Enron. Scott Sullivan, WorldCom's CFO, exploits ambiguities in the accounting rules to, among other things, classify routine expenditures as capital investments. That is, outgoing money is treated as though it is an ongoing investment that will return a profit in the future. Using these basic tricks, Sullivan manages to make it appear as though WorldCom's revenue increases by some $9 billion.

When Enron collapses, the country turns its furious attention to accounting tricks. Are there other companies that seem to be too successful to be real? WorldCom's deviousness is quickly uncovered. In April of 2002, the board fires Ebbers, but the company is already in ruins. The accounting scandal comes to light in June, and by July, the company files for bankruptcy. WorldCom lays off a fourth of its employees, and the stock, which once traded at sixty-five dollars a share—drops to nine cents a share. At the time of its bankruptcy, WorldCom has about $104 billion dollars in assets. This makes it a far larger loss than Enron, which had only $63.4 billion in assets. WorldCom's collapse means billions of investors' dollars are down the drain.

The early 2000s see a host of accounting scandals similar to those at Enron and WorldCom. In fact, the Enron and WorldCom scandals spark an interest in seeing where else these illicit accounting methods might be working their magic.

Attention turns to Global Crossing, a firm born in 1999 from the merger of an American telecom company and a Bermuda-based fiber optics company. The company gets off to a fantastically good start, and is valued on the stock market at $75 billion in its first year. As with Enron and World-Com, the sheen of success hides a rotten core. Global Crossing is beset by the same issues facing WorldCom and the entire telecommunications industry. As with Enron and WorldCom, management uses accounting tricks to bamboozle stockholders. For example, Global Crossing exchanges network capacity with other carriers. These trades don't produce any real value, but Global Crossing marks them up as revenue anyway. One company Global Crossing swaps networks with, Qwest, uses exactly the same practice, adding more than $4 billion in revenue from network swaps. By 2002, Global Crossings is in bankruptcy and Qwest's stock has fallen from sixty dollars a share to a dollar a share.

THE OUTRAGE

The Enron scandal and its progeny turn heads. A February 2002 survey reveals that 28 percent of Americans are "following the Enron story very closely" and another 28 percent are following it "fairly closely," a rarity for business stories, which usually attract little interest.[13] But for an angry public, Enron represents a set of questions. How did the company manage it? How could a monumental fraud go unnoticed for so long? Why did no one blow the whistle?

One of the most obvious partners in the collapse is the accounting firm Arthur Andersen. Arthur Andersen has been well paid to audit Enron, WorldCom, Qwest, and other corruption-riddled companies. Once the epitome of honest, independent auditing services, Arthur Andersen turned increasingly to consulting to boost its profits. In 1989, the firm's consulting arm, Arthur Andersen Consulting, becomes independent from its auditing services, but auditors profit handsomely if they persuade auditing clients to hire Andersen for consulting. Andersen's consultants, in turn, offer advice that will help assure a clean audit. With this arrangement, Andersen is heavily incentivized to offer positive audits. As a final blow to objectivity, Arthur Andersen hires the entire internal auditing section of Enron, totaling forty people. Auditor independence is no longer even a pretense.

The economics of the relationship between Enron and Andersen are revealing. In a single year, 2000, Enron pays Andersen $52 million, about half of which is for consulting. Enron cannot pull off its massive accounting manipulation scheme without a compliant auditor, and Andersen knows it needs to keep Enron as a customer if they are to keep their company alive. Anyone who gets in the way of the relationship is quickly dismissed: in February of 2001, an Andersen auditor is fired when he starts asking too many questions about Enron's financials. As soon as the Andersen partner in charge of Enron, David B. Duncan, hears that the Federal Communications Commission is going to start investigating Enron's books, he orders "an expedited effort to destroy documents."[14] For days, Enron employees work to destroy the evidence.

Enron's board of directors has been similarly willfully blind. A biting congressional report alleges that "the Board witnessed numerous indications of questionable practices by Enron management over several years, but chose to ignore them to the detriment of Enron shareholders, employees and business associates."[15] The board even created special-purpose entities—essentially company branches—that hid the company's financial failures. This is the same board that signs off on Skilling's plan when he has an interoffice affair with a secretary, for whom he divorces his wife, and whom he wants to promote to a position with an annual salary of $600,000.

Bankers and lawyers, too, are neck deep in the various scandals. Banking analysts are expected to provide objective reports about stock prospects, but there is more money to be made in the sideline work, such as underwriting contracts. "Bringing in the big bucks is primary to an analyst's success," explains a Goldman Sachs executive, "and actually being able to pick a stock takes a second."[16] As firms slyly realize, falsifying positive reports opens up investment banking opportunities. The finance firms that underwrote Enron's bonds and stock made $323 million between 1986 and 2001. By pretending that everything is fine, the bankers keep the faucet on and let the money pour in. Similarly, J. P. Morgan, Deutsche Bank, and Bank of America hid their concerns about WorldCom and worked to sell $12 billion worth of suspect paper. Lawyers are also incentivized to hide issues. Even when Enron is rotten to the core and on the verge of collapse, the law firm of Vinson & Elkins finds nothing wrong with Enron's accounting.

These companies are also close to the political world. Enron donates millions to various politicians.[17] The White House hosts Enron execs across three presidencies. Global Crossing's founder, Gary Winnick, plays golf with President Clinton and has Presidents Nixon, Reagan, and Bush over to his mansion. Bernie Ebbers is close with Mississippi House Speaker Tim Ford. Furthermore, the media sensationalize the dramatic successes of the big-money executives, instead of asking the tough questions about where all the money is coming from. Jeff Skilling and Andrew Fastow are publicly lauded for years. Fastow receives *CFO* magazine's CFO Excellence Award in 1999. *CEO* magazine names Enron's board of directors among the nation's top five. In 1996, WorldCom tops the *Wall Street Journal*'s list of the best corporations in returns to shareholders in the past ten years. Enron gets away with its scam for far longer than it should have, in part because the media are cheering them on.

In February of 2002, the Special Investigative Committee of the Board of Directors of Enron Corporation releases its findings on the scandal.[18] As the news spreads, public outrage rises, Congress vows to investigate. Enron races to destroy all evidence of criminality by the wholesale shredding of reams of documents and the destruction of computer hardware. Nonetheless, the executives of Enron are pursued by the FBI and the Department of Justice, who issue subpoenas compelling them to testify, but nearly all invoke the Fifth Amendment and remain silent.

Skilling, in contrast, decides to defend himself before Congress. He's not an accountant, he argues, and he'd trusted the people he hired to guide him. Skilling and Fastow are among the Enron execs who claim that they had no warning. Watkins, the original whistleblower, also testifies before Congress. She accuses Skilling and Fastow of bypassing the board and using Lay as a scapegoat. Watkins's claims lack evidence, much of which has been shredded or erased, so the situation remains unclear. Eventually, the smoking gun is found: investigators find a copy of the Watkins memo (that somehow avoided the shredder) showing that it had been circulated among the Enron execs and within Arthur Andersen. Claims of ignorance suddenly seem disingenuous.

A handful of company executives try to slip into the shadows, finding positions in consulting, investment management, or other ventures.[19] Chief Risk Officer Rick Buy and Chief Accounting Officer Rick Causey leave Enron for good, and Ken Lay is forced out of his director position. Public pressure even forces U.S. Securities and Exchange Commission chairman Harvey Pitt to resign.

Fastow, Skilling, and Lay, however, face the harshest punishments. In 2004, Fastow is indicted by a grand jury on ninety-eight criminal counts, including obstruction of justice. During his final hearing on January 14, 2004, he pleads guilty as part of a plea bargain. He's charged instead with two conspiracy counts involving wire and securities fraud. He will serve ten years in prison and relinquish $23.8 million of his assets. (It is estimated that Fastow was enriched by some $37 million while at Enron.)

Prosecutors decide to stage a "mega-trial" in 2006.[20] Jeff Skilling is charged the following month. The Enron Task Force unleashes a forty-two-count indictment against him, a set of charges that could mean 325 years in prison. Unfazed, Skilling pleads not guilty. Lay, meanwhile, is charged with misleading Arthur Andersen about Enron's plans and lying to banks. He initially pleads not guilty, but in a press conference staged by his defense lawyers, he admits responsibility.

The Arthur Andersen firm is also under fire for destroying documents related to Enron. On May 6, 2002, Arthur Andersen is charged with obstructing the investigation into Enron, and soon after is tried and found guilty. Though the conviction is later vacated by the Supreme Court because of vague jury instructions, Arthur Andersen's reputation is in ruins. It surrenders its accounting license to the SEC and ultimately declares bankruptcy. [21]

Public criticism is as scathing as prosecutors' charges, attributing the Enron and WorldCom scandals to systematic failings. With billions of dollars lost from Americans' savings, trust in big business plummets. In July 2002 the *Washington Post* publishes an article describing corporate America:

> A rogue's gallery of crooked corporate chieftains, avaricious auditors, bumbling board barons and feckless federal fraud foes has tumbled out of the cascade of business scandals that blacken the image and threaten to sap the vitality of American capitalism. The most well-run casino in the world suddenly looks like a shoddy set-up for suckers.[22]

Others, meanwhile, worry that the scandal will do more than shake people up; it might dry up the U.S. innovation pipeline, essential to America's financial success. If the nation's innovation declines, university president William R. Brody tells Congress, then it would fall behind China, India, and western Europe in important high-tech areas. After all, the United States has already shifted from being the leader in exports to a net importer. Americans are feeling the impact, too; family income for most Americans stayed flat toward the end of the twentieth century. The scandals, which illicitly siphon so much wealth into the hands of a very few, experts concede, may be playing a role in the larger issue of America's economic future.

THE REFORM

For legislators, the answer to the problem lies in better corporate governance and accountability. Democrats and Republicans break party lines to support a bill that would crack down on corporate crime. New York attorney general Eliot Spitzer is an especially vocal advocate, earning the 2002 title "Crusader of the Year" by *Time* magazine. The media, too, decry greed in corporate governance as a major cause of recent scandals.

The movement for legislative action culminates in the passage of the Sarbanes-Oxley Act (SOX) in July 2002, the most extensive financial legislation since the securities laws of the Great Depression era.[23] The explicit goal of the legislation is "to protect investors by improving the accuracy and reliability of corporate disclosures,"[24] in other words, to make sure companies are honest about their finances. SOX achieves this goal by improving corporate governance and reforming the relationship between public companies and their auditors.[25] The new law requires public companies to have an approved internal code of ethics; ensures that CEOs and CFOs personally attest to the accuracy of their financial statements; increases the level of financial statement disclosure; includes protections for whistleblowers who report suspected fraud or financial misconduct to their superiors; and restricts share trading by corporate officers.

The act's criminal provisions are tough. Title IX of SOX, called the White-Collar Crime Penalty Enhancement Act of 2002 (WCCPA), beefs up sentencing for corporate crimes. SOX also clearly criminalizes several actions that had been overlooked by previous reform efforts, such as the destruction of documents and audit records. SOX also establishes a new quasi-public authority called the Public Company Accounting Oversight Board (PCAOB), which keeps a close eye on the auditors of public companies and has the power to regulate, investigate, and punish auditing firms that do not comply with the rules and standards set by the PCAOB. Most importantly, the board prohibits auditing firms from auditing and consulting for the same client.[26]

The effects of SOX are felt almost immediately by businesses nationwide. Companies pay fines, white-collar criminals face jail, and financial transparency becomes an expectation. Management is compelled to clean up its accounting practices, and earnings estimates are more likely to stay honest and conservative. Financial reporting practices are improved. In 2005, for example, *USA Today* describes Tyco International this way: "The plush Park Avenue headquarters is gone. So is the liquidity crisis. So are the million-dollar birthday bashes, the eight digit bonuses for the senior executives and the acquisition binge that pushed Tyco's debt load to the breaking point."[27]

The reforms have their costs. For example, Section 404 of SOX requires companies to have their internal control systems for managing financial and accounting information verified by an independent auditor. This quickly earns distain for being an incredibly expensive process, with the costs of audits, insurance premiums, legal opinions, and independent director salaries ranging from hundreds of thousands to millions of dollars.[28] The first year the law is in effect, Fortune 1000 companies spend over $5 billion to comply with SOX. Though General Electric reports costs of $30 million to document and update internal control systems, the burden falls particularly hard on smaller companies with a valuation under $1 billion, which spend 30 percent more to meet SOX standards. SOX becomes a lush new income stream for accountants and lawyers, earning it nicknames like the Accountants Relief Act, and the Consultants & Lawyers Full Employment Act.

Furthermore, foreign governments seek to protect their auditors from legal claims in this toxic environment, and European companies are keen to avoid SOX-regulated listings. As one European company finance director complains, "If we knew Sarbanes was coming, we never would have listed [in the United States]."[29] The costs and dangers of SOX lead many private companies to avoid SOX's daunting regulations by declining to go public. And in 2004, over 20 percent of public companies in the United States consider going private to avoid SOX.

Attorneys and auditors, not wanting to follow the path of Arthur Andersen, become far less willing to allow for client input on audits. Credit rating agencies track their every move, and investors demand clearer financial statements from their managers. A growing sense of distrust sweeps corporate America. In 2005, the Financial Accounting Standards Board (FASB) publishes a chilling report: companies and auditors are "afraid of the new regime,"[30] but they are unable to voice their concerns for fear of legal, regulatory, and media-based scrutiny. "The watchdogs," the *Financial Times* declares, "are out of control."[31]

In order to mitigate some of these negative effects, an important reform of SOX comes in 2007, when audit standards are modified, cutting annual costs for many firms by 25 percent or more. Nonetheless, the law remains particularly burdensome for small and medium-sized businesses that are traded publicly. In order for the law to work, it needs more flexibility. As scholar Suraj Srinivasan says, "Flexibility—being able to exempt some smaller companies from the mandate and make it easier for others to implement—is an important quality to keep in mind when we discuss future regulation."[32]

In 2008, the financial crisis throws the entire financial system into dire straits, and Congress responds in 2010 with the Dodd-Frank Act. While Dodd-Frank aims to increase Wall-Street regulation, it provides an opportunity to reform SOX by adding in some of that flexibility. Now, smaller companies with a market capitalization of less than $75 million are exempted from the much-loathed Section 404.[33] The act also initiates a "bounty program," which rewards whistleblowers with 10 to 30 percent of any monetary sanction recovered from a corrupt company. The reforms go hand in hand with the older 1977 Foreign Corrupt Practices Act (FCPA), which criminalized corporate corruption at the international level.

BEYOND REFORM

The central question remains: does SOX work? In early 2005, the *New York Times* concludes that 51 percent of companies that went public in 2004 now have poor corporate governance practices, *up* from 37 percent in 1999 after a wild year in the stock market, but *down* from 63 percent in 2002. "The quality of governance has deteriorated in [private companies gone public],"[34] notes the analyst. Though the twelve-point drop in companies with poor governance from 2002 to 2004 shows that progress is being made, a majority of companies going public still do not have good governance.

SOX supporters, however, point to a Financial Executives Research Foundation report finding that 71 percent of financial management staff agree that SOX is somewhat effective or very effective at reducing fraud.[35] They also claim that SOX makes markets more efficient in three ways. First, a 2005 survey found that 83 percent of large-company CFOs agree that SOX increases investor confidence. When investors are more confident in a company's claims about their earnings, it leads to stronger stock return reactions following the release of quarterly earnings reports. Second, another study found that SOX limits the risk of overconfident CEOs and turns them from a potential liability into an asset for most companies. When leaders who are inclined to take risks must operate within specific rules, they are more likely to propel a company forward than down a dangerous path that could end up hurting the company. Third, data also suggest that SOX has increased corporate innovation as measured by the quantity and quality of patents put out by the companies most impacted by SOX.[36]

Despite some companies reporting that they considered going private to avoid the law when it first took effect, the number of private companies going public remains healthy and strong today. And most of the firms that considered publicly delisting were already smaller and more susceptible to fraud, precisely the sorts of companies, scholars argue, that shouldn't have played in public markets to begin with.

However, the numbers tell only half of the story. Even though some companies put out more patents, other research shows that U.S. companies bound by SOX "significantly reduced . . . the sum of their capital and R&D expenditures, in comparison with their non-U.S. counterparts" after the law is adopted.[37] Perhaps SOX does dis-incentivize risk taking and

investment. The costs of compliance also remain incredibly high. Protiviti, a consultancy, finds that the average cost of SOX compliance is over $1
million.[38] It varies by the size of an organization: smaller companies valued at less than $100 million spend an average of $800,000, while a majority of organizations valued at $20 billion or greater spend over $2 million
on compliance. Most companies also report that the number of hours they
spend on SOX compliance continues to increase year over year.[39]

Some financial thinkers are worried for other reasons. What if SOX has
just shifted the way in which fraud is perpetrated? After all, from 1990 to
2005, financial instruments have become more complex, and companies
have found clever ways to avoid regulators. Ownership and control becomes fuzzy, and investors can't track who's in charge of what. Additionally, the whistleblower protection measures of SOX are relatively toothless in practice. The burden of proof is initially placed on the employee
making the claim, so while many complaints are filed, few make it to
litigation, and only a minority of those that do are decided on the side of
the employee alleging fraud.[40]

As a result, some criticize SOX for being "largely cosmetic," failing to
"address the profound changes in financial markets."[41] Meanwhile, new
financial entities like hedge funds—young, diverse, and daring—threaten
to outmaneuver current regulations. Greed, as with all vice, is difficult to
regulate through criminal law. The law is helping, but stories of corporate
downfall still riddle the news. Perhaps something more needs to be done.

There is little consensus on what that additional reform might be. On
the one hand, some still don't think the law goes far enough. New statistics worsen the fear; a 2010 study finds that "[n]early one in four house-
holds was victimized by white collar crime within the previous year."[42]
Some contend the whistleblower protection measures of the law do not
do enough to incentivize employees to come forward with allegations of
fraud.[43] For example, the law requires that companies collect anonymous
complaints, but does not require that they respond to them in any way.
There are still instances of employees who thought they would have protection after reporting fraud but still lose their jobs. A 2005 report declares
that "[it] will take more than beefed up internal financial controls to guarantee sterling corporate performance."[44]

On the other hand, some criticize the law for going too far. In particular,
the SOX's internal audit rules remain burdensome. Richard Chambers,
the CEO of the Institute of Internal Auditors (IIA), suggests that auditors
under SOX should focus only on a few key things: the effectiveness of
a company's organization of documents, internal controls tests, and the
like. Anything else, says Chambers, represents too much involvement.

Not everyone is pleased with the criminal penalties either. Many white-
collar criminals receive the same sentences as those given to violent drug

dealers, murderers, and rapists, which they argue is unfair. Further, research shows that prison does little or nothing to deter white-collar criminals, who are actually more likely to repeat their offenses than those who are not imprisoned. In light of this, perhaps punishment for corporate criminals should be economic, just like the nature of their crimes. Others defend the harsh sentences and dispute findings that prison does not deter white-collar crime. No matter what the deterrent statistics, they argue, prison is morally stigmatizing—an appropriate punishment for such coldly calculated crime.

Of course, scandals still occur. Though some use this to argue for more regulation, some say an apparent increase in financial scandals since SOX is a sign that the law works. Increased accountability and transparency is uncovering a greater percentage of the fraud that has always existed, and ultimately this will deter corporate America from engaging in shady practices in the first place.

The stoic faces behind the Enron and WorldCom scandals still loom large, and Americans continue to watch white-collar crime cases closely. For now, SOX remains highly influential. The PCAOB has become an integral part of corporate America's regulatory framework, and SOX seems to have made companies more honest about their accounts. It has, however, come with high compliance costs, and it remains unclear whether those costs are outweighed by less fraud and more transparent and efficient markets. Flexibility may remain a key feature of future legislation—a reminder that, as crime evolves in innovative corporate America, the law must evolve with it.

Conclusion

Trigger Crimes and Social Progress

Previous chapters have reviewed several dozen "trigger crimes" that have arisen since the early 1900s. In this final chapter, we step back to examine the common pattern of tragedy, outrage, and reform that we see repeated in these cases. Our study of trigger crimes and the tragedy-outrage-reform dynamic suggests that there is explanatory power in distinguishing among three kinds of trigger crime.

NEW PROBLEMS, NEW SOLUTIONS, AND CHANGING NORMS

Some tragedies become trigger crimes because they focus public attention, and outrage, on a new societal problem that has only now become crystalized in the public's mind. Other tragedies reflect longstanding problems, but problems that now seem to have a plausible solution within reach. A final group of cases concern an old problem where a solution has been available in the past, but what has changed is a shift in societal norms regarding the importance of solving the problem.

New Problems. The 1911 Triangle Factory fire is an example of a new-problem case. Prior to the late 1800s, Americans made their own garments. A rush of immigrants came to New York with the new century, bringing a large talent pool of tailors, drapers, and engineers and cheap labor. Now there is a product demand, a talent collection, and the bodies to run the machines, all amassed in the same compact area. By 1910, an estimated 70 percent of the clothing worn by U.S. women originates in

New York's Garment District.¹ The factories are housed in the new electri-
cally run steel buildings that are quickly built to house them. Even the engineering of such buildings is new. *Skyscraper*, a term that was originally
used in the 1880s to describe a building of ten to twenty floors, becomes
far more feasible when steel manufacturing grows sophisticated enough
to supplant iron around 1895. All this progress creates conditions that allow the horrendous tragedy of the Triangle Factory fire.

Such an advent of a new sort of societal problem is a common stimulus
for trigger cases. The 1937 Sulfanilamide Crisis spawns a regime of drug
safety that has not been needed in a world with limited commercial development and distribution of medicines. The 1972 TWA airplane bombings
trigger a new focus on airline security only because hijackings have arisen
as a growing problem.

New Solutions. The 1964 Genovese murder-witness scandal is an example of a new-solutions case. About the time of the Genovese attack,
AT&T implemented 6-1-1 as a universal customer service request number and 4-1-1 as a universal directory-assistance number. Adding a third
short number, 9-1-1, for emergency calls becomes a relatively quick, easy,
and cheap solution to the problem of contacting local police.² At the time,
rotary telephones are used, and 9-1-1 is both easy to remember and quick
to dial. (AT&T's willingness to provide this service may not have been
entirely altruistic. Without a universal number, people in emergencies
sometimes called the operator, an AT&T employee, who had to stop other
business to determine the proper police station to call and its phone number. The new nationwide emergency number is funded through a small
additional charge placed on nearly everyone's phone bill. The reform is
thought to save the company millions of dollars.)

The availability of a new solution to an old problem is a common pattern in trigger-crime cases. The advent of DNA as an investigative tool in
the 1986 Leicestershire murder cases comes about because a researcher
at a nearby university is at the time studying the uniqueness of each
individual's DNA. Similarly, when the FBI tried to fight the Mafia, there
were no laws that allowed them to attack the organization as a whole. But
a legal solution to the problem was developed, and soon Federal RICO
statutes are followed by state reforms all around the country.

Changing Norms. The 1969 Santa Barbara oil spill and Cuyahoga River
fire are examples of changing-norms cases. There have been notorious environmental disasters before the 1969 Santa Barbara oil spill and
Cuyahoga River fire but little social or political will to pay the price to
avoid them. Rachel Carson's 1962 book, *Silent Spring*, helps prime the
pump of public concern by giving Americans a frightening view into a
world of environmental degradation. DDT sprayed on crops kills the tar-

get insects but also kills many other creatures. It enters the human body and is retained in fat cells, causing cancer and other serious health problems. *Silent Spring* stays on the *New York Times* bestseller list for eighty-six weeks, and its message is widely disseminated before the oil spill. The notion of Americans killing themselves by killing the environment becomes a palpable concern.

The 1980 Cari Lightner death is another, somewhat different kind of example of a changing-norms case. Instead of the relatively quick public shift seen with the environmental trigger crimes, social norms against drunk driving took a long slog of concerted effort to change.

In the ten years before Cari Lightner's 1980 death, 250,000 people died in drunk-driving incidents, and most Americans knew someone who was injured or killed. "Alcohol was involved in nearly 60 percent of fatal crashes and we were banging our heads against the wall," remembers Jim Fell, an employee for the National Traffic Safety Administration. "Then, all of a sudden, a woman named Candy Lightner [Cari's mother] came along, kicking and screaming about her daughter who had been killed."[3] Victims and their families start using MADD as a resource, which allows MADD to link all the individual harms into a national wrong that has previously gone unnoticed. As the strands knit together into a single stream of outrage, the politicians start listening. By 1982, less than two years after MADD's founding, one hundred MADD chapters exist around the country, with more forming daily. Forty-one states establish task forces and commissions to assess each state's drunk-driving problem and propose solutions.[4] By 1983, 129 new anti-drunk-driving laws are in place around the nation.

MADD's very personal approach changes the political dynamics. MADD insists that legislators stop treating drunk driving as an unfortunate reality. The community comes to reject the notion that, as Candy Lightner puts it, drunk driving "is the only socially acceptable form of homicide."[5]

The same sort of change in social norms can be seen as the determinative factor in other cases as well. Domestic violence was simply tolerated as the way of the world until the appalling events of the 1983 Tracey Thurman beating helped trigger people's appreciation that that reality must change. Tracy becomes fearful for her life from her estranged husband who repeatedly attacks her and vows to kill her. She consistently pleads with police to intervene, but the police refuse, seeing the regular beatings as a private matter. When Buck Thurman nearly kills his wife with the police on the scene doing nothing, Tracey sues the township and wins. The resulting publicity promotes a dramatic shift away from public tolerance of domestic violence, which leads to nationwide reform.

Stalking offenses show a similar history. Stalking has been going on for decades. When Rebecca Schaeffer is killed by a violent stalker, the brutality of the violence finally awakens a great national cry for change.

EXPLORING THE TRAGEDY-OUTRAGE-REFORM DYNAMIC

Why do some tragedies produce broad outrage while others, often of a very similar nature, do not? Why do some outrages produce reform while others, often with greater claims to outrageousness, do not?

The Triangle Factory fire was a horrendous event, but it was hardly the only horrendous event of its nature. Eight years earlier, the Iroquois Theatre fire on December 30, 1903, in Chicago kills six hundred people. When firefighters respond to the blaze, they think the theater is in fact closed. No flames are visible, and the doors seem locked. In fact, so many bodies are stacked up against the inward opening exits that the doors are as tight as though they were locked. The only person to serve any jail time in relation to the disaster is a nearby saloon owner who robs some of the dead bodies while his establishment serves as a makeshift morgue. Why is it the Triangle Factory fire that sparks such outrage and reform, rather than the Iroquois Theatre fire?

One may observe the same phenomenon with regard to the 1969 Santa Barbara oil spill and Cuyahoga River fire. These were hardly the first environmental disasters. Indeed, for a century, the residents of Cleveland, Ohio, have tolerated their river regularly catching fire—at least eleven different times on record. The fire of 1952 is particularly destructive, blazing for three days and causing $1.8 million worth of damage. The Cuyahoga isn't the only river known to catch fire. Michigan's Rouge River, the Schuylkill River of Philadelphia, the Buffalo River in Buffalo, and the Chicago River have all been known to burn, as well as both Baltimore and New York harbors. Why is it that it is the 1969 Cuyahoga River fire that inspires outrage and reform?

The same is true of drunk driving before the 1980 Cari Lightner death. No one bothered keeping national records of drunk-driving deaths before 1980, but a survey of local records shows the enormous extent of the problem. In one day in that period, just after midnight a Florida barber crosses the street and is struck by a drunk twenty-three-year-old house painter. Three minutes later, in South Carolina, a drunk twenty-seven-year-old slams into a middle-aged woman. Less than an hour later, a drunk Texas driver going the wrong way down the highway kills another driver. And on it goes until fifty-four people are dead in the single day due to impaired driving.[6] Before the year ends, the death toll will be in excess of twenty-one thousand. Cari Lightner's death is just one of a continuing flood of victims. Why is it her death that triggers reform and not others before it?

The dynamic can be observed for many other trigger cases: the 1993 death of Polly Klaas is an appalling crime, but her death was far from the first at the hands of a violent career criminal. Recall Kimber Reynolds who was killed just a year before. Why did the death of Polly seem to make a difference?

The 1983 Tracey Thurman beating is hardly an unusual event. Authorities didn't bother keeping statistics on domestic violence before that time, but the available evidence suggests the extent of the problem. When Kansas City looked at its homicide statistics in 1971, it found that 40 percent of homicides were spouse killings. In nearly half of those killings, police had been previously called to the home at least five times.[7] A 1975 National Family Violence Survey Found that serious domestic abuse occurred in 16 percent of American families every year.[8]

Nor are the egregious facts of the Tracey Thurman case particularly unique. In a 1955 case, Sandra Baker is afraid of her husband, a New York City policeman. She gets an order of protection, but despite the order, he threatens and beats her again and again. When Sandra again calls the police, they refuse to take action against the husband, saying the protection order is "no good" and "only a piece of paper." When Sandra again takes the matter to court, she is told her husband is not coming to the hearing because he is sick. But she sees him in the building, and she asks to remain in the court office because she is afraid of him. She is told she cannot stay and when she emerges from the office he shoots her. Yet it is the Tracey Thurman case that ends up inspiring broad national reform, rather than any of the thousands of earlier egregious cases. Why should this be so?

Which Tragedies Will Produce Broad Public Outrage? Which Instances of Public Outrage Will Produce Reform?

Producing Public Outrage. There are lots of tragedies, but not all of them generate outrage. What are the circumstances that produce outrage in one case and not in another case that may seem equally outrageous?

The three categories of cases described above can provide part of the answer to these questions (although the three-part typology ought not be pushed too far[9]). For example, it may be easiest to generate outrage in cases where a new problem has arisen because the danger or suffering is not something that people have come to accept as an unfortunate part of their lives. Simply because it is new and different, it gains attention and calls out for a solution.

For similar reasons, the old problem–new solution cases are less likely to produce public outrage. People have come to accept the danger or suffering as simply an unfortunate part of their reality. It is only the availability of a new solution that can shake people from their lethargy.

The changing-norms cases are similar in that the past acceptance of the danger or suffering might minimize the outrage of some people. It is the power of the changed norm that is doing the work in these cases to generate outrage, even though a case similar to the trigger case did not generate outrage in the not-too-distant past.

Converting Outrage into Reform. There are lots of things that people get outraged about that do not produce reforms. What circumstances make some outrages produce reform while others do not?

Once there is public outrage, it may be easiest to convert that outrage into reform in cases of newly available solutions to old problems. As noted above, producing outrage in these cases is the hard part. The new availability of a solution makes the reform step easy.

The case studies suggest that one can also successfully convert outrage into reform in the new-problem cases and the changing-norms cases, but here the move to successful reform faces a complex situation: each outrage must compete with many other outrages to be the one to get the special attention of the political powers that will produce the legal reform. The legislative leaders may make their reform selections on their own, but more often than not, they are responding to the judgment of others: newspapers and other news organizations, influential lobbying groups, celebrities and other public figures and, increasingly, social media. How can one current outrage become the outrage that wins the reform lottery?

A number of factors, such as the extent of news media coverage, are obvious in their important effect, but other important factors are less obvious, and some factors have an outsized effect that make them particularly important.

Dramatic Images. Perhaps a trigger-crime outrage can win the lottery just by being so spectacularly and visually outrageous—like the burning women falling from the sky in the Triangle Factory fire or the Cuyahoga River burning. Dramatic photographs for the media outlets can be compelling: oil-covered birds on the beach and piles of dead dolphins washing ashore. After the attacks on 9/11, the news services publish painful images of the Twin Towers billowing dense black smoke into a pristine blue sky. These are striking images that will give that outrage special attention. The larger point is that the same rules that affect publicity campaigns, such as dramatic visual images, also affect public opinion in cases of specific trigger-crime outrages.

Influential Victims. Another factor that can give one outrage an advantage over others is who it affects. The Santa Barbara oil spill damages a neighborhood with a good deal of money and influence. The residents clearly have the means and connections to get legislative attention and to whip up broader public support in ways not available to less influential victims. Richard Nixon is the U.S. president at the time and has his unofficial White House in nearby San Clemente. President Nixon visits the site of the oil spill: "It is sad that it was necessary that Santa Barbara should be the example that had to bring it to the attention of the American people."[10] (A corollary to the advantage of influential victims is that a tragedy can be converted into reform even without broad social outrage. Public outrage can certainly help, but legislative leaders can be influenced more directly.) In related fashion, the Triangle Factory fire comes out well in the reform contest by occurring in New York City, the home of Randolph Hearst. The Hearst papers and their syndicates around the country cover the fire for weeks.

Devoted Publicity Manager. But compare the influential-victim path to the drunk-driving reform. It is not politically influential victims that create the outrage and reform. It is the relentless publicizing by Cari Lightner's mother that does the job and compensates for her lack of political influence. The process here is slow but steady. Without singularly dramatic images or particularly influential victims, the building of outrage and the move to reform takes time: societal norms have to be changed first.

Pump Primers. A common pattern revealed by the trigger-crimes collection is the presence of a previous tragedy, often not too long before the trigger case, that in a sense primes the pump for the trigger case's outrage to produce the broad reform. For example, the Iroquois Theatre fire eight years earlier primed the pump for the public outrage and reform triggered by the Triangle Factory fire. Similarly, the outrage and reforms that follow the 1932 Lindbergh kidnapping are made possible in part because of the public sensitivity to the problem provided five years earlier with the kidnapping of twelve-year-old Marion Parker, who is tortured to death. Just one year before Polly Klaas is abducted and killed in 1993, Kimber Reynolds is killed by a career criminal. There is an attempt to address the problem of offenses by repeat offenders, but the effort fails. The exercise does, however, seem to prime the pump for a stronger, more focused, reaction to reform that comes with the Polly Klaas killing.[11]

Luck. There are only so many reform projects that a legislature can undertake at any given time. A tragedy may have the bad luck of occurring at the same time as an even greater tragedy, which then siphons off public outrage and clogs up the channels of reform. So there is a certain amount of luck involved in the path from trigger crime to legal reform. In some cases, the path from tragedy to reform can benefit from good luck. On the day that the Triangle Factory burns, Frances Perkins, then secretary of the New York City Committee on Public Safety and later secretary of labor under President Roosevelt, is in a restaurant nearby. She is drawn to the commotion and witnesses the horrifying events of the fire. It is hard to imagine that her witnessing the events does not influence her resolve to do what she can to prevent future occurrences.

Ultimately, to get from tragedy to reform requires quite a few elements to be in place, both in prompting outrage and in converting that outrage into action. So there is a certain amount of "perfect storm" quality in the process—a specific combination of conditions must exist at the same time or in a certain relation to one another to actually produce reform.

Legislative Reform Versus Real-World Change

The tragedy, outrage, and reform process is not complete with the enactment of legislation. The legal reforms simply mark the end of the first phase. Legal change may have little or no effect on the real world.

In the case of the Triangle Factory fire, for example, the same defendants are brought to court again several years later for a similar incident and get a similar trivial punishment. In 1913, Blanck and Harris, the owners of the Triangle Shirtwaist Factory, are running a new factory where the doors are again being chained, trapping 150 women inside without means of escape in case of fire. The violation is discovered before a tragedy occurs. The result: Blanck is fined twenty-five dollars. Later that same year, on December 23, Blanck is again found to be in violation of the law and issued a warning, but on this occasion is not fined.

In the Lightner drunk-driving case, two weeks after being released from custody for killing Cari Lightner, Busch is again a licensed driver. While drunk, he crashes into a car stopped at a red light, totaling both cars. In 1992, Busch is again in court, for his sixth drunk-driving conviction. He is fined $583, and his driver's license is suspended for nine months.[12]

Laws on the books can have no effect unless witnesses, prosecutors, judges, juries, sentencing guideline commissions, and others take the offense more seriously and play their part in making the system work to actualize the new legal rules.

The notion of "trigger crimes" suggests a step function—a point of dramatic legal change—which is probably an accurate description of the legal-reform phase of the process: the tragedy triggers a legal reform that did not previously exist. But in the subsequent phase, after the legislation is in place, the process of changing actual practice is more like a continuous curve than a step function. Real-world change requires a collective and interactive process, as in building a skyscraper. Steelworkers, carpenters, electricians, and plumbers must all do their work on each level before they can get to the next level. In a similar fashion, getting beyond legal reform to actual changing of practice on the ground requires that witnesses, prosecutors, judges, jurors, and all other participants in the criminal justice system must come to share the new norm if it is to be enforced.

The law reform–social change dynamic is a bit of a chicken-and-egg problem. The new norm's internalization by criminal justice system participants and others depends to a large extent on the criminal justice system's enforcement of it backed by community support. But that enforcement and support depends to a large extent on these people and others internalizing the new norm. Increasing enforcement of the legal rules and increasing internalization of the new norm must move ahead together, incrementally—building the building floor by floor.

Going Too Far

When a trigger crime's outrage is translated into legal reform, it is not uncommon for that reform to go too far. The reasons for this might be explained by several phenomena, two of which one might call the "reform hysteria dynamic" and the "bureaucratic momentum dynamic."

The Reform Hysteria Dynamic. It is common that in the heat of the moment, the energy and momentum that creates legislative reform ends up carrying the reforms too far.

The dynamic is illustrated by what has been called the "crime du jour" problem. A particular headline criminal case leads to the creation of a new offense, such as *carjacking*. Does anyone doubt that it was illegal to pull someone out of their vehicle and then take their car before the offense of carjacking was put on the books? Or, for another example, *home invasion* is now a new separate crime. Is home invasion any different from what was *aggravated burglary*? These are not new offenses; they are already fully criminalized. Adding the new name to an old offense gives legislators a chance to show that they share their constituents' concerns and are "doing something" about them. Unfortunately, the only real effect is to create confusion and ambiguity, as the criminal code now punishes the same conduct under two separate somewhat differently defined offenses.

The same political motivations tend to exaggerate the punishment grade of offenses created or amended in response to public upset about the crime du jour. Everyone understands that crimes vary in seriousness. We want more serious crimes to be punished more severely than lesser offenses. But when the crime-du-jour dynamic causes the legislature in the heat of the moment to exaggerate a crime's seriousness, it throws off the criminal code's internal structure that classifies offenses according to their relative seriousness. Over time, the crime-du-jour process creates serious internal inconsistencies and disproportionalities in the grading among different offenses. The dynamic is made worse by the fact that it creates a continuing upward spiral: after one crime du jour exaggerates the grading for an offense, the next crime du jour uses the exaggerated grading of the first as the new baseline from which the grading of the next crime du jour must be exaggerated.[13]

The same dynamic behind the crime-du-jour problem—the tendency of the uproar that sparks reform to go too far—is seen in new-problem cases and in changing-norm cases. The Polly Klaas abduction, by a man who had six previous convictions for violent felonies, ends up making three-strikes statutes a national phenomenon. But life without parole is not necessarily an appropriate sentence for every instance of three strikes. William Rummel, for example, was given life where his "third strike" was not returning to fix the air-conditioning for a bar owner who had paid him $120. His previous two strikes were of similar seriousness.[14]

The Reverend Dempsey–inspired war on drugs actually makes sense under the circumstances of the moment. Illicit drugs are destroying entire communities, and the criminal justice system seems unable or unwilling to slow the plague. But when legal reform is finally put into motion, initially in the form of the Rockefeller drug laws in New York and later in federal reforms, the legislation goes too far. In one case, student Clarence Aaron, a football player at Southern University in Baton Rouge with no criminal record, is given three life terms for introducing a buyer and seller for a cocaine deal, even though he never possesses or touches any of the drugs involved.[15]

The Bureaucratic Momentum Dynamic. Another common dynamic that tends to lead to going too far is found in those reforms that create governmental bureaucracies, typically to solve a new problem or a problem recently appreciated because of changed norms. The difficulties seem to arise, first, because government agencies, once established, tend to seek to build their empire. That is, as good bureaucrats, they tend to focus on what additional areas of our lives they can bring within their mandate. Further, because each government agency tends to focus on a particular interest—the interest they were created to promote and protect—it thereby exaggerates the value of that interest as against all other interests.

For example, no one can dispute that the Cuyahoga River fire and the Santa Barbara oil spill make strong cases for the creation of the federal Environmental Protection Agency, but many people argue today that the EPA has gone too far, not only in expanding its reach but also in its balance of environment interests as against competing interests. In 2013, Marietta Industrial Enterprises, a company in Ohio, is fined $50,000, and the president of the company, Scott Elliott, is jailed. The company, among other things, crushes medium carbon ferromanganese. Unknown to Elliot, the workers turn off the fans while the processing is going on. This is not a violation of any rule as the employees use other containment methods instead. After a time, Elliot learns that the fans are being turned off, and he instructs the workers that the fans should be left on. From then on, the fans are left on. Elliot's crime? He did not report the nonuse of the fans to the EPA. The EPA rule states that if the fans are not working properly, then the company is obliged to report the fact. The company is criminally prosecuted for its failure to report.[16] The EPA has come a long way from simply preventing environmental disasters like the Santa Barbara oil spill or the Cuyahoga River fire.

There are seventy-seven departments within the EPA that operate largely free of congressional restraint.[17] In 1972, the Clean Water Act covers navigable waterways. By 2015, the EPA has produced a 299-page document, titled the "Waters of the United States Rule," that seems to expand its jurisdiction to every bit of water no matter how small that is "within 4,000 feet of the high tide line or the ordinary high water mark of a traditional navigable water, interstate water, the territorial seas, impoundments, or covered tributary."[18] Congressman Steve Scalise, for example, complains that the "EPA's attempt to redefine 'navigable waterways' to include every drainage ditch, backyard pond and puddle is a radical regulatory overreach that threatens to take away the rights of property owners and will lead to costly litigation and lost jobs."[19]

The same bureaucratic-momentum dynamic may be seen in other areas as well. For example, the building-safety codes inspired by the Triangle Factory fire have proved themselves to be invaluable. However, building safety is not cost free. Wider stairways and hallways mean smaller usable spaces. Specialty materials cost extra. Many people argue that homelessness in cities is driven partly by codes that dramatically increase housing costs. In El Paso County, Colorado, wildfires destroyed 488 homes in 2013. Fire codes that had imposed on builders and home owners seemed smart when they were adopted in 2009. But when it came time to rebuild, few could afford to do so due to the cost of compliance. The county had to choose between no homes or homes that did not meet the existing standards.[20] The county relaxed their fire codes.

For another example, the federalization of criminal law inspired by the Lindbergh kidnapping and the Dillinger bank robberies has proved extremely valuable in effectively fighting crimes that individual states cannot handle. Nonetheless, that federalization has also shown what some people see as excesses. In one case, Idaho's Snake River runs through a federal park area. Tom and Scott Lindsey launch their rafts to go fishing on the river at 7:00 a.m., rather than 9:00 a.m., which federal regulations specify. That night, they camp on a gravel bank below the high-water mark, where no federal park permit is required. They cook on a gas stove; by regulation open fires are not permitted. The following day law enforcement agents helicopter in to arrest the brothers for two felonies:

camping without a permit and building a campfire without a permit. They are taken into custody, but the federal district court judge dismisses the case, saying that the federal agents did not have authority over state lands. The government appeals and the Ninth Circuit Court of Appeals decides that the Forest Service is entitled to enforce its regulations on the state river because such is necessary to protect the adjacent federal land. The prosecutor declines to retry the brothers.[21]

Less Danger in New-Solution Cases. The going-too-far problem seems less common in the new-solution cases, perhaps because there may be less danger of overreach. Frequently, we are happy to let the new solution go as far as it can go.

The creation of the 9-1-1 emergency call system, triggered by the 1964 Genovese killing witness scandal, has been wildly successful, and there seems little reason to rein it in. People call 9-1-1 about 2 million times a month. Seventy percent of those calls come from cell phones.[22] Similarly, having professional and well-trained medical examiners, triggered by the 1915 Chloroform-killer case, has only increased their effectiveness in solving crimes and avoiding public health threats. WITSEC, triggered by the 1967 Calabrese intimidation, has made it easier to gain the cooperation of reliable witnesses and, if anything, has not been made available enough. Criminal profiling, triggered by the 1950s New York City "Mad Bomber" case, has become increasingly sophisticated and can increasingly predict where a perpetrator lives as well as their personal characteristics. Again, there seems little interest in limiting the use of this investigative tool. DNA testing, pioneered in the 1986 Leicestershire murders, has become increasingly inexpensive and ever more reliable. The process has been expanded into forensic DNA typing of pet hairs, seed pods, pond slime, and a host of other biologicals that can provide compelling reliable evidence in criminal investigation and prosecution.[23]

CONCLUSION

The stories and analyses here demonstrate that, oddly, some crimes— trigger crimes—can make our world better. For a variety of reasons, these crimes prompt public outrage—when previous others, equally bad, did not—and that outrage produces legal and social reform when previous instances of public outrage did not. Sometimes the heat or momentum of the reform energy goes too far, and the tendency of government bureaucracies to expand their empire leads to overreach, but these excesses are often caught and corrected.

Particularly striking in this view of the tragedy–outrage reform dynamic is what it reveals about the nature of social progress. We may like to think that our triumphs of progress are the result of a planned, orderly, and rational process of democratic government. But in truth it is often chaotic and unpredictable, brought about by a seemingly random or at least unpredictable cast of characters and events. Who would have guessed that a single kidnapping would create the federalization of criminal law, that a particular sniper would lead to the creation of SWAT teams, or that an attack on a New York street would inspire the national 9-1-1 system? Could anyone guess that the beating of a high school dropout would change our views on domestic abuse? A failed bombing attempt that hurt no one would inspire a regime of airport security? A group of deaths of some fragile old people, that might or might not have been intentional, brought down the lucrative patronage position for coroners. Or that a concerned pastor would change our nation's drug policies?

As chaotic as our social progress may seem, the trigger-crime stories are comforting in the apparent inevitability of American progress. As unpredictable as our social and political life may seem, over time our democratic society does effectively identify problems and produce solutions. Our progress may be messy but it is relentless.

Notes

CHAPTER ONE

1. The following account draws from: Leon Stein, *Triangle Fire* (New York: J. B. Lippincott, 1962); "How Regulation Came to Be: The Triangle Shirtwaist Fire," by dsteffen at http://www.dailykos.com/story/2010/03/21/846135/-How-regulation-came-to-be-The-Triangle-Shirtwaist-Fire.

2. *Triangle Fire*, 14.

3. http://www.perno.com/amer/docs/The%20Triangle%20Shirtwaist%20Factory%20Fire.htm.

4. *Triangle Fire*, 15.

5. *Triangle Fire*, 20.

6. *Triangle Fire*, 23.

7. *Triangle Fire*, Opposite from table of contents.

8. *Triangle Fire*, 29.

9. This narrative is drawn from the following sources: http://trianglefire.ilr.cornell.edu/legacy/legislativeReform.html; http://triangleshirtwaisthd.weebly.com/main-event.html; http://trianglefire.ilr.cornell.edu.

10. *Triangle Fire*, 139.

11. *Triangle Fire*, 139.

12. *Triangle Fire*, 140.

13. *Triangle Fire*, 141.

14. Information in this paragraph is drawn from the following source: http://trianglefire.ilr.cornell.edu/supplemental/timeline.html (Timeline).

15. "How Regulation Came to Be," 7.

16. "How Regulation Came to Be," 8.

17. http://francesperkinscenter.org/?page_id=574.

18. http://trianglefire.ilr.cornell.edu/legacy/legislativeReform.html.

19. "Triangle Shirtwaist Factory Fire (1911)," *New York Times*, March 11, 2011, 1.

20. http://magazine.sfpe.org/professional-practice/history-fire-protection-engineering.

21. http://nlsd.net/index2.html.

22. https://www.utexas.edu/safety/fire/safety/historic_fires.html.

23. http://www.nfpa.org/newsandpublications/nfpa-journal/2014/july-august-2014/features/inside-threat.

24. http://workingperson.me/2015/02/a-brief-history-of-fr/.

25. http://www.scientificadvisory.com/ses.html.

26. http://www.consumerwatch.com/household/appliances/coffeemakers.php.

27. Information in this section is drawn from the following sources: http://www.epa.gov/region9/greenbuilding/codes/standards.html; https://www.fema.gov/building-codes.

28. http://www.census.gov/popclock/.

29. http://www.economist.com/blogs/graphicdetail/2013/02/daily-chart-7.

CHAPTER TWO

1. This portion of the narrative is drawn from the following sources: Centers for Disease Control and Prevention, "Death Investigation Systems," last updated October 26, 2016, http://www.cdc.gov/phlp/publications/coroner/death.html; Centers for Disease Control and Prevention, "Medicolegal Officers," last updated October 26, 2016, http://www.cdc.gov/phlp/publications/coroner/medicolegal.html; M. Chalabi, "What Does It Mean to Die of Natural Causes?" *FiveThirtyEight*, August 13, 2015, https://fivethirtyeight.com/features/what-does-it-mean-to-die-of-natural-causes/; "Civil Service Board Again Aids Riordan," *New York Times*, January 29, 1918, http://query.nytimes.com/mem/archive-free/pdf?res=9E01E2DD103FE433A2575AC2A9679C946996D6CF; Colin Evans, *Blood on the Table: The Greatest Cases of New York City's Office of the Chief Medical Examiner* (New York: Berkley Publishing Group, 2012); Deborah Blum, *The Poisoner's Handbook* (New York: Penguin, 2010); Gregory J. Davis, "The Medical Examiner and Coroner Systems," *Medscape*, last updated December 4, 2015, http://emedicine.medscape.com/article/1785357-overview#showall; M. Hansen, "Body of Evidence—When Coroners and Medical Examiners Fail to Distinguish Accidents from Murders from Suicides, a Botched Autopsy Can Be the Death of a Fair Trial, an Insurance Settlement or a Civil Suit," *ABA Journal* 115 (1995): 60–67, 69, accessed August 28, 2015, http://www.jstor.org/stable/27835826; Randy Hanzlick, "Overview of the Medicolegal Death Investigation System in the United States," in *Medicolegal Death Investigation System: Workshop Summary*, 7–11 (Washington, DC: The National Academies Press, 2003); "Hylan Puts Norris in Riordan's Place," *New York Times*, January 31, 1918, http://query.nytimes.com/mem/archive-free/pdf?res=9900E5DB133DE533A25752C3A9679C946996D6CF; "Killed 8 in Home, He Tells Perkins," *New York Times*, February 3, 1915; "Move for Riordan by Civil Service," *New York Times*, January 28, 1918, http://query.

nytimes.com/mem/archive-free/pdf?res=9D01E7DD103FE433A2575BC2A9679 C946996D6CF; Murderpedia, "Carl Menarik," accessed June 27, 2017, http:// murderpedia.org/male.M/m/menarik-carl.htm; National Conference of Commissioners on Uniform State Laws, *Model Post-mortem Examinations Acts* (Chicago: National Conference of Commissioners on Uniform State Laws, 1954); National Institute of Justice and National Research Council, "The Medical Examiner and Coroner Systems: Current and Future Needs," in *Strengthening Forensic Science in the United States: A Path Forward*, 241–52, Bibliogov, 2009; Arun Rath, "Is the 'CSI Effect' Influencing Courtrooms?" *National Public Radio*, February 5, 2011, http:// www.npr.org/2011/02/06/133497696/is-the-csi-effect-influencing-courtrooms; Roger Roess and Gene Sansone, *The Wheels That Drive New York: A History of the New York City Transit System* (Heidelberg: Springer Publishing, 2013).

2. Blum, *The Poisoner's Handbook*, 7.
3. "Killed 8 in Home," 9.
4. Blum, *The Poisoner's Handbook*, 6.
5. "Killed 8 in Home," 9.
6. Blum, *The Poisoner's Handbook*, 7.
7. Blum, *The Poisoner's Handbook*, 7.
8. Blum, *The Poisoner's Handbook*, 7.
9. Blum, *The Poisoner's Handbook*, 12.
10. Blum, *The Poisoner's Handbook*, 8.
11. Blum, *The Poisoner's Handbook*, 13.
12. Blum, *The Poisoner's Handbook*, 6.
13. Blum, *The Poisoner's Handbook*, 22.
14. Blum, *The Poisoner's Handbook*, 23.
15. Blum, *The Poisoner's Handbook*, 17.
16. Blum, *The Poisoner's Handbook*, 18.
17. Blum, *The Poisoner's Handbook*, 24.
18. "Carl Menarik."
19. Evans, *Blood on the Table*, 10.
20. Evans, *Blood on the Table*, 10.
21. Blum, *The Poisoner's Handbook*, 21.
22. Blum, *The Poisoner's Handbook*, 21.
23. Blum, *The Poisoner's Handbook*, 20.
24. Blum, *The Poisoner's Handbook*, 21.
25. Roess and Sansone, *The Wheels That Drive New York*, 200–03.
26. Blum, *The Poisoner's Handbook*, 27.
27. Blum, *The Poisoner's Handbook*, 22.
28. "Move for Riordan by Civil Service."
29. Blum, *The Poisoner's Handbook*, 24.
30. "Civil Service Board Again Aids Riordan,"
31. "Civil Service Board Again Aids Riordan."
32. "Hylan Puts Norris in Riordan's Place."
33. Blum, *The Poisoner's Handbook*, 25.
34. National Institute of Justice and National Research Council, "The Medical Examiner and Coroner Systems: Current and Future Needs."

35. National Institute of Justice and National Research Council, "The Medical Examiner and Coroner Systems: Current and Future Needs," 242.

36. National Conference of Commissioners on Uniform State Laws, *Model Postmortem Examinations Acts*.

37. Davis, "The Medical Examiner and Coroner Systems."

38. Centers for Disease Control and Prevention, "Death Investigation Systems."

39. Chalabi, "What Does It Mean to Die of Natural Causes?"

40. Rath, "Is the 'CSI Effect' Influencing Courtrooms?"

41. Hanzlick "Overview of the Medicolegal Death Investigation System in the United States," 7.

CHAPTER THREE

1. This portion of the narrative draws on the following sources: Sara Beale, "Federalizing Crime: Assessing the Impact of the Federal Courts," in *The Federal Role in Criminal Law*, edited by James Strazzella (Thousand Oaks, CA: Sage Publications, 1996), http://scholarship.law.duke.edu/cgi/viewcontent.cgi?article=2045&context=faculty_scholarship; Emily Berman, "New FBI Rules Go Too Far," *Huffington Post*, June 22, 2011, http://www.huffingtonpost.com/emily-berman/new-fbi-rules-go-too-far_b_881602.html; Horace L. Bomar, "The Lindbergh Law," *Law and Contemporary Problems* 1 (1934): 435–44, http://scholarship.law.duke.edu/lcp/vol1/iss4/5; L. Chiasson, *The Press on Trial: Crimes and Trials as Media Events* (Westport, CT: Greenwood Press, 1997); James B. Comey, "FBI Budget Request for Fiscal Year 2017," February 26, 2016, https://www.fbi.gov/news/testimony/fbi-budget-request-for-fiscal-year-2017; "Dillinger Slain in Chicago; Shot Dead by Federal Men in Front of Movie Theatre," *New York Times*, July 22, 1934, http://www.nytimes.com/learning/general/onthisday/big/0722.html#article; Julia Dohan, "Criminal Law—Federal Bank Robbery Act—A Scheme Whereby Funds Are Withdrawn from a Federally Insured Bank by Means of Forged Checks Constitutes Stealing and Purloining within the Meaning of the Federal Bank Robbery Act," *Villanova Law Review* 28 (1983): 786–804; Dale V. Every, *Charles Lindbergh His Life* (New York: D. Appleton and Company, 1927); Federal Bureau of Investigation, "A Brief History," http://www.fbi.gov/about-us/history/brief-history; Federal Bureau of Investigation, "Today's FBI: Facts and Figures 2013–2014," https://www.fbi.gov/file-repository/stats-services-publications-todays-fbi-facts-figures-facts-and-figures-031413.pdf/view; Federal Bureau of Investigation, "Famous Cases and Criminals: John Dillinger," March 27, 2015, https://www.fbi.gov/history/famous-cases/john-dillinger; Federal Bureau of Investigation, "Lindbergh Kidnapping," https://www.fbi.gov/history/famous-cases/lindbergh-kidnapping; Elliot Gorn, *Dillinger's Wild Ride: The Years That Made America's Public Enemy Number One* (New York: Oxford University Press, 2009); Walter L. Hixson, *Murder, Culture and Injustice: Four Sensational Cases in American History* (Akron: Akron University Press, 2011); Illinois State Case Studies, "The Lindbergh Case" (n.d.), http://my.ilstu.edu/~ftmorn/cjhistory/casestud/lindy.html; Ludovic Kennedy, *The Airman and the Carpenter: The*

Lindbergh Kidnapping and the Framing of Richard Hauptman (New York: Penguin, 1986); Douglas Linder, "The Trial of Richard 'Bruno' Hauptmann: An Account," *Famous Trials,* http://famous-trials.com/hauptmann/1389-home; Dary Matera, *John Dillinger: The Life and Death of America's First Celebrity Criminal,* (Boston: Da Capo Press, 2010); Shahid M. Shahidullah, *Crime and Policy in America: Laws, Institutions, and Programs* (Lanham, MD: University Press of America, 2008); Lee Tien, "Peekaboo, I See You: Government Authority Intended for Terrorism Is Used for Other Purposes," *Electronic Frontier Foundation,* October 26, 2014, https://www.eff.org/deeplinks/2014/10/peekaboo-i-see-you-government-uses-authority-meant-terrorism-other-uses; United States Congress, "Congressional Record," 1932, https://archive.org/details/congressionalrec75eunit; United States History, "Unemployment Statistics during the Great Depression," http://www.u-s-history.com/pages/h1528.html; University of Missouri–Kansas City, "The Testimony of Bessy Gow," http://law2.umkc.edu/faculty/projects/ftrials/Hauptmann/gowtest.html; K. Weiser, "John Dillinger: Public Enemy #1," *Legends of America,* August 2015, http://www.legendsofamerica.com/20th-johndillinger.html; Sidney Whipple, *The Lindbergh Crime* (New York: Blue Ribbon Books, 1935).

2. University of Missouri–Kansas City, "The Testimony of Bessy Gow,"

3. Kennedy, *The Airman and the Carpenter,* 83.

4. Every, *Charles Lindbergh His Life,* vi.

5. Chiasson, *The Press on Trial,* 117.

6. Linder, "The Trial of Richard 'Bruno' Hauptmann."

7. Linder, "The Trial of Richard 'Bruno' Hauptmann."

8. Linder, "The Trial of Richard 'Bruno' Hauptmann."

9. Linder, "The Trial of Richard 'Bruno' Hauptmann."

10. Linder, "The Trial of Richard 'Bruno' Hauptmann."

11. Linder, "The Trial of Richard 'Bruno' Hauptmann."

12. Kennedy, *The Airman and the Carpenter,* 105.

13. Linder, "The Trial of Richard 'Bruno' Hauptmann."

14. Illinois State Case Studies, "The Lindbergh Case."

15. Bomar, "The Lindbergh Law," 435.

16. Bomar, "The Lindbergh Law," 436.

17. Beale, "Federalizing Crime," 41.

18. United States Congress, "Congressional Records," 13283.

19. United States Congress, "Congressional Records," 13289.

20. Bomar, "The Lindbergh Law," 437.

21. Linder, "The Trial of Richard 'Bruno' Hauptmann."

22. Shirley Graham. "Anatomy of the Lindbergh Kidnapping," *Journal of Forensic Science* 42(3) (1997): 368–77, https://www.ncjrs.gov/App/publications/abstract.aspx?ID=172046.

23. Clark Sellers, "Handwriting Evidence Against Hauptmann," *Journal of Criminal Law and Criminology* 27(6) (March–April 1937): 874, http://www.google.com/url?sa=t&rct=j&q=&esrc=s&source=web&cd=1&cad=rja&uact=8&ved=0ahUKEwiM7JjmtpXVAhXIZiYKHR46C6gQFggiMAA&url=http%3A%2F%2Fscholarlycommons.law.northwestern.edu%2Fcgi%2Fviewcontent.cgi%3Farticle%3D2693%26context%3Djclc&usg=AFQjCNFaeOgVznyLtAAImKTPEFKZ9ty4HQ.

24. Weiser, "John Dillinger: Public Enemy #1."

25. Weiser, "John Dillinger: Public Enemy #1," 2.

26. Weiser, "John Dillinger: Public Enemy #1," 3.

27. Gorn, *Dillinger's Wild Ride*.

28. Federal Bureau of Investigation, "Famous Cases and Criminals: John Dillinger."

29. Gorn, *Dillinger's Wild Ride*.

30. United States History, "Unemployment Statistics."

31. Federal Bureau of Investigation, "Famous Cases and Criminals: John Dillinger."

32. "Dillinger Slain in Chicago; Shot Dead by Federal Men in Front of Movie Theatre."

33. Shahidullah, *Crime and Policy in America*, 63.

34. United States Congress, "Congressional Records," 2946.

35. United States Congress, "Congressional Records," 2947.

36. United States Congress, "Congressional Records." 2947.

37. United States Congress, "Congressional Records." 2947.

38. Dohan, "Criminal Law," 788.

39. Beale, "Federalizing Crime," 40.

40. Shahidullah, *Crime and Policy in America*, 61.

41. Federal Bureau of Investigation, "A Brief History."

42. Federal Bureau of Investigation, "A Brief History."

43. Federal Bureau of Investigation, "A Brief History."

44. Comey, "FBI Budget Request for Fiscal Year 2017."

45. Federal Bureau of Investigation, "Today's FBI: Facts and Figures 2013–2014,"

46. Berman, "New FBI Rules Go Too Far."

CHAPTER FOUR

1. This portion of the narrative draws from the following sources: Christopher P. Adams and Van V. Bratner, "Estimating the Cost of New Drug Development: Is It Really $802 Million?" *Health Aff* 25 (2006): 420–28; Heather M. Alger et al., "Data Gaps in Toxicity Texting of Chemicals Allowed in Food in the United States," *Reproductive Toxicology* 42 (December 2013): 85–94; Carol Ballentine, "Sulfanilamide Disaster," *FDA Consumer*, June 1981, https://www.fda.gov/aboutfda/whatwedo/history/productregulation/sulfanilamidedisaster/; Gary S. Becker, "Power to the Patients," *American Enterprise Institute*, May 1, 2004, https://www.aei.org/publication/power-to-the-patients/; Pam Belluck, "Judge Strikes Down Age Limits on Morning-After Pill," *New York Times*, April 5, 2013, http://www.nytimes.com/2013/04/06/health/judge-orders-fda-to-make-morning-after-pill-available-over-the-counter-for-all-ages.html; Joseph A. DiMasi, "What's Time Got to Do with It?" *Health Aff* 25 (2006): 1188; "Food Advisory Committee Meeting on Infant Formula," FDA, https://www.fda.gov/ohrms/dockets/ac/02/briefing/3852b1_01.htm; "Food Safety Modernization Act and Animal Feed,"

FDA, https://www.fda.gov/AnimalVeterinary/Products/AnimalFoodFeeds/ ucm347941.htm; "Report Brief—The Future of Drug Safety: Action Steps for Congress," *Institute of Medicine*, September 2006; Ronald Hamowy, "Medical Disasters and the Growth of the FDA," *Independent Policy Report*, February 2010, www.independent.org/pdf/policy_reports/2010-02-10-fda.pdf; "Harvey W. Wiley: Pioneer Consumer Activist," *FDA Consumer*, January–February 2008, https://www.fda.gov/AboutFDA/WhatWeDo/History/CentennialofFDA/ HarveyW.Wiley/ucm081121.htm; "The Inadequate Response of the FDA to the Crisis of AIDS in the Blood Supply," *Legal Electronic Document Archive at Harvard Law School*, https://dash.harvard.edu/bitstream/handle/1/8965576/ lrussell.html?sequence=2; Charles O. Jackson, *Food and Drug Legislation in the New Deal*, (Princeton, NJ: Princeton University Press, 1970); C. W. Jackson, A. H. Sheehan, and J. G. Reddan, "Evidence-Based Review of the Black-Box Warning for Droperidol," *Am J. Health Syst Pharm* 64(11) (June 1, 2007): 1174–86; Sharon B. Jacobs, "Crises, Congress, and Cognitive Biases: A Critical Examination of Food and Drug Legislation in the United States," *Colorado Law Scholarly Commons* 64 (2009): 599–629; Wallace F. Janssen, "The Story of the Laws Behind the Labels," *FDA Consumer*, June 1981, https://www.fda.gov/aboutfda/whatwedo/ history/overviews/ucm056044.htm; Rebecca Leung, "FDA: Harsh Criticism from Within," *CBS News*, February 15, 2005, http://www.cbsnews.com/news/fda-harsh-criticism-from-within/; Andrew Martin and Andrew Pollack, "F.D.A. Says Food from Cloned Animals Is Safe," *New York Times*, December 29, 2006, http:// www.nytimes.com/2006/12/29/business/29fda.html; Barbara J. Martin, *Elixir: The American Tragedy of a Deadly Drug* (Lancaster, PA: Barkberry Press, 2014); Michelle Meadows, "Promoting Safe and Effective Drugs for 100 Years," *FDA Consumer*, January–February 2006, https://www.fda.gov/AboutFDA/WhatWeDo/ History/ProductRegulation/PromotingSafeandEffectiveDrugsfor100Years/; Morton Meyers, "Art of Dyeing," in *Happy Accidents: Serendipity in Major Medical Breakthroughs in the 20th Century* (New York: Arcade Publishing, 2007), https:// books.google.com/books?id=pbgtAgAAQBAJ&pg=PT59&lpg=PT59&dq=frankl in+delano+Roosevelt+junior+sulfanilamide&source=bl&ots=_Q9RfGbkao&sig= 8ctk8u0TcTsUzUKEpqj6g6zqN4I&hl=en&sa=X&ved=0ahUKEwjTwPOSwY3SA hXIJiYKHcPXDggQ6AEIiwEwFw#v=onepage&q=franklin%20delano%20Roosevelt%20junior%20sulfanilamide&f=false; Myllys et al., "Association of Changes in the Bacterial Ecology of Bovine Mastitis with Changes in the Use of Milking Machines and Antibacterial Drugs," *Acta Vet Scand.* 35(4) (1995): 363–69; Lars Noah, "The Little Agency That Could (Act with Indifference to Constitutional and Statutory Strictures)," *Cornell L. Rev.* 93 (2007–2008): 901–25; "Parents Warned of Additives Link," *BBC News*, September 6, 2007, http://news.bbc.co.uk/2/hi/ health/6979976.stm; "Preemie Outrage: Cost of Drug That Prevents Premature Birth to Rise from $10 to $1500," *Daily Mail*, March 9, 2011, http://www.daily-mail.co.uk/news/article-1364747/Preemie-outrage-Cost-makena-drug-prevents-premature-birth-rise-10-1500-KV-Pharmaceuticals.html; "Ron Paul: FDA and Big Pharma 'Are in Bed Together,'" *InfoWars*, April 10, 2012, https://www. infowars.com/ron-paul-fda-and-big-pharma-are-in-bed-together/; Jeffrey E. Shuren, "The Modern Regulatory Administrative State: A Response to Changing

Circumstances," *Harv. J. on Legis.* 38 (2001): 291; U.S. Congress, "Elixir Sulfa-nilamide. Letter from the Secretary of Agriculture Transmitting in Response to Senate Resolution No. 194, a Report on Elixir Sulfanilamide-Massengill," *75th Congress*, November 16, 1937, https://archive.org/stream/CAT10509199/CAT10509199_djvu.txt; Susan Thixton, "FDA Proposed Pet Food Regulations," *TruthAboutPetFood*, November 7, 2013, http://truthaboutpetfood.com/fda-pro posed-pet-food-regulations/.

2. Martin, "Elixir: The American Tragedy," 4.
3. Meyers, "Art of Dyeing," chap. 4.
4. Jackson, *Food and Drug Legislation*, 153.
5. Ballentine, "Sulfanilamide Disaster."
6. Martin, "Elixir: The American Tragedy," 29.
7. Martin, "Elixir: The American Tragedy," 58.
8. Ballentine, "Sulfanilamide Disaster."
9. U.S. Congress, "Elixir Sulfanilamide."
10. Ballentine, "Sulfanilamide Disaster."
11. Ballentine, "Sulfanilamide Disaster."
12. Martin, "Elixir: The American Tragedy," 83.
13. Martin, "Elixir: The American Tragedy," 85.
14. Ballentine, "Sulfanilamide Disaster."
15. Ballentine, "Sulfanilamide Disaster."
16. Hamowy, "Medical Disasters," 8.
17. Ballentine, "Sulfanilamide Disaster."
18. Hamowy, "Medical Disasters," 9.
19. Martin, "Elixir: The American Tragedy," 142.
20. Martin, "Elixir: The American Tragedy," 142.
21. Martin, "Elixir: The American Tragedy," 142.
22. Martin, "Elixir: The American Tragedy," 143.
23. Martin, "Elixir: The American Tragedy," 143.
24. Janssen, "The Story of the Laws Behind the Labels."
25. Janssen, "The Story of the Laws Behind the Labels."
26. Janssen, "The Story of the Laws Behind the Labels."
27. "Harvey W. Wiley: Pioneer Consumer Activist."
28. Meadows, "Promoting Safe and Effective Drugs for 100 Years."
29. Jacobs, "Crises, Congress, and Cognitive Biases," 604–07.
30. Ballentine, "Sulfanilamide Disaster."
31. Ballentine, "Sulfanilamide Disaster."
32. Jacobs, "Crises, Congress, and Cognitive Biases," 605.
33. Jacobs, "Crises, Congress, and Cognitive Biases," 605.
34. Jacobs, "Crises, Congress, and Cognitive Biases," 605.
35. Janssen, "The Story of the Laws Behind the Labels."
36. Robert K. Plumb, "Deformed Babies Traced to a Drug: 'Harmless' Tablet Given to Mothers Abroad Is Cited as Infants' Crippler," *New York Times*, April 11, 1962.
37. Title 21, Food and Drugs: Parts 1 to 99, Revised as of April 1, 2012, https://www.gpo.gov/fdsys/pkg/CFR-2012-title21-vol1/pdf/CFR-2012-title21-vol1.pdf.

38. Plumb, "Deformed Babies Traced to a Drug."
39. Belluck, "Judge Strikes Down Age Limits."
40. Adams and Bratner, "Estimating the Cost of New Drug Development."
41. DiMasi, "What's Time Got to Do with It?"
42. Becker, "Power to the Patients."
43. "Preemie Outrage: Cost of Drug That Prevents Premature Birth to Rise from $10 to $1500."
44. "Report Brief—The Future of Drug Safety"
45. Meadows, "Promoting Safe and Effective Drugs for 100 Years.
46. Meadows, "Promoting Safe and Effective Drugs for 100 Years.
47. Myllys et al. "Association of Changes."
48. "Parents Warned of Additives Link."
49. Martin and Pollack, "F.D.A Says Food from Cloned Animals Is Safe."
50. Alger et al. "Data Gaps in Toxicity Texting."
51. Jacobs, "Crises, Congress, and Cognitive Biases," 599–600.
52. Jacobs, "Crises, Congress, and Cognitive Biases," 629.

CHAPTER FIVE

1. This account is drawn from the following sources: Flourish Abumere, "Effectiveness of Criminal Profiling," *Academia.edu* (n.d.), http://www.academia.edu/2333675/Effectiveness_of_Criminal_Profiling; Richard Buck et al., "Profile of Serial-Arson Suspect—Family, Friends Describe Troubled Boy, Impulsive Adult," *Seattle Times*, February 8, 1993, http://community.seattletimes.nwsource.com/archive/?date=19930208&slug=1684304; Michael Cannell, *Incendiary: The Psychiatrist, The Mad Bomber and the Invention of Criminal Profiling* (New York: Minotaur Books, 2017); Michael Cannell, "Unmasking the Mad Bomber," *Smithsonian*, April 2017, http://www.smithsonianmag.com/history/unmasking-the-mad-bomber-180962469/; Jack Claridge, "Criminal Profiling & Its Use in Crime Solving," *Explore Forensics*, October 28, 2015, http://www.exploreforensics.co.uk/criminal-profiling-and-its-use-in-crime-solving.html; John Douglas et al., "Criminal Profiling from Crime Scene Analysis," *US Department of Justice*, 1986, http://www.all-about-forensic-psychology.com/support-files/criminal-profiling-from-crime-scene-analysis.pdf; Federal Bureau of Investigation, "FBI 100: The Unabomber," April 24, 2008, https://archives.fbi.gov/archives/news/stories/2008/april/unabomber_042408; Don Foster, *Author Unknown: On the Trail of Anonymous* (New York: Henry Holt and Co., 2000); Lucinda Franks, "Don't Shoot," *The New Yorker* (July 22, 1996): 26–31, http://archives.newyorker.com/?i=1996-07-22#folio=026; Phil Gast, "Land That Belonged to 'Unabomber' for Sale," *CNN*, December 5, 2010, http://www.cnn.com/2010/US/12/04/montana.unabomber.property/; Michael M. Greenburg,, *The Mad Bomber of New York: The Extraordinary True Story of the Manhunt That Paralyzed a City* (New York: Union Square Press, 2011); Gripped for Glory Blog, "Out of the Ashes We Rise," November 12, 2010, http://grippedforglory.blogspot.com/2010/11/out-of-ashes-we-rise-part-i.html; David Heinzmann, "As Chicago Killings Surge, the Unsolved Cases Pile Up,"

Chicago Tribune, September 9, 2016, http://www.chicagotribune.com/news/local/breaking/ct-chicago-homicide-clearance-rate-20160909-story.html; Debbie Howlett, "FBI Profile: Suspect Is Educated and Isolated," *USA Today*, November 13, 1996, http://usatoday30.usatoday.com/news/index/una12.htm; Jolayne Houtz, "The Two Sides of Arsonist Paul Keller," *Seattle Times*, May 4, 1993, http://community.seattletimes.nwsource.com/archive/?date=19930504&slug=1699416; John P. Jarvis and Amber J. Scherer, "Criminal Investigative Analysis: Practitioner Perspectives (Part One of Four)," *FBI Law Enforcement Bulletin*, https://leb.fbi.gov/2014/june/criminal-investigative-analysis-practicioner-perspectives-part-one-of-four; Anne E. Kornbult and Gene Mustain, "Survivors Share the Pain," *Daily News*, April 7, 1996, http://www.nydailynews.com/archives/news/survivors-share-pain-article-1.726438; The Learning Network, "Dec. 7, 1941: Japan Attacks Pearl Harbor," *New York Times*, December 7, 2011, https://learning.blogs.nytimes.com/2011/12/07/dec-7-1941-japan-attacks-pearl-harbor/?_r=0; Casey McNerthney, "How Was Serial Seattle Arsonist Paul Keller Caught?" *Seattle Local News*, http://blog.seattlepi.com/seattle911/2009/11/12/how-was-serial-seattle-arsonist-paul-keller-caught/; Laurence Miller, "Hostage Negotiations: Psychological Strategies for Resolving Crises," *PoliceOne*, May 22, 2007, https://www.policeone.com/standoff/articles/1247470-Hostage-negotiations-Psychological-strategies-for-resolving-crises/; Ian Sample, "Psychological Profiling 'Worse than Useless,'" *The Guardian*, September 14, 2010, https://www.theguardian.com/science/2010/sep/14/psychological-profile-behavioural-psychology; Louis B. Schlesinger, "Psychological Profiling: Investigative Implications from Crime Scene Analysis." *J. Psychiatry & L.* 37 (2009): 73–84; Brent E. Turvey, *Criminal Profiling: An Introduction to Behavioral Evidence Analysis* (Cambridge, MA: Academic Press, 2011); "Wave of Arson Puts Seattle Residents on Guard," *New York Times*, November 27, 1992, http://www.nytimes.com/1992/11/27/us/wave-of-arson-puts-seattle-residents-on-guard.html; Colin Wilson, *Manhunters: Criminal Profilers and Their Search for the World's Most Wanted Serial Killers* (New York: Skyhorse Publishing, 2014); Lea Winerman, "Criminal Profiling: The Reality behind the Myth," *American Psychological Association* 35(7) (July/August 2004): 66.

2. Greenburg, *The Mad Bomber of New York*, 1–2.
3. Foster, *Author Unknown.*
4. Greenburg, *The Mad Bomber of New York*, 10–11.
5. The Learning Network, "Dec. 7, 1941: Japan Attacks Pearl Harbor."
6. Greenburg, *The Mad Bomber of New York*, 12.
7. Greenburg, *The Mad Bomber of New York*, 45.
8. Greenburg, *The Mad Bomber of New York*, 48.
9. Greenburg, *The Mad Bomber of New York*, 49.
10. Greenburg, *The Mad Bomber of New York*, 53.
11. Greenburg, *The Mad Bomber of New York*, 54.
12. Greenburg, *The Mad Bomber of New York*, 59.
13. Greenburg, *The Mad Bomber of New York*, 63.
14. Greenburg, *The Mad Bomber of New York*, 65.
15. Greenburg, *The Mad Bomber of New York*, 66.
16. Greenburg, *The Mad Bomber of New York*, 76–77.
17. Cannell, *Incendiary*, 95.

18. Cannell, "Unmasking the Mad Bomber."
19. Greenburg, *The Mad Bomber of New York*, 92.
20. Greenburg, *The Mad Bomber of New York*, 93.
21. Greenburg, *The Mad Bomber of New York*, 95.
22. Greenburg, *The Mad Bomber of New York*, 95.
23. Greenburg, *The Mad Bomber of New York*, 96.
24. Greenburg, *The Mad Bomber of New York*, 98–99.
25. Greenburg, *The Mad Bomber of New York*, 103.
26. Greenburg, *The Mad Bomber of New York*, 108.
27. Greenburg, *The Mad Bomber of New York*, 111–12.
28. Greenburg, *The Mad Bomber of New York*, 127.
29. Greenburg, *The Mad Bomber of New York*, 138.
30. Greenburg, *The Mad Bomber of New York*, 141–42.
31. Greenburg, *The Mad Bomber of New York*, 145.
32. Greenburg, *The Mad Bomber of New York*, 146.
33. Greenburg, *The Mad Bomber of New York*, 155.
34. Greenburg, *The Mad Bomber of New York*, 86.
35. Greenburg, *The Mad Bomber of New York*, 88.
36. Greenburg, *The Mad Bomber of New York*, 212.
37. Greenburg, *The Mad Bomber of New York*, 212.
38. Greenburg, *The Mad Bomber of New York*, 213.
39. Greenburg, *The Mad Bomber of New York*, 214.
40. Greenburg, *The Mad Bomber of New York*, 215.
41. Wilson, *Manhunters.*
42. Turvey, *Criminal Profiling*, 35.
43. Greenburg, *The Mad Bomber of New York*, 218.
44. Jarvis and Scherer, "Criminal Investigative Analysis."
45. Jarvis and Scherer, "Criminal Investigative Analysis."
46. Schlesinger, "Psychological Profiling," 73.
47. Schlesinger, "Psychological Profiling."
48. Winerman, "Criminal Profiling."
49. Winerman, "Criminal Profiling."
50. Winerman, "Criminal Profiling."
51. This portion of the narrative is drawn from the following sources: "FBI 100: The Unabomber"; Mustain, "Survivors Share the Pain"; Howlett, "FBI Profile."
52. Howlett, "FBI Profile."
53. Franks, "Don't Shoot."
54. Gast, Phil, "Land That Belonged to 'Unabomber' for Sale."
55. Franks, "Don't Shoot."
56. In the words of one psychologist, "Behavioral profiling has never led to the direct apprehension of a serial killer, a murderer, or a spree killer, so it seems to have no real-world value." Sample, "Psychological Profiling 'Worse than Useless.'"
57. This narrative is drawn from the following sources: "Wave of Arson Puts Seattle Residents on Guard"; Houtz, "The Two Sides of Arsonist Paul Keller"; McNerthney, "How Was Serial Seattle Arsonist Paul Keller Caught?"; Gripped for Glory Blog, "Out of the Ashes We Rise."

58. Buck et al., "Profile of Serial-Arson Suspect."
59. Abumere, "Effectiveness of Criminal Profiling."
60. Claridge, "Criminal Profiling and Its Use in Crime Solving."
61. Abumere, "Effectiveness of Criminal Profiling."
62. Claridge, "Criminal Profiling and Its Use in Crime Solving."
63. Miller, "Hostage Negotiations: Psychological Strategies for Resolving Crises."
64. Douglas et al., "Criminal Profiling from Crime Scene Analysis."
65. Winerman, "Criminal Profiling."
66. Heinzmann, "As Chicago Killings Surge, the Unsolved Cases Pile Up."

CHAPTER SIX

1. This portion of the narrative is drawn from the following sources: 18 U.S.C. § 3237(a) (2012); Howard Abadinsky, *Organized Crime* (Chicago: Nelson-Hall, 1994); Dan Bryan, "The American Mafia in the Early 20th Century," *American History USA*, last modified March 8, 2012, https://www.americanhistoryusa.com/mafia-early-20th-century/; Sean Gardiner and Pervaiz Shallwani, "Mafia Is Down—but Not Out," *Wall Street Journal*, February 18, 2014, https://www.wsj.com/articles/mafia-in-new-york-city-is-down-but-not-out-1392778841; Jack Kelly, "How America Met the Mob," *Buffalo Police Then and Now*, accessed June 29, 2017, http://www.bpdthenandnow.com/howamericametthemob.html; John Kerry and Hank Brown, *The BCCI Affair: A Report to the Committee on Foreign Relations*, United States Senate (Washington, DC: U.S. G.P.O., 1993); Arnold H. Lubasch, "17 Found Guilty in 'Pizza' Trial of a Drug Ring," *New York Times*, March 3, 1987, http://www.nytimes.com/1987/03/03/nyregion/17-found-guilty-in-pizza-trial-of-a-drug-ring.html; Peter Maas, *The Valachi Papers* (New York: G. P. Putnam's Sons, 1968); "Organized Crime," *Interpol.int.*, https://www.interpol.int/Crime-areas/Organized-crime/Organized-crime; Allen Pusey, "Nov. 14, 1957: Mob Bosses Raided at Apalachin," *ABA Journal*, last modified November 1, 2014, http://www.abajournal.com/magazine/article/nov._14_1957_mob_bosses_raided_at_apalachin; Gil Reavill, *Mafia Summit: J. Edgar Hoover, the Kennedy Brothers, and the Meeting That Unmasked the Mob* (New York: Thomas Dunne Books, 2013; Thomas Reppetto, *Bringing Down the Mob: The War Against the American Mafia*) (New York: Holt Paperbacks, 2007); Alain L. Sanders, "Law: Showdown at Gucci," *Time*, August 21, 1989; "Organized Crime," *United States Attorney's Bulletin* 60 (November 2012), https://www.justice.gov/usao/eousa/foia_reading_room/usab6006.pdf; "United Nations Convention against Transnational Organized Crime and the Protocols Thereto," *United Nations Office on Drugs and Crime*, http://www.unodc.org/unodc/en/treaties/CTOC/index.html.
2. Kelly, "How America Met the Mob."
3. Bryan, "The American Mafia in the Early 20th Century."
4. Pusey, "Nov. 14, 1957: Mob Bosses Raided at Apalachin."
5. Kelly, "How America Met the Mob."
6. Reavill, *Mafia Summit*, 86.

7. Reavill, *Mafia Summit*, 95.

8. Kelly, "How America Met the Mob."

9. Reavill, *Mafia Summit*, 109.

10. Reavil, *Mafia Summit*, 109.

11. Reavil, *Mafia Summit*, 106.

12. Reavil, *Mafia Summit*, 71.

13. Reavil, *Mafia Summit*, 71.

14. Maas, *Valachi Papers*, 30.

15. Mass, *Valachi Papers*, 31.

16. Maas, *Valachi Papers*, 62.

17. Maas, *Valachi Papers*, 64.

18. Maas, *Valachi Papers*, 32.

19. Maas, *Valachi Papers*, 33.

20. Maas, *Valachi Papers*, 34.

21. Maas, *Valachi Papers*, 34.

22. Maas, *Valachi Papers*, 35.

23. Maas, *Valachi Papers*, 37.

24. Maas, *Valachi Papers*, 36.

25. Maas, *Valachi Papers*, 30.

26. Maas, *Valachi Papers*, 40.

27. Maas, *Valachi Papers*, 45.

28. Maas, *Valachi Papers*, 9.

29. Reppetto, *Bringing Down the Mob*, 208–09.

30. Reppetto, *Bringing Down the Mob*, 95.

31. Letiza Paoli, *The Oxford Handbook of Organized Crime* (Oxford: Oxford University Press, 2015), 291.

32. Sanders, "Law: Showdown at Gucci."

33. Reppetto, *Bringing Down the Mob*, 96–97.

34. 18 U.S.C. § 3237(a) (2012).

35. Reppetto, *Bringing Down the Mob*, 214–15.

36. Reppetto, *Bringing Down the Mob*, 213–16.

37. This portion of the narrative draws from the following sources: John Floyd, "Introduction: RICO State by State: A Guide to Litigation Under the State Racketeering Statues, Second Edition," *American Bar Association* 2 (November 2012), http://www.americanbar.org/publications/gpsolo_ereport/2012/november_2012/introduction_rico_state_by_state.html; Donald Rebovich et al., "Local Prosecution of Organized Crime: The Use of State RICO Statues," *U.S. DOJ, Bureau of Justice Statistics*, October 1993.

38. This portion of the narrative is drawn from the following source: Jennie Cohen, "Major Mob Busts in U.S. History," *History.com*, January 21, 2011, http://www.history.com/news/major-mob-busts-in-u-s-history.

39. Lubasch, "17 Found Guilty in 'Pizza' Trial of Drug Ring."

40. Reppetto, *Bringing Down the Mob*, 221.

41. Reppetto, *Bringing Down the Mob*, 281.

42. Reppetto, *Bringing Down the Mob*, 291.

43. *See, e.g.*, Gardiner and Shallwani, "Mafia Is Down—but Not Out."

44. Gardiner and Shallwani, "Mafia Is Down—but Not Out."

45. This portion of the narrative is drawn from the following source: G. Robert Blakey and John R. Blakey, "Civil and Criminal RICO: An Overview of the Statute and Its Operation" *Defense Counsel Journal* 54 (1996).

46. This portion of the narrative is drawn from the following source: Kenneth Carlson and Peter Finn, "Prosecuting Criminal Enterprises," *Bureau of Justice Statistics, US DOJ,* November 1993, https://www.ncjrs.gov/pdffiles1/Digitization/142524NCJRS.pdf.

47. Reppetto, *Bringing Down the Mob,* 291.

48. "BCCI's Criminality," Federation of American Scientists, 1992, https://fas.org/irp/congress/1992_rpt/bcci/04crime.htm.

49. "BCCI's Criminality," Federation of American Scientists.

50. Department of Justice, "Nine FIFA Officials and Five Corporate Executives Indicted for Racketeering Conspiracy and Corruption," May 27, 2015, https://www.justice.gov/opa/pr/nine-fifa-officials-and-five-corporate-executives-indicted-racketeering-conspiracy-and.

51. Gardiner and Shallwani, "Mafia Is Down—but Not Out."

52. This portion of the narrative is drawn from the following sources: "Organized Crime," *Interpol.int.,* http://interpol.int/Crime-areas/Organized-crime/Organized-crime; "Legislative Arrangements to Outlaw Serious and Organized Crime Groups—Chapter 4 (Legislation Targeting Participation in an Organized Crime Group)," *Parliament of Australia,* August 17, 2009, 53–96, http://www.aph.gov.au/Parliamentary_Business/Committees/Joint/Former_Committees/acc/completed_inquires/2008-10/laoscg/report/index; Rebecca Payne, "Combating the Organized Crime Threat to the Healthcare System: Lessons Learned from Eurasian Organized Crime Prosecutions," *United States Attorneys Bulletin* 60, US DOJ Office for United States Attorneys (November 2012).

53. See, for example "13163 Mexico—Agreement Regarding the Sharing of Forfeited Assets," *US Department of State,* September 4, 2001, https://www.state.gov/s/l/tias/2001/130466.htm.

54. United Nations Convention against Transnational Organized Crime and the Protocols Thereto.

CHAPTER SEVEN

1. Fortner, *The Black Silent Majority: The Rockefeller Drug Laws and the Politics of Punishment* (Cambridge, MA: Harvard University Press, 2015), 131.

2. This portion of the narrative is drawn from the following sources: Vanessa Barker, *The Politics of Imprisonment: How the Democratic Process Shapes the Way America Punishes Offenders* (New York: Oxford University Press, 2009); G. Beschner et al., *Life with Heroin: Voices from the Inner City* (Lexington, MA: D.C. Heath and Company, 1985); Robert Bremmer, *Children and Youth in America* (Cambridge, MA: Harvard University Press, 1974); Thalif Deen, "Despite U.N. Treaties, War on Drugs a Losing Battle," *MintPress News,* February 28, 2015, http://www.mintpressnews.com/despite-u-n-treaties-war-against-drugs-a-losing-battle/202674/; "The Drug Laws That Changed How We Punish," *National Public Radio,* Febru-

ary 14, 2013, http://www.npr.org/2013/02/14/171822608/the-drug-laws-that-changed-how-we-punish; "Drug Use and Crime," *National Bureau of Justice State Prison Inmate Survey*, 1986; "The Drug War, Mass Incarceration and Race," *Drug Policy Alliance*, February 10, 2016, http://www.drugpolicy.org/resource/drug-war-mass-incarceration-and-race; Erin Durkin, "New York City Drug Overdose Deaths Up 73% over Last Five Years, with Heroin Claiming the Most Victims," *New York Daily News*, August 9, 2016, http://www.nydailynews.com/new-york/new-york-city-drug-overdose-deaths-73-years-article-1.2744675; Fortner, *The Black Silent Majority*; Michael J. Fortner, "How the Black Middle Class Pushed for Harsher Drug Laws," *Dailybeast*, September 14, 2015, http://www.thedailybeast.com/articles/2015/09/14/how-the-black-middle-class-pushed-for-harsher-drug-laws.html; Blanche Frank, "An Overview of Heroin Trends in New York City: Past, Present and Future," *Mount Sinai Journal of Medicine* 67 (October/November 2000), www.drugpolicy.org/docUploads/meth340.pdf; Stephen Gutwillig, "Federal vs. State Laws," *Los Angeles Times*, March 10, 2009, http://www.latimes.com/la-oew-gutwillig-imler10-2009mar10-story.html#page=1; "History of Mandatory Minimum Penalties and Statutory Relief Mechanisms," in *2011 Report to the Congress: Mandatory Minimum Penalties in the Federal Criminal Justice System, United States Sentencing Commission*, http://www.ussc.gov/sites/default/files/pdf/news/congressional-testimony-and-reports/mandatory-minimum-penalties/20111031-rtc-pdf/Chapter_02.pdf; Danielle, Kurtzleben, "Data Show Racial Disparity in Crack Sentencing," *U.S. News and World Report*, August 3, 2010, https://www.usnews.com/news/articles/2010/08/03/data-show-racial-disparity-in-crack-sentencing; Mike Levine, "Drug Use Drops for America's Youth, Rises for Over 50 Crowd," *ABC News*, September 4, 2013, http://abcnews.go.com/US/drug-drops-americas-youth-rises-50-crowd/story?id=20155714; Christopher Mascharka, "Mandatory Minimum Sentences: Exemplifying the Law of Unintended Consequences," *Fla. St. U. L. Rev.* 28 (2001): 935; M. Mauer, "The Changing Racial Dynamics of the War on Drugs," *The Sentencing Project*, April 2009; Seth Motel, "6 Facts about Marijuana," *Pew Research*, April 14, 2015, http://www.pewresearch.org/fact-tank/2015/04/14/6-facts-about-marijuana/; "New York—Race and Hispanic Origin for Selected Large Cities and Other Places: Earliest Census to 1990," *U.S. Census Bureau*, https://www.census.gov/population/www/documentation/twps0076/NYtab.pdf; "Prescription Drug Abuse Epidemic; Painkillers Driving Addiction, Overdose," *National Safety Council*, 2017, http://www.nsc.org/learn/NSC-Initiatives/Pages/prescription-drug-abuse.aspx; Natalie Shibley, "Squashing Superfly: A Harlem Minister Fights Dope," *Religions of Harlem*, April 7, 2011, http://religionsofharlem.org/2011/04/07/squashing-superfly-a-harlem-minister-fights-dope/; Ian_Simpson, "Crack Sentences Reduced, Thousands to Go Free," *Reuters*, November 1, 2011, http://www.reuters.com/article/us-cocaine-crack-newspro-idUSTRE7A04X320111101.

3. This portion of the narrative is drawn from the following sources: William Raspberry, "Vigilantes Wage War on Junkies," *New Pittsburgh Courier*, February 19, 1972, http://search.proquest.com/docview/202567991?accountid=14707; Michael J. Fortner, "Must Jesus Bear the Cross Alone?: Reverend Oberia Dempsey and His Citizen's War on Drugs," *Journal of Policy History* 27 (2015): 118–56; Malcolm W. Browne, "Pastor Organizes Militia to Combat Crime in Harlem,"

New York Times, October 21, 1967; Natalie Shibley, "Squashing Superfly: Claims Harlem Has 40,000 Dope Addicts," *Chicago Daily Defender*, October 10, 1962; "Cop Slain, 2 Attack Lawlessness in Harlem," *New York Amsterdam News*, November 14, 1970, 16; "Harlem Vigilantes Move on Pushers," *Chicago Daily Defender*, June 23, 1965, 2; "Says Harlemites Arm Themselves Because of Crime Rise in Area," *New York Amsterdam News*, October 21, 1967, 7; "Churches in Harlem Hurt by Crime," *Washington Afro-American*, January 21, 1969; Oberia Dempsey, "Dope Battle Lost: The War Goes On," *New York Amsterdam News*, November 2, 1968; Brian Mann, *How the Rockefeller Drug Laws Changed America*, North County Public Radio, January 24, 2013, http://www.northcountrypublicradio.org/news/story/21316/20130124/how-the-rockefeller-drug-laws-changed-america.

4. Bremmer, *Children and Youth in America*, 1402.

5. Fortner, *The Black Silent Majority*, 179.

6. Bremmer, *Children and Youth in America*, 1404.

7. Mann, "The Drug Laws That Changed How We Punish."

8. Fortner, "How the Black Middle Class Pushed for Harsher Drug Laws."

9. Fortner, "How the Black Middle Class Pushed for Harsher Drug Laws."

10. Fortner, "How the Black Middle Class Pushed for Harsher Drug Laws."

11. Fortner, *The Black Silent Majority*, 142.

12. Fortner, *The Black Silent Majority*, 142.

13. "New York—Race and Hispanic Origin for Selected Large Cities and Other Places."

14. Frank "An Overview of Heroin Trends in New York City."

15. Barker, "The Politics of Imprisonment" (no page numbers).

16. Fortner, *The Black Silent Majority*, 148.

17. Shibley, "Squashing Superfly."

18. Shibley, "Squashing Superfly."

19. Fortner, *The Black Silent Majority*, 148.

20. Fortner, *The Black Silent Majority*, 142.

21. Fortner, *The Black Silent Majority*, 149.

22. "Harlem Vigilantes Move on Pushers."

23. Dempsey, "Dope Battle Lost."

24. "Churches in Harlem Hurt by Crime."

25. "Claims Harlem has 40,000 Dope Addicts."

26. Beschner et al., *Life with Heroin*, 4.

27. Mann, *How the Rockefeller Drug Laws Changed America*.

28. Fortner, *The Black Silent Majority*, 179.

29. This portion of the narrative draws from the following sources: Lewis Cole, *Never Too Young to Die* (New York: Pantheon Books, 1989); F. Martin Harmon, *Charles "Lefty" Driesell: A Basketball Legend* (Macon, GA: Mercer University Press, 2014); Dan Baum, *Smoke and Mirrors: The War on Drugs and the Politics of Failure* (New York: Back Bay Books, 1997); "Triumph to Turmoil," *Baltimore Sun*, June 18, 2006, http://articles.baltimoresun.com/2006-06-18/sports/0606180233_1_bias-march-11-cocaine; Michael Weinreb, "The Day Innocence Died," *ESPN*, 2008, http://www.espn.com/espn/eticket/story?page=bias; Jonathan Easley, "The Day the Drug War Really Started," *Salon*, June 19, 2011, http://www.salon.com/2011/06/19/len_bias_cocaine_tragedy_still_affecting_us_drug_law/; Sally

Jenkins and Michael Wilbon, "The Strange Final Week of Len Bias's Life," *Washington Post*, August 19, 1986, http://articles.latimes.com/1986-08-19/sports/sp-16982_1_len-bias, and basketball-reference.com.

30. Cole, *Never Too Young to Die*, 22.
31. Weinreb, "The Day Innocence Died,"
32. Weinreb, "The Day Innocence Died,"
33. Weinreb, "The Day Innocence Died."
34. Cole, *Never Too Young to Die*, 96.
35. Jenkins and Wilbon,"The Strange Final Week of Len Bias's Life."
36. Weinreb, "The Day Innocence Died," 10.
37. Harmon, *Smoke and Mirrors*, 225.
38. Cole, *Never Too Young to Die*, 69.
39. Cole, *Never Too Young to Die*, 69.
40. Harmon, *Smoke and Mirrors*, 233.
41. Harmon, *Smoke and Mirrors*, 226.
42. Harmon, *Smoke and Mirrors*, 231.
43. Harmon, *Smoke and Mirrors*, 225
44. Harmon, *Smoke and Mirrors*, 230.
45. Harmon, *Smoke and Mirrors*, 228.
46. Forntline: PBS, "Thirty Years of America's Drug War," http://www.pbs.org/wgbh/pages/frontline/shows/drugs/cron/.
47. Harmon, *Smoke and Mirrors*, 233.
48. Harmon, *Smoke and Mirrors*, 234.
49. Harmon, *Smoke and Mirrors*, 234.
50. Harmon, *Smoke and Mirrors*, 234.
51. Harmon, *Smoke and Mirrors*, 235.
52. Harmon, *Smoke and Mirrors*, 232.
53. Harmon, *Smoke and Mirrors*, 235.
54. Harmon, *Smoke and Mirrors*, 235.
55. "History of Mandatory Minimum Penalties and Statutory Relief Mechanisms."
56. Harmon, *Smoke and Mirrors*, 228.
57. Thirty Years of America's Drug War."
58. Cole, *Never Too Young to Die*, 150.
59. This portion of the narrative draws from the following source: "Crack Cocaine Mandatory Minimum Sentences," *Families Against Mandatory Minimums*, accessed June 8, 2016, http://famm.org/projects/federal/us-congress/crack-cocaine-mandatory-minimum-sentences/.
60. Simpson, "Crack Sentences Reduced, Thousands to Go Free."
61. Levine, "Drug Use Drops for America's Youth, Rises for Over 50 Crowd."
62. This portion of the narrative draws from the following narratives: Samuel Oakford, "Portugal's Example: What Happened After It Decriminalized All Drugs, from Weed to Heroin," *Vice News*, April 19, 2016; Michael Spector, "Getting a Fix," *The New Yorker*, October 17, 2011, http://www.nydailynews.com/new-york/new-york-city-drug-overdose-deaths-73-years-article-1.2744675.
63. Oakford, "Portugal's Example."
64. Spector, "Getting a Fix."

65. Oakford, "Portugal's Example."

66. Information in this portion of the narrative is drawn from the following source: "State Medical Marijuana Laws," *National Conference of State Legislatures*, April 21, 2017, http://www.ncsl.org/research/health/state-medical-marijuana-laws.aspx.

67. Motel, "6 Facts about Marijuana."

68. "America's New Drug Policy Landscape" (Pew Research Center: U.S. Politics & Policy. April 2, 2014).

69. Jonathan P. Caulkins, Beau Kilmer, Mark A. R. Kleiman, Robert J. Mac-Coun, Greg Midgette, Pat Oglesby, Rosalie Liccardo Pacula, and Peter H. Reuter, *Considering Marijuana Legalization: Insights for Vermont and Other Jurisdictions* (Santa Monica, CA: RAND Corporation, 2015).

70. Gutwillig, "Federal vs. State Laws."

71. "Prescription Drug Abuse Epidemic; Painkillers Driving Addiction, Overdose."

72. "Prescription Drug Abuse Epidemic; Painkillers Driving Addiction, Overdose."

73. Eddie Small, "Bronx Leads Heroin Overdose Deaths Citywide," DNA Info, August 10, 2016.

CHAPTER EIGHT

1. This portion of the narrative is drawn from the following sources: C. D. Batson and J. M. Darley, "'From Jerusalem to Jericho': A Study of Situational and Dispositional Variables in Helping Behavior," *JPSP* 27 (1973): 100–108, accessed from http://faculty.babson.edu/krollag/org_site/soc_psych/darley_sa-marit.html; Kevin Cook, *Kitty Genovese: The Murder, the Bystanders, the Crime That Changed America* (New York: W.W. Norton & Company, 2014); Federal Communications Commission, "9-1-1 and E9-1-1 Services,' last updated April 14, 2017, https://www.fcc.gov/general/9-1-1-and-e9-1-1-services; Martin Gansberg, "37 Who Saw Murder Didn't Call the Police," *New York Times*, March 27, 1964, http://www.nytimes.com/1964/03/27/37-who-saw-murder-didnt-call-the-po lice.html; Intelligence Transportations Systems Joint Program Office, "Success Stories: Next-Generation 9-1-1," June 24, 2015, http://www.its.dot.gov/ng911/; Brendan Keefe and John Kelly, "911's Deadly Flaw: Lack of Location Data," *USA Today*, February 22, 2015, https://www.usatoday.com/story/news/2015/02/22/cellphone-911-lack-location-data/23570499/; Rich Kinsey, "Witnesses Later Help Solve Murder of Kitty Genovese (part 2)," *Michigan Live*, April 3, 2014, http://www.mlive.com/news/ann-arbor/index.ssf/2014/04/kitty_genovese_part_2.html; David J. Krajicek, "The Killing of Kitty Genovese: 47 Years Later, Still Holds Sway over New Yorkers," *New York Daily News*, March 13, 2011, http://www.ny dailynews.com/news/crime/killing-kitty-genovese-47-years-holds-sway-new-yorkers-article-1.123912; Robert D. McFadden, "Winston Moseley, Who Killed Kitty Genovese, Dies in Prison at 81," *New York Times*, April 4, 2016, https://www.nytimes.com/2016/04/05/nyregion/winston-moseley-81-killer-of-kitty-

genovese-dies-in-prison.html; Motorola Solutions, "4 Key Things to Know About Text to 9-1-1," last accessed July 10, 2015, https://www.motorolasolutions.com/en_us/communities/fresh-ideas.entry.html/2015/07/10/4_key_things_to_know-7EBv.html; Jim Rasenberger, "Kitty, 40 Years Later," *New York Times*, February 8, 2004, http://www.nytimes.com/2004/02/08/nyregion/kitty-40-years-later.html; GovTrack, "S. 800 (106th): Wireless Communications and Public Safety Act of 1999," last accessed June 30, 2017, https://www.govtrack.us/congress/bills/106/s800/text; Charles Skoller, *Twisted Confessions: The True Story Behind the Kitty Genovese and Barbara Kralik Murder Trials* (Austin, TX: Bridgeway Books, 2008); U.S. Department of State, "Emergencies 911 Abroad," https://travel.state.gov/content/dam/students-abroad/pdfs/911_ABROAD.pdf; "What Really Happened the Night Kitty Genovese Was Murdered?" *National Public Radio*, March 3, 2014, http://www.npr.org/2014/03/03/284002294/what-really-happened-the-night-kitty-genovese-was-murdered.

2. Skoller, *Twisted Confessions*, 10.
3. Skoller, *Twisted Confessions*, 19.
4. Skoller, *Twisted Confessions*, 21.
5. Krajicek, "The Killing of Kitty Genovese."
6. Skoller, *Twisted Confessions*, 24.
7. Rasenberger, "Kitty, 40 Years Later."
8. Cook, *Kitty Genovese.*
9. Gansberg, "37 Who Saw Murder Didn't Call the Police."
10. Gansberg, "37 Who Saw Murder Didn't Call the Police."
11. Gansberg, "37 Who Saw Murder Didn't Call the Police."
12. Gansberg, "37 Who Saw Murder Didn't Call the Police."
13. Gansberg, "37 Who Saw Murder Didn't Call the Police."
14. Cook, *Kitty Genovese*, 156–57.
15. Cook, *Kitty Genovese*, 158.
16. "What Really Happened the Night Kitty Genovese Was Murdered?"
17. Kinsey, "Witnesses Later Help Solve Murder of Kitty Genovese (part 2)."
18. This portion of the narrative is drawn from the following sources: Sarah Stone, "How Did "911" Become the Emergency Call Number in North America?," *Today I found out.com*, July 7, 2014, http://www.todayifoundout.com/index.php/2014/07/911-become-emergency-call-number-united-states/; National Emergency Number Association, "9-1-1 Origin & History, National Emergency Number Association," 2014, https://www.nena.org/?page=911overviewfacts; Random History, "40 Interesting Facts About . . . 911 Emergency Calls," August 13, 2014, http://facts.randomhistory.com/911-emergency-calls-facts.html.
19. Cook, *Kitty Genovese*, 166.
20. Cook, *Kitty Genovese*, 167.
21. Cook, *Kitty Genovese*, 167.
22. Cook, *Kitty Genovese*, 166.
23. Cook, *Kitty Genovese*, 168.
24. Cook, *Kitty Genovese*, 168.
25. Babson and Darley, "'From Jerusalem to Jericho.'"
26. Stone, "How Did "911" Become the Emergency Call Number?"
27. Federal Communications Commission, "9-1-1 and E9-1-1 Services."

28. GovTrack, "Wireless Communications and Public Safety Act of 1999."

29. Federal Communications Commission, "9-1-1 and E9-1-1 Services."

30. Motorola Solutions, "4 Key Things to Know About Text to 9-1-1."

31. Random History, "40 Interesting Facts About . . . 911 Emergency Calls,"

32. Motorola Solutions, "4 Key Things to Know About Text to 9-1-1."

33. John Kelly and Brendan Keefe, "Driver Clings to Life but the 911 Dispatcher Can't Find Her," *USA Today*, February 22, 2015, http://www.geovisible.com/911s-deadly-flaw.html.

34. Intelligence Transportations Systems Joint Program Office, "Success Stories: Next-Generation 9-1-1."

35. U.S. Department of State, "Emergencies 911 Abroad."

CHAPTER NINE

1. This portion of the narrative draws from the following sources: Austin History Center, Letter by Charles Whitman, July 31, 1966, alt.cimedia.com/statesman/specialreports/whitman/letter.pdf; Radley Balko, *Rise of the Warrior Cop: The Militarization of America's Police Forces* (New York: PublicAffairs, 2014); Jimmy Breslin, "Gates on Gates: L.A.'s Top Gun: CHIEF: My Life in the LAPD," *Los Angeles Times*, May 24, 1992, http://articles.latimes.com/1992-05-24/books/bk-265_1_daryl-gates; "Charles Whitman Copies of 1966 Letters," https://supernaught.com/products/charles-whitman-copies-of-1966-letters; Jerry Cohen and William S. Murphy, *Burn, Baby, Burn! The Los Angeles Race Riot, August 1965* (New York: E. P. Dutton, 1966); Pamela Colloff, "96 Minutes," *Texas Monthly*, August 2006, http://www.texasmonthly.com/articles/96-minutes/; Robert Conot, *Rivers of Blood, Years of Darkness* (New York: Bantam, 1967); Spencer Crump, *Black Riot in Los Angeles: The Story of the Watts Tragedy*, (Glendale, CA: Trans-Anglo Books, 1966); Steven L. Danver, *Revolts, Protests, Demonstrations, and Rebellions in American History 3* (Santa Barbara, CA: ABC-CLIO, 2010); Darrell Dawsey, "To CHP Officer Who Sparked Riots, It Was Just Another Arrest," *Los Angeles Times*, August 19, 2009, http://articles.latimes.com/1990-08-19/local/me-2790_1_chp-officer; Robert M. Fogelson, *The Los Angeles Riots of 1965* (North Stratford, NH: Ayer, 1988); Matthew Harwood, "One Nation under SWAT: How America's Police Became an Occupying Force," *Salon*, August 14, 2014, http://www.salon.com/2014/08/14/one_nation_under_swat_how_americas_police_became_an_occupying_force_partner/; Gerald Horne, *Fire This Time: The Watts Uprising and the 1960s* (Cambridge, MA: Da Capo Press, 1997); Tom Hundley, "U.S. Drafts Military in Drug Battle," *Chicago Tribune*, February 11, 1990, http://articles.chicagotribune.com/1990-02-11/news/9001120710_1_crop-substitution-cocaine-production-drug-battle/3; Martin Kidston, "'Troops to COPS' Bill Would Help Veterans Become Police Officers," *Independent Record*, April 30, 2009, http://helenair.com/news/local/troops-to-cops-bill-would-help-veterans-become-police-officers/article_c0a2c107-ff9b-5d2d-8856-986267033e93.html; Gary M. Lavergne, *A Sniper in the Tower: The Charles Whitman Murders* (Denton, TX: University of North Texas Press, 1997); John McConahay and David Sears, *The Politics of Violence: The New*

Urban Blacks and the Watts Riot (Boston: Houghton Mifflin, 1973); The McCone Commission, "144 Hours in August 1965," in *Violence in the Streets,* edited by Shalon Endleman (Chicago: Quadrangle Books, 1968); "National Security Decision Directive Number 221: Narcotics and National Security," *The White House,* April 8, 1986 (declassified on April 20, 2005), http://fas.org/irp/offdocs/nsdd/nsdd-221.pdf; John Pennella and Peter Nacci, "Department of Justice and Department of Defense Joint Technology Program: Second Anniversary Report," *National Institute of Justice, U.S. Department of Justice,* February 1997, https://www.ncjrs.gov/pdffiles/164268.pdf; "Police Stockpile Weapons, Preparing for Riots, *"New York Times,* March 2, 1968, http://jfk.hood.edu/Collection/White%20Materials/Preparation/Prep%20013.pdf; "The Rise and Fall of the Symbionese Liberation Army," *PBS.org,* February 16, 2005, http://www.pbs.org/wgbh/amex/guerrilla/peopleevents/e_kidnapping.html; Raphael Sonenshein, *Politics in Black and White: Race and Power in Los Angeles* (Princeton, NJ: Princeton University Press, 1994), accessed from https://books.google.com/books?id=JrqH8TdEmroC&pg=PA85&lpg=PA85&dq=Sam+Yorty+watts+riots&source=bl&ots=ENT09dJzTT&sig=qBlf1BexkfoUmqpAQz6CADiDUC8&hl=en&sa=X&ved=0ahUKEwisgui19cfTAhUhsVQKHasLA6M4FBDoAQgsMAI#v=onepage&q=watts%20riots&f=false; Bernard Trainor, "Role in Drug War for National Guard," *New York Times,* January 7, 1989, http://www.nytimes.com/1989/01/08/us/role-in-drug-war-for-national-guard.html; Ed Vaughn, "National Guard Involvement in the Drug War," 1992, https://groups.google.com/forum/#!topic/rec.boats/WLu-sD4Ba5w.

2. Dawsey, "To CHP Officer Who Sparked Riots."
3. McConahay and Sears, *The Politics of Violence,* 5.
4. McConahay and Sears, *The Politics of Violence,* 4.
5. The McCone Commission, "144 Hours in August 1965," 2.
6. Horne, *Fire This Time,* 56.
7. Crump, *Black Riot in Los Angeles,* 19.
8. Horne, *Fire This Time,* 26–27.
9. Horne, *Fire This Time,* 50.
10. Horne, *Fire This Time,* 58.
11. Cohen and Murphy, *Burn, Baby, Burn!,* 60.
12. Cohen and Murphy. *Burn, Baby, Burn!,* 61.
13. "Cohen and Murphy, *Burn, Baby, Burn!,* 62.
14. The McCone Commission, "144 Hours in August 1965," 321.
15. Cohen and Murphy, *Burn, Baby, Burn!,* 81.
16. Cohen and Murphy, *Burn, Baby, Burn!,* 82.
17. Horne, *Fire This Time,* 60.
18. Home, *Fire This Time,* 60.
19. Sonenshein, *Politics in Black and White,* 77.
20. Cohen and Murphy, *Burn, Baby, Burn!,* 88.
21. McConahay and Sears, *The Politics of Violence,* 6.
22. Horne, *Fire This Time,* 59.
23. Horne, *Fire This Time,* 59.
24. Horne, *Fire This Time,* 58.
25. Horne, *Fire This Time,* 66.

26. Danver, *Revolts, Protests, Demonstrations, and Rebellions in American History*, 980.

27. McConahay and Sears, *Politics of Violence*, 7.

28. The McCone Commission, "144 Hours in August 1965," 326.

29. McConahay and Sears, *Politics of Violence*, 7.

30. Horne, *Fire This Time*, 71–72.

31. Conot, *Rivers of Blood*, 349.

32. Horne, *Fire This Time*, 146.

33. Crump, *Black Riot in Los Angeles*, 71–74.

34. Crump, *Black Riot in Los Angeles*, 74.

35. Crump, *Black Riot in Los Angeles*, 90.

36. Crump, *Black Riot in Los Angeles*, 93.

37. "Charles Whitman Copies of 1966 Letters."

38. Lavergne, *A Sniper in the Tower*, 126–27.

39. Colloff, "96 Minutes."

40. Lavergne, *A Sniper in the Tower*, 134.

41. Lavergne, *A Sniper in the Tower*, 134.

42. Colloff, "96 Minutes."

43. Lavergne, *A Sniper in the Tower*, 164–65.

44. Colloff, "96 Minutes."

45. Colloff, "96 Minutes."

46. Lavergne, *A Sniper in the Tower*, 111.

47. Lavergne, *A Sniper in the Tower*, 266.

48. Balko, *Rise of the Warrior Cop*, 53.

49. Balko, *Rise of the Warrior Cop*, 61.

50. Balko, *Rise of the Warrior Cop*. 61.

51. Balko, *Rise of the Warrior Cop*, 61.

52. Balko, *Rise of the Warrior Cop*, 61.

53. Balko, *Rise of the Warrior Cop*, 62.

54. Balko, *Rise of the Warrior Cop*, 63.

55. "Police Stockpile Weapons, Preparing for Riots."

56. Balko, *Rise of the Warrior Cop*, 63.

57. Balko, *Rise of the Warrior Cop*, 63.

58. Breslin, "Gates on Gates."

59. Balko, *Rise of the Warrior Cop*, 79.

60. "The Rise and Fall of the Symbionese Liberation Army."

61. This portion of the narrative is drawn from the following sources: Balko, *Rise of the Warrior Cop*, 126–29; Miles Corwin, "The Shootout on East 54th Street: Violence: Twenty Years Ago, the LAPD and the Symbionese Liberation Army Exchanged Fire at a Home in South-Central," *Los Angeles Times*, May 18, 1994, http://articles.latimes.com/1994-05-18/local/me-59109_1_east-54th-street; Nate Blakeslee, "Tulia: Race, Cocaine, and Corruption in Small Texas Town," New York Public Affairs, 2005.

62. Balko, *Rise of the Warrior Cop*, 130.

63. Balko, *Rise of the Warrior Cop*, 131–32.

64. Harwood, "One Nation under SWAT."

65. "National Security Decision Directive Number 221."

66. Balko, *Rise of the Warrior Cop*, 51–57.

67. Balko, *Rise of the Warrior Cop*, 175.

68. Trainor, "Role in Drug War for National Guard."

69. Hundley, "U.S. Drafts Military in Drug Battle."

70. Vaughn, "National Guard Involvement in the Drug War."

71. Balko, *Rise of the Warrior Cop*, 180.

72. Balko, *Rise of the Warrior Cop*, 188.

73. Balko, *Rise of the Warrior Cop*, 189–90.

74. Balko, *Rise of the Warrior Cop*, 191.

75. Pennella and Nacci, "Department of Justice and Department of Defense Joint Technology Program: Second Anniversary Report."

76. Kidston, "'Troops to COPS' Bill Would Help Veterans Become Police Officers."

77. This portion of the narrative draws from the following source: Bob Parker, "How the North Hollywood Shootout Changed Patrol Arsenals," *Police: The Law Enforcement Magazine*, February 28, 2012, http://www.policemag.com/channel/weapons/articles/2012/02/how-the-north-hollywood-shootout-changed-patrol-rifles.aspx.

78. This portion of the narrative draws from the following sources: Kyung Lah, "How a 1997 Bank Robbery Led to Police Militarization," *CNN News*, August 18, 2014, http://outfront.blogs.cnn.com/2014/08/18/how-a-1997-bank-robbery-led-to-police-militarization/; Parker, "How the North Hollywood Shootout Changed Patrol Arsenals."

79. Balko, *Rise of the Warrior Cop*, 229.

80. Balko, *Rise of the Warrior Cop*, 253.

81. This portion of the narrative draws from the following source: Mark Schone et al., "108 Hours: Inside the Hunt for the Boston Marathon Bombers," *NBC News*, April 11, 2014, http://www.nbcnews.com/storyline/boston-bombing-anniversary/108-hours-inside-hunt-boston-marathon-bombers-n76956.

82. Balko, *Rise of the Warrior Cop*, 244–45.

83. This portion of the narrative draws from the following sources: Balko, *Rise of the Warrior Cop*, 245–47; Janelle Stecklein, "Tulia Drug Busts: 10 Years Later, Some Still Haunted by Controversial Drug Case," *Amarillo Globe News*, July 19, 2009, http://amarillo.com/stories/071909/new_news1.shtml#.VY1Vju1Viko.

84. Balko, *Rise of the Warrior Cop*, 248.

CHAPTER TEN

1. This section is drawn from the following sources: Michael A. Bellesiles and Christopher Waldrep, *Documenting American Violence* (Oxford: Oxford University Press, 2006); Steve Cichon, "Feb. 19, 1965: Pascal Calabrese, Later the First Federally Protected Witness, Robs City Hall," *Buffalo News*, February 19, 2015, http://history.buffalonews.com/2015/02/19/feb-19-1965-first-federally-protected-witness-robs-city-hall-gunpoint/; Peter Earley, *WITSEC: Inside the Federal Witness Protection Program* (New York: Bantam Dell, 2002); Nora V. Demleitner, "Witness

Protection in Criminal Cases: Anonymity, Disguise, or Other Options," *Am. J. Comp. L. Supp.* 46 (1998): 641; Raneta J. Lawson, "Lying, Cheating, and Stealing at Government Expense: Striking a Balance Between the Public Interest and the Interests of the Public in the Witness Protection Program," *Ariz. St. L. J*, 224 (1992): 1429; Risdon N. Slate, "The Federal Witness Protection Program: Its Evolution and Continuing Growing Pains," *Crim. Jus. Ethics* 16 (1997): 20; U.S. Marshals Service, "Witness Security Program," http://www.usmarshals.gov/witsec/index.html.

2. Michael Bellesiles and Christopher Waldrep, *Documenting American Violence: A Sourcebook* (New York: Oxford University Press, 2005), 300–01.

3. Earley, *WITSEC*, 47.
4. Earley, *WITSEC*, 33.
5. Earley, *WITSEC*, 1.
6. Earley, *WITSEC*, 3.
7. Earley, *WITSEC*, 44.
8. Earley, *WITSEC*, 47.
9. Cichon, "Feb. 19, 1965."
10. Earley, *WITSEC*, 48.
11. Earley, *WITSEC*, 51.
12. Earley, *WITSEC*, 51.
13. Earley, *WITSEC*, 51–52.
14. Earley, *WITSEC*, 55.
15. Earley, *WITSEC*, 56.
16. Earley, *WITSEC*, 55–56.
17. Earley, *WITSEC*, 62.
18. Earley, *WITSEC*, 60.
19. Earley, *WITSEC*, 68.
20. Earley, *WITSEC*, 69.
21. Earley, *WITSEC*, 71.
22. Earley, *WITSEC*, 77.
23. Earley, *WITSEC*, 89.
24. Earley, *WITSEC*, 91.
25. Earley, *WITSEC*, 92.
26. Lawson, "Lying, Cheating, and Stealing at Government Expense," 1430.
27. 18 U.S.C. § 3481 (1976).
28. Earley, *WITSEC*, 92.
29. Lawson, "Lying, Cheating, and Stealing at Government Expense," 1430.
30. Earley, *WITSEC*, 93.
31. Earley, *WITSEC*, 99.
32. This portion of the narrative is drawn from the following source: Office of the Inspector General, U.S. Department of Justice, "The Federal Bureau of Prisons' Witness Security Program," October 2008, https://oig.justice.gov/reports/BOP/a0901/final.pdf.
33. Slate, "The Federal Witness Protection Program," 21.
34. Slate, "The Federal Witness Protection Program."
35. This portion of the narrative is drawn from the following source: Slate, "The Federal Witness Protection Program (quoting S. Rep. No. 617, 91st Cong., 1st Sess. 59-60 [1969]).

36. See, for example, *Doe v. United States*, 231 Ct. Cl. at 716.

37. See *Garcia v. United States*, 666 F.2d 960 (5th Cir.), *cert. denied*, 459 U.S. 832 (1982).

38. Lawson, "Lying, Cheating, and Stealing at Government Expense," 1431.

39. Lawson, "Lying, Cheating, and Stealing at Government Expense," 1430.

40. Slate, "The Federal Witness Protection Program," 20–21.

41. Slate, "The Federal Witness Protection Program," 20.

CHAPTER ELEVEN

1. This section is drawn from the following sources: Rachel Carson, *Silent Spring* (New York: Houghton Mifflin, 1962); Keith Clarke and Jeffrey J. Hemphill, "The Santa Barbara Oil Spill, a Retrospective," *Yearbook of the Association of Pacific Coast Geographers*, vol. 64, edited by Darrick Danta, University of Hawaii Press, 2002, 157–62; "Compliance and Enforcement Annual Results 2011 Fiscal Year," *EPA*, 2012; E. Devaney, "The Evolution of Environmental Crimes Enforcement at the United States Environmental Protection Agency," Presentation at the Third International Conference on Environmental Enforcement, 1994; Benjamin Goad, "EPA Piles up Billions," *TheHill*, February 7, 2014, http://thehill.com/regulation/energy-environment/197839-epa-touts-billions-in-fines; Sean Hackbarth, "Full Stream Ahead: Why EPA's Water Rule Goes Too Far," *U.S. Chamber of Commerce*, May 27, 2015, https://www.uschamber.com/above-the-fold/full-stream-ahead-why-epa-s-water-rule-goes-too-far; Investor's Business Daily, "Puddles, Potholes Under Government Control—Has EPA Gone Too Far?" *Climate Change Dispatch*, May 29, 2015, http://climatechangedispatch.com/puddles-potholes-under-government-control-has-epa-gone-too-far/; Nicolas Loris, "The Many Problems of the EPA's Clean Power Plan and Climate Regulations: A Primer," *Heritage Foundation*, July 7, 2015, http://www.heritage.org/environment/report/the-many-problems-the-epas-clean-power-plan-and-climate-regulations-primer; Harvey Molotch, "Oil in Santa Barbara and Power in America," *Sociological Inquiry* 40 (January 1970): 131–44; Kim Phillips-Fein and Julian E. Zelizer, *What's Good for Business: Business and American Politics since World War II* (New York: Oxford University Press, 2012); "The Rhetoric of Ecology," *Life* 8(8) (March 6, 1970); Daniel Riesel, *Environmental Enforcement: Civil and Criminal* (New York: Law Journal Press, 1997); Lily Rothman, "Here's Why the Environmental Protection Agency Was Created," *Time*, March 22, 2017, http://time.com/4696104/environmental-protection-agency-1970-history/; "The Santa Barbara Declaration of Environmental Rights," *Edhat*, January 28, 1970, www.edhat.com/site/tidbit.cfm?nid=147298; Santa Barbara Wildlife Care Network, "Oil Contamination: Santa Barbara's 1969 Oil Spill," August 20, 2002, http://web.archive.org/web/20030727101744/http://www.silcom.com/~sbwcn/spill.shtml; Michael Scott, "After the Flames: The Story behind the 1969 Cuyahoga River Fire and Its Recovery," *Cleveland.com*, January 4, 2009, http://blog.cleveland.com/metro/2009/01/after_the_flames_the_story_beh.html; University of California, Santa Barbara, "1969 Santa Barbara Oil Spill," 2005, http://www2.bren.ucsb.edu/~dhardy/1969_Santa_Barbara_Oil_Spill/About.html.

2. Santa Barbara Wildlife Care Center, "Oil Contamination: Santa Barbara's 1969 Oil Spill."

3. Molotch, "Oil in Santa Barbara and Power in America," 132.

4. University of California, Santa Barbara, "1969 Santa Barbara Oil Spill."

5. This portion of the narrative is drawn from the following sources: American Public Works Association, "The Reversal of the Chicago River," http://www2.apwa.net/about/awards/toptencentury/chica.htm; "America's Sewage System and the Price of Optimism," *Time*, August 1, 1969, http://content.time.com/time/magazine/article/0,9171,901182,00.html; Julie Grant, "How a Burning River Helped Create the Clean Water Act," *The Allegheny Front*, April 17, 2015, http://www.alleghenyfront.org/how-a-burning-river-helped-create-the-clean-water-act/; "Killer Smog Claims Elderly Victims," *History.com*, http://www.history.com/this-day-in-history/killer-smog-claims-elderly-victims; John Roberts, "Garbage: The Black Sheep of the Family—A Brief History of Waste Regulation in the United States and Oklahoma," *Oklahoma Department of Environmental Quality*, 2015, http://www.deq.state.ok.us/lpdnew/wastehistory/wastehistory.htm.

6. "America's Sewage System and the Price of Optimism."

7. Carson, *Silent Spring*, 32.

8. Phillips-Fein and Zelizer, *What's Good for Business*, 215.

9. "The Santa Barbara Declaration of Environmental Rights."

10. "The Rhetoric of Ecology," 36.

11. Rothman, "Here's Why the Environmental Protection Agency Was Created."

12. 42 U.S.C. §§ 7401-7642.

13. 42 U.S.C. § 7413(c)(1).

14. Devaney, "The Evolution of Environmental Crimes Enforcement."

15. Riesel, *Environmental Enforcement: Civil and Criminal*.

16. 33 U.S.C. §§ 401 *et seq.*

17. 18 U.S.C. § 3063.

18. Clean Air Act § 306(b) (42 U.S.C. § 7606(b)).

19. EPA 2011 Annual Report, https://www.epa.gov/sites/production/files/2016-12/documents/fy16-enforcement-annual-results-data-graphs.pdf#page=12.

20. EPA 2011 Annual Report.

21. Hackbarth, "Full Stream Ahead: Why EPA's Water Rule Goes Too Far."

22. Hackberth, "Full Stream Ahead: Why EPA's Water Rule Goes Too Far."

23. This portion of the narrative draws from the following source: "MIE Fined, President to Serve Jail Time," *Marietta Times*, December 7, 2013, http://www.mariettatimes.com/news/local-news/2013/12/mie-fined-president-to-serve-jail-time/.

24. This portion of the narrative draws from the following source: Kate Wilke, "The 5 Most Polluted Waterways in the United States," *OutwardOn*, April 12, 2016, http://www.outwardon.com/article/the-5-most-polluted-waterways-in-the-united-states/.

25. Scott, "After the Flames."

26. Scott, "After the Flames."

27. Scott, "After the Flames."

CHAPTER TWELVE

1. This portion of the narrative is drawn from the following sources: Air Transportation Security Act of 1974, PL 93–366 (S 39), PL 93–366, August 5, 1974, 88 Stat 409; "Aviation Impact Reform: Data & Analysis—Empowering Those Who Seek Transparency, Accountability, and Reform at FAA," *FAA History*, 1985, http://aireform.com/faa-history-records/faa-history-pages/faa-history-1985/; "Aviation Security Advisory Commission," *Transportation Security Administration*, https://www.tsa.gov/for-industry/aviation-security; "New Challenges New Duties," in *The Federal Aviation Administration: A Historical Perspective, 1903–2008, FAA.gov*, https://www.faa.gov/about/history/historical_perspective/media/historical_perspective_ch4.pdf; Public Law 99-83, 99th Congress, International Security and Development Cooperation Act 1985, 22 USC 2151, August 8, 1985, http://www.gpo.gov/fdsys/pkg/STATUTE-99/pdf/STATUTE-99-Pg190.pdf; "Timeline of Security Measures," *Transportation Security Administration*, http://www.tsa.gov/video/evolution/index.html; "TSA Evolution Timeline," http://www.tsa.gov/video/evolution/TSA_evolution_timeline.pdf.

2. This portion of the narrative is drawn from the following sources: "1972: TWA Jet Explodes at Las Vegas Airport," *BBC*, http://news.bbc.co.uk/onthisday/hi/dates/stories/march/8/newsid_4268000/4268151.stm; "Bomb T.W.A. Jet; Device Is Found on United Plane," *Chicago Tribune*, March 9, 1972, http://archives.chicagotribune.com/1972/03/09/page/1/article/bomb-t-w-a-jet-device-is-found-on-united-plane; "Bombing of TWA Plane at McCarran Led to New Security," *Las Vegas Sun*, March 9, 2005, http://lasvegassun.com/news/2005/mar/09/bombing-of-twa-plane-at-mccarran-led-to-new-securi/; Bill McKenna and Ashley Semler, "Hijacking Epidemic in America: 1961–1972," *BBC*, July 11, 2013, http://www.bbc.com/news/av/magazine-23233105/hijacking-epidemic-in-america-1961-1972; Susan Nasr, "How Bomb-Sniffing Dogs Work," *HowStuffWorks*, http://science.howstuffworks.com/bomb-sniffing-dog.htm; Richard Witkin, "T.W.A. Plotters Reported Silent," *New York Times*, March 10, 1972, http://www.nytimes.com/1972/03/10/archives/twa-plotters-reported-silent-airline-asserts-no-contact-was-made.html.

3. This portion of the narrative is drawn from the following sources: Robert T. Holden, "The Contagiousness of Aircraft Hijacking," *American Journal of Sociology* 91 (1986): 874–904; "Johnson Recalls Hijacking 40 Years Later," *The Times Dispatch*, November 14, 2012, http://www.thetd.com/freepages/2012-11-14/news/story2.php; "New Challenges New Duties," in *The Federal Aviation Administration: A Historical Perspective, 1903–2008, FAA.gov*, https://www.faa.gov/about/history/historical_perspective/media/historical_perspective_ch4.pdf.

4. This portion of the narrative is drawn from the following source: "Experts Say L.A. Terminal Bomb Most Destructive Used at Airport," *Los Angeles Fire Department Archive*, August 7, 1974, http://www.lafire.com/famous_fires/1974-0806_Explosion-LAX/1974-0807_Explosion-LAX.htm.

5. This portion of the narrative is drawn from the following sources: William Smith, "Terror Aboard Flight 847," *Time*, June 24, 2001, http://content.time.com/time/magazine/article/0,9171,142099,00.html; "TWA Flight 847 Is Hijacked by Terrorists," *History.com*, http://www.history.com/this-day-in-history/twa-

flight-847-is-hijacked-by-terrorists; "Hijacking of TWA Flight 847," *Aviation On-line,* http://avstop.com/history/majorevents/flight847.html.

6. Smith, "Terror Aboard Flight 847."

7. "Hijacking of TWA Flight 847."

8. This portion of the narrative is drawn from the following sources: Jessica Ravitz and Laura Smith-Spark, "Lockerbie Bombing 25 Years on: Victims Honored on Both Sides of the Atlantic," *CNN,* December 21, 2013, http://www.cnn.com/2013/12/21/world/europe/lockerbie-anniversary/; Jesse Greenspan, "Remembering the 1988 Lockerbie Bombing," *History.com,* December 20, 2013, http://www.history.com/news/remembering-the-1988-lockerbie-bombing; "Pan Am Flight 103 Disaster: Terrorist Bombing [1988]," *Encyclopaedia Britannica,* http://www.britannica.com/event/Pan-Am-flight-103-disaster; "Pan Am Flight 103 Fast Facts," *CNN,* December 29, 2014, http://www.cnn.com/2013/09/26/world/pan-am-flight-103-fast-facts/.

CHAPTER THIRTEEN

1. This section is drawn from the following sources: The American Presidency Project, "Ronald Regan, Executive Order 12358—Presidential Commission on Drunk Driving," April 14, 1982, http://www.presidency.ucsb.edu/ws/?pid=42395; Laurie Davies, "25 Years of Saving Lives," *Driven* (Fall 2005): 9–17; Nancy Faber, "Clarence Busch, the Drunk Driver Who Inspired a Movement, Faces Prison after Another Accident," *People,* October 14, 1985, http://people.com/archive/clarence-busch-the-drunk-driver-who-inspired-a-movement-faces-prison-after-another-accident-vol-23-no-16/; James Fell and Robert Voas, "Mothers Against Drunk Driving (MADD): The First 25 Years," *Traffic Injury Prevention* 7(3) (2006): 195–212, http://www.researchgate.net/profile/Robert_Voas/publi cation/6804716_Mothers_Against_Drunk_Driving_(MADD)_the_first_25_years/links/0912f50c7339d46b82000000.pdf; Final Report, PCAA Presidential Commission on Drunk Driving, November 1983, https://babel.hathitrust.org/cgi/pt?id=mdp.39015034427750;view=1up;seq=5; Find Law, "Underage DUI: Zero Tolerance Laws," accessed June 15, 2017, http://dui.findlaw.com/dui-laws-resources/underage-dui-zero-tolerance-laws.html; Paul Galloway, "Booze and Death Travel Our Roads: Courts Look the Other Way," *Chicago Tribune,* June 30, 1985, http://articles.chicagotribune.com/1985-06-30/features/8502120240_1_drunk-cari-lightner-candy-lightner/3; Governors Highway Safety Association, "Alcohol Impaired Driving," 2016, http://www.ghsa.org/html/stateinfo/laws/impaired_laws.html; "The History of Drunk Driving Laws in the U.S.," *LifeSafer,* January 22, 2013, http://www.lifesafer.com/blog/the-history-of-drunk-driving-laws-in-the-u-s/; Knight-Ridder Newspapers, "Drunken Driver Who Killed MADD Founder's Daughter in Another Accident," *Bangor Daily News,* April 19, 1985, https://news.google.com/newspapers?id=qs48AAAAIBAJ&sjid=MS 4MAAAAIBAJ&pg=1272%2C1396656; Michael Laurence, "The Development of California Drunk-Driving Legislation," *California Department of Justice: Earl Warren Legal Institute,* 1998; Candace Lightner, "Cari's Story," *We Save Lives: Your Partners*

in Highway Safety, 2016, http://wesavelives.org/caris-story/; Candy Lightner, "The Death of Cari Lightner," *Candy Lightner: Making a Difference*, Blogspot, January 8, 2009, http://candylightnermadd.blogspot.com/2009/01/death-of-cari-lightner.html; MADD, "Administrative License Revocation Overview," June 2012, http://www.madd.org/laws/law-overview/Administrative_License_Revocation_Overview.pdf; MADD, "In Honor of . . . ," accessed July 6, 2017, http://fliphtml5.com/uxdn/xowb/basic; MADD, "Penalties for Drunk Driving Vehicular Homicide," May 2012, http://www.madd.org/laws/law-overview/Vehicular_Homicide_Overview.pdf; MADD, "Why We're Here: Millie Webb," August 15, 2016, http://www.madd.org/local-offices/tn/blog/voices-of-victims-blogs/why-were-here-millie-webb.html; National Council on Alcohol and Drug Dependence, "Driving While Impaired—Alcohol and Drugs," 2017, https://ncadd.org/learn-about-alcohol/drinking-and-driving; Gerald D. Robin, *Waging the Battle Against Drunk Driving: Issues, Countermeasures, and Effectiveness* (Westport, CT: Greenwood Press, 1991); Ivy Scarborough, *Winning Against DUI: A Handbook for Victims of Drunk Driving and Antidrunk Driving Advocates*, Humboldt, TN, 1996, http://www.ivyscarborough.com/_assets/WinningAgainstDUI.pdf; Maria Wilhelm, "A Grieving, Angry Mother Charges That Drunken Drivers Are Getting Away with Murder," *People*, June 29, 1981, http://people.com/archive/a-grieving-angry-mother-charges-that-drunken-drivers-are-getting-away-with-murder-vol-15-no-25/; Times Wire Services, "Catalyst for MADD Arrested Again: Drunk Driver Served 9 Months in Fatal 1980 Accident," *Los Angeles Times*, April 19, 1985, http://articles.latimes.com/1985-04-19/news/mn-14951_1_drunk-driver.

2. MADD, "In Honor of . . . ."
3. Wilhelm, "A Grieving, Angry Mother."
4. Wilhelm, "A Grieving, Angry Mother."
5. Robin, *Waging the Battle Against Drunk Driving*, 8.
6. Laurence, "The Development of California Drunk-Driving Legislation," 4.
7. Laurence, "The Development of California Drunk-Driving Legislation," 5.
8. Laurence, "The Development of California Drunk-Driving Legislation," 6.
9. MADD, "In Honor of . . . ."
10. Davies, "25 Years of Saving Lives," 10.
11. Robin, *Waging the Battle Against Drunk Driving*, 9.
12. Davies, "25 Years of Saving Lives," 10.
13. Robin, *Waging the Battle Against Drunk Driving*, 9.
14. Davies, "25 Years of Saving Lives," 11.
15. Laurence, "The Development of California Drunk Driving Legislation," 6.
16. Robin, *Waging the Battle Against Drunk Driving*, 9.
17. The American Presidency Project, "Ronald Regan, Executive Order 12358."
18. Final Report, PCAA Presidential Commission on Drunk Driving.
19. This portion of the narrative is drawn from the following additional sources: "Judge Refuses to Reduce Bail," *Associated Press News Archive*, May 2, 1985, http://www.apnewsarchive.com/1985/Judge-Refuses-To-Reduce-Bail/id ac5138413321321f25c50c48f45625ea; "Man Who Triggered Start of MADD Gets Four Year Term," *Lodi News-Sentinel*, October 17, 1985, https://news.google.com/newspapers?id=jxYzAAAAIBAJ&sjid=RzIHAAAAIBAJ&pg=6631%2C5923005; United Press International, "Man Who Sparked MADD Crusade Arrested

Again," *SunSentinel*, April 19, 1985, http://articles.sun-sentinel.com/1985-04-19/news/8501150202_1_candy-lightner-new-arrest-drivers.

20. Galloway, "Booze and Death Travel Our Roads."

21. Scarborough, *Winning Against DUI*, 33.

22. Fell and Voas, "Mothers Against Drunk Driving (MADD): The First 25 Years."

23. Find Law, "Underage DUI: Zero Tolerance Laws."

24. MADD, "Why We're Here: Millie Webb."

25. Fell and Voas, "Mothers Against Drunk Driving: The First 25 Years."

26. This section is drawn from the following sources: International Alliance for Responsible Drinking, "BAC and BrAC Limits," http://www.iard.org/policy-tables/bac-brac-limits/; John Lacey, Carlos Rodriguez-Iglesias, and Connie Wiliszowsk, "Legislative History of .08 Per Se Laws," *National Highway Traffic Safety Administration*, June 2001, http://ntl.bts.gov/lib/26000/26000/26071/DOT-HS-809-286.pdf.

27. Fell and Voas, "Mothers Against Drunk Driving: The First 25 Years."

28. Davies, "25 Years of Saving Lives."

29. This portion of the narrative is drawn from the following source: MADD, "Ignition-Interlocks: Every State, for Every Convicted Drunk Driver," August 2016, http://www.madd.org/laws/law-overview/Draft-Ignition_Interlocks_Overview.pdf.

30. This portion of the narrative is drawn from the following sources: David Berg, "Dram Shop Laws: Bar Owner Liability for Drunk Driving Accidents," *AllLaw.com*, 2017, http://www.alllaw.com/articles/nolo/auto-accident/dram-shop-laws.html; Deborah B. Goldberg, "Imposition of Liability on Social Hosts in Drunk Driving Cases: A Judicial Response Mandated by Principles of Common Law and Common Sense," *Marq. L. Rev.* 69 (1986): 251, http://scholarship.law.marquette.edu/mulr/vol69/iss2/6.

31. This portion of the narrative is drawn from the following source: Michael Jamison, "Over-Serving Charges in DUI Crash: Conviction Changes Landscape for Bartenders," *The Missoulian* (Missoula, MT) June 27, 2010, http://missoulian.com/news/local/over-serving-charges-in-dui-crash-conviction-changes-landscape-for/article_53bb9d52-81a8-11df-88fb-001cc4c002e0.html.

32. This portion of the narrative is drawn from the following source: Sean Dooley, "Let Kids Drink at Your House and You Could Go to Jail, Maine Couple Warns," *ABC News 20/20*, June 14, 2013, http://abcnews.go.com/US/social-host-law-kids-drink-house-jail-maine/story?id=19391725.

33. This portion of the narrative is drawn from the following sources: National Highway Traffic Safety Commission, "Fatalities Analysis Reporting System," http://www-fars.nhtsa.dot.gov/Trends/TrendsAlcohol.aspx; MADD, "History of Drunk Driving," 2017, http://www.madd.org/drunk-driving/about/history.html?referrer=http://www.madd.org/statistics/; NIH, "Alcohol-Related Traffic Deaths Fact Sheet," updated October 2013, http://report.nih.gov/nihfactsheets/ViewFactSheet.aspx?csid=24.

34. This portion of the narrative is drawn from the following sources: "Gov. Corzine Signs Law Granting Immunity to Underage Drinkers Seeking Medical Help for Others" *The Star-Ledger*, October 2, 2009, http://www.nj.com/news/

index.ssf/2009/10/gov_corzine_signs_law_granting.html; Maggie Koerth-Baker, "Driving Under the Influence, of Marijuana," *New York Times*, February 17, 2014, http://www.nytimes.com/2014/02/18/health/driving-under-the-influence-of-marijuana.html; William Bosker et al., "A Placebo-Controlled Study to Assess Standardized Field Sobriety Tests Performance during Alcohol and Cannabis Intoxication in Heavy Cannabis Users and Accuracy of Point of Collection Testing Devices for Detecting THC in Oral Fluid," *Psychopharmacology (Berl)* 223(4) (October 2012): 439–46, *Springer.com*, published online May 13, 2012, http://www.ncbi.nlm.nih.gov/pmc/articles/PMC3456923/.

35. National Council on Alcohol and Drug Dependence, "Driving While Impaired—Alcohol and Drugs."

CHAPTER FOURTEEN

1. This section is drawn from the following sources: Richard Bonnie, John Jeffries Jr., and Peter Low, *A Case Study in the Insanity Defense: The Trial of John W. Hinckley, Jr.* (Eagan, MN: Foundation Press, 2008); Randy Borum and Solomon M. Falero, "Empirical Research on the Insanity Defense and Attempted Reforms: Evidence Toward Informed Police," *Law and Human* Behavior 23(1) (1999): 375–94; Lincoln Caplan, "The Insanity Defense," *The New Yorker*, July 2, 1984, http://www.newyorker.com/magazine/1984/07/02/the-insanity-defense; Lincoln Caplan, *The Insanity Defense and the Trial of John W. Hinckley, Jr.* (New York: Laurel, 1984); Kimberly Collins, Gabe Hinkebein, and Staci Schorgl, "The John Hinckley Trial & Its Effect on the Insanity Defense," *University of Michigan–Kansas City*, http://law2.umkc.edu/faculty/projects/ftrials/hinckley/hinckleyinsanity.htm; Emanuel Francone, "Insanity Defense," *Legal Information Institute*, July 2016, https://www.law.cornell.edu/wex/insanity_defense; Paul L. Montgomery, "Lennon Murder Suspect Preparing Insanity Defense," *New York Times*, February 9, 1981, http://www.nytimes.com/1981/02/09/nyregion/lennon-murder-suspect-preparing-insanity-defense.html; "Shock and Anger Flash Through the United States," *Palm Beach Post*, March 31, 1981, A9.

2. Caplan, "The Insanity Defense," 54.

3. Caplan, "The Insanity Defense," 54–55.

4. Caplan, *The Insanity Defense and the Trial of John W. Hinckley, Jr.*, 35.

5. Caplan, "The Insanity Defense," 55.

6. Caplan, "The Insanity Defense," 55.

7. Caplan, "The Insanity Defense," 56.

8. Caplan, "The Insanity Defense," 56.

9. Caplan, "The Insanity Defense," 58.

10. Caplan, *The Insanity Defense and the Trial of John W. Hinckley, Jr.*, 11–12.

11. This portion of the narrative is drawn from the following additional sources: Michael T. Cahill and Paul H. Robinson, *Criminal Law* (New York: Aspen Publishers, 2011); "From Daniel M'Naghten to John Hinckley: A Brief History of the Insanity Defense," *PBS Frontline*, http://www.pbs.org/wgbh/pages/

frontline/shows/crime/trial/history.html; Valerie P. Hans and Dan Slater, "John Hinckley Jr. and the Insanity Defense: The Public's Verdict," *Cornell Law Faculty Publications* 334 (1983), http://scholarship.law.cornell.edu/facpub/334; Doug Linder, "The Trial of John W. Hinckley, Jr.," *University of Michigan–Kansas City*, 2008, http://law2.umkc.edu/faculty/projects/ftrials/hinckley/hinckleyaccount.html; Denise Noe, "The John Hinckley Case: Verdict and Uproar," *Crime Library*, https://archive.li/LKQrC.

12. Linder, "The Trial of John W. Hinckley, Jr."

13. Noe, *The John Hinckley Case: Verdict and Uproar.*

14. Collins, Hinkebein, and Schorgl, "The John Hinckley Trial & Its Effect On the Insanity Defense."

15. Collins, Hinkebein, and Schorgl, "The John Hinckley Trial & Its Effect On the Insanity Defense."

16. "From Daniel M'Naghten to John Hinckley: A Brief History of the Insanity Defense."

17. "From Daniel M'Naghten to John Hinckley: A Brief History of the Insanity Defense."

18. See also *United States v. Brawner*, 471 F.2d 969 (1972).

19. Chapter IV: Offenders with Mental Disease or Defect—Insanity Defense Reform Act of 1984—Amends the Federal criminal code to make it an affirmative defense to a Federal prosecution that at the time of the commission of the acts constituting the offense, the defendant, as a result of mental disease or defect, was unable to appreciate the nature and quality or the wrongfulness of his acts. Authorizes a special verdict of "not guilty only by reason of insanity" for any criminal defendant who raises the issue of insanity by notice as currently provided. . . . Establishes a new civil commitment procedure for persons found not guilty only by reason of insanity. Prohibits expert witness opinion in court as to the mental state of the defendant when the crime was committed. Summary as of 10/10/1984, filed in H. Rept 98-1159.

20. Francone, "Insanity Defense."

21. 18 U.S. Code §17—Insanity Defense, http://www.law.cornell.edu/uscode/text/18/17.

22. See Morris B. Hoffman and Stephen J. Morse, "The Insanity Defense Goes Back on Trial," *New York Times*, July 30, 2006, http://www.nytimes.com/2006/07/30/opinion/30hoffman.html.

23. See Mental Health America, "Position Statement 57: In Support of the Insanity Defense," June 8 2014, http://www.mentalhealthamerica.net/positions/insanity-defense.

24. Mental Health America, "Position Statement 57: In Support of the Insanity Defense."

25. This portion of the chapter draws on the following sources: Robinson and Williams, *Mapping American Criminal Law: Variations Across the 50 States*, chapter 17 (insanity) (2018); Lisa Callahan, Connie Mayer, and Henry J. Steadman, "Insanity Defense Reform in the United States—Post-Hinckley," *Mental and Physical Disability Law Reporter* 11(1) (1987): 54–59; Paul H. Robinson, *Criminal Law: Case Studies & Controversies* (New York: Little, Brown & Co. Law & Business, 2012, 590).

26. For a summary of the insanity defense formulations across the states, see Robinson and Williams, *Mapping American Criminal Law*, chapter 17 (insanity).

27. See American Bar Association, Standing Committee on Association Standards for Criminal Justice, Report to the House of Delegates, August 1984, Standard 7-6.1, Commentary p. 327.

28. See, for example, *State v. Strasburg*, 1110 P.1020 (Wash. 1910) and *State v. Korell*, 690 P.2d 992 (Mont. 1984).

29. This portion of the narrative is drawn from the following sources: Timothy Roche, "Andrea Yates: More to the Story," *Time*, March 18, 2002, http://content. time.com/time/nation/article/0,8599,218445,00.html; Treatment Advocacy Center, "How Many Individuals with Serious Mental Illness Are in Jails and Prisons?" November 2014, http://www.treatmentadvocacycenter.org/storage/doc uments/backgrounders/how%20many%20individuals%20with%20serious%20 mental%20illness%20are%20in%20jails%20and%20prisons%20final.pdf.

30. The case was retried for different reasons in 2006.

31. See Michael D. Thompson, "In 'Cures' Bill, Keys to Further Criminal Justice Improvements," *The Council of State Governments*, December 22, 2016, https:// csgjusticecenter.org/jc/enactment-of-cures-bill-exemplifies-keys-to-advancing-criminal-justice-improvements/.

32. Borum and Falero, "Empirical Research on the Insanity Defense and Attempted Reforms," 387.

33. Callahan, Mayer, and Steadman, "Insanity Defense Reform in the United States—Post-Hinckley," 59.

34. Borum and Falero, "Empirical Research on the Insanity Defense and Attempted Reforms," 381.

35. Bonnie, Jeffries, and Low, *A Case Study in the Insanity Defense*, 127–28 (quoting *The Moral Basis of the Insanity Defense*, 69 A.B.A.J. 194, 196–97 [1983]).

36. Bonnie, Jeffries, and Low, *A Case Study in the Insanity Defense*, 133.

37. This portion of the narrative is largely drawn from the following sources: Borum and Falero, "Empirical Research on the Insanity Defense and Attempted Reforms"; Cahill and Robinson, *Criminal Law*.

38. See, for example, Paul H. Robinson, *Intuitions of Justice and Utility of Desert* (New York: Oxford University Press, 2013).

CHAPTER FIFTEEN

1. This portion of the narrative is drawn from the following sources: "1991 Inside Edition Report (Robert John Bardo Murder Trial)," November 16, 2015, https://www.youtube.com/watch?v=HuCvI263ZVA; Andrea Ford, "Suspect on Tape Tells of Actress's Last Words." *Los Angeles Times*, October 2, 1991, http:// articles.latimes.com/1991-10-22/local/me-114_1_bardo; "Interview with Brad Siberling, Annika Einhorn," *CNN Larry King Live—Transcripts*, September 30, 2002, http://transcripts.cnn.com/TRANSCRIPTS/0209/30/lkl.00.html; Mike Tharp, "In the Mind of a Stalker," *U.S. News & World Report* 112(6) (1992): 28; Frank Wilkins, "The Death of Rebecca Schaeffer," *Reel Reviews*, http://www.franksreel reviews.com/shorttakes/shaeffer/shaeffer.htm.

2. Tharp, "In the Mind of a Stalker."

3. Wilkins, "The Death of Rebecca Schaeffer."

4. Tharp, "In the Mind of a Stalker."

5. Orit Kamir, *Every Breath You Take: Stalking Narratives & the Law* (Ann Arbor: University of Michigan Press, 2001), 176.

6. "Interview with Brad Siberling, Annika Einhorn."

7. Ford, "Suspect on Tape Tells of Actress's Last Words."

8. Tharp, "In the Mind of a Stalker."

9. Wilkins, "The Death of Rebecca Schaeffer."

10. Ford, "Suspect on Tape Tells of Actress's Last Words."

11. For example, one article titled "California Law Targets Obsessed Fans, Vengeful Lovers," published in *State Legislatures* in October of 1991, explains, "The usual stalking victim, however, is a woman terrorized by a vengeful ex-husband or boyfriend. . . . Although men are stalked less often than women, male victims of harassment received some notoriety in the movie 'Fatal Attraction'"; Kamir, *Every Breath You Take*, 180.

12. This portion of the narrative is drawn from the following source: Jerry Greene, "Dolphins' Baty and Wife Living on Time Borrowed from Stalker, *Baltimore Sun*, October 20, 1991, http://articles.baltimoresun.com/1991-10-20/sports/1991293162_1_stagner-baty-kathleen.

13. Cal. Pen. Code §646.9.

14. Kamir, *Every Breath You Take*, 180.

15. See National Institute of Justice, "Domestic Violence, Stalking, and Anti-Stalking Legislation: An Annual Report to Congress under the Violence Against Women Act," April 1996.

16. Cal. Pen. Code §646.9 (West 1990).

17. C. E Abeyta-Price, Laura Curliss, and Kathleen McAnaney, "From Imprudence to Crime: Anti-Stalking Laws," *Notre Dame Law Review* 68(4) (1993).

CHAPTER SIXTEEN

1. This account is drawn from the following sources: Joel Brinkley, "House Study Finds Officers at Fault in Beirut Bombing," *New York Times*, December 20, 1983, http://www.nytimes.com/1983/12/20/world/house-study-finds-officers-at-fault-in-beirut-bombing.html; Stephen J. DiGregoria, "If We Don't Bring Them to Court, the Terrorists Will Have Won: Reinvigorating the Anti-Terrorist Act and General Jurisdiction in a Post-Daimler Era," *Brooklyn Law Review* 82(1) (2016), accessed from http://brooklynworks.brooklaw.edu/cgi/viewcontent.cgi?article=1527&context=blr; William E. Farrell, "A Marine Is Killed and Three Others Are Hurt in Beirut," *New York Times*, October 1, 1982, http://www.nytimes.com/1982/10/01/world/a-marine-is-killed-and-three-others-are-hurt-in-beirut.html; Dante B. Fascell, "Combatting International Terrorism: The Role of Congress," *Ga. J. Int'l. & Compl. L.* 16 (1986): 655; The Federal Bureau of Investigation, "A Brief History of the FBI," https://www.fbi.gov/about-us/history/brief-history; The Federal Bureau of Investigation, "Crime and Terror

Have Gone Global. And So Have We," https://www.fbi.gov/about-us/inter national_operations; Timothy J. Geraghty, *Peacekeepers at War: Beirut 1983—The Marine Commander Tells His Story* (Lincoln, NE: Potomac Books, 2009); Eric M. Hammel, *The Root: The Marines in Beirut, August 1982–February 1984* (Pacifica, CA: Pacifica Military History, 1993); Jane Mayer, "Ronald Reagan's Benghazi," *The New Yorker*, May 5, 2014, http://www.newyorker.com/news/daily-comment/ronald-reagans-benghazi; Naval History Blog: U.S. Naval Institute, "Beirut Marine Barracks Bombing: October 23, 1983," October 23, 2013, http://www.navalhistory.org/2013/10/23/beirut-marine-barracks-bombing-october-23-1983; Glenn E. Robinson, "Palestine Liberation Organization," *Oxford Islamic Studies Online*, http://www.oxfordislamicstudies.com/article/opr/t236/e0618.

2. Hammel, *The Root*, 292.

3. Hammel, *The Root*, 293.

4. Hammel, *The Root*, 295.

5. Robinson, "Palestinian Liberation Organization."

6. *See* Associated Press, "Casualties of Mideast Wars," *Los Angeles Times*, March 8, 1991, http://articles.latimes.com/1991-03-08/news/mn-2592_1_civil-war.

7. Robinson, "Palestinian Liberation Organization."

8. Naval History Blog: U.S. Naval Institute, "Beirut Marine Barracks Bombing: October 23, 1983."

9. *See* Micah Zenko, "When Reagan Cut and Run," *Foreign Policy*, February 7, 2014, http://foreignpolicy.com/2014/02/07/when-reagan-cut-and-run/.

10. Brinkley, "House Study Finds Officers at Fault in Beirut Bombing."

11. Brinkley, "House Study Finds Officers at Fault in Beirut Bombing."

12. Brinkley, "House Study Finds Officers at Fault in Beirut Bombing."

13. Brinkley, "House Study Finds Officers at Fault in Beirut Bombing."

14. Brinkley, "House Study Finds Officers at Fault in Beirut Bombing."

15. *See* University of Texas Archives, "Message to the Congress Transmitting Proposed Legislation to Combat International Terrorism," April 26, 1984, http://www.reagan.utexas.edu/archives/speeches/1984/42684a.htm.

16. Fascell, "Combating International Terrorism," 657.

17. This portion of the narrative is drawn from the following sources: Library of Congress, "Summaries for the Comprehensive Crime Control Act of 1984," June 28, 1984, https://www.govtrack.us/congress/bills/98/hr5963/summary; The Federal Bureau of Investigation, "Timeline of Terrorist Events from April 18, 1983 to September 20, 1984," https://www.fbi.gov/stats-services/publications/terror/image/page28.jpg/view; The Federal Bureau of Investigation, "Testimony of Louis J. Freeh, Director, FBI, "Terrorism to the United States," https://www2.fbi.gov/congress/congress01/freeh051001.htm.

18. See *United States v. Yunis*, 681 F. Supp. 896, 903 (D.D.C. 1988).

19. See Kenneth Noble, "Lebanese Suspect in '85 Hijacking Arrested by the F.B.I. While at Sea," *New York Times*, September 18, 1987, http://www.nytimes.com/1987/09/18/world/lebanese-suspect-in-85-hijacking-arrested-by-the-fbi-while-at-sea.html.

20. This portion of the narrative is drawn from the following source: Philip Shenon, "U.S. Will Not Seek Death in Hijacking," *New York Times*, January 19,

1987, http://www.nytimes.com/1987/01/19/world/us-will-not-seek-death-in-hijacking.html.

21. See The Federal Bureau of Investigation, "Statement before the Subcommittee on Border, Maritime, and Global Counterterrorism House Homeland Security Committee Washington DC," October 4, 2007, https://www.fbi.gov/news/testimony/the-fbi2019s-legal-attache-program.

22. This portion of the narrative is drawn from the following sources: James Benjamin and Richard Zabel, "In Pursuit of Justice: Prosecuting Terrorism in the Federal Courts," *Human Rights First*, May 2008; Deborah Feyerick and Phil Hirschkorn, "Jury Convicts Four on All Charges in Embassy Bombings," *CNN*, May 29, 2001, http://www.cnn.com/2001/LAW/05/29/embassy.bombings.verdict/; Benjamin Weiser, "In Embassy Bombings Case, Putting a Face on Men Confronting Death," *New York Times*, April 22, 2001, http://www.nytimes.com/2001/04/22/nyregion/in-embassy-bombings-case-putting-a-face-on-men-confronting-death.html.

23. This portion of the narrative is drawn from the following additional sources: Bootie Cosgrove-Mather, "Shoe Bomber Pleads Guilty," *CBS*, October 2, 2002, http://www.cbsnews.com/news/shoe-bomber-pleads-guilty/; Pam Belluck, "Threats and Responses: The Bomb Plot; Unrepentant Shoe Bomber Is Given a Life Sentence for Trying to Blow Up Jet," *New York Times*, January 31, 2003, http://www.nytimes.com/2003/01/31/us/threats-responses-bomb-plot-unrepentant-shoe-bomber-given-life-sentence-for.html; "Richard Reid Fast Facts," *CNN Library*, December 23, 2014, http://www.cnn.com/2013/03/25/us/richard-reid-fast-facts/.

24. See Peter Zimite, "US-POLITICS: FBI Seeks Expansion of Foreign Operations," *Inter Press Service*, August 5, 1996, http://www.ipsnews.net/1996/08/us-politics-fbi-seeks-expansion-of-foreign-operations/.

CHAPTER SEVENTEEN

1. This section is drawn from the following sources: Caroline Bettinger-Lopez et al., "Domestic Violence in the United States: A Preliminary Report prepared for Rashida Manjoo," *U.N. Special Rapporteur on Violence Against Women*, April 18, 2011; Cynthia Daniels et al., *Feminists Negotiate the State: The Politics of Domestic Violence* (Lanham, MD: University Press of America, 1997); Janet E. Findlater and Dawn van Hoek, "Prosecutors and Domestic Violence: Local Leadership Makes a Difference," *Mich. B. J.* 73 (1994): 908; Linda Mills, *Violent Partners: A Breakthrough Plan for Ending the Cycle of Abuse* (New York: Basic Books, 2009), 27, accessed from https://books.google.com/books?id=-0zma38wndwC&pg=PA24&dq=tracey+thurman+testifying+before+Congress&hl=en&sa=X&ei=wnFkVfm3DaW_sQSymYOgDQ&ved=0CCQQ6AEwAQ#v=onepage&q=tracey%20thurman%20testifying%20before%20Congress&f=false; National Center on Domestic and Sexual Violence, "The History of the Violence Against Women Act," September 2009, http://www.ncdsv.org/images/OVW_HistoryVAWA.pdf; Office on Violence Against Women, "2012 Biennial Report to Congress on the Effectiveness of Grant

Programs Under the Violence Against Women Act," http://www.justice.gov/ sites/default/files/ovw/legacy/2014/03/13/2012-biennial-report-to-congress. pdf; Elizabeth Schneider, *Battered Women and Feminist Lawmaking* (New Haven, CT: Yale University Press, 2002); Suzanne Tomkins, "20 Years of Domestic Violence Advocacy, Collaborations, and Challenges: Reflections of a Clinical Law Professor," *Buffalo Journal of Gender, Law and Social Policy* 22 (2013–2014): 1.

2. Jeannie Park, Susan Schindehette, and Maria Speidel, "Thousands of Women, Fearing for Their Lives, Hear a Scary Echo in Tracey Thurman's Cry for Help," *People*, October 9, 1989, http://www.people.com/people/archive/ article/0,,20121378,00.html.

3. This subsection is drawn from the following sources: 101st Congress, Second Session on Legislation to Reduce the Growing Problem of Violent Crime Against Women, "Women and Violence: Hearings before the Committee on the Judiciary United States Senate," August 29 and December 11, 1990; Nancy Blodgett, "Violence in the Home," *ABA Journal*, May 1, 1987, 66–69, accessed from https://books.google.com/books?id=pjK22zjVqm0C&pg=PA66&lpg=PA 66&dq=Violence+in+the+Home+blodgett+aba&source=bl&ots=vIWZLr75Hh& sig=7itkNhPaBCqlwbOlLD7ggTPNA40&hl=en&sa=X&ved=0ahUKEwjM6eDPt ffUAhUEbj4KHSOiCK0Q6AEIIjAA#v=onepage&q=Violence%20in%20the%20 Home%20blodgett%20aba&f=false; Brennan, Patricia, "A Cry for Help," *Washington Post*, October 1, 1989, https://www.washingtonpost.com/archive/lifestyle/ tv/1989/10/01/a-cry-for-help/b6d4472a-51a1-4c09-9781-f1805a20cd5f/?utm_ term=.7ed5eb45d27e; Rachel Gottlieb and Bryan Mortytko, "Thurman's Ex-wife Seeks Court Order to Keep Him Away," *Courant Correspondent*, April 4, 1996, http://articles.courant.com/1996-04-04/news/9604040303_1_probation-court-papers-superior-court; Park, Schindehette, and Speidel, "Thousands of Women, Fearing for Their Lives"; Dick Polman, "Maimed Wife Strikes Blow for Justice," *Chicago Tribune*, May 18, 1986, http://articles.chicagotribune.com/1986-05-18/ features/8602040789_1_tracey-thurman-city-police-officers-sin/2; *Thurman v. City of Torrington*, 595 F. Supp. 1521, 1524–1526 (D. Conn. 1984).

4. Park, Schindehette, and Speidel, "Thousands of Women, Fearing for Their Lives."

5. Park, Schindehette, and Speidel, "Thousands of Women, Fearing for Their Lives."

6. Park, Schindehette, and Speidel, "Thousands of Women, Fearing for Their Lives."

7. Polman, "Maimed Wife Strikes Blow for Justice."

8. Polman, "Maimed Wife Strikes Blow for Justice."

9. 101st Congress, "Women and Violence," 99.

10. Polman, "Maimed Wife Strikes Blow for Justice."

11. Polman, "Maimed Wife Strikes Blow for Justice."

12. Polman, "Maimed Wife Strikes Blow for Justice."

13. Park, Schindehette, and Speidel, "Thousands of Women, Fearing for Their Lives."

14. Polman, "Maimed Wife Strikes Blow for Justice."

15. Polman, "Maimed Wife Strikes Blow for Justice."

16. This subsection is drawn from the following additional sources: Roslyn Muraskin, ed., *Women and Justice: Development of International Policy* (New York: Taylor and Francis, 1999), 111, accessed from https://books.google.com/books?id=JGOOAgAAQBAJ&pg=PA110&lpg=PA110&dq=buck+Thurman&source=bl&ots=LzQRdjrR1c&sig=LeQ0Vz-02u71MXB2tY_hzrA_rMY&hl=en&sa=X&ved=0ahUKEwjXy7LnkL3SAhULs1QKHRQyD6s4ChDoAQhQMAk#v=onepage&q=copyright&f=false.

17. See 42 U.S.C. § 1983.

18. Polman, "Maimed Wife Strikes Blow for Justice."

19. Polman, "Maimed Wife Strikes Blow for Justice."

20. This subsection is drawn from the following additional sources: Jay Bobbin, "'Tracey Thurman Story' a True Tragedy," *Orlando Sentinel*, October 2, 1989, http://articles.orlandosentinel.com/1989-10-02/lifestyle/8910013571_1_tracey-thurman-story-met-tracey-buck; Jerry Buck, "Nancy McKeon Takes 'Tracey Thurman' Seriously," *Pittsburgh Press*, October 1, 1989, https://news.google.com/newspapers?nid=1144&dat=19891001&id=y8obAAAAIBAJ&sjid=jWMEAAAAIBAJ&pg=3530,1068750&hl=e; "Equal Rights Amendment," *West's Encyclopedia of American Law*, 2005, http://www.encyclopedia.com/topic/Equal_Rights_Amendment.aspx; Deborah Geigis, "Tracey Thurman Motuzick," *Hartford Courant*, March 15, 1992, http://articles.courant.com/1992-03-15/news/0000204455_1_domestic-violence-domestic-abuse-family-violence-prevention; Indiana Coalition Against Domestic Violence, "History of Battered Women's Movement," September 1999, http://www.icadvinc.org/what-is-domestic-violence/history-of-battered-womens-movement/; Chris Parker, "No Nonsense, No Bitterness, Better Policing," *Republican-American*, June 8, 2008.

21. Buck, "Nancy McKeon Takes 'Tracey Thurman' Seriously."

22. Parker, " No Nonsense, No Bitterness, Better Policing."

23. Blodgett, *Violence in the Home*, 67.

24. Felony and Misdemeanor Master Crime List, Massachusetts Sentencing Commission, December 2015, http://www.mass.gov/courts/docs/admin/sentcomm/mastercrimelist.pdf.

25. This subsection is drawn from the following source: Donna Cassata, "Former Wife of Ex-SEC Official Tells Her Story in Book: Once a Battered Wife Hiding in Closet, She Now Reaches Out to Others," *Los Angeles Times*, May 15, 1988, http://articles.latimes.com/1988-05-15/news/mn-4183_1_charlotte-fedders.

26. This subsection is drawn from the following source: Tamar Lewin, "What Penalty for a Killing in Passion?" *New York Times*, October 21, 1994, http://www.nytimes.com/1994/10/21/us/what-penalty-for-a-killing-in-passion.html.

27. This subsection is drawn from the following sources: "Domestic Violence Milestones," *Hartford Courant*, November 1, 2009, http://articles.courant.com/2009-11-01/news/dv-timeline.art_1_abusive-spouses-violence-law-violence-against-women-act; Sandra Norman-Eady, "Summary of Family Violence," *OLR Research Report*, October 2, 2009, https://www.cga.ct.gov/2009/rpt/2009-R-0349.htm.

28. National Center on Domestic and Sexual Violence, "The History of the Violence Against Women Act."

29. National Center on Domestic and Sexual Violence, "The History of the Violence Against Women Act."

30. By the National Institute of Justice.

31. See Victim Protection, Support and Assistance, "Stop Violence Against Women," 2003, http://hrlibrary.umn.edu/svaw/domestic/explore/6support. htm.

32. See Tony Dokoupil, "Why Domestic Violence Prevention Programs Don't Work," *NBC News*, May 23, 2014, http://www.nbcnews.com/storyline/nfl-controversy/why-domestic-violence-prevention-programs-dont-work-n217346.

33. This subsection draws from the following source: Sarah Mervosh, "Witnesses Say Deanna Suffered Years of Abuse before Slaying," *Dallas Morning News*, May 20, 2015, https://www.dallasnews.com/news/crime/2015/05/20/witnesses-say-deanna-cook-suffered-years-of-abuse-before-slaying.

34. Mervosh, "Witnesses Say Deanna Suffered Years of Abuse before Slaying."

35. Shannan Catalano, "Intimate Partner Violence, 1993–2010," *Bureau of Justice Statistics*, November 27, 2012, NCJ 239203, https://www.bjs.gov/index. cfm?ty=pbdetail&iid=4536.

36. Lawrence Greenfeld et al., "Violence by Intimates: Analysis of Data on Crimes by Current or Former Spouses, Boyfriends, and Girlfriends," *Bureau of Justice Statistics, U.S. Department of Justice*, March 1998, https://www. google.com/url?sa=t&rct=j&q=&esrc=s&source=web&cd=2&ved=0ahUKE wjD7dyZr7nVAhUG_IMKHZTVCDgQFggsMAE&url=https%3A%2F%2Fbjs. gov%2Fcontent%2Fpub%2Fpdf%2Fvi.pdf&usg=AFQjCNE_GiCJDl28eJKhJK p7e9jXxI2Usg; Catalano, "Intimate Partner Violence, 1993–2010."

37. See Alanna Vagianos, "30 Shocking Domestic Violence Statistics That Remind Us It's an Epidemic," *Huffington Post*, February 13, 2015, http://www. huffingtonpost.com/2014/10/23/domestic-violence-statistics_n_5959776.html.

38. Mills, *Violent Partners*, 34, https://www.google.com/url?sa=t&rct=j&q =&esrc=s&source=web&cd=2&ved=0ahUKEwjD7dyZr7nVAhUG_IMKHZTVC DgQFggsMAE&url=https%3A%2F%2Fbjs.gov%2Fcontent%2Fpub%2Fpdf%2Fvi. pdf&usg=AFQjCNE_GiCJDl28eJKhJKp7e9jXxI2Usg.

39. Mills, Linda, *Violent Partners: A Breakthrough Plan for Ending the Cycle of Abuse* (New York: Basic Books 2009): 27, accessed from https://books.google. com/books?id=-0zma38wndwC&pg=PA24&dq=tracey+thurman+testifying+ before+Congress&hl=en&sa=X&ei=wnFkVfm3DaW_sQSymYOgDQ&ved=0C CQQ6AEwAQ#v=onepage&q=tracey%20thurman%20testifying%20before%20 Congress&f=false.

CHAPTER EIGHTEEN

1. This section is drawn from the following sources: Lisa Calandro et al., "Evolution of DNA Evidence for Crime Solving—A Judicial and Legislative History," *Forensic Magazine*, January 6, 2005, http://www.forensicmag.com/articles/2005/01/evolution-dna-evidence-crime-solving-judicial-and-legislative-history; Ian Cobain, "Killer Breakthrough—the Day DNA Evidence First Nailed

a Murderer," *The Guardian*, June 7, 2016, https://www.theguardian.com/uk-news/2016/jun/07/killer-dna-evidence-genetic-profiling-criminal-investigation; Simon A. Cole, *Suspect Identities: A History of Fingerprinting and Criminal Identification*, Cambridge, MA: Harvard University Press, 2002; Michelle Hibbert, "DNA Databanks: Law Enforcement's Greatest Surveillance Tool?" *Wake Forest Law Review* 34 (1999): 767–825; Nathan James, "DNA Testing in Criminal Justice: Background, Current Law, Grants, and Issues," *Congressional Research Service*, December 6, 2012, accessed from https://fas.org/sgp/crs/misc/R41800.pdf; Robert Mackay, "'Genetic Fingerprinting' Is Hailed in Britain, *Schenectady Gazette*, March 27, 1987, https://news.google.com/newspapers?nid=1917&dat=19870327&id=cQwhAAAAIBAJ&sjid=hHIFAAAAIBAJ&pg=845,6297032&hl=en; National Institute of Justice, "The Future of Forensic DNA Testing: Predictions of the Research and Development Working Group," November 2000, https://www.ncjrs.gov/pdffiles1/nij/183697.pdf; Joseph Wambaugh, *The Blooding: The Dramatic True Story of the First Murder Case Solved by DNA* (New York: William Morrow and Company, 1989).

2. Wambaugh, *The Blooding*, 31.

3. Wambaugh, *The Blooding*, 28.

4. Wambaugh, *The Blooding*, 41.

5. Wambaugh, *The Blooding*, 48.

6. Wambaugh, *The Blooding*, 96.

7. Wambaugh, *The Blooding*, 109.

8. Wambaugh, *The Blooding*, 119.

9. Wambaugh, *The Blooding*, 121.

10. Wambaugh, *The Blooding*, 124.

11. Wambaugh, *The Blooding*, 126.

12. Wambaugh, *The Blooding*, 130–31.

13. Wambaugh, *The Blooding*, 134.

14. Wambaugh, *The Blooding*, 147.

15. This portion of the narrative is drawn from the following source: "Discovering DNA Fingerprinting," October 11, 2012, http://m.geschool.net/532368/blog/post/discovering-dna-fingerprinting.

16. "Discovering DNA Fingerprinting."

17. Wambaugh, *The Blooding*, 151.

18. Cobain, "Killer Breakthrough—The Day DNA Evidence First Nailed a Murderer."

19. Wambaugh, *The Blooding*, 154.

20. Wambaugh, *The Blooding*, 159–63.

21. Wambaugh, *The Blooding*, 164.

22. Wambaugh, *The Blooding*, 168.

23. Wambaugh, *The Blooding*, 170.

24. Wambaugh, *The Blooding*, 169.

25. Wambaugh, *The Blooding*, 170–71.

26. Wambaugh, *The Blooding*, 214.

27. Wambaugh, *The Blooding*, 224.

28. Wambaugh, *The Blooding*, 234.

29. Wambaugh, *The Blooding*, 234.

30. Wambaugh, *The Blooding*, 179.

31. Wambaugh, *The Blooding*, 235.

32. Wambaugh, *The Blooding*, 237.

33. Wambaugh, *The Blooding*, 201.

34. Wambaugh, *The Blooding*, 245.

35. Wambaugh, *The Blooding*, 282.

36. This portion of the narrative is drawn from the following sources: Terri Sundquist, "How a Magazine Ad Helped Convict a Rapist," *Promega Connections*, July 11, 2014, http://www.promegaconnections.com/how-a-magazine-ad-helped-convict-a-rapist/; Jeff Weiner, "Should Serial Rapist Go Free? No Decision after Hearing," *Orlando Sentinel*, October 10, 2014, http://www.orlandosentinel.com/news/breaking-news/os-tommie-lee-andrews-rapist-hearing-20141010-story.html.

37. This portion of the narrative is drawn from the following sources: Peter Baker, "In Grim Distinction, Va. Killer Is First to Die Based on DNA Testing," *Washington Post*, April 28, 1994, http://www.washingtonpost.com/wp-dyn/content/article/2010/03/16/AR2010031602456.html; "The DNA 'Wars' Are Over," *PBS Frontline*, June 21, 2017, http://www.pbs.org/wgbh/pages/frontline/shows/case/revolution/wars.html.

38. "The DNA 'Wars' Are Over."

39. Baker, "In Grim Distinction, Va. Killer Is First to Die Based on DNA Testing."

40. This portion of the narrative is drawn from the following source: The Innocence Project, "David Vasquez," http://www.innocenceproject.org/cases-false-imprisonment/david-vasquez.

41. *See Jones v. Murray*, 962 F.2d 302 (4th Cir. 1992), accessed from https://casetext.com/case/jones-v-murray-2.

42. This portion of the narrative is drawn from the following sources: Council for Responsible Genetics, "Forensic DNA Collection: A Citizen's Guide to Your Rights Scenarios and Responses," http://www.councilforresponsiblegenetics.org/pageDocuments/I6W7Q3D7RM.pdf; National Conference of State Legislators, "DNA Arrestee Laws," 2013, http://www.ncsl.org/Documents/cj/ArresteeDNALaws.pdf.

43. Cole, *Suspect Identities*, 294–95

44. This section is drawn from the following source: Mark Johnson, "DNA Data Bank Gives Police New Weapon," *Deseret News*, February 18, 1998, http://www.deseretnews.com/article/613916/DNA-data-bank-gives-police-new-weapon.html?pg=all.

45. Johnson, "DNA Data Bank Gives Police New Weapon."

46. Johnson, "DNA Data Bank Gives Police New Weapon."

47. See Office of the Inspector General, "Combined DNA Index System Operational and Laboratory Vulnerabilities: Statement on Compliance with Laws and Regulations," May 2006, https://oig.justice.gov/reports/FBI/a0632/laws.htm.

48. Johnson, "DNA Data Bank Gives Police New Weapon."

49. See The Federal Bureau of Investigation, "CODIS—NDIS Statistics: Measuring Success," 2017, https://www.fbi.gov/services/laboratory/biometric-analysis/codis/ndis-statistics.

50. See Peter Finn, "Revolution Underway in Use of DNA Profiles," *Washington Post*, November 16, 1997, http://www.washingtonpost.com/wp-srv/local/daily/march99/dna97.htm.

51. This portion of the narrative is drawn from the following sources: Cole, *Suspect Identities*, 296–300; "The Evidence: O.J. Simpson," *CNN*, http://www.cnn.com/US/OJ/evidence/index.html; William Thompson, "Proving the Case: The Science of DNA: DNA Evidence in the O.J. Simpson Trial," *U.Colo. L. Rev.* 67 (1996): 827.

52. See "'DNA Analysis Backlog Elimination Act of 2000," Public Law 106–546—Dec. 19, 2000, December 19, 2000, accessed from http://www.gpo.gov/fdsys/pkg/PLAW-106publ546/pdf/PLAW-106publ546.pdf.

53. See *United States v. Kincade*, 379 F.3d 813 (9th Cir. Cal. 2004).

54. This portion of the narrative is drawn from the following source: *Maryland v. King*, 133 S. Ct. 1 (U.S. 2012).

55. Eyewitness misidentification is the greatest contributing factor to wrongful convictions, proven by DNA testing playing a role in more than 70 percent of convictions overturned through DNA testing nationwide. The Innocence Project, "Eyewitness Identification," https://www.innocenceproject.org/causes/eyewitness-misidentification/.

56. See The Innocence Project, https://www.innocenceproject.org/.

57. See The Innocence Project, "DNA Exonerations in the United States," 2017, https://www.innocenceproject.org/dna-exonerations-in-the-united-states/.

58. See The Innocence Project, "Frequently Asked Questions," http://www.innocenceproject.org/faqs.

59. "Innocence Project 25th Anniversary," Innocence Project: 2017, https://www.innocenceproject.org/contact/#faq_section.

60. Cole, *Suspect Identities*, 297.

61. This portion of the narrative is drawn from the following sources: Andrew Blankstein and Jean Guccione, "'CSI' Effect or Just Flimsy Evidence," *Los Angeles Times*, March 18, 2005, http://articles.latimes.com/2005/mar/18/local/me-jurors18; Arun Rath, "Is the 'CSI Effect' Influencing Courtrooms?" *NPR News*, February 5, 2011, http://www.npr.org/2011/02/06/133497696/is-the-csi-effect-influencing-courtrooms; Donald Shelton, "The 'CSI Effect': Does It Really Exist?" *National Institute of Justice Journal* 259 (March 17, 2008), http://www.nij.gov/journals/259/pages/csi-effect.aspx.

CHAPTER NINETEEN

1. This portion of the narrative is drawn from the following sources: James Austin et al., "Three Strikes and You're Out: The Implementation and Impact of Strike Laws," 2, accessed from https://www.ncjrs.gov/pdffiles1/nij/grants/181297.pdf; "Before Being Sentenced to Die, Killer Disrupts a Courtroom," *New York Times*, September 27, 1996, http://www.nytimes.com/1996/09/27/us/before-being-sentenced-to-die-killer-disrupts-a-courtroom.html; Joe Domanick, *Cruel Justice: Three Strikes and the Politics of Crime in America's Golden State*

(Berkeley: University of California Press, 2005); Kevin Fagan, "20 Years after Polly Klaas Killing, Attitudes Change," *SF Gate*, October 2, 2013, http://www. sfgate.com/crime/article/20-years-after-Polly-Klaas-killing-attitudes-4861976. php#photo-5264786; Daniel Katkin, "Habitual Offender Laws: A Reconsideration," *Buff. L. Rev.* 21 (1971–1972): 99–120, accessed from http://heinonline.org/HOL/ Page?handle=hein.journals/buflr21&div=13&g_sent=1&collection=journals#118; David R. Lacourse, "Three Strikes, You're Out: A Review," *Washington Policy Center*, January 1, 1997, http://www.washingtonpolicy.org/publications/detail/ three-strikes-youre-out-a-review; Kenneth W. Mentor, "Habitual Offender Laws: Three Strikes and You're Out," *Kenneth W. Mentor*, accessed from http://kenmen tor.com/papers/3strikes.htm; Jay Robert Nash, *The Great Pictorial History of World Crime, Volume 2* (Lanham, MD: Rowman & Littlefield, 2009); *People v. Davis*, 46 Cal. 4th 539, 208 P. 3D78, 94 Cal. Rptr. 3D 322, accessed from http://scocal.stanford. edu/opinion/people-v-davis-33016; "A Primer: Three Strikes—The Impact After More Than a Decade," *Legislative Analyst's Office: California's Nonpartisan Fiscal and Policy Advisor*, http://www.lao.ca.gov/2005/3_strikes/3_strikes_102005.htm; "Richard Allen Davis," *Murdapedia.com*, http://murderpedia.org/male.D/d/ davis-richard-allen.htm; Jeffrey Toobin, "The Man Who Kept Going Free," *The New Yorker*, March 7, 1994, 38–53, accessed from http://archives.newyorker. com/?i=1994-03-07#folio=038; Michael Vitiello, "Three Strikes Laws: A Real or Imagined Deterrent to Crime?" *Human Rights Magazine* 29 (2002), accessed from https://www.americanbar.org/publications/human_rights_magazine_home/ human_rights_vol29_2002/spring2002/hr_spring02_vitiello.html.

2. *See* "Resistance and Revolution: The Anti-Vietnam War Movement at the University of Michigan," 1965, 1972, "Induction Statistics," accessed from http:// michiganintheworld.history.lsa.umich.edu/antivietnamwar/exhibits/show/ex hibit/item/73.

3. Toobin, "The Man Who Kept Going Free," 40.
4. Toobin, "The Man Who Kept Going Free," 47.
5. *People v. Davis*, 3.
6. *People v. Davis*, 5.
7. *People v. Davis*, 5.
8. *People v. Davis*, 7.
9. *People v. Davis*, 10.
10. Domanick, *Cruel Justice*, 105.
11. Domanick, *Cruel Justice*, 117.
12. *People v. Davis*, 11.
13. *People v. Davis*, 12.
14. *People v. Davis*, 13.
15. *People v. Davis*, 14.

16. This portion of the narrative is drawn from the following sources: Elizabeth Gleick, "America's Child," *People*, December 20, 1993, http://www.people.com/ people/archive/article/0,,20107057,00.html; "Polly's Story," Polly Klaas Foundation, http://www.pollyklaas.org/about/pollys-story.html; "The Sad Case of Polly Klaas," *Newsweek*, December 12, 1993, http://www.newsweek.com/sad-case-polly-klaas-190468; "With Song and Poetry, a Farewell to a Kidnapped Girl Named Polly," *New York Times*, December 11, 1993.

17. "Before Being Sentenced to Die, Killer Disrupts a Courtroom."

18. Domanick, *Cruel Justice*, 154.

19. *People v. Davis*, 28.

20. This portion of the narrative is drawn from the following source: Jennifer Edwards Walsh, *Three Strikes Law: Historical Guides for Controversial Issues in America* (Westport, CT: Greenwood Press, 2007).

21. *People v. Davis*, 25.

22. See "Crime and Punishment: Three Strikes and You're Out," *Retro Report*, December 2, 2013, https://www.retroreport.org/video/transcript/crime-and-punishment-three-strikes-and-youre-out/.

23. Domanick, *Cruel Justice*, 37–41.

24. Domanick, *Cruel Justice*, 86.

25. Lacourse, "Three Strikes, You're Out: A Review."

26. Domanick, *Cruel Justice*, 129–32.

27. Domanick, *Cruel Justice*, 78–79.

28. Domanick, *Cruel Justice*, 134.

29. See *People v. Sup. Ct. (Romero)*, 13 Cal.4th 497 (Cal. 1996).

30. See *People v. Williams*, 17 Cal.4th 148 (Cal. 1998).

31. See Matt Taibbi, "Cruel and Unusual Punishment: The Shame of Three Strikes Law," *Rolling Stone*, March 27, 2013, http://www.rollingstone.com/politics/news/cruel-and-unusual-punishment-the-shame-of-three-strikes-laws-20130327.

32. Domanick, *Cruel Justice*, 4.

33. Austin et al., "Three Strikes and You're Out!," 2.

34. Arkansas, Colorado, Connecticut, California, Delaware, Florida, Georgia, Illinois, Indiana, Montana, Maryland, New Jersey, S. Carolina, Tennessee, Louisiana, New Jersey, New Mexico, N. Carolina, Pennsylvania, Texas, Virginia, Washington, West Virginia, and Wisconsin.

35. This portion of the narrative is drawn from the following source, "Massachusetts Cop Was Killed by Career Criminal Out on Parole Despite Three Life Sentences," *Fox News*, December 29, 2010, http://www.foxnews.com/us/2010/12/29/mass-cop-killed-career-criminal-parole-despite-life-sentences.html.

36. This portion of the narrative is drawn from the following sources: Robinson and Williams, *Mapping American Criminal Law: Variations Across the 50 States*, ch. 2 (2018); Hayley H. Fritchie, "*State v. Noble*: Mandatory Minimum Madness in Louisiana," *Tul L. Rev.* 89 (2015): 933; Cole Heyer, "Comparing the Strike Zone of 'Three Strikes and You're Out' Laws for California and Georgia,' *Suffolk University Law Review* 45 (1994): 1230–31; Michael Vitiello, "Three Strikes: Can We Return to Rationality," *J. Crim. L & Crimonology* 87 (1997): 395, accessed from http://scholarly-commons.law.northwestern.edu/cgi/viewcontent.cgi?article=6910&context=jclc.

37. This portion of the narrative is drawn from the following sources: Matthew Albright, "Delaware to Scale Back Three-Strikes Laws," *Journal Sentinel Online*, June 21, 2016, http://www.jsonline.com/story/news/politics/2016/06/21/three-strikes-laws/86188402/; "Bill Clinton Regrets 'Three Strikes,'" *BBC News*, July 16, 2015, http://www.bbc.com/news/world-us-canada-33545971; Riley Yates, "Few Criminals Sentenced under Three-Strikes Law," *The Morning Call*,

January 4, 2014, http://articles.mcall.com/2014-01-04/news/mc-pa-three-strikes-law-rarely-used-20140104_1_three-strikes-law-life-terms-michael-tony-lane.

38. See Naomi Goodro, "Career Criminals Targeted: The Verdict Is In, California's Three Strike Laws Are Effective." *Golden Gate University Law Review* (2007): 468.

39. See *Ewing v. California*, 538 U.S. 11, 14 (2003).

40. Vitiello, "Three Strikes Law: A Real or Imagined Deterrent to Crime?"

41. See Robinson, Paul. "Life Without Parole Under Modern Theories of Punishment," in *Life Without Parole: America's New Death Penalty?* (New York: New York University Press, 2012), 140.

42. Robinson, *Distributive Principles of Criminal Law* (Oxford: Oxford University Press, 2008), chaps. 3, 4, and 8.

43. This portion of the narrative is drawn from the following sources: California Innocence Project, "Three Strikes of Injustice," https://californiainnocenceproject.org/2012/10/three-strikes-of-injustice/; Kelly Duane de la Vega and Katie Galloway, "'Three Strikes of Injustice,'" *New York Times*, October 8, 2012, http://www.nytimes.com/2012/10/09/opinion/three strikes-of-injustice.html.

44. Duane de la Vega and Galloway, "'Three Strikes of Injustice.'"

45. This portion of the narrative is drawn from the following sources: "Bill Clinton Regrets 'Three Strikes' bill"; Fritchie, "*State v. Noble*"; Sake Knafo and Ryan J. Reilly, "These 32 People Are Spending Their Lives in Prison for Nonviolent Crimes," *Huffington Post*, November 13, 2013, http://www.huffingtonpost.com/2013/11/13/life-without-parole_n_4256789.html; Robinson, "Life Without Parole Under Modern Theories of Punishment," 145–46.

46. This portion of the narrative is drawn from the following sources: "California Proposition 36, Changes in the "Three Strikes" Law (2012)" *Ballotpedia*, http://ballotpedia.org/California_Proposition_36,_Changes_in_the_%22Three_Strikes%22_Law_(2012); Brooke Donald, "Stanford Law's Three Strikes Project Works for Fair Implementation of New Statute," *Stanford News*, June 6, 2013, http://news.stanford.edu/news/2013/june/three-strikes-project-060613.html; Aaron Sankin, "California Prop 36, Measure Reforming State's Three Strikes Law, Approved by Wide Majority of Voters," *Huffington Post*, November 7, 2012, http://www.huffingtonpost.com/2012/11/07/california-prop-36_n_2089179.html.

CHAPTER TWENTY

1. "9/11: Timeline of Events," *History.com*, http://www.history.com/topics/9-11-timeline.

2. Philip Sheewell, "9/11: Voices from the Doomed Planes," *The Telegraph*, London. September 11, 2011.

3. Remarks by the President George W. Bush after Two Planes Crash into World Trade Center, http://georgewbush-whitehouse.archives.gov/news/releases/2001/09/20010911.html.

4. Amateur footage of South Tower Collapse, https://www.youtube.com/watch?v=gJbGm7GE1tA.

5. Jason Burke, *The 9/11 Wars*, New York: Penguin Books, 2012, 27.

6. Lawrence Wright, *The Looming Tower* (New York: Alfred Knopf, 2007), 133.

7. Burke, *The 9/11 Wars*, 21.

8. Wright, *The Looming Tower*, 4

9. Kevin McCoy, "9/11 Death and Injury Total Still Rising," *USA Today*, September 9, 2015.

10. See Institute for the Analysis of Global Studies, "How Much Did the September 11 Terrorist Attack Cost America?," http://www.iags.org/costof911.html.

11. See Neil deGrasse Tyson, "The Horror, the Horror," *Hayden Planetarium*, http://www.haydenplanetarium.org/tyson/read/2001/09/12/the-horror-the-horror.

12. Burke, *The 9/11 Wars*, 27.

13. Burke, *The 9/11 Wars*, 28.

14. Burke, *The 9/11 Wars*, 44–45.

15. The 9/11 Commission, "The 9/11 Commission Report," 1–2.

16. See Public Law 107–40, 107th Congress, September 18, 2001, accessed from http://www.gpo.gov/fdsys/pkg/PLAW-107publ40/pdf/PLAW-107publ40.pdf.

17. Stephen J. Schulhofen, "Rethinking the Patriot Act: Keeping America Safe and Free," *The Century Foundation*, 27–29, https://tcf.org/assets/downloads/20050615-rethinking-the-patriot-act.pdf.

18. "Timeline: How the Anthrax Terror Unfolded," *NPR.org*, February 15, 2011, http://www.npr.org/2011/02/15/93170200/timeline-how-the-anthrax-terror-unfolded; Ronald Standler, "Brief History of the USA PATRIOT Act of 2001," September 27, 2008, http://www.rbs0.com/patriot.pdf, p. 5.

19. "Address to a Joint Session of Congress and the American People," President George W. Bush, United States Capitol, September 20, 2001, http://georgewbush-whitehouse.archives.gov/news/releases/2001/09/20010920-8.html.

20. Howard Ball, *The USA Patriot Act: A Reference Handbook*, (ABC-CLIO), August 2004, 47.

21. See Stephen J. Schulhofen, "Rethinking the Patriot Act: Keeping America Safe and Free," 3.

22. See "President Bush Signs Anti-Terrorism Bill," *PBS NewsHour*, October 26, 2011, http://www.pbs.org/newshour/updates/terrorism-july-dec01-bush_terrorismbill/.

23. See "About: Transportation Security Administration," *TSA.gov*, last accessed June 26, 2017, http://www.tsa.gov/about-tsa.

24. This portion of the narrative draws from the following sources: Susan N. Herman, *Taking Liberties: The War on Terror and the Erosion of American Democracy* (Oxford: Oxford University Press, 2014); "Patriot Act Gag Power Is Unconstitutional, ACLU Tells Court," *American Civil Liberties Union*, August 15, 2007, https://www.aclu.org/news/patriot-act-gag-power-unconstitutional-aclu-tells-court.

25. This portion of the narrative is drawn from the following sources: Lorenzo Franceschi-Bicchierai, "The 10 Biggest Revelations from Edward Snowden's Leaks," *Mashable.com*, June 5, 2014, http://mashable.com/2014/06/05/edward-snowden-revelations/; Glenn Greenwald, "NSA Collecting Phone Records of

Millions of Verizon Customers Daily," *The Guardian,* June 6, 2013, http://www.theguardian.com/world/2013/jun/06/nsa-phone-records-verizon-court-order; "Goodbye Section 215: Patriot Act Key Surveillance Provisions Expire," *RT.com,* June 1, 2015, http://rt.com/usa/263745-patriot-act-expiration-surveilance/.

26. Of both parties.

27. See James Ball, "NSA Monitored Calls of 35 World Leaders after US Official Handed Over Contacts," *The Guardian,* October 25, 2013, http://www.theguardian.com/world/2013/oct/24/nsa-surveillance-world-leaders-calls.

CHAPTER TWENTY-ONE

1. This section draws from the following sources: Ken Brown and Ianthe J. Dugan, "Arthur Andersen's Fall from Grace Is a Sad Tale of Greed and Miscues," *Wall Street Journal,* June 7, 2002, https://www.wsj.com/articles/SB1023409436545200; William R. Bufkins and Bala G. Dharan, "Red Flags in Enron's Reporting of Revenues and Key Financial Measures," *Social Science Research Network* (2010): 97–100; Adam Clymer, "Enron's Many Strands: Public Opinion; Worries About Pensions Show a Rise," *New York Times,* February 22, 2002, http://www.nytimes.com/2002/02/22/business/enron-s-many-strands-public-opinion-worries-about-pensions-show-a-rise.html; Clemense Ehoff and Dahli Gray, "Sarbanes-Oxley and Dodd Frank: Then There Was Fraud," *Journal of Business and Economics Research* 13(1) (2015); Kurt Eichenwald and Diana B. Henriques, "Enron's Many Strands: The Company Unravels; Enron Buffed Image to a Shine Even as It Rotted From Within," *New York Times,* February 10, 2002, http://www.nytimes.com/2002/02/10/business/enron-s-many-strands-company-unravels-enron-buffed-image-shine-even-it-rotted.html; Kurt Eichenwald and Richard A. Oppel, "Enron's Collapse: The Overview; Arthur Andersen Fires an Executive for Enron Orders," *New York Times,* January 16, 2002, http://www.nytimes.com/2002/01/16/business/enron-s-collapse-overview-arthur-andersen-fires-executive-for-enron-orders.html; Jamie L. Gustafson, "Cracking Down on White-Collar Crime: An Analysis of the Recent Trend of Severe Sentences for Corporate Officers," *Suffolk U. L. Rev.* 40 (2007): 685; Julia Hanna, "The Costs and Benefits of Sarbanes-Oxley," *Forbes.com,* March 10, 2014, http://www.forbes.com/sites/hbsworkingknowledge/2014/03/10/the-costs-and-benefits-of-sarbanes-oxley/; Paul M. Healy and Krishna G. Palepu, "The Fall of Enron," *Journal of Economic Perspectives* 17(2) (2003): 3–26; Michael Holt, "The Sarbanes-Oxley Act," *Elsevier Online,* October 12, 2005; Jane Hughes and Scott MacDonald, *Separating Fools from Their Money: A History of American Financial Scandals* (Piscataway, NJ: Transaction Publishers, 2011); Daniel Luedtke, "Progression in the Age of Recession: Restorative Justice and White-Collar Crime in Post-Recession America," *Brooklyn Journal of Corporate, Financial & Commercial Law* 9(1) (2014): 311–14.

2. Hughes and MacDonald, *Separating Fools from Their Money,* 194.

3. Bufkins and Dharan, "Red Flags in Enron's Reporting of Revenues and Key Financial Measures."

4. Hughes and MacDonald, *Separating Fools from Their Money,* 195.

5. Hughes and MacDonald, *Separating Fools from Their Money*, 195.

6. *See* "Enron Scandal: The Fall of a Wall Street Darling," *Investopedia*, December 2, 2016, http://www.investopedia.com/updates/enron-scandal-summary/#ixzz4coKIjDv6.

7. Healy and Palepu, "The Fall of Enron," 10.

8. Eichenwald and Henriques, "Enron's Many Strands."

9. Eichenwald and Henriques, "Enron's Many Strands."

10. Eichenwald and Henriques, "Enron's Many Strands."

11. Hughes and MacDonald, *Separating Fools from Their Money*, 197.

12. Larry Siegel, "Criminology: Theories, Patterns and Typologies" (Belmont, CA: Thompson Wadsworth, 2007), 403.

13. Clymer, "Enron's Many Strands: Public Opinion."

14. Eichenwald and Oppel, "Enron's Collapse: The Overview."

15. Hughes and MacDonald, *Separating Fools from Their Money*, 207.

16. Hughes and MacDonald, *Separating Fools from Their Money*, 208.

17. This portion of the narrative is drawn from the following source: Michael Weisskopf, "Enron's Democrat Pals," *Time*, August 17, 2002, http://content.time.com/time/business/article/0,8599,338580,00.html.

18. See William Powers, "Report of the Special Investigation Committee," *Special Investigative Committee, Enron Board of Directors*, February 1, 2002, i.cnn.net/cnn/2002/LAW/02/02/enron.report/powers.report.pdf.

19. This portion of the narrative is drawn from the following additional source: Kurt Eichenwald, *Conspiracy of Fools: A True Story* (New York: Broadway Books, 2005), 664–75.

20. Hughes and MacDonald, *Separating Fools from Their Money*, 198.

21. Though the decision is later overturned by the U.S. Supreme Court, which rules that the jury was given instructions that were too broad.

22. Hughes and MacDonald, *Separating Fools from Their Money*, 222.

23. This portion of the narrative is drawn from the following source: Frank O. Bowman, "The Sarbanes-Oxley Act and What Came After," *Federal Sentencing Reporter* 15(4) (2002–2003): 231–33.

24. This portion of the narrative draws from the following sources: "Go Directly to Jail: White Collar Sentencing After the Sarbanes-Oxley Act," *Harv. L. Rev.* 122 (2008–2009): 1728–49; Public Law 107-24, July 30, 2002, accessed from https://www.sec.gov/about/laws/soa2002.pdf.

25. Ultimately, criminal provisions are put in place by members of the Senate Judiciary Committee and their counterparts from the House, while the civil regulatory provisions are taken from the Senate and House banking committees. The chairmen of the latter, Senator Paul Sarbanes (D-MD) and Representative Michael Oxley (R-OH), are the bill's namesakes.

26. See, for example, Public Company Accounting Oversight Board Homepage, accessed June 27, 2017, http://pcaobus.org/Pages/default.aspx.

27. Hughes and MacDonald, *Separating Fools from Their Money*, 243.

28. This portion of the narrative draws on the following sources: Leonce Bargeron et al., "Sarbanes-Oxley and Corporate Risk-Taking," *Journal of Accounting and Economics* 49 (2010): 34–52; Curtis Verschoor, "Has SOX Been Successful?" *AccountingWEB*, September 5, 2012, http://www.accountingweb.com/practice/

practice-excellence/has-sox-been-successful. Note that the Jumpstart Our Business Startups Act (JOBS Act), passed in 2012, eliminates the SOX Section 404 requirements for entities that meet the definition of an emerging growth company.

29. Hughes and MacDonald, *Separating Fools from Their Money*, 237.

30. Hughes and MacDonald, *Separating Fools from Their Money*, 237.

31. Hughes and MacDonald, *Separating Fools from Their Money*, 237.

32. Hanna, "The Costs and Benefits of Sarbanes-Oxley."

33. Incorrigible Section 404 of SOX for smaller companies, or public companies with less than a $75 million market capitalization.

34. Hughes and MacDonald, *Separating Fools from Their Money*, 238.

35. "Breaking the Cycle of Fraud: What Senior Financial Executives Should Do," *Financial Executives Research Foundation* 2015, www.financialexecutives.org/ferf/download/2015%20Final/2015-001.pdf.

36. This portion of the narrative draws from the following sources: Yuqi Gu and Ling Zhang, "The Impact of the Sarbanes-Oxley Act on Corporate Innovation," *Journal of Economics and Business* 90 (2017): 17–30; Daniel Richman, "Federal White Collar Sentencing in the United States: A Work in Progress," *Law and Contemporary Problems* 76 (2013): 53–73, available at https://scholarship.law.duke.edu/lcp/vol76/iss1/4.

37. Bargeron et al., "Sarbanes-Oxley and Corporate Risk-Taking," 35.

38. See Francine McKenna, "The State of Sarbanes-Oxley Compliance According to Protiviti," *Forbes.com*, June 21, 2011, http://www.forbes.com/sites/francinemckenna/2011/06/21/the-state-of-sarbanes-oxley-compliance-according-to-protiviti/. Please note that this report reflects figures from, or prior to, a 2011 survey.

39. "Fine-Tuning SOX Costs, Hours, and Controls: Assessing the Results of Protiviti's 2017 Sabanes-Oxley Compliance Survey," *Protiviti*, 2017, 4, 5, and 13.

40. Holt, "The Sarbanes-Oxley Act," 56.

41. Hughes and MacDonald, *Separating Fools from Their Money*, 244.

42. Luedtke, "Progression in the Age of Recession."

43. This portion of the narrative draws from the following sources: Miriam A. Cherry, "Whistling in the Dark? Corporate Fraud, Whistleblowers, and the Implications of the Sarbanes-Oxley Act for Employment Law," *Washington Law Review* 79 (2004): 1029; Jisoo Kim, "Confessions of a Whistleblower: The Need to Reform the Whistleblower Provision of the Sarbanes-Oxley Act," *J. Marshall L. Rev.* 43 (2009): 241.

44. Hughes and MacDonald, *Separating Fools from Their Money*, 248.

CONCLUSION

1. Lauren Benet Stephenson, "The History of the New York City Garment District," Zady Inc., 2015, https://zady.com/features/the-history-of-the-new-york-city-garment-district.

2. The narrative is drawn from the following sources: Sarah Stone, "How Did '911' Become the Emergency Call Number in North America? Today I Found

Out," July 7, 2014, http://www.todayifoundout.com/index.php/2014/07/911-become-emergency-call-number-united-states/; "9-1-1 Origins and History, National Emergency Number Association," 2013, https://www.nena.org/?page=911overviewfacts; "40 Interesting Facts About . . . 911 Emergency Calls," *Random History.com*, August 7, 2014.

3. James C. Fell and Robert B. Voas, "Mothers Against Drunk Driving (MADD): The First 25 Years," Pacific Institute for Research and Evaluation, March 2006.

4. Gerald D. Robin, *Waging the Battle Against Drunk Driving: Issues, Countermeasures, and Effectiveness* (Westport, CT: Greenwood Press, 1991), 9.

5. Robin, *Waging the Battle*, 9.

6. Andrew H. Malcolm, "Drinking and Driving: New Year's Eve 1981, *New York Times*, December 31, 1982.

7. "History of Battered Women's Movement," Indiana Coalition Against Domestic Violence, March 25, 2009, http://www.icadvinc.org/what-is-domestic-violence/history-of-battered-womens-movement/.

8. Cathy Young, "Domestic Violence: An In-Depth Analysis," Independent Women's Forum, September 30, 2005, http://www.iwf.org/news/2432535/Domestic-Violence:-An-In-Depth-Analysis.

9. There is a limit to the tightness of the categories. A single case may have bits of more than one category, for example.

10. K. C. Clarke and Jeffrey J. Hemphill, "The Santa Barbara Oil Spill, a Retrospective," *Yearbook of the Association of Pacific Coast Geographers*, edited by Darrick Danta, University of Hawai'i Press, vol. 64, 2002, 157–62.

11. Of course, in some instances, two cases are so close in time and intertwined in their effect that it would be hard to see only one of them as the trigger case. This occurs, for example, with the trigger for the development of SWAT teams in the militarization of police: the 1965 riots in Watts and the case of sniper Charles Whitman, who used superior firepower to keep police at bay. Another example, already discussed above, is the Santa Barbara oil spill, which was followed only six months later by the Cuyahoga River fire.

12. Ivy Scarborough, "Winning Against DUI: A Handbook for Victims of Drunk Driving and Antidrunk Driving Advocates," 33, 1996, http://www.ivyscarborough.com/_assets/WinningAgainstDUI.pdf.

13. For a more detailed discussion of the crime du jour dynamic, see Paul H Robinson, "The Rise and Fall and Resurrection of American Criminal Codes, *University of Louisville Law Review* 53 (2015): 173, 181; Paul H Robinson and Michael T Cahill, "The Accelerating Degradation of American Criminal Codes" *Hastings Law Journal* 56 (2005): 633; Paul H. Robinson, Thomas Gaeta, Matthew Majarian, Megan Schultz, and Douglas M. Weck, "The Modern Irrationalities of American Criminal Codes: An Empirical Study of Offense Grading," *J. Crim. L. & Criminology* 100 (2010): 709, 718–28.

14. See Paul H Robinson, *Criminal Law Case Studies*, fifth ed. (Minneapolis, MN: West Academic, 2015), 38–46.

15. Seth Ferranti, "The Ugly Truth of Mandatory Drug Sentencing," *The Fix.com*, May 22, 2012, https://www.thefix.com/content/Getting-life-selling-drugs-seth-ferranti7314?page=all.

16. EPA, *Environmental Crimes Case Bulletin* 3, December 2013.

17. "Puddles, Potholes under Government Control—Has EPA Gone Too Far?" *Investor's Business Daily,* May 29, 2015, *Climate Change Dispatch.com,* http://climatechangedispatch.com/puddles-potholes-under-government-control-has-epa-gone-too-far/.

18. "Puddles, Potholes under Government Control."

19. "Puddles, Potholes under Government Control."

20. Ryan Maye Handy, "El Paso County Weakened Some Fire Codes after Destructive Black Forest Fire," *The Gazette,* October 30, 2015.

21. Paul H. Robinson and Michael T. Cahill, *Law Without Justice: Why Criminal Law Doesn't Give People What They Deserve* (Oxford: Oxford University Press, 2006), 187–92.

22. "9-1-1 Origins and History."

23. Some people have expressed concern about the creation of DNA databases as raising potential privacy problems.

Index

Trans World Airlines. *See* TWA
trigger crimes, xii, 14, 309–20
TSA (Transportation Security
Administration), 290–91
Tulsa, Oklahoma, 49–50
TWA (Trans World Airlines), 173–74;
bomb threat, 173–75; hijacking of
Flight 847, 177–78

Unabomber, 74–75
Uniform Drinking Age Act, 190–91
United Airlines Flight 175. *See* planes
hijacked on 9/11
United Airlines Flight 93. *See* planes
hijacked on 9/11
United States v. Brawner (insanity
defense), 202–3
"Uniting and Strengthening America
by Providing Appropriate Tools
Required to Intercept and Obstruct
Terrorism" Act. *See* Patriot Act
University of Texas, Austin, 136–39
U.S. Department of Justice's
Organized Crime and Racketeering
Section, 149
U.S. Marshals Service, 153, 156

Valachi, Joe (RICO), 85–89
Valley of the Drums, 168
Vandermeer, Walter (Dempsey), 97,
111
VAWA. *See* Violence Against Women
Act
Violence Against Women Act
(VAWA), 261, 233

War on Drugs, 110, 144, 179, 318
War on Terror, 279–92
Washington Post, 74, 104, 208, 302
Watkins, Harold Cole (sulfanilamide),
50
Watkins, Sharon (Enron), 296
Watts, California, 128–40; cost of riots,
135; deaths in riots, 135; Human
Relations Commission (HRC),
130–33; reputation of police in, 128;
riots, 128–35, 140

Watts riots, timeline of: beginning of
unrest, 127–29; curfew imposed, 134;
fires begin, 131; Human Relations
Commission (HRC) meeting, 130–
31; National Guard, 132–33; rioting
ends, 135; snipers are shooting
firemen, 132; unrest becomes a riot,
131; unrest grows rapidly, 129–30
weak enforcement of laws, 24–25
white collar crime, increased legal
penalties, 303
Whitman, Charles, 136–40; brain
tumor, 140; number of victims, 140
Wickersham Commission, 46
Winecoff Hotel (hotel fire), 12
wiretaps, 150, 289, 291
WITSEC (Witness Security Program),
156, 320. *See also* witness protection
program
witness protection program, 150;
becoming law, 156; before formal
organization, 154–55; building
new identities, 155; criticisms of,
158; failures of, 158–59; need for
permanent protection for witnesses,
153; new identity for Calabrese,
153; Organized Crime Control
Act, 156; protection of Calabrese,
151–53; protection of families, 151,
153–54, 155–56; size of, 158; success
of, 159; Title V, 156; U.S. Marshals
Service, 156; WITSEC (Witness
Security Program), 156–58
Witness Security Program. *See*
WITSEC
Woman in Red (Dillinger). *See* Sage,
Anna
worker safety, 13–14
World Trade Center, 279–82
WorldCom, 298–99, 302, 307

Yates, Andrea, 206–7
Yorty, Sam (mayor of Los Angeles),
131–32
Yunis, Fawaz (hijacker), 218

Zero tolerance laws, 191

About the Authors

Paul H. Robinson, JD, is Colin S. Diver Professor of Law at the University of Pennsylvania Law School. Robinson is one of the world's leading criminal law scholars, a prolific writer and lecturer, and has published articles in virtually all of the top law reviews. A former federal prosecutor and counsel for the U.S. Senate Subcommittee on Criminal Laws and Procedures, he was the lone dissenter when the U.S. Sentencing Commission promulgated the current federal sentencing guidelines. He is the author or editor of fourteen books, including *Intuitions of Justice and the Utility of Desert* (2013), *Distributive Principles of Criminal Law* (2008), and *Law Without Justice: Why Criminal Law Doesn't Give People What They Deserve* (2005).

Sarah Robinson works as a writer and researcher and has coauthored several books. She obtained a master's in counseling while serving as a sergeant in the U.S. Army. History, people, and the evolution of thought are her main points of interest. The Robinsons have five children.

Other General Interest Books by Paul H. Robinson

Mapping American Criminal Law: Variations across the 50 States
(with Tyler Williams)

*Shadow Vigilantes: How Distrust in the Justice System Breeds a New
Kind of Lawlessness* (with Sarah Robinson)

*Law Without Justice: Why Criminal Law Doesn't Give People What
They Deserve* (with Michael Cahill)

Pirates, Prisoners & Lepers: Lessons from Life Outside the Law
(with Sarah Robinson)

Would You Convict? Seventeen Cases that Challenged the Law

Selected Scholarly Books by Paul H. Robinson

Intuitions of Justice & the Utility of Desert

*Distributive Principles of Criminal La Structure and Function in
Criminal Law: Who Should Be Punished How Much?*

Structure and Function in Criminal Law

Justice, Liability, and Blame: Community Views and the Criminal Law

Criminal Law Defenses (2 vols.)

Criminal Law: Case Studies & Controversies (4ᵗʰ ed.)

Criminal Law (2nd ed.) (with Michael Cahill)

Criminal Law Conversations (editor, with Steve Garvey & Kim Ferzan)